Logical   Using reason and evidence to support an assertion; that which proceeds according to a rational plan.

Nonlogical   Unrelated to logic or reason; having to do with emotions or tastes. (Compare "illogical.")

Objective   Expressing opinions based solely on observation; not distorted by personal feelings.

Pejorative   Unfavorable, denigrating.

Premise   A proposition or statement from which reasoning proceeds and from which a conclusion is drawn.

Rhetoric   Written or spoken communication that seeks to persuade.

Rhetorical question   A question asked merely for effect with either no answer expected or an obvious answer implied. Rhetorical questions do not constitute evidence.

Semantics   The meaning of language. A semantic dispute is one in which there is disagreement about the meanings of words.

Subjective   Expressing opinions based on personal feelings rather than on observation.

Valid   Following the rules of logic. A valid argument is one in which the conclusion necessarily follows from the premises.

Value judgment   An assertion that something is good or bad in a moral or esthetic sense.

Value statement   A statement that makes a declaration about the worth or value of something.

A Contemporary Rhetoric

A Contemporary Rhetoric

Third Edition

Maxine Hairston

University of Texas at Austin

Houghton Mifflin Company Boston
Dallas Geneva, Ill. Hopewell, N. J. Palo Alto London

Cover and interior calligraphy by Tim Girvin

Edward Hopper, American, 1882–1967.
Hotel Lobby, 1943. Oil on canvas, 32¼ × 40¾ in.
Courtesy Indianapolis Museum of Art, William
Ray Adams Memorial Collection.

Four drawings for painting *Hotel Lobby*. Conte on paper. Collection of Whitney Museum
of American Art, New York. Photograph by Geoffrey Clements.

Contents

Preface

From its first edition in 1974 *A Contemporary Rhetoric* has been a comprehensive text designed not only to introduce students to the writing process and help them set standards for their writing but also to help them become critical readers and careful thinkers as well as effective writers. It emphasizes that writing is not simply a specialized skill but an important tool for discovery and mastery of knowledge and an essential component of almost every intellectual and professional activity. Every year more students seem to realize this, and consequently they hope that their composition courses will help them to become proficient in the kind of writing they know will be important in their lives as citizens and consumers as well as in their roles as lawyers, engineers, managers, teachers, or business women and men. This text provides practical writing strategies and realistic writing assignments so they may achieve that goal.

The text is rhetorically based; that is, it tries to show writers the best means of persuasion available to them in any writing situation. Thus it introduces writers to the primary rhetorical concerns of audience, purpose, and voice, and it devotes substantial time to explaining the strategies writers can use when working in the three rhetorical categories of invention, arrangement, and style. It also points out to students that they are natural rhetoricians and that they can call upon their inherent powers to think, explain, and persuade to develop their potential as writers. The text demonstrates that the ability to write is not magical or mystical, nor does it depend on mastering a complex set of rules; writing is a disciplined and creative intellectual activity that can be taught and can be learned by ordinary people who are willing to work at it.

In the third edition of a *A Contemporary Rhetoric* I have expanded the initial chapter of the second edition, "Writing: A Short Course," into two chapters in order to give students a more comprehensive introduction to the writing process. The first chapter lists, explains, and illustrates the qualities of good writing, and then gives students specific and research-based information about how professional writers actually work. It also outlines the stages of the writing process, drawing a visual analogy with painting. The second chapter shows students how to define their audience and purpose, gives them a battery of specific strategies for generating and discovering material for their writing, makes extensive suggestions about good ways to organize writing, and concludes with a comprehensive section on transitions and coherence in writing.

In this edition I have expanded the section on sentence combining and introduced a new approach to looking at paragraph unity. I have also expanded the section on Rogerian or non-threatening argument and shown new applications for it. Finally, I have extended the scope of the book by adding a complete chapter on the research paper, a chapter that incorporates search strategies worked out by professional research librarians and includes fifty annotated research topics especially chosen for undergraduates. Throughout the third edition I have brought in new examples from both student and professional writers, and I have revised some theme assignments to make them more useful and more relevant to current concerns. I have also included several full-length student papers in the exercises.

I believe the third edition of *A Contemporary Rhetoric* reflects my growth in the past four years as a rhetorician, a writer, and a teacher of writing, and I attribute much of that growth to my association and interaction with a number of outstanding professional people now working in composition. Among them are my valued friend and colleague Michael Keene; my stimulating and cooperative colleagues at the University of Texas, James Kinneavy, Stephen Witte, Lester Faigley, and John Ruszkiewicz; and at least a dozen people whose writing, scholarship and conversation have kept me thinking and creating: Linda Flower, Ellen Nold, Andrea Lunsford, Nancy Sommers, Win Horner, Sondra Perl, Richard Young, Richard Larson, Ed Corbett, Joe Williams, John Warnock, and Frank D'Angelo. I appreciate deeply the steady encouragement and solid judgment of the staff at Houghton Mifflin. I also want to thank my reliable and patient typist, Sarah Hindsman Williams, and acknowledge the following colleagues who reviewed and made suggestions for this edition: K. E. Dubs, University of Oregon; Helen R. Fogelquist, Los Angeles City College; Eric H. Gould, University of Denver; Richard Hankins, Baldwin-Wallace College; Penny Hirsch, Northwestern University; Jack Holliday, Pan American University; David P. Press,

University of Wisconsin-Milwaukee; Robert L. Root, Jr., Central Michigan University; Ronald Strahl, Indiana University; William B. Stone, University of Illinois at Chicago Circle; Michael Stugrin, University of Pittsburgh; Douglas M. Trank, University of Iowa; and James D. Young, Georgia Institute of Technology.

To the Student

A major purpose of this textbook is to help you feel good about your writing. You can develop the confidence to handle these various writing tasks that most of us face regularly in our personal and professional lives, and you can learn that even though writing is hard work it can also be fun—stimulating and satisfying in a number of ways. To gain confidence and ease in writing—and doing so may certainly take you more than one or even two college terms—doesn't necessarily require that you learn more grammar rules or that you practice writing more complex sentences or using more sophisticated paragraph structures. What it does require, however, is that you learn the basic principles of rhetoric—that is, the art of using language to persuade and convince.

Although you may not realize it, you already know a great deal about rhetoric. Almost without thinking about it, you analyze your audience when you are talking to someone and adjust your style and vocabulary to that audience. You also know almost instinctively which kinds of arguments or appeals are most likely to work with each audience. You may, in fact, already be quite skilled at persuading people to see your point of view or give you what you want. So you at least partially understand and use the principles of rhetoric when you speak. This text will help you to learn more about those principles and show you ways to put them to work when you write. It will also help you to understand and evaluate the way other people use rhetoric in speech or in writing to inform or persuade you.

These two abilities—to be able to practice and to understand the principles of rhetoric—are two sides of the same coin. Anyone who wants to function well in our information-based society needs to become adept at both of them. As Aldous Huxley wrote in *Brave New World Revisited*,

"An education for freedom is, among other things, an education in the proper uses of language." In our era of rapid and radical change in communication technology, Huxley's statement takes on greater force every year. For that reason, this is a text devoted to thinking and reasoning as well as to writing, and many of the discussions and writing assignments focus on the critical analysis of rhetoric and on the fallacies and devious strategies that sometimes creep into it.

The goals of this text, then, are simultaneously simple and ambitious. They are these:

1. To help you understand rhetorical principles so that you can adapt your writing to various audiences and various purposes.
2. To help you to communicate information clearly and present ideas persuasively.
3. To help you to understand and feel comfortable with the writing process.
4. To help you become an intelligent and critical reader who can follow and judge an argument, analyze and evaluate persuasion, and make intelligent criticisms about what you read.

To attain the first three goals you need to become a *competent writer*, that is, someone whose writing is clear and easy to understand. Even though you may have only modest verbal skills, you can, through effort and patience and practice, learn to be a competent writer. I hope this text will help you not only to develop your competence but, if possible, to move beyond it to become a really good writer. And I hope it will help you to master the habits of straight thinking that must underlie good writing.

To attain the fourth goal of becoming a good critic of rhetoric, you will have to learn to stretch your imagination and put yourself in the place of other writers. Who are they writing for, what do they intend to achieve with that audience, and how do they do it? When you can read with those questions in mind as well as write with them in mind, you'll be on your way to mastering the complex art of rhetoric.

Because the art of rhetoric is one that can be learned and practiced by ordinary people, it can easily be turned to dishonest and dishonorable purposes. For this reason some critics, ancient and modern, have attacked those who teach rhetoric, claiming that it gives writers and orators a bag of tricks with which to deceive. Such an argument is as short-sighted as one that condemns freedom of the press because some people abuse it, or gene splicing because it may produce some potentially dangerous mutations. All learning carries risk with it, and no one should scorn to study rhetoric because unscrupulous people have sometimes put it to bad uses. In fact, that is all the more reason to study it in order to protect your own interests. The best place to start such a study is with your own writing.

Writing: A Short Course, Part I

Some of the perennial questions that bother both students and teachers when they begin a writing course are "Where should we start? What are the most important abilities and concepts a person needs to master when he or she starts to write?" These questions can generate a storm of argument, but for a good reason we are not likely to find simple answers to them. The reason is that people who are starting to write need to know a number of things all at once, because even relatively simple writing tasks require that the people doing them have mastered not one but several writing abilities.

But no one can master all these abilities at once, so we have to set priorities and focus first on those that seem to be the most important for the novice writer. In my judgment they are as follows:

1. Recognizing and appreciating good writing.
2. Understanding the writing process.
3. Learning how to get started writing.
4. Learning how to organize writing.
5. Learning how to unify writing.

These first two chapters will give you guidelines for developing these basic abilities, and once you grasp these main principles, you should be able to approach writing your first papers with some confidence. At least you will understand what you are supposed to be doing even if you do it rather awkwardly and slowly the first few times. Gradually, as you master these abilities and begin to supplement these early lessons with more complex ones, you will begin to write easily without always consciously thinking about what you are doing. But studied practice has to come first.

In fact, you are probably already fairly well prepared to write that first paper even if you have not done much writing in high school, because all writing starts with the mind and the emotions, not with a pencil or pen or typewriter. For a long time you have been using your interpersonal skills to communicate with people in conversations or letters. You have ideas or opinions and you tell people about them by using language that comes naturally to you. You state your position on issues and support it by drawing on your experience or on another natural skill, the ability to reason.

This strong desire that all of us have to make others understand us should serve you well as you write. Now you just need to organize your ideas more carefully and to think deliberately about how you can use the right words and the right examples to make your points. The process is necessarily slower and more painstaking than talking, and no one claims that if you can talk well you can also automatically write well. But the two processes are closely connected, and you can use those already well developed communication skills when you start to write. And remember that even beginning writers do many more things right than they do wrong.

What Is Good Writing?

The purpose of this section is to give you a working definition of good writing that will help you to set standards by which you can judge your writing and to understand some important goals of a college writing course. The definition is limited in that it refers only to *expository writing,* that is, nonfiction writing that presents and explains ideas. Expository writing always takes place in a specific situation; that is, someone writes it for a specific audience and for a specific purpose. Thus we have to make our first judgments about any piece of expository writing by asking this question: Does it achieve its purpose for its intended audience? If it does, it is effective writing; if it does not, it is ineffective, no matter how attractive it may seem when considered out of context. So when we judge a piece of writing we must first try to decide if it accomplishes what the author intended. After we decide that question, we can look for other features that affect its general quality.

All expository writing has an audience and a purpose

Characteristics of Good Writing

Fortunately, it is not difficult to identify characteristics that are common to good expository writing and to pinpoint the features that most readers want to find.

First, they want writing to be *significant.* It should tell them something they want or need to know.

Good writing is significant, clear, unified, economical, developed, and grammatical

Second, they want writing to be *clear*. They don't want to have to reread it several times to find out what it means.

Third, they want writing to be *unified* and *well organized*. They don't want the author to lead them off in several directions so that they get no sense of an underlying plan.

Fourth, they want writing to be *economical*. They don't want to feel that the writer is being unnecessarily long winded and wasting their time.

Fifth, they want writing to be *adequately developed*. They want the author to support key points and keep any promises he or she makes.

Sixth, they want writing to be *grammatically acceptable*. They don't want to find distracting mistakes in usage or mechanics.

These characteristics are basic to any kind of effective nonfiction writing. But for nonfiction writing to be not only satisfactory and efficient but also a pleasure to read, it should have at least one more quality: vigor. That term is easier to illustrate than to define, but in general one can say that vigorous writing makes the reader sense the writer's presence. Often it has a visual quality and a definite rhythm, and it reflects the writer's energy and his or her interest in the topic. The selections on pages 459–474 of the Appendix illustrate vigorous writing.

Qualities of significant writing

Significance Writing is significant when the reader enjoys it, learns something from it, or fills some need by reading it. When writing serves any of those purposes, it is worth doing, even if it is not profound or original. As a student writer, you shouldn't underestimate your own resources for making your writing significant. You have had experiences that other people would enjoy hearing about, and almost certainly you have valuable information about some activity or interest that someone would like to read about. You also hear the news, read the papers, and react to events and issues. You can incorporate all of this material into your writing to make it interesting and significant to your readers.

What most readers are apt to consider insignificant and trivial, a waste of their time, is "canned writing," that is, writing that states the obvious or only repeats conventional ideas or sentiments that are already so familiar to the reader that they make no impression. Such writing is pointless. The student who produces it usually has no real interest in the topic and is just going through motions in order to meet a requirement. The instructor who reads it does so for the same reason: to meet a requirement. Papers written under these conditions are really "teacher papers." Full of generalities and clichés, they bore both the people who write them and the people who read them. Here is a rather typical opening paragraph from a "teacher paper":

> A person's basic morals are formed during childhood. Almost from the time you are born you are told what is right and what is wrong. The family is the most dominant force in the shaping of a child's morals. Parents try to guide their children according to their own morals. Society is another strong force in shaping morals, and people tend to have those values which society had while they were growing up. Today the media also have a strong influence on morals.

Although the writing is clear and correct, the content is so hackneyed that no reader would voluntarily continue past the first two sentences. And students shouldn't expect their writing instructors or their fellow students to read such papers either—they're not worth anyone's time.

On the other hand, here is an opening paragraph on a comparably broad topic, but it engages the reader's interest and promises to say something worth reading:

> The demonstrations and riots of the 1960s dramatically brought civil rights issues home to Americans. Fifteen years ago it was not uncommon to hear of a man who had lost his life because he believed that black Americans should have the same rights as white Americans. Today the battlefields are quiet, and to a casual observer, it might appear that the Civil Rights Movement has obtained its objectives. How accurate would such a statement be? To put it another way, is America now totally "color blind"?

Probably the best way to make your writing worth reading is to choose a topic that interests you, one that hasn't been written about so often that there's nothing new to say about it. If you can't do that, at least try to find something personal and specific to say about the assigned topic.

Qualities of clear writing

Clarity When people complain about bad writing, they frequently single out lack of clarity as the fault that annoys them most. When writing is vague and obscure, it taxes their patience and wastes their time, and if they have no strong incentive for trying to figure out what the writer is saying, they'll quickly stop reading. Clarity is relative, of course; informed and skilled readers with large vocabularies often have no trouble reading material that many other readers would find confusing. But even very skilled readers value clarity; they don't want their reading to be any harder to understand than it must be, given the subject matter.

Most writers would tell you that nothing is more important than writing clearly, and nothing is more difficult. To write clearly you have to pay attention to everything: audience, sentence structure, diction, organization, transitions, choice of examples, and half a dozen other considerations. So much is involved that most of the writing advice in this book is really advice on how to write clearly. Learning to do so may be a long process, but it is not a mysterious one. With persistence, most writers can master it.

Qualities of unified writing

Unity and organization When you go to hear someone give a talk and leave thinking, "That speaker really got to the point. She was easy to follow and didn't waste anyone's time," you have heard a unified speech. When you read a piece of writing that stays directly on the topic and moves purposefully from one point to the other without jolts, interruptions, or digressions, you get the same impressions. That kind of writing is satisfying to read and usually easy to understand.

In tightly unified writing, each sentence in a paragraph develops or supports the main idea of the paragraph and connects in some way with any sentences that come before and after it. All the sentences seem to fit with each other in a logical sequence. In poorly unified writing, however, the sentences often seem to be jumbled; they could be moved around and rearranged without its making much difference. The paragraphs in tightly unified writing also fit with each other logically. Just as no irrelevant sentences go off at a tangent in a good paragraph, no disconnected paragraphs pop up unexpectedly in a good essay.

We call this quality in writing *coherence,* a word that comes from the verb *cohere,* which literally means "to stick together." Writers create coherence in their writing in two principal ways, ways that will be explained in the next chapter.

Qualities of economical writing

Economy Many student writers find it difficult to believe that they should write economically because they so often have been asked to write papers of a specified length—1,000 words, 2,500 words, 10 pages, and so on—and have worried about finding enough to say to produce the specified number of words. Consequently they have acquired the habit of thinking that they should write as much as they can, and they may find it hard to realize that their wordiness is more likely to annoy readers than to impress them. But it's true. To busy people—and that includes your writing instructor—time is their most valuable commodity, and they resent having to wade through puffed-up writing that takes twice as long as it needs to make a point. Thus it pays for student writers to learn to think in terms of maximum, not minimum, numbers of words and to cultivate the writing and rewriting habits that will help them to overcome wordiness. Later chapters will suggest specific ways to do this.

Qualities of well-developed writing

Adequate development Early in any piece of writing, the writer establishes a contract with the reader. That contract can take various forms: a title that predicts, an opening question that must be answered, a thesis statement to be developed, or an anecdote or reference to be explained. The contract becomes the writer's *commitment,* an obligation to the reader. Good writers meet that obligation by answering questions they have raised and by explaining and developing the assertions they have made.

In other chapters of this book, you will find an expanded discussion of this important component of any writing task and suggestions about how to set up your writing commitments and how to meet them. For this introductory discussion it is enough to say that good writers don't make extravagant commitments that they can't meet in the space they have to work in and they follow through on any commitments they do make. They achieve these goals by keeping two cautions in mind. First, they choose limited topics, and second, they make limited commitments. And in both instances they develop their main ideas with reports, anecdotes, evidence, and specific details that help their readers to visualize the problem and grasp the issues. Other sections of this text will explain and demonstrate how one goes about this kind of development.

Qualities of grammatical writing

Acceptable usage I recently did a survey of professional people like bankers, lawyers, business executives, judges, and administrators to find out how they reacted to finding grammatical mistakes in the writing that they had to read in the course of their work. Although most of them indicated that the quality they valued most in writing is clarity, all agreed that they also expect writers to know and observe the rules of good English usage and that they get upset when they don't. A survey made at the University of Texas in 1975 showed that professors in every discipline felt the same way.

The responses of these people don't mean that they expect the grammar and mechanics to be perfect in every report or paper; in fact, they probably aren't sure what "perfect" grammar is. They do, however, expect writers to have as good a command of the conventions of English usage and punctuation as the average educated public speaker or writer has. They want writing to meet the standards that they—and you—learned as high school and college students.

Mechanics

Use the handbook and glossary

Learning all the hundreds of rules that govern writing the English language is no easy task, but you have been working at it for several years. By this time you should have a reasonably good grasp of the fundamentals. Now that you are writing on the college level, your teachers should be able to assume that they do not need to spend hours of class time reteaching punctuation or basic sentence structure. Most teachers, however, are realistic enough to know that many students have some persistent grammatical problems. For this reason, there is a short handbook and glossary of usage in the Appendix to this text, to which you can turn for help with specific problems.

Students who make major errors in writing often do it not from ignorance, however, but from indifference, carelessness, or forgetfulness. They are simply not convinced that writing correctly is important enough to justify the amounts of time and effort it requires. It would be reassuring to agree with those who say that mechanics are really not important, that what you write and how you put your words together matter far more than such details as a comma fault, an occasional sentence fragment, or a misplaced modifier. Such an assertion is partially justified. Focusing your attention on saying something worthwhile and saying it forcefully and clearly *are* much more important than devoting most of your energies to turning out an absolutely "correct" composition. A paper can be totally trivial even though the spelling, handwriting, and grammar are flawless. But it is poor logic to say that because content is more important than mechanics, then mechanics do not matter. They do, and for several reasons.

Poor mechanics steal attention from content

First, poor grammar and punctuation in a paper draw a disproportionate amount of attention to themselves. In some ways the situation is analogous to that of running a household: more than one person has complained that the most frustrating thing about housekeeping is that much of the time you are doing invisible work. No one notices it unless it is *not* done.

When reading your papers, college teachers seldom think, "What nice punctuation!" or "This student certainly spells well." They take those skills for granted and concentrate their attention on other elements of your writing: clarity, coherence, and sound thinking. If, however, you have neglected the niceties of grammar and spelling, the errors will divert their attention from what you are doing right to what you are doing wrong—and that is certainly not where you want it. Both you and the housekeeper have a better chance of getting credit for the important things you do if you take care of the relatively unimportant ones as a matter of course.

The toleration level of teachers varies. Some are fairly permissive about the more common lapses in grammar; some are very strict. Most college teachers, however, have reasonable standards. They no longer worry about all the fine points of usage. Nevertheless, they still frown on comma splices and sentence fragments, insist that you differentiate between adverbial and adjectival forms, and want subjects and verbs to agree and modifying phrases to come in the right place. And they care about spelling, not because they equate intelligence with good spelling, but because they know other people do.

The second reason you should be concerned about writing correctly is that you need to form good habits now when the penalties for writing incorrectly are not so severe as they will be later. In a composition course, you will be writing several papers; if you have problems, you have a chance to solve them as you go along and gradually bring your work up to the level of standard English. In upper-division courses, however, your grade may depend on the one or two papers you turn in. Under those circumstances, a poorly written paper can cost you dearly.

Learning mechanics now costs less

The crucial test comes when you begin to write the letters and applications that could affect your future. At that point careless grammar and misspelling say to your prospective employer or to the admissions officer, "Here is a sloppy and irresponsible person who is totally indifferent to the impression made on me." Harsh and unreasonable as such a judgment may seem, it is a predictable one. People in authority do judge you by your writing.

The final hazard of faulty mechanics is that they can interfere with communication. The failure to put commas in the proper places can completely alter the sense of a statement. Misplaced modifiers can make sentences comically ambiguous. Run-on sentences or the failure to insert quotation marks where they are needed can confuse your readers. Thus, faulty mechanics not only distract and annoy your readers, they can also deceive them.

Poor mechanics interfere with communication

Spelling Pay attention to your spelling. After eight or ten years of studying spelling, you should know whether you are a reasonably competent speller. If you are not, don't just shrug off your deficiencies by saying, "Well, I never could spell." If you had mastered all the skills required to drive a car except that of backing it, you wouldn't say, "Oh, I'll just settle for this. Backing up is too hard." You would practice backing until you mastered it because you would be handicapped in your driving if you did not. You will be equally handicapped in writing if you refuse to do whatever is necessary to correct your spelling.

There are several steps you can take to improve your spelling. First, invest in one of the standard dictionaries and keep it on your desk or work table. Get in the habit of looking up any word about which you have the slightest doubt. If you are not sure whether there are two *r*'s in *embarrass,* look it up; if you are confused about whether *pursue* is spelled with a *u* or *e,* check it. Words with unaccented vowel syllables, such as "sep-*a*-rate," "com-*pro*-mise," "mil-*i*-tant," and "ul-*ti*-mate," are frequent troublemakers because there is no way to be sure which vowel to use without checking. Most word endings with an *ize* sound are spelled *ise,* but *emphasize* is not, so you may have to check on those too. All this is a nuisance, of course, but absolutely necessary if you are serious about improving your spelling.

Keep a list of words you misspell

You should also form the habit of keeping a list of the correctly spelled versions of words you have missed on papers. The flash card system is handy since it allows you to consult them in alphabetical order, or you may put the list in the back of your English notebook. In addition, make it a practice to pay particular attention to the spelling of key words in an assignment. Teachers have little patience with the student who is so careless as to consistently spell Hemingway with two *m*'s, to write a paper on John Stuart Mill and use the spelling "Mills" throughout, or to forget to put in the second *l* every time *syllogism* is used.

Find a study skills program

There may be some spelling aids available on campus. Ask your teacher if your college offers a study skills program that includes instruction in spelling, if there is an English laboratory set up to help you, and if the bookstores carry inexpensive, programmed workbooks for improving your spelling. As a last resort, you can always find one of those fortunate souls who are naturally good spellers and ask for help in checking over the final draft of your work.

Finally, if you consistently have difficulty with punctuation or spelling don't worry about mechanics while you are writing your first draft. Once you get started writing, if the ideas are coming quickly and you're forming your sentences rather easily, stopping to fret about whether everything is correct may make you lose the creative energy you've worked up. You will do better to keep going until you have finished the first draft and to put off editing for mistakes until the final stages of the writing process.

The Problem of Models for Student Writing

Most people would agree in principle with these standards for good writing—after all, when they *read* they want the material to be significant, clear, unified, economical, and adequately developed, and they expect correct usage and spelling. Many college students, however, don't seem to believe that their instructors really want them to write clearly and economically and to say something honest and direct. Instead, they think college professors expect them to produce polished writing on scholarly topics and major issues, using an abstract and high-level vocabulary and a complex and elegant style. No wonder students are afraid to write! Very few people, including their professors, are qualified to do what students frequently expect of themselves, and yet students often assume that they are the only ones who can't live up to these high expectations.

Misconceptions about models for writing

Such misconceptions about "college-level writing" come from a number of sources. First, many students have read little contemporary nonfiction except for their high school textbooks, so they have no models of effective persuasive or explanatory expository writing by which to judge their own efforts. Even if they do read clear and interesting articles in magazines like *Esquire, Ebony, Newsweek*, or *Sports Illustrated*, they do not think of them as good models to imitate because they are popular, not scholarly. In fact, however, such articles often make excellent models for college writers because their authors have mastered the art of writing readable prose.

A second reason that students have trouble identifying models for their own writing is that they sometimes encounter wordy and ponderous writing in their textbooks or academic journals and assume that the style is typical of academic prose. Moreover, often it is just the article that students find the hardest to read that impresses them most. And because they are inexperienced readers, they seldom say to themselves, "I am having a hard time reading this book or article because it is badly written." Rather they say, "I must be stupid because I am having such a hard time reading this article. What's more, this must be important stuff because the author uses so many big words and long sentences."

Although an essay or book may be important and worth reading *even though* it is hard to understand, no one should be impressed by a piece of writing *because* it is hard to understand. Readers who allow themselves to be dazzled and intimidated by overblown and confusing writing are like the people in the Hans Christian Andersen fairy tale who were afraid to say that the emperor, who was supposed to be wearing a robe of beautiful cloth, actually was naked. Because these spectators had been told that the robe was made of a wonderful fabric which was invisible to those who were stupid or not fit to hold office, they did not have the nerve to say they couldn't see the fabulous robe. In the same way, timid readers are sometimes afraid to say, "I don't understand what that means" for fear they will be thought stupid or unfit to be around educated people. So by their silence they help to encourage unclear writing—worse, they sometimes try to imitate it to impress people.

As a student, you will almost inevitably have to read much writing that is dense and difficult to understand—for example, works by Marx, Dewey, Kant, Hegel, and others. Although there is little use in complaining—after all we can't go back and ask those thinkers to write more clearly—you certainly shouldn't think that such cumbersome prose is a good model. Above all, don't try to imitate it.

Use clear writing as a model

What you should use for models are those serious books and articles that you can read and understand with comparatively little trouble, and there are certainly many of those. Historians like Bruce Catton and Arthur Schlesinger, or philosophers like Bertrand Russell, economists like John Kenneth Galbraith, and literary critics like Wayne Booth and Cleanth Brooks demonstrate that you don't have to write badly to say something important.

You can also learn something about clear writing from the simple language of magazine articles written for people who have similar interests but who come from a wide variety of educational and income groups. For instance, here are two examples from vastly different magazines:

Everyone who has ever taken up a fishing pole or a hunting piece has known hunters and fishing types who are invariably lucky when the rest of us are coming home empty-handed. A little investigation would show, I'm convinced, that almost all of that habitual "luck" is an ancient mixture of toil and guile. To be sure, the most innocent tenderfoot townie alive can bag a ten-point buck once in a while without actually having the remotest notion of what he's doing. But the man who brings his deer or turkey home every season when most of his buddies are sitting around a stove somewhere cracking their knuckles and bemoaning the lack of game does not depend on luck. Fishing and hunting reward the chap who knows where to be, at what hour, and what to do after he gets to that place to be.[1]

The man who began the King Ranch and one of America's most durable families had no family ties himself. In 1833, at the age of nine, he was apprenticed to a jeweler in New York City. He never saw his family again and never divulged anything about them except that they were Irish. The young boy could not abide the close, tedious work of the jeweler's shop or the rigid medieval bonds of apprenticeship. Even at that age he was drawn toward open spaces. At eleven he stowed away on a sailing ship bound for Mobile and for the next ten years he worked on steamboats in the rivers and coastal waters of the eastern Gulf of Mexico. The steamboaters were his parents and the frontier was his schoolroom. The boy learned its tough and demanding lessons well, and he grew into a young man with a quick mind and quicker fists.[2]

The language in both examples is clear, simple though not elementary, and seems to flow as naturally as everyday speech. In most cases, that is the kind of language you should use when you write. Don't switch over to a complicated, stilted style and use words you're really not familiar with just because you are putting those words on paper.

In fact, one way to test the readability of your prose is to read a sentence out loud after you've written it and ask yourself, "Does that sound like me? Would I talk like that, even in serious conversation?" If the answer is no, you should revise and simplify the sentence.

Good writing is readable

As you take more college courses, you will be reading more and more nonfiction of all kinds, and if you read critically you will learn to distinguish good writing from poor writing. You know now what to look for. In informative or persuasive prose, those

[1] Richard Starnes, "Dry Run," *Field and Stream*, July 1976, p. 10.
[2] William Broyles, Jr., "The Last Empire," *Texas Monthly*, October 1980, p. 158.

features of good writing combine to produce one quality: *readability*. If you put your best efforts into reading a piece of writing—and that is an important "if"—and if the subject is not so complicated or specialized that it is over your head, you have a right to expect that you will be able to understand what the writer is saying. So trust your instincts about good writing and also your taste. If you like what you're reading, it is probably well written.

What Happens When People Write

People who are taking writing courses in the 1980s are lucky because they are nearly the first generation of students who have the chance to benefit from the research and investigation into the writing process that has been done in the past ten years. That research, which is continuing, has helped us to understand at least partially how writers work and what happens during the writing process. We are also beginning to identify some of the significant differences between the writing behaviors of skilled and unskilled writers and to draw some conclusions that can help apprentice writers work more effectively. And as we find out more about how writers work, we also find out more about how they don't work. As a result, we can now dispel some of the popular myths that seem to surround the act of writing for many people.

Myths about writing

Dispelling Some Myths

The myth about inspiration Many nonwriters believe that "real" writers are gifted people who write in a frenzy of inspiration. They are so talented that they do not have to spend much time or effort on their writing. Instead, they wait around until they are in the mood to write and then when an idea strikes them, they pour the words out onto the paper in a spurt of creativity. The myth also holds that because such people are geniuses, their inspired writing is always good. They don't have to revise their work or write anything more than once; they get it right the first time. And the more inspired they are, the better their writing is.

Most writing is not inspired

We might call this view of the writing process the Magic Touch Theory. Even in the past, practicing writers would have told you that this is a fairy tale, and now research confirms what they knew from experience. But some people like to believe the fairy tale because it gives them a good excuse for not working at their writing. Since they're not geniuses and never have any inspirations, they reason, no one should expect much of them. But the myth of the Magic Touch is almost pure fantasy. Those of us who write and teach writing know that very ordinary people can and do become good writers.

Writing is not a rule-governed activity

The myth about rules At the other extreme are people who believe that they would be good writers if they just knew enough rules. They think that writing is a rule-governed activity and that if they could learn all the rules that professional writers know they would not have any more problems with their writing. These people frequently excuse their poor writing by saying that they are still working at learning the rules; they assume that once they master them, they will become good writers.

Practicing writers can also demolish this myth. No writer ever produced good work because he or she worked hard at memorizing rules or formulas. Although it's certainly true that effective writers must be able to spell, punctuate, and construct correct sentences, most writers don't think about rules as they write. They may think about them as they *rewrite*, but rules have no power to help writers generate ideas or organize them into readable form.

The Habits of Writers

How good writers work

Most good writers are not geniuses who write in bursts of inspiration, nor are they human computers who produce discourse according to a set of rules. Rather, the average productive writer is a steady worker who acts pretty much as other people do when they have a job to do. And though different individuals have different ways of approaching writing tasks, my research has convinced me that we can draw these generalizations about how effective writers behave:

   1. Effective writers don't count on inspiration; they write whether they feel like it or not. They write regularly, and usually they write according to a schedule.

2. Effective writers usually write in a specific place, and they like to use the same tools each time—typewriter or pencil. The details of writing are important to them—the kind of paper, the location of their desk, the clothes they wear, the atmosphere of the room—so they try to create a favorable environment for their work.

3. Effective writers depend on deadlines to keep them working; they make commitments that will force them to write and to get their work in by a certain date.

4. Effective writers often procrastinate writing and feel guilty about doing so.

5. Effective writers usually work slowly. Many of them consider 1,500 words (five double-spaced, typed pages) a good day's work.

6. Effective writers usually make some kind of plan before they start to write, but they keep their plan flexible and they replan as they work.

7. Effective writers often have trouble starting to write, but many of them have developed strategies for overcoming this problem.

8. Effective writers expect to get new insights as they work; they know that writing is an act of discovery, and they develop their ideas by writing.

9. Effective writers stop frequently to reread and reflect on what they have already written; they know that such rereading stimulates them to continue writing.

10. Effective writers revise their work *as* they write, and they expect to do two or more drafts of their writing.

11. Effective writers are careful observers, and they have a system for collecting ideas or material that may be useful to them.

12. Effective writers do not always enjoy writing—usually they can find something else they would rather be doing—but they get satisfaction from *having written*.[3]

All these data suggest that when people write they engage in a process that is inexact, messy, sometimes unpredictable, often astonishing, and frequently tedious. By its nature, it defies precise

[3] The bibliography of works from which these conclusions were drawn is on page 33.

analysis; nevertheless we can find certain patterns in the writing process, patterns that seem to correspond to those common to other creative endeavors in fields such as art, music, architecture, or scientific discovery.

The Stages of the Writing Process

Researchers and theorists who have studied and speculated about the creative process believe that it takes place in four stages: preparation, incubation, illumination and execution, and verification. In writing, those stages seem to look like this:

Preparing to write

1. *Preparation* For writers, there are probably two parts to the preparation stage. The first includes just about everything a person has engaged in before he or she starts on a writing assignment—education, personal experiences, sports, work, reading, family life. All these areas of one's life provide potential writing material, and the more alert and thoughtful one is about his or her experiences, the better prepared that person is to write.

The second part of the preparation stage in writing begins when a writer identifies the writing task. This stage may include choosing and narrowing a topic or clarifying an assignment made by someone else. It also requires identifying audience and purpose; for whom are you writing and why are you writing? When the writer has answered those questions, he or she can begin to employ various strategies for generating material, strategies that will be explained at length in Chapter 2. The writer may also start thinking about ways to organize the material and exploring ways to develop it; a later chapter will also focus on these concerns. The activity at this stage of the process might be compared to feeding information into a computer from which one will later write a program or solve a problem.

Incubating ideas

2. *Incubation* After spending as much time and energy as they can afford on the preparation stage, many writers just stop working or thinking directly about their writing task and let all the accumulated material "cook" in their subconscious mind. They turn their attention to something else and seem not to be working, but beneath the surface their subconscious faculties are busy examining, evaluating, and sorting the information and memories the writer has stored.

Executing the plan

3. *Illumination and execution* After an incubation period the writer usually returns to the task with a fairly clear idea of what he or she wants to do and with some sense of how to proceed. The writer begins to work and a piece of writing comes into existence, not easily and not without many starts and stops, but at the end of this stage a writer has a first draft. Usually a writer has to repeat this stage of the process several times before producing the final draft. There will be more later about drafts and strategies for revision.

Checking

4. *Verification* Finally, like a scientist checking the results of an experiment or an architect inspecting a completed building, the writer has to edit his or her writing by checking spelling, punctuation, and any possible lapses in usage. This last task involves cleaning up and polishing the final product before submitting it for examination.

The Generative Power of the Process

This sketchy overview may make the writing process seem more simple and straightforward than it really is. The fact is that when writers are working on a major project, the first and third stages often mingle, overlap, or alternate. Probably most writers begin by planning, making preliminary outlines, or sketching out a design for their article or book. Many writers, however, do not plan their project completely before they start writing because they don't know exactly how they want it to develop. And because they know from experience that fresh ideas and a clearer vision of their goal will come to them as they write, they frequently move back and forth between the preparation and execution stages. Often, even while authors are writing they are planning ahead, and sometimes the ideas they have as they write may cause them to rethink and to change the work they have already done.

Writing is not a linear process

Thus the stages of the writing process are not strictly linear; that is, they do not start at stage 1 and move in a straight line through stage 4; rather, they move in uneven and often halting steps, frequently taking detours or backtracking. Like a building or a musical composition or a painting, a piece of writing evolves through a series of stages, all of which represent the steps of development necessary for creating the final product. There seem to be particularly striking similarities between the way painters plan and develop their work and the way writers go about producing a piece of writing.

For instance, if we look at the working sketches for the painting *Hotel Lobby*, by the famous American painter Edward Hopper, we can infer a good deal about the process by which the painting developed. In Figure 1 we see a rough sketch, comparable to an early draft of a piece of writing. Clearly, Hopper has in mind at this stage the main features and overall design of his painting, but apparently he has not yet decided how he is going to develop the details or what relationship the figures in the painting will have to each other. At this stage, the figure sitting alone at the right side of the picture seems to be a man, but we can tell little about him or about the man and woman at the left of the picture except that they appear to be talking to each other.

Figure 2 is a more advanced draft of *Hotel Lobby*. Now the figures become clearer and the relationship among them begins to emerge. We sense an air of intimacy between the man and woman on the left as the man puts his arm on the woman's chair and leans toward her. This intimacy emphasizes the isolation of the female figure sitting alone at the extreme left and of the white-haired man on the right who seems to be despondent as he stares straight ahead. At this stage, Hopper has apparently also thought more about the composition of the painting, and for reasons of balance and emphasis, he has added the heavy dark vertical panel at the left of the picture.

Figures 3 and 4 show Hopper's practice sketches for individual details in the picture. One might compare these to individual passages of narration or description or to a separate introductory paragraph that a writer might identify as needing special attention, to be worked on in isolation from the whole text. From these sketches we see that Hopper has decided to add the figure of a girl who did not appear in the early drafts, and we get the first hint that the older woman is going to appear isolated, rather than in an intimate pose.

Figure 5 shows the final version of the painting, substantially different from the versions we saw in Figures 1 and 2. Now the elderly man stands upright, paying no attention to the older woman, apparently his wife. The man across the room has become an attractive young woman who is absorbed in her reading

Figure 1

Figure 2

Figure 5 *Hotel Lobby*

and ignores the older couple. The second woman on the left has disappeared. As one critic puts it, "In the evolution from drawings to the final painting, Hopper apparently tried to accentuate the sense of non-communication, to reveal a poignant lack of emotional interaction."[4] Like a writer, Hopper began with an idea and put it into rough draft form, but he found his real focus as he worked. With each succeeding draft—and there may have been more than those in Figures 1,2,3, and 4—the work of art developed into the final, rich version in which we see the three isolated figures framed and set off by a background of strong geometric patterns.

Analogy between writing and painting

Similarly, the writer who wants to produce a careful and thoughtful essay or paper begins by sketching out his or her ideas in rough draft form and gradually develops them into a final polished document. Of course, no practicing writer has time to do several drafts of every piece of writing, and not every writing task warrants the time and effort required to write several drafts. But when you really care about doing a good job and are willing to invest the necessary time, you are most apt to develop your full potential if you follow the work patterns common to creative people in other fields.

So the creative process is not a great mystery. We can identify the stages that professionals go through, and amateurs and students can develop their own abilities by watching what the masters do and by practicing the same routines. It is probably true that in every field, only those few who have that elusive quality of natural talent will go to the very top—only a few Edward Hoppers or Joan Didions or Bjorn Borgs seem to be born into this world. But the difference between the successful students who mastered their craft and those who dropped out of the running may well be the difference between those who cultivated good habits and those who lapsed into poor ones.

Think of yourself as a working writer

As you write the papers for this composition course, try to get in the habit of thinking of yourself as a working writer, not as a student who is doing writing assignments. Experiment to find out what kind of tools suit you best and what kind of writing environment you like. Decide whether you are a morning writer or a

[4] Gail Levin, *Edward Hopper: The Art and the Artist* (New York: W. W. Norton & Co., Inc., published in association with the Whitney Museum of American Art, 1980), p. 49.

night writer, and establish a routine for yourself. Condition yourself to think of writing a paper or a report as a process having several stages, not an isolated task that you complete in one sitting. And think of all the papers you write as steps in your development as a writer, a development that will continue for many years after you graduate from college. The chances are good that at times you will be a practicing writer when you become a professional person, and if now you can start to develop the habits and attitudes of effective writers, in a few years you should find that you are a competent and confident writer who can put your ideas into readable prose.

The next chapter of the book will help you to get started as a writer.

Exercises

1. *What is good writing?* Here are several paragraphs taken from both professional and student writing. Which paragraphs are good, and why? What are the features that detract from the paragraphs you do not like?

   a. A revolution is under way. Most Americans are already well aware of the gee-whiz gadgetry that is emerging, in rapidly accelerating bursts, from the world's high-technology laboratories. But most of us perceive only dimly how pervasive and profound the changes of the next twenty years will be. We are at the dawn of the era of the smart machine—an "information age" that will change forever the way an entire nation works, plays, travels, and even thinks. Just as the industrial revolution dramatically expanded the strength of man's muscles and the reach of his hand, so the smart-machine revolution will magnify the power of his brain. But unlike the industrial revolution, which depended on finite resources such as iron and oil, the new information age will be fired by a seemingly limitless resource—the inexhaustible supply of knowledge itself. Even computer scientists, who best understand the galloping technology and its potential, are wonderstruck by its implications.[5]

---

[5] "And Man Created the Chip," *Newsweek*, June 30, 1980, p. 50.

b. Almost every city today has a number of western stores. These stores sell nothing but western clothes, and you can find a large selection of cowboy boots there. Prices range from about one hundred dollars to five or six hundred dollars a pair. For a good pair of bull or cowhide boots, you should plan to spend $125–$150. If you wait for a good sale, you can get these same boots for $90–$100. In addition, some individuals will hand-make your boots. These are considerably more expensive, usually $200–$225 minimum but if you have the money they are well worth the price. A good bootmaker will have you come in before he even starts on the boot. He will measure your foot in every direction and then custom fit the boot to your foot. A custom made boot will last a lot longer than a machine made boot. [*student paragraph*]

c. Scholarships provide a chance for underprivileged and independent students to go to college. Furthermore they seek out people of intelligent potential who wouldn't have thought of going to college. Many people because of their past environment and background don't consider going to college until scholarship agencies contact them through schools, advertisements, and other various means. This includes the basic function of scholarships which is to allow people to go to college that can't afford it. Also young people who wish to make it on their own find it possible through scholarships. All of these various opportunities that all types of scholarships offer emphasizes the importance of personal achievements and therefore promotes it. [*student paragraph*]

d. If a culture is restricted from keeping pace with society, the individuals of that society lose their definition and sense of purpose. They have no choice except to search for meaning in an outmoded cultural reference that does not account for any new symbols and ideas a society conceives and adopts over time. The society becomes confused and stumbles awkwardly, out of step with reality. . . . Any fiber that clashes with the status quo is discarded in deference to strands that complement the reactionary web that is suffocating the life out of our democracy.[6]

[6] Mark McKinnon, "Slouching Toward Camelot," *The Daily Texan*, October 16, 1980, p. 2.

e. You've seen them along the highway. Those cars and trucks parked sporadically along the major thoroughfares of the state and overflowing with anything and everything under the sun. Home-painted signs saying "FRESH FRUIT—GREAT BUYS" or "FRESH SEAFOOD—FROM $1.99 A POUND" entice weary travelers to stop and shop for a bargain. Other merchants don't need signs to point to their wares—you can spot their purple and red polka-dotted bean-bag chairs or their ten foot stuffed Pink Panther dolls from a mile away. [*student paragraph*]

2. *Models*

a. Find a paragraph that seems to you to be particularly well written. Clip it out and tape it to a sheet of paper, or copy it onto a sheet, being sure in either case to give the source. Beneath it write a short paragraph explaining why you think the paragraph is a good one.

b. From a book or magazine select a paragraph that you find difficult to understand and try to analyze why you are having trouble with it. Does the problem seem to be with you because you do not have adequate background or reading skills, or with the author because she or he does not write well? Can you think of a way in which the author could have made the paragraph easier to understand?

3. Rewrite these sentences to make them clearer and more vigorous:

a. The size of the growth rate will depend on consumers' perception of the quality of the available product as well as on the effectiveness of marketing strategies.

b. I cannot account for the accuracy of the depiction of such emotions.

c. Students would be cognizant of the fact that they had command of the technique.

d. The rules may not be enforced unless and until there is a finding of public health necessity.

e. Raising the interest rate is required in order to assure the continued viability of the credit union movement and to assure the availability of consumer loans.

4. In a sentence or two write out an example that you could use to support each of these abstract statements:

a. Addiction to television strikes all age groups.

b. Prosperity is a relative term.

c. Owning a foreign car can be a real headache.

d. Social competition starts very early.

e. The word *busing* has taken on new meaning in the last few years.

5. Comment on the quality and the readability of the following two student papers. Do they meet the criteria set up for good writing (pp. 3–8), and are they comparatively easy to read? Give reasons for your answers.

Paper A was written for an audience of ten- to twelve-year-old children to explain what computer programmers can do. Paper B was written for a general audience, such as readers of an airline magazine.

A. *Computer Programming: May the Force Be With You*

Imagine yourself the pilot of a two-billion dollar rocket ship, with R2D2 and C3PO at your side. All around you flies the mysterious black beauty of space. Your mission: travel to Einsteina, a newly discovered planet in the Andromeda galaxy. You will record information about the planet's geology, biology and chemistry. On your trip back to the earth, you will use the ship computer to determine if Einsteina would support a colony of scientists. Your skill as a computer programmer will determine the success of the mission.

In today's world and in the future, women and men who program computers are important to almost all areas of life. Here is a list of just a few things that you can do as a computer programmer:

• Create special effects for movies like *Star Wars*
• Help design cities of the future

- Keep library or business records
- Create computer-designed art
- Help design a submarine
- Develop new methods of teaching

As you can see, programmers are involved in solving problems in most areas of life. Since good problem solvers are needed everywhere, programmers can work for almost any type of business, government or educational institution. Whether you want to live in Hawaii, France, Egypt, or in the U.S.A., your skills as a programmer will find you a job.

By now you may have decided that you might enjoy being a computer programmer. So let's talk about what a programmer actually does at work.

Computer programmers solve problems. Then they teach the computer to solve the same kind of problem. You see, computers can only do what they are told to do—sort of like a dumb robot. But they think much faster than people do. And once you tell a computer how to do something, it will remember it until it is told to forget it.

So there are four basic steps to programming:

1. Solve the problem
2. Write the steps to the solution
3. Write the steps in computer language
4. Teach the steps to the computer

Computers don't read English or Spanish. Computers read a special language. Actually there are many computer languages. Cobol is a computer language used to solve business problems. Scientists use a computer language called Fortran. These languages are like English, but shorter. They are also like math.

Let's look at a simple computer program.

Program Addition (This program adds numbers.)

A = 5;
B = 10;
C = 16;
D = A + B + C
Print D

Now this program is typed to the computer on a keyboard that looks like a typewriter keyboard. The computer will read the program and remember the value of each letter. When it sees the word "print", the computer will type out the number 31 on the screen. This program is one that you could do without a computer, but as the problems become more difficult, you can see the value of using a computer. You could ask the computer to add one thousand numbers, and it would print the answer faster than you can turn on a light switch.

Solving more difficult problems requires more time and thought on the programmer's part. But once the program is "fed" into the computer, the computer will print the answer in a very short time. And the next time you want to solve the same problem, you don't have to start at the beginning. Just ask the computer. It will still have the answer stored in its memory.

You can see that computers save people time and energy. So you can understand that people who program computers are important to many different parts of life. The next time you turn on the television, or ride in the car, or talk on the phone, remember: a computer programmer was one of the people who made it possible.

Mike Williams

B. *The Wild West Hero: America's Oldest Cover Up*

You are watching a western on TV when an uneasy feeling creeps down your spine as two gunslingers approach each other on a deserted, dusty street. A haunting silence falls over the town as horrified townspeople watch quietly from their hiding places. The wind kicks up and time stands still as you are shown the icy-cold eyes of the gunfighters staring through one another. You sit up in your chair as you peer at the faces of two hard men; two poker-faced men who are putting each other through a bittersweet hell. The picture shifts to two hands nervously hovering above their guns, when all at once they both draw. Gunshots are heard, smoke is seen and you watch as an angry, unbelieving man with gritted teeth falls in slow motion with hand over heart. A cloud of dust arises upon impact with the ground and as the dust slowly filters back to the ground, our villain dies. A feeling of relief gradually replaces your uneasiness and you smile because your hero, Quick Carl, is still alive.

Somehow, the preceding gunfight seems terribly beautiful when seen on television, but unfortunately gunfights probably very seldom happened that way. In fact, most modern beliefs about western legend and heroes are not quite true, even though we might wish them to be so. Legend builds many champions of the west up to be brave, rugged and always ready for a challenge. In reality, many western heroes appear to be quite pathetic when you contrast what they were supposed to be with what they really were.

For example, let's take the case of Calamity Jane, best remembered out of Hollywood in the figure of Jean Arthur. According to a Robert Sherrill book, *The Saturday Night Special*, legend portrays Jane as being a crack shot, a scout for the Army, a pony express rider and also being very beautiful. Unfortunately, Sherrill says, accurate history tells another story: her real name was Martha Jane Canary; her mother, Charlotte Canary, ran a brothel called "The Bird Cage," in which Calamity Jane apprenticed. Jane was not the gun-toting beauty she is now made out to be. Sherrill tells us that historian Bruce Nelson who specializes in studying her adventures cites that "her services to the Army were in a quite different capacity from that mentioned" in her autobiography. "Citizens of Deadwood who knew Jane well described her as a common harlot—and one of such coarse and forbidding appearance as to frighten away all save the tipsiest miner."

"Coarse and forbidding" are two adjectives historians might have also used in describing Belle Starr, yet another heroine of wild west fame. The legendary Belle Starr (Myra Bill Shirley) epitomized the frontier woman, gracious but with a will of iron, and always loyal to her man. According to legend, Belle was quite handy with a six-gun and rifle; however, the manner of her death seems to question that. She was shot down from behind by her son who used a charge of buckshot to knock her off her horse and a charge of turkeyshot to finish her off. Sherrill's *Saturday Night Special* also tells us that the real Belle Starr was a known whore and an ugly one at that. She had two illegitimate children—a boy who grew up to be her incestuous lover and murderer, and a girl who followed in mother's prostitute footsteps.

Belle Starr's son was not the only backshooter in the west. A young man named Billy the Kid, about whom Hollywood has made no fewer than twenty-one movies, was also a come-from-behind artist. In each of Hollywood's movies about him, the hero is represented by tall, handsome actors such as Paul Newman, who was the last person to portray Billy the Kid. A more accurate description of Billy, according to Peter Lyon in *The Wild, Wild West*, would be a "slight, short, buck-toothed, narrow-shouldered youth whose slouch added to his unwholesome appearance." As mentioned earlier, Billy usually killed from ambush; his only recorded face-to-face gun murder was of an unarmed man.

The Wild Bill Hickok legend began at Rock Creek, Nebraska, where Bill had supposedly wiped out singlehandedly the "McCanles Gang" of nine "desperadoes, horse-thieves, murderers, and cutthroats," according to Harper's Monthly. Using six-gun, rifle, and Bowie knife, Hickok supposedly took on the gang and received eleven bullets in his body.

However, once again Sherrill's *Saturday Night Special* gives a more correct version of the story; it seems that Hickok was hiding behind a calico curtain in a trading post when he gunned down Dave McCanles. The other members of the "gang" consisted of McCanles' twelve-year old son, a young cousin, and a young employee who blundered into the fight. The son did nothing more than run to his dying father while the other two were wounded in the gunplay and attempted to run away. The latter two were not successful as some of Hickok's friends murdered one boy with a hoe and the other with a shotgun blast. Ironically, Hickok's triumph over the "McCanles Gang" has been referred to sometimes as being "the greatest one man gunfight in history." In later years, Sherrill finds Wild Bill in Abilene Kansas in 1871 where he had been hired to enforce the law. Some say he spent most of his nights sleeping with the whores in the section of Abilene called "Devil's Half Acre," while others complained that he spent the rest of his time protecting "professional gamblers, madams, and salonkeepers from irate and dissatisfied customers who thought they had been cheated—as indeed they probably had."

If after reading this you feel like you've been cheated by Hollywood and possibly previous history courses, you're probably right. However, don't feel bad; Hollywood has taken practically everyone for a ride, and the problem of legend being passed off as fact is still with us today. Our present society has the tendency to dramatize personalities and happenings in movies and on television. Who will be the heroes of tomorrow? Possibly the "Godfathers" and hoodlums of today, but it is really hard to say. It isn't hard to guess that whoever they are, they will be given more credit than they deserve.

Reggie Rice

6. Proofread the following student paper carefully, and correct any errors in punctuation, spelling, grammar, or word choice.

I do not believe America should have tax supported hospitals. Establishing tax supported hospitals would raise taxes considerably thus increasing the burdon already on the tax payers. In countries that have state supported hospitals such as Sweden, the tax payers put 57 per cent of there whole income toward taxes. The tax payers in this country on the average put 37 percent of there total income toward taxes. I can see where tax supported hospitals could quite easily get out of hand. With the cost of medical expences as they are today, if everyone that needed medical attention was put in the hospital, the hospitals would go broke. For the cost of maintaining a tax supported hospital would be astronomical, more than the American people can afford to pay. Also with the increased number of patients there would be a shortage of hospitals and staff. Hospital efficiency would decrease resulting in poorer health care on everyones part.

With the assumption that people are attracted to the medical profession for prestige and economic opportunities. What would happen if this incentive was taken away? Students thinking of persuing a medical career might be discouraged from putting up with all the school needed to become a doctor. After eight years of school and two years as an intern they would expect more than a job at a government hospital. Afterall they could easily get that position now by joining the service after medical school. I don't think the world would ever have enough experienced doctors. Can we afford to loose these potential doctors of the future?

The establishment of tax supported hospitals would also hurt the private physicians practice. For people would tend to go for the cheaper medical care. This in turn could deprive a patient from receiving the better care a private specialist has to offer. Bringing the efficiency of medical care down as a whole just to reach more people does not seem justified.

I dont think that free health care is the solution for helping the poor. If the government could build more training facilities, and give more scholarships to deserving students, then our doctor and nurse output would increase and eventually medical care would find its way into the areas that it is so badly needed. I believe the solution for better medical care lies in producing more doctors and bringing medical care to the people, rather than lowering the present status and cost to include more people. I'm not saying we should turn our backs on these people, for they do need help, but I don't think tax supported hospitals are the solution.

Suggested Writing Assignments

Theme 1

Purpose To give you practice in writing the kind of simple, straightforward, and concrete language that you are likely to use when you speak. Your main purpose is to communicate clearly an impression or an experience to an interested person whom you know quite well.

Procedure Write one or two paragraphs on one of the following topics. Use simple language and concentrate on finding words that will appeal to your audience's senses and examples that will illustrate your point. Check your writing as you go to see that you are focusing on *one* point, and be sure that you have such clear links between your sentences that your reader cannot get lost. Remember that these paragraphs are chiefly descriptive, not argumentative.

Topics

a. Describe the ceramic piece or jewelry you are making.
b. Narrate your experience in getting a new muffler or bumper for your car.

   c. Describe a particularly attractive place where you have skied, backpacked, canoed, or biked.

   d. Write your impression of a recent movie, concert, play, or television program.

Theme 2

Purpose To give you practice in using clear, direct, and concrete language in a comparatively short and simple expository paper. Your main purpose is to *explain* an idea or opinion clearly.

Procedure Choose one of the following topics and write a short paper for an audience of your classmates. Try to stick to informal language and to illustrate your points. Before you start, brainstorm your topic and then write down a brief summary, thesis sentence, or list of points to help you organize your thoughts.

Topics

   a. How a student can economize on clothes (or on groceries or transportation).

   b. The advantages of living in an apartment.

   c. Why I pay fifteen dollars for a haircut—or, why I refuse to pay fifteen dollars for a haircut.

   d. The television ad that I hate the most.

   e. The advantages—or disadvantages—of owning a foreign car.

Bibliographical Sources for Pages 16–17 (The Habits of Writers)

Barzun, Jacques. "A Writer's Discipline." *Writing, Editing, and Publishing.* Chicago: University of Chicago Press, 1971. Pp. 5–17.

Britton, James. "The Composing Processes and the Functions of Writing." *Research in Composing.* Ed. Charles Cooper and Lee Odell. Urbana: National Council of Teachers of English, 1978. Pp. 13–28.

Cowley, Malcolm, ed. *Writers at Work: The Paris Review Interviews,* 1st series. New York: The Viking Press, 1958.

Didion, Joan. "On Keeping a Notebook." *Slouching Towards Bethlehem*. New York: Delta Books, 1968. Pp. 131–40.

————. "Why I Write." *New York Times Book Review*, December 5, 1976, pp. 2, 98–99.

Emig, Janet. "A Review of the Literature." *The Composing Processes of Twelfth Graders*. Urbana: National Council of Teachers of English, 1971. Pp. 7–27.

Galbraith, John Kenneth. "Writing, Typing, and Economics." *Atlantic Monthly*, March 1978. Pp. 102–105.

Kazin, Alfred. "An Interview with Alfred Kazin." *Composition and Teaching*. San Jose, California: San Jose State University, 1978. Pp. 2–29.

McPhee, John. Introduction to *The John McPhee Reader*. New York: Vintage Books, 1977. Pp. xiv–xxvii.

Murray, Donald. *A Writer Teaches Writing*. Boston: Houghton Mifflin Company, 1968.

Pianko, Sharon. "Reflection: A Critical Component of the Composing Process." *College Composition and Communication*, October 1979. Pp. 275–78.

Plimpton, George, ed. *Writers at Work: The Paris Review Interviews*, 2nd series. New York: The Viking Press, 1963.

————, ed. *Writers at Work: The Paris Review Interviews*, 3rd series. New York: The Viking Press, 1967.

————, ed. *Writers at Work: The Paris Review Interviews*, 4th series. New York: The Viking Press, 1976.

Publishers Weekly staff, eds. *The Author Speaks*. New York and London: R.R. Bowker and Company, 1977.

Robertson, Nan. "Barbara Tuchman: A Loner at the Top of Her Field." *The New York Times*, February 27, 1979. P. C10.

Sommers, Nancy. "Revision in the Composing Process: A Case Study of Student Writers and Experienced Writers." Unpublished paper delivered at the annual meeting of the Modern Language Association, 1978.

Stallard, Charles. "An Analysis of the Writing Behaviors of Good Student Writers." *Research in the Teaching of English*, Summer 1974. Pp. 206–18.

Steinbeck, John. *Journal of a Novel*. London: Pan Books, 1970.

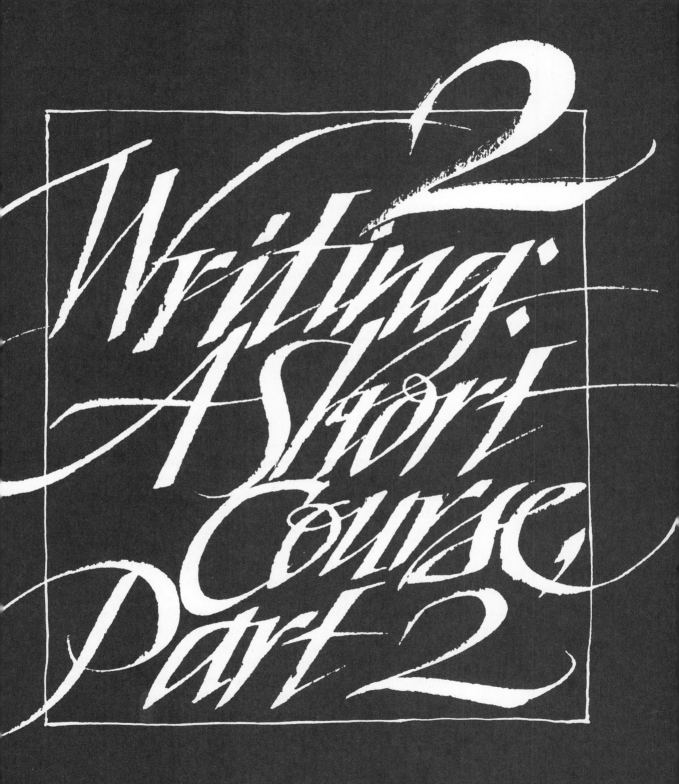

Preparing to Write

Probably the best break you can give yourself when you need to write a paper is to start early enough so that you can allow ample time for preparation. Professional writers have recognized this for years, and consequently many of them spend more time preparing to write than they do actually writing. They know that brainstorming their topic, sketching out a plan, or making preliminary notes helps them generate ideas and discover insights they didn't know they had. Amateur writers, on the other hand, often wait until the last minute before they start writing and thus do not give themselves time to tap their creative powers and to let their ideas develop. They don't realize what rich resources they have within themselves, nor do they know how to get to these resources. But there are strategies both for developing those resources and for tapping them. This chapter will explain what they are.

The advantage of an early start

Preparation: Stage One

People who must write a lot have developed special strategies for adding to their reserves of material and keeping themselves well prepared for whatever writing tasks they may need to do. For example, many writers keep a file of clippings they have built up by regularly scanning newspapers and magazines for items of special interest. Most of them also have some system for taking notes and are never without pen or pencil and something to write on, usually a small notebook. Many working writers also make special efforts to break out of their regular routines occasionally so that they can observe and talk to people whose jobs and style of living are very different from theirs. They seek experience and try to develop a kind of personal radar system that picks up signals from everything that is going on around them.

Strategies for finding material

As an apprentice writer, you can enrich your own stock of working material by cultivating the same kinds of habits. Moreover, doing so doesn't necessarily require that you travel widely or spend a great deal of money. Rather, you need to learn to mine your environment for everything it has to offer. Talk to the person who fixes your dishwasher or refrigerator; listen to the conversation going on next to you in the airport; pick up a foreign language magazine on the newsstand or in the library and see how its ads and illustrations differ from ours; check your campus newspaper to see what unusual outings the recreational sports department is offering; go to a meeting of the Sierra Club or the Pre-law Association and find out what they talk about; pay special attention to the signs you see on campus or in public buildings. In other words, put your intellectual antennae out to discover what is going on around you—you'll be surprised at how much activity you find, and how many anecdotes, narratives, and examples you can draw from it later on.

Preparation: Stage Two

Preliminary decisions So your general preparation to write goes on all the time. Specific preparation to write starts when you receive or choose your writing task. At that point you need to do three things.

Define your writing task

First, *define your writing task as precisely as possible.* If the assignment has several parts, write them down in order. If it gives you several options, choose the one that gives you the best chance to write concretely about something you know and to draw on your experience for illustration. Think about the commitment you will make in the paper and limit it to one you can handle. (See p. 17, Chapter 1.)

Define your audience

Second, *define your audience.* Two of the most important questions that working writers ask themselves are "Who is my audience for this piece, and why are they going to read it?" No writer can really make intelligent decisions about his or her writing without knowing the answer to those questions; yet inexperienced writers often start a paper without giving a thought to who, other than their composition instructor, would be reading it. They "blue-sky" it, throwing their words to some vague and general reader who puts no demands nor limitations on them, and the result bores everyone, including themselves.

The problem of audience is so important that it will be a major concern in Chapter 3. For now, just keep in mind that identifying your audience specifically is an essential part of getting ready to write.

Define your purpose   Third, *define your purpose*. Probably the four most common purposes for which people write nonfiction are *to inform, to persuade, to entertain,* or *to demonstrate competence* (papers and essay exams in courses). Sometimes you may have more than one purpose in a paper, or sometimes you may find that you switch your purpose after you start to write. Nevertheless, before you start preparing to write you should have a clear idea what it is you want to do in your paper; otherwise, you are likely to waste a lot of time. Chapter 3 will say much more about purpose and will discuss some of the important ways in which it affects how you organize and develop your writing.

Strategies for Discovery

Stocking your brain with a wide variety of experiences and information takes time, but it's a satisfying process, particularly if you're a naturally curious person and like to talk to people and to read. But one does not accumulate a stock of resources for writing in an orderly fashion, and consequently the data that you may want to draw on for a specific writing task often cannot be called up on command. They may lie hidden in dark corners, maybe close to the bottom of your mind, or may have gotten wedged in with other information you don't want. The problem is how to get to them and bring them to the surface of your mind where you can examine them and see if you want to use them.

The problem is an important one, especially for inexperienced writers who must work on a schedule that doesn't allow them time to consider a topic at their leisure and wait to see what may develop from it. They need exploratory strategies that will help them probe into their memories and information banks and stir up some intellectual action that will generate ideas for their writing. Those strategies should be comparatively simple so that they can be put to use immediately, and they should yield results quickly. The strategies described here meet both these requirements.

Strategy 1: Writing As every practicing writer knows, writing itself is the best device anyone has for generating and discovering ideas. The very act of writing, of seeing words on paper, seems to help stimulate the brain and help writers make connections

The magic of writing

that they had not seen before. If there is any magic about writing, this is the moment at which it seems to be working. For this reason, sometimes the best tactic for getting started is just to start writing and see what develops. Even if your first efforts don't lead anywhere, almost certainly they will help you break the inertia barrier. And once you realize what a powerful generative device writing can be, you will expect to get new insights and inspirations as you work.

But the magic of this kind of writing is unreliable, and writers who wait until they start writing to think about what they want to say often find that inspiration fizzles out before they can complete their work. For that reason, it's a good idea to try several other kinds of probes and have a stock of strategies at your disposal when you start to write.

Learning to brainstorm

Strategy 2: Brainstorming Brainstorming is a free-association technique for stirring up intellectual energy. Writers can engage in it singly or in groups but either way, the method is essentially the same. You begin with a word or an idea and start writing down everything and anything that it brings to mind. You continue free associating at an intense pace for a predetermined period of time—usually fifteen to twenty minutes—recording your thoughts as you go.

In group brainstorming, one person acts as recorder and writes down everyone's ideas. No one worries about correct grammar or spelling or about explaining or justifying anything that is said. The important thing is to get down a lot of ideas as quickly as they can surface. Individuals who brainstorm by themselves go about it the same way, writing down their ideas as fast as they come.

Two principles govern brainstorming:

First, everything that comes out in a brainstorming session is a right answer. You should not dismiss any suggestion as trivial, irrelevant, impractical, or inappropriate. At this point in the discovery process, writers haven't yet discovered what they want to say or exactly what they want to do, so how can any suggestions be "wrong"?

Second, ideas piggy-back on each other. When those who are doing the brainstorming come up with an idea, they are not necessarily responding to the original stimulus; rather, they may be taking off from a second, third, or fourth level of association that may seem remote from the original. One of the benefits of brainstorming is that it starts chains of thought, and sometimes those chains lead to places that are more interesting than the original starting point.

Strategy 3: Focused freewriting You probably know from experience that sometimes original ideas and insights seem to pop into your head when you are engaged in casual conversation with someone. Such revelations can really be astonishing; you find that you didn't know what you were thinking until the words came out of your mouth. Apparently the very act of putting words together stirs up your subconscious and brings to the surface useful bits of information that fit with the topic you're discussing. That's one principle underlying brainstorming.

Getting started with freewriting

Casual, unstructured writing, or freewriting, can produce the same results. When you freewrite, you sit down at the typewriter with a supply of cheap paper or at a desk with a reliable pen and lined paper or a notebook. Then you just start writing whatever comes into your head and keep going for at least ten minutes. If you stall and can't think of something to say, just write "I'm stalled, I'm stalled—can't think of anything" until something comes into your head. Usually that won't take long.

Sometimes writers will write about just anything that comes into their head when they are using freewriting as a strategy for breaking through a temporary writing block. But when you are using it to generate material on a particular topic, you need to do *focused freewriting*. At the top of your paper write down your topic, even though it's a broad one, and take off from there.

In freewriting it's important to keep moving and keep skimming off the ideas that come into your head. Don't stop to edit or correct your writing or to pause and reflect on what you have written. If you stop to think about what you're writing and cross out something or decide to change a word or a phrase, you might censor out some thought that could start a productive chain of ideas. At this point you don't want to make any decisions about what's right or wrong, useful or not useful. You just want to generate material.

Peter Elbow, the teacher who introduced the idea of freewriting in a book called *Writing Without Teachers*, suggests that after a session of freewriting you stop to sum up the main point of what you have written in just one sentence; he calls that summary the "center of gravity" in the piece. Then after resting, start free-writing again, using that "center of gravity" as the takeoff point for the next ten- to fifteen-minute freewriting session. You can continue this for three or four sessions until you have discovered some points you want to make in your writing and worked up momentum to get started.

Finding your main points by capsuling

Strategy 4: Capsuling The theory behind *capsuling* as a strategy for discovering what you want to say is that by forcing yourself to put the chief points of your topic into a condensed statement, you will find the specific ideas you want to emphasize. One way to go about it is to imagine that someone has asked you what you are going to write about for an assigned paper. You give that person your general topic and get the response, "That's awfully broad—what are you going to say about it?" When someone asks you that question, usually you will find that you're embarrassed to reply with generalities so vague that nobody would find them interesting. So you have to come up with specifics, and often those specifics will give you a basis for your paper.

Using the journalist's questions

Strategy 5: The journalist's questions People who are learning to write newspaper articles are often advised by their teacher or their boss to start investigating their topics by asking six basic questions:

1. *Who* is doing the action?
2. *What* is happening or what happened?
3. *Where* is the event taking place?
4. *When* did it happen or when will it happen?
5. *Why* did it happen or why will it happen?
6. *How* will it affect those involved?

If you answer these questions fully, you will find that you can generate a surprising amount of material on a topic.

Strategy 6: Anecdotes or narratives Sometimes it is possible to get started writing on a subject by focusing on a person or

Using a narrative to get started

event connected with the subject and creating an anecdote or narrative that will suggest a line of thought that you want to pursue. People who write novels sometimes work this way. For instance, Joan Didion describes one such incident in her writing career:

> This second picture [that suggested a situation] was of something actually witnessed. A young woman with long hair and a short white dress walks through the casino at the Riviera in Las Vegas at one in the morning. She crosses the casino alone and picks up a house telephone. I watch her because I have heard her paged and recognize her name: she is a minor actress I see around Los Angeles from time to time, in places like Jax and once in the gynecologist's office in the Beverly Hills Clinic, but have never met. I know nothing about her. Who is paging her? Why is she here to be paged? How exactly did she come to this? It was precisely this moment in Las Vegas that made *Play It As It Lays* begin to tell itself to me.[1]

The way in which Didion noticed this scene and responded to it illustrates that kind of personal radar mentioned at the beginning of this chapter. Didion makes the process sound rather mysterious, but actually the strategy can work just as well for a person writing nonfiction. Primarily it requires that you train yourself to be alert to what is going on around you and that you think of everything as potential material for your writing.

Strategy 7: Prism thinking At some time you may have seen a movie or read a book in which several narrators relate the same event, each recounting it from his or her own point of view. Such accounts dramatize the truth that a person's opinions or interpretation of an event vary tremendously according to that person's relationship to that event. If we are involved in an action or situation, we view it as a *participant*; if we are watching someone else who is involved, we view it as a *spectator*; and if we are neither actually involved nor directly watching, but only giving a detached account of the action or situation, we view it as a *reporter*. I call this exercise of looking at an event or topic from these three

Looking at your topic from three angles

[1] Joan Didion, "Why I Write," *New York Times Book Review*, December 10, 1975, p. 3.

angles *prism thinking.* It can be an excellent device for generating ideas about a topic.

Strategy 8: Research and serendipity Sometimes the best way to start preparing to write a paper is to do the obvious: go to the library and start researching your topic. In Chapter 12 you will find a detailed explanation of how to get started on your research and a guideline to the resources available to you in most libraries. But your most valuable asset for research may be one not found in any library or stored in any computer. It is *serendipity,*[2] the ability to find good things, apparently by accident. The ability is more than luck: it is a cultivated intuition for looking in the right place at the right time to discover something you didn't really know was there but somehow are not surprised to find. To discover something by serendipity, you cannot have tunnel vision that is always focused on your goal. Rather, you have to stay alert, glancing at peripheral, apparently irrelevant items as you work, always receptive to stimuli coming at you from unexpected directions. Serendipity is closely tied to one's system of personal radar, but it also increases as you learn more about a topic. The more you know and the better prepared you are, the more likely you are to make happy discoveries.

Finding ideas by happy accidents

Finally, you can look ahead to Chapter 9, "Modes of Argument," to get ideas about how you might probe a topic. The strategies for developing an argument that are discussed in that chapter come from the father of rhetorical theory, Aristotle, and they can be just as useful for finding something to say on a topic as they are for constructing a logical paragraph.

Using the modes of argument

At this point, what you need to be doing most is writing. Once you do that, you can begin to test the strategies from this section and discover which works best for you.

Organizing Your Writing

As you have been generating ideas for writing and gathering material to support those ideas, you may also have been considering

---

[2] The English writer Horace Walpole coined the term in 1754, taking it from the Eastern legend about the three princes of Serendip who kept unexpectedly encountering good fortune while they were on a quest for treasure.

Why you should plan ahead

how you could organize your thoughts into an effective paper. Like any other complex activity that involves coordinating several parts or steps into a unified whole—for example, building a boat, planning a trip, or creating a fine meal—writing a paper requires that you make some kind of plan. Only geniuses in any field should try to "wing it," that is, count on inspiration and sheer luck to guide them as they improvise step by step. The rest of us are likely to wind up in disaster if we don't plan ahead.

Five Planning Strategies

But insisting that you need a plan does not mean that you can use only the traditional organizing devices, the sentence outline and the thesis sentence. Rather, it means that you need to work out some method for giving a *pattern* to your writing, for imposing order on it so that your reader can follow your ideas without getting lost. Professional writers have several strategies for developing a plan, but the ones they rely on most often are the outline, the thesis sentence, the preliminary abstract, the section-by-section summary, and the working list. Let's take a look at how each of these works and what their advantages are.

1. The outline Only a few professional writers use outlines, but those that do swear by them. The eminent psychologist B. F. Skinner, for instance, says that he makes an outline that winds up being so detailed that it is almost like the finished prose. The *New Yorker* reporter and essayist John McPhee uses an elaborate system of taking notes on index cards, then arranging the cards into the parts of what he calls a "logical" outline that controls the structure of his essay.

For the person who enjoys making an outline, it is probably the ideal organizational tool. Outlines force you to think through your whole paper before you start and to decide whether you have enough supporting material, which points you want to use, and how you are going to arrange them. Also, if you make a careful and detailed outline, you will probably save yourself substantial writing time because you will have to do less revising. A formal sentence outline for a paper about college women might look like this:

Writing a formal outline

Changing Trends Among College Women

I. In the past ten years, the number of women going to college has steadily increased.
   A. Now, for the first time, more than half of all college students are women.
   B. The greatest percentage increase has been among women from 25 to 34.
   C. The number of women getting preprofessional and graduate degrees has doubled in ten years.
      1. Women's applications to law and medical schools are up dramatically.
      2. Women now enroll in traditionally all-male institutions like the Harvard Business School and the Wharton School of Finance.
II. This change in patterns has come about for several reasons.
   A. The women's movement of the 1970s encouraged women to seek economic independence.
      1. More and more women have realized that marriage does not guarantee security.
      2. Women have begun to realize that without an education they can get only low-status, low-paying jobs.
   B. Also as a result of the women's movement, more women plan careers as part of their long-term life plans.
   C. The rising divorce rate has caused many women to go back to school to seek new interests and improve their job credentials.
   D. Our society is now putting more stress on education for everybody.
III. This change in patterns is affecting colleges and universities in several ways.
   A. Schools are under pressure to change their curricula to provide more courses on topics of interest to women.
   B. Schools are under pressure to provide more flexible course scheduling to accommodate women students who cannot live on campus.

C. Schools are going to have to provide some kind of subsidized child-care facilities for student parents or they will lose enrollment.

For long, complex writing tasks, this kind of outline works particularly well because it gives you a feeling of having your subject under control before you start, and you shouldn't have much trouble starting to write after you have put this much time into thinking out your organization. You have also generated good material.

Formal sentence outlines have their drawbacks, however. Many of us can't seem to sustain the drive to follow one through all the way to the end of a project, and we feel constrained by the requirements to have all the bits of our composition fit into symmetrical patterns—the requirement that you can't have an "a" without a "b" seems particularly irksome. And we feel that outlines constrain our thinking too—they are like blueprints that don't allow room for change or innovation as a piece of writing progresses. For that reason a less formal and more adaptable kind of outline seems to work best for many people. For instance, a writer might find it more practical to plan the paper outlined above with this kind of informal outline:

*Making an
informal outline*

Changing Trends Among College Women

More women than ever going to college:
Biggest increase among 25 to 34
More women in law school and med school—more in graduate school
Places that used to be all-male now enroll women (give examples)
Reasons for increase in women in college:
Women's movement—economic independence, sense of own identity
Finding out marriage no guarantee—average woman works 25 years out of her life
See other women stuck in low-paying jobs like clerks and typists
Degrees women got 10 or 20 years ago are outdated
Increased divorce rate making women go back to college—

previously many were discouraged from going by husbands
and families. Now it's necessary.
What it will do to the colleges:
Administrators will have to pay more attention to women stu-
dents and be more flexible about some of the rules
Women are going to want day-care centers on campus

This kind of loose structure will still give you a good organizational plan, but it's much easier to construct because you don't
have to make everything fit into slots. And because you don't
have so much time and energy invested in it, you will probably
be more willing to make changes in it as new ideas occur to you.

2. Thesis sentences Another kind of organizing tool that can be
extremely useful is the thesis sentence. It should be a tight,
though not necessarily brief, statement that summarizes the main
points you are going to make in your paper. You do not have to
begin your paper with it, or even use it in your writing, but it
does provide a working guideline that can keep you on the track.
For example, a thesis sentence for a paper on better safety at city
swimming pools could read:

*Constructing
thesis sentences*

> In order to improve safety and prevent drownings at our city
> pools, the city should hire only guards who are certified
> through the Red Cross Water Safety Instruction Course and
> who are mature enough to get respect and obedience from
> swimmers; we should also hire enough guards to cover every
> area of the pools at all times and require that they stay on
> their guard stations while they are on duty.

If you followed this thesis through and expanded each section
with supporting details and illustrations, you should be able to
turn out a tight and logically developed paper.
Here are some other good thesis sentences taken from student
papers:

> Although the government should not ban the advertising of
> junk foods on television, the TV industry and the Federal
> Trade Commission should work together to put some controls

on such advertising because junk foods have almost no nutritional value, they damage people's bodies, and the ads for them encourage children to form bad eating habits.

Local police should stop arresting people for "victimless crimes," such as prostitution, nude dancing, using drugs, and gambling because such acts cause no damage to other people or property, they persist regardless of penalties, and making them crimes encourages more serious crimes such as blackmail and bribery.

Students starting college should realize the importance of academic achievement, of not carrying more courses than they can handle well, of attending class regularly, and of pacing their studying.

If you write such a thesis sentence *ahead of time*, you should have little trouble turning out a well-organized paper.

A poor thesis sentence, however, is little help to the writer, regardless of when it is written. For example, the following thesis sentences show that their authors have very little idea of how they are going to develop their papers.

The Open Records Law of 1974 has caused many problems.

I am going to describe some of the ways women are oppressed.

The United States should not withdraw from the United Nations.

Sentences like these give a writer no guidance for organization since they are really no more than statements of opinion.

3. Preliminary abstracts A tight, one-paragraph preliminary abstract of your paper can, *if written ahead of time*, serve the same organizing function as a thesis sentence. It may work better because you have room to include more details. Moreover, writing this kind of summary paragraph can be useful in another way; when you learn to write concise abstracts of your work, you are getting practice for writing the kind of abstract or précis that you need to prepare when you are writing technical reports, proposals,

Writing an abstract

or articles to submit for publication or to a meeting. And although a good abstract is difficult to write because it usually requires that you condense all your main points into about one hundred words, you have developed a valuable skill once you have mastered this art of condensation. This ability to condense material into capsule form is also a real asset for newspaper, radio, and television reporters.

A person roughing out a summary paragraph for the paper on better safety at the city swimming pools might produce one like this:

> The best way to improve safety and prevent drownings at our city pools is to hire more lifeguards and to be sure all guards are well trained, mature, and responsible. In the past, several people have drowned because there were not enough guards at crowded pools. Also, in the past many guards had no training in water safety procedures, and they were not mature enough to maintain the discipline that one must have for a safe pool. More mature guards would also be more likely to stay at their stations and not mix with the swimmers. Such a hiring program would be more expensive, but it would save lives.

Summarizing by sections

4. Section-by-section summary This device works especially well for longer papers that you want to block out but are really not ready to outline in detail. Suppose, for example, that you were going to write a paper on the local real estate market for your economics class. You choose as your audience the employees of a national company that is moving its plant to your city; your purpose is to give them complete and accurate information about what to expect if they plan to buy houses. Your summary would look something like this:

1. The price of houses in the area is at about the national average. Prices are not yet as inflated as they are in California or some parts of Texas, but they have been increasing at a rate of about 12 percent a year.
2. Fairly difficult to finance a house unless purchaser can make

a down payment of about 20 percent to 25 percent. If you can afford a large down payment, some property on which mortgages can be assumed at a lower than the going interest rate. Current interest rate running about four points below the prime rate.

3. Not easy to find good rental houses in the city; apartments also scarce because of large student population. Anyone planning to rent should start looking early and sign a lease as soon as possible. Give approximate rents.

4. Good buys in houses available if you are willing to live in south or east part of town, the less fashionable areas. Also some large, four-bedroom, three-bath houses available at reasonable prices if you are willing to live about 15 miles out of town and commute. Give typical prices. Warn that public transportation in the area is poor—not really practical to plan to ride the bus.

5. Suggest that someone in family come to the city several months ahead of time to negotiate for a house or apartment.

This kind of plan gets down your main points on paper where you can study them and think about how you want to add to or modify them. After you write them out, you may also decide to rearrange them. For instance, in this summary, the fourth section might work better as the second section. Also, the very act of writing out a summary will help you generate ideas for developing your paper.

Preparing a working list

5. A working list A final method of organization is to make a list of the points you want to cover, grouped or subdivided in some way. This method is perhaps the most open-ended and flexible because you can add to various parts of the list as you work or rearrange and regroup items if you find an unexpected pattern developing. It's rather like making an elaborate packing list when you are moving or going on a trip. You write down your categories, leaving plenty of space under each one. Then as you prepare to write, you jot items down under the proper heading. Sometimes you get them down in the order you want to use them, but sometimes you have to shift them. And even after you begin to write, it's a good idea to keep the list close at hand and add new points to it when you think of them.

For me, this system seems to work best for almost any kind of writing. Combined with free writing and brainstorming, it helps me to generate a body of material and get it into usable form more quickly than any other method I've tried. I am not an outliner, and I used to feel guilty because I wasn't. Now, however, I've discovered that I am a much more efficient writer when I make lists than I am when I outline, and I realize that individual writers have to choose the methods that best suit their temperament.

For example, here is the working list I used to organize this section of Chapter 2:

Need for Planning

Need a pattern to let your reader know what to expect

Complex activities require a plan or they bog down

Need to be flexible—not a blueprint

Different kinds of plans work for different people—don't always have to outline

Ways to Organize

Outlines—formal, informal, sometimes cause problems

Thesis sentences

Preliminary abstracts

Section-by-section summary

Open-ended lists

Other Helps to Organization

Need a title to condition reader's expectations

Have a pattern—classification, comparison/contrast, etc.

Plans shouldn't get too elaborate or you get attached to them

Lead-in to next section on cohesion

If you were to check the text of this section against this list you would find that it does not correspond exactly, but it comes very close. Since I was writing the list only for myself, I didn't worry about parallel structure or complete sentences. I just put down ideas as they came to me, but I made the wording complete enough so that I wouldn't forget the point I wanted to make. In the actual writing, I changed the order of points a little and added some other points that I didn't think of until I began to write; however, the essentials of the section are on the list.

Other Aids to Organization

Titles When you give your paper a title that accurately reflects its content, you increase your chances of writing a well-organized paper. A title, after all, is a promise to the reader, and if you make that promise before you begin to write, you are more likely to stick to the point. At this preliminary stage, your title will be a tentative one, a working guide that may have to be rewritten later, but it will help you to anchor your paper.

Organizing by titles and controlling patterns

Controlling patterns Writers and teachers sometimes talk about *structure* in an essay, a term that describes the way a piece of writing is put together or its underlying pattern or design. Writers plan their writing in order to give it this structure, which acts as a controlling pattern that holds it together. If, as a writer, you can decide ahead of time what kind of controlling pattern you want to use, you will find that you have a powerful organizational device that will almost take over and plan your paper for you.

Chapters 5 and 10 talk about the patterns of exposition you can use to develop assertions and arguments: *definition*, *cause and effect*, *classification*, *comparison*, *induction*, and *deduction*. These patterns, and others—for instance, *question and answer* or *problem and solution*—parallel our natural thought processes. We are familiar with them and our minds move easily along the tracks that they lay down. We sense an underlying design, a path that leads us along to a destination. And if you establish any of these patterns in your writing and hold to it (or them) as you work, your writing is not likely to get out of control. So when you are planning your paper, think about these natural patterns. Would any of them work well with your topic? If so, you are already ahead on planning your paper.

A Caution About Planning

But now that I have made the case for planning as an important part of most writing tasks, I want to add a caution: don't invest so much time and energy in your plans that you are unwilling to discard them if you don't like the way they are working out or if a better one occurs to you. A plan shouldn't be like an elaborate blueprint that commits you to executing it to the last detail. If you labor over a plan too long and include an excessive number of details, you may get attached to it and not be able to see its shortcomings when you actually put it into operation. Also you are less likely to have your personal radar extended to catch any unexpected creative "blips" that might come your way or to be ready for serendipity to lead you in a new direction. If you were planning a trip, you would probably be cautious enough not to put down such a big deposit that you couldn't afford to cancel if you changed your mind; think of your writing plans in the same way.

Keep your plans flexible

Finally, the conflict between careful planning and a creatively flexible approach to writing comes down to the traditional tension between freedom and discipline. Before starting on any significant project you need to make plans, thoughtful and careful plans. You need to take them seriously and to consult them as you work. But you also need to be flexible and open to new ideas and new possibilities, ready to adjust your plan when that is desirable. You will probably do your best writing when you can combine these approaches.

Unifying Your Writing

Four Unifying Strategies

Readers are perverse creatures who, if given the slightest opportunity, will manage to get lost when they are reading. If they encounter a gap between one point and the next, they lose track of

Remember that your reader can easily get lost

the narrative or argument. If they don't get clear directional signals to guide them between sentences and between paragraphs, they will head off in the wrong direction. If the author does not put in the right word to show the relationship between ideas, they will put in the wrong one. And if they cannot sense an underlying pattern in a piece of writing, they are likely to get confused and quit reading.

The truth is that most readers are lazy, and they won't work at trying to follow what they read. And because they won't, as a writer you have to take the responsibility for making your writing so well unified, so coherent, that a reader will move through it without losing his or her way. You can use a variety of strategies, direct and indirect, to give your writing that kind of unity.

Designs help to control writing

1. **Structural design** The best unifying devices for any writing are the natural thought patterns mentioned in the previous section. A paper built around a cause-and-effect pattern or an assertion-and-support pattern, for example, will often hold together with little or no transitional "glue," just as a carefully constructed rock fence holds together because the pieces of rock fit, not because of the mortar that has been applied from the outside.

In addition to using what seem like natural designs, you can also use stylistic patterns such as *parallel structure*. Notice that the first paragraph in this section uses this device, starting several consecutive sentences with "If they . . . . "

Downshifting (pp. 147–149) and *Commitment and Response* (pp. 164–165) are also two structural designs that act as powerful unifiers: more on them in the chapter on paragraphs.

Using predictions

2. **Predictions** Another indirect way to tie the parts of your paper together is to make a series of predictions to your reader and then carefully follow through on them. For example, James Austin, who writes about chance and creativity, begins a key paragraph, "We can readily distinguish four varieties of chance. . . . " then goes on to talk about Chance I, Chance II, Chance III, and Chance IV. As long as he follows through on his prediction, he has little chance of losing his reader. A writer can get the same effect with ordinal numbers—*first, second, third,* and so on—or with sequence words: *next, subsequently, finally,* and so on.

Repeat words or phrases

3. Repetition Most of us consciously try to avoid repeating the same word or phrase in several consecutive sentences and dig into our memories to come up with substitutes because we don't want our writing to sound monotonous. But repetition can serve as an effective linking device if we use it deliberately with an eye to creating a pattern. See the previous examples of parallelism, for instance. A writer can also consciously repeat a key word in order to furnish readers a series of cues or signals that will keep them moving in the right direction. For example:

> *Country music* is symbolized for most people by Nashville, and it's a fitting symbol without being an exclusive one. "*Country music*" suggests a music of the land. Nashville is a city and a growing one, and so, too, the mainstream *country music* of 1976 is a music by and for urbanized people who may come from the land and remember it with an idealized affection, but who also want to put the brute realities of rural poverty behind them. If much contemporary *country music* strikes purists as slick and false, that's because its hard-core fans want not so much a recollection of how it used to be out on the back forty as an aural Hallmark card. [italics added][3]

A writer can also use a *repeated pronoun* to create a pattern and a continuity that will hold writing together. For example:

> *She* has daydreams of a privileged life. . . . *She* is rather glad to imagine herself without a job. *She* would get up at seven-thirty, not five-thirty. *She* would see her husband off, her children off, maybe drive the latter to school herself, then have a quiet breakfast. *She* would delight in her aloneness—no one on either side of her, working the assembly line. *She* would watch television, meet a friend at a shopping mall, have lunch with her, come home and do some planting or weeding or "fixing" food or "just plain relaxing." That last option is the one *she* favors most when *she* evokes her daytime

[3] John Rockwell, "Blues, and Other Noises, in the Night," *Saturday Review*, September 4, 1976.

dreams while standing and inspecting an endless stream of towels. [italics added][4]

Unify with a metaphor

A third effective way to use repetition as a unifying device is to build a passage around a central image or metaphor. For example:

> In a sense we have come to our nation's Capitol to *cash a check*. When the architects of our republic wrote the magnificent words of the Constitution and Declaration of Independence they were signing a *promissory note* to which every American was to fall heir. This note was a promise that all men would be guaranteed the inalienable rights of life, liberty, and the pursuit of happiness.
>
> It is obvious today that America has *defaulted* on this *promissory note* insofar as her citizens of color are concerned. Instead of honoring this sacred obligation, America has given the Negro people a *bad check*; a *check* which has come back marked *"insufficient funds."* But we refuse to believe that the *bank of justice* is *bankrupt*. We refuse to believe that there are *insufficient funds* in the great *vaults* of opportunity of this nation. So we have come *to cash this check*—a *check* that will give us upon demand the riches of freedom and the security of justice. [italics added][5]

We can classify the three transitional strategies discussed above as *indirect* strategies, as they grow out of the style and structure of writing rather than from deliberate attempts to join the parts of writing. Most of the time you should rely on these indirect strategies as much as you can because writing seems smoother and tighter when its unity comes from the underlying structure rather than from the more obvious external devices that we call transitions. But such external devices are also necessary and fill important functions for any writer.

4. Hooks, links, and directional signals All of us rely heavily on a group of particular words and phrases when we want to show

---

[4] Robert Coles and Jane Hallowell Coles, *Women of Crisis* (New York: Dell Publishing Co., Inc., 1978), pp. 234–235.
[5] Martin Luther King, Jr., "I Have a Dream," copyright 1963 by Martin Luther King, Jr.

relationships or give directions in our writing. We call these terms *transitional words*, and although we have dozens of them to work with, they show only a limited number of relationships. We can classify them according to these seven categories:[6]

1. Coordination or Similarity. Signaled by *likewise, just as, in the same way, similarly*, and so on.

   Example: *Just as* she is unable to finish a project, she is unable to sustain a friendship.

2. Contrast or Qualification. Signaled by *but, however, yet, although, in spite of, nevertheless*, and so on.

   Example: Jones has just married his third and youngest wife; *in spite of* this, he continues to preach against divorce.

3. Alternation. Signaled by *or, either, on the other hand*, and so on.

   Example: *Either* we build more low-cost houses, *or* we will have a city of slums.

4. Inclusiveness or Accumulation. Signaled by *moreover, for example, in addition*, and so on.

   Example: Stanfield lives a degenerate and indolent life; *moreover*, he has no desire to change.

5. Consequence. Signaled by *consequently, therefore, thus, so, as a result*, and so on.

   Example: The governor proposes to triple the tuition at medical schools and do away with low-interest loans; *as a result*, poor students may have to drop out of school.

6. Causation. Signaled by *because, for*, and sometimes *since*.

[6] This list is adapted from W. Ross Winterowd, "The Grammar of Coherence," in *Contemporary Rhetoric: A Conceptual Background with Readings*, ed. W. Ross Winterowd (New York: Harcourt Brace Jovanovich, Inc., 1975), pp. 229–231.

Example: *Since* Jerry does not do well on machine-scored tests, he cannot get into graduate school.

7.   Sequence or Ranking. Signaled by numbers or sequence words such as *first, second, sooner, finally, next,* and so on.

Example: *First* we must win the primary; *later* we can raise funds.

Seven different groups of transition words send out seven different kinds of signals. For that reason, when you need to show a connection between parts of your writing, you can't, figuratively speaking, just reach into a sack of assorted transitional terms and pick one. If you operate that way, you have six chances to go wrong and give your reader a faulty signal. For transition words give out powerful signals that condition your reader to expect certain content to follow; if it does not, the reader gets confused or frustrated, and the whole communication between you can break down.

Transition words are not interchangeable

For example, the word *although* conditions the reader to expect a qualification that contradicts or counteracts the main idea. Here is a sentence in which the signal word is functioning correctly:

Although Scully never graduated from college, he is a tremendously successful businessman.

In the next sentence, however, the reader would say, "What's going on? I don't see the contradiction."

Although Scully never graduated from college, he has never held a good job.

One also couldn't casually substitute *moreover* or *therefore* or *but* for *although*; they all give specific signals that wouldn't work in this sentence.

Therefore, a general list of transition words won't help you much. Rather, you need to be conscious of the relationship you want to signal between sentences or parts of sentences and pick a term from the right group. When you do pick the right words, you move your readers along from one idea to the other, giving good directional signals and gently nudging them in the direction you want them to go. Here are two student paragraphs that show how it's done:

1. The attitudes I take toward Frisbee are dual. *First,* I consider each flight as an individual act, unrelated to how badly or well I threw the disc last time. *Second,* I try to achieve a balance between concentrating too much and not concentrating enough. *If* I lack the first attitude, I feel a little ashamed when the Frisbee fails to reach its intended target; *this feeling* can make me throw even worse the next time, specifically *because* of my fear that *that* will happen, *and so on* in a vicious circle. *On the other hand,* *if* I congratulate myself too much on a good throw, I'm inclined to demand the *same* performance from myself each time. *This* is *also* self-defeating. *Therefore,* I try to isolate each flight as something to be experienced anew. [italics added]

2. *Other* dangers are not as immediately recognizable *although these* are hazards you face every time you dive. Yet *these* dangers—*such as* nitrogen narcosis, the bends, and air embolism—are easily avoided by a diver who has successfully completed a diver training certification course. *This training* is available from many places, *some* of which are local dive shops, *some* university courses, and *some* YMCA's. Without *this certification* you cannot rent equipment or have scuba tanks filled. [italics added]

Here is a choppy student paragraph in which the writer fails to keep the reader moving along smoothly by putting in good links and directional signals.

Practically anybody can get diabetes. Diabetes overlooks sex, race, creed, and color. Diabetes does seem to have a special preference for women over 30. One of the most unusual aspects of the disease is the apparent link to marriage and motherhood. The highest number of deaths from diabetes is among married women. The more children a woman has the more susceptible she is to diabetes.

The writer also has problems with wordiness and order, and the poor transitions magnify them.

Tying It All Together

Even very experienced writers seldom completely master all the diverse strategies for shaping writing into the smooth, easy-flowing, and apparently effortless prose that is the mark of a skillful writer. Most of us admit that we have to revise and tinker with sentences and paragraphs for a long time, patching here and joining there in order to get them to hang together reasonably well. It's never easy. But if you can keep two principles in mind, they may help.

Two guiding principles for unifying your writing

1. Each sentence or paragraph that you write should leave a little residue, a little trace, out of which the next sentence or paragraph develops. It can be an expectation, a hint, a repeated word, or a pattern, but there should be something. Sentences and paragraphs in a piece of discourse should not be truly separate units that don't relate to each other.
2. Between all the units you construct, you should have some kind of hook, real or implied. It can be repetition, parallelism, sequence, or pattern, or it can be a signal word—*therefore, nevertheless, also,* or one from some other group. Whatever you use, the reader should be able to feel the connection. You should try never to have two units so isolated that if one of them came at the bottom of a page and the next one came at the top of the next page, the reader would do a double take and say "Is there something missing?"

You can sense both these principles at work in the following passage, in which the writer has used so many hooking and linking strategies that a diagram of them would look like the wiring in the back of a television set. Yet he has done it so skillfully that the reader moves along, quite unconscious of the signals and hooks.

People who think cowboys are realists generally think so because the cowboy's speech is salty and apparently straightforward, replete with the wisdom of natural men. What that generally means is that cowboy talk sounds shrewd and perceptive, and so it does. In fact, however, both the effect and the intention of much cowboy talk is literary: cowboys are aphorists. Whenever possible, they turn their observations into aphorisms. Some are brilliant aphorists, scarcely inferior to Wilde or La Rochefoucauld; one is proud to steal from them. I plucked a nice one several years ago, to wit: "A woman's love is like the morning dew: it's just as apt to fall on a horseturd as it is on a rose." In such a remark the phrasing is worth more than the perception, and I think the same might be said for the realism of most cowboys. It is a realism in tone only: its insights are either wildly romantic, mock-cynical, or solemnly sentimental. The average cowboy is an excellent judge of horseflesh, only a fair judge of men, and a terrible judge of women, particularly "good women."[7]

It is probable that McMurtry himself wasn't wholly conscious of putting in ties and links as he wrote. Rather, he made the basic unity of the piece come out of the logical structure and out of the natural development of his topic. At least that's the way it seems. And that's the effect that everyone who is trying to be a good writer should strive for.

Exercises

1. *Gathering information*

   a. Take a small notebook or $3'' \times 5''$ cards with you and set out to overhear deliberately some interesting conversations. Some likely listening places are the lounge in the student union, the waiting area at an airport or bus station, the local pizza and beer parlor, the laundromat, or the check-out line at the grocery store.

   b. Interview someone whose job provides opportunities to

[7] Larry McMurtry, *In a Narrow Grave* (New York: Simon & Schuster, Inc., 1968), pp. 148–149.

meet many different kinds of people; for example, a cab driver, an admissions officer at your school, a nurse who works in the emergency room at the hospital, or a bartender in a local bar. Talk with that person about his or her job and find out what kinds of experiences make it interesting. Take notes that would help you to write a descriptive anecdote about working at such a job.

2. *Preparing to write*

a. Identify the probable audience for each of these written documents and state that audience's reason for reading the document.

   • an application for a scholarship
   • a brochure on how to establish credit
   • an article on women alcoholics

b. Identify the purpose a writer might have in writing the following essays. Compare your answers with those of two other people in your class.

   • an article on home computers
   • an article on pregnancy among teen-agers
   • an article on job opportunities for engineers

3. *Generating ideas*

Here are three topics that could yield some interesting material for a paper:

   • Buying or Building a Home in the 1980s
   • Career Goals for Women in the 1980s
   • Dressing for Success

Choose the one that you find most interesting and see how much material you can generate by using the following strategies for discovering what you know:

a. *Brainstorming.* For fifteen minutes write down every idea that comes to you about your topic. Remember that in brainstorming no idea is wrong or irrelevant.

b. *Focused freewriting.* Formulate a statement about your chosen topic—for example, "Trends in home buying are going to change in the 1980s"—and then start writing about that statement. Write for ten minutes without taking your pen from the paper or stopping to reflect on what you are writing.

c. *Capsuling.* After thinking about your topic for ten or fifteen minutes, write a brief abstract or summary of the main points you want to make.

d. *Journalist's questions.* Write down brief answers to these questions about your topic: who, what, where, when, why, how?

e. *Anecdotes.* Write down a personal anecdote or narrative of either your own or someone else's experience that you could use to illustrate some point about your topic.

f. *Prism thinking.* Write three sentences about the topic that reflects these three differing viewpoints: that of a participant, that of a spectator, and that of a reporter.

4. *Organizing your ideas*

Write a formal or informal outline, a controlling thesis sentence, a one-paragraph abstract or summary, or a subdivided list that would help you to organize one of these writing tasks:

a. a brochure on nutrition for low-income families

b. a letter to a judge appealing a suspension of your driver's license for receiving four speeding tickets in one year

c. a proposal for expanding and reorganizing student parking facilities on your campus

d. letter to parents requesting apartment (no dorms)

5. Analyze the controlling patterns of the following student paragraphs. If necessary, review p. 52 to refresh your memory about organizational patterns.

a. From small towns to big cities across the United States

there is an increasing need for a federally funded day care program to look after the children of the multitude of mothers who work outside the home. According to recent estimates, five out of six million preschool children of working mothers in the U.S. do not have adequate day care facilities. Some children are taken to unlicensed facilities providing substandard care, while others are left at home to provide for themselves. The following statistics dramatize the problem.

• The number of married women with preschool age children who hold jobs has doubled since 1960.

• Among women who are widowed, divorced, or separated from their husbands, slightly more than half with preschool children are in the labor force.

• In total, about six million pre-school children have working mothers, and almost 27 million children under 18 have mothers employed outside the home.

b. If you have ever watched the lid on a saucepan full of boiling water cooking the vegetables for dinner, you may have noticed that the lid moves up and down. This is not magic, it is steam pressure. Imagine kernels in a popcorn popper. When heated the kernels pop and expand, taking up far more room than before. Water behaves like this when heated also, because steam is just water that takes up more room, expanding and building up pressure unless it can escape. The whistle on a kettle works from built up steam pressure which must escape through the spout. The steam engine is like a huge kettle, but the pressure is used to push pistons and turn wheels instead of just blowing a whistle.

c. Have you ever wondered what it would be like to meet Houston Oiler Earl Campbell? To actually sit down and talk with him for a few minutes? Many people only dream of such an opportunity, but talking to Earl Campbell, Roger Staubach, or Reggie Jackson is just an everyday happening for a sportswriter.

6. Analyze the unifying devices, both direct and indirect, in this complete short essay written to accompany a two-page layout of photographs of oil field workers.

Working the Rigs

No one really likes the work. No one really likes getting out in the Texas sun and skinning his knuckles on heavy sections of steel pipe or wrestling with a spinning chain or climbing to the top of a rig where a single slip can lead to a ninety-foot fall or mixing drilling mud that gets in work clothes and combines with the grease, sweat, and oil to make a smell that no amount of washing can remove. No one likes to put up a rig in one isolated spot then take it down later only to put it up again in another isolated spot miles away. And no one likes the long hours and graveyard shifts and the endless driving back and forth to the job and coming home, as one roughneck put it, to "warmed over coffee and an asleep old lady."

Then why do people do it? They may like the money: when there's plenty of work, as there is today, roughnecks can make $15,000 to $25,000 in a year. They may like the people they work with. They may take pride in their toughness and satisfaction from knowing they can do a particular dirty and dangerous job better than the next man. And they may like the life that surrounds the oil rigs—the high school football games, the fishing trips in a pickup with a camper on the back, the beers on Saturday night, the long Sunday dinners after a morning in the Baptist church. But no one really likes the work.[8]

7. Rewrite these student paragraphs to make them more unified:

a. If you were to change television channels again, you might find a rather innocent type of cartoon such as Walt Disney's Mickey Mouse or Donald Duck. You probably remember watching these when you were a child. This type of cartoon usually contains little or no violence. Often it subtly teaches children a moral. Some of these cartoons may contain a little violence, but it is presented in the form of slapstick comedy. Mickey Mouse and Donald Duck were popular in the '50s and are still popular today.

---

[8] *Texas Monthly*, October 1978, p. 124.

b. We have found that Braille, the traditional method of teaching the blind to read, is becoming outdated. Learning and using it is a slow procedure. The cost of paper is soaring and once symbols have been punched the paper is not reusable. This causes a large waste of costly material. Books typed in Braille are unusually bulky and hard to handle.

8. Analyze the controlling pattern and the unifying devices in this student paper. Does the paper seem to be well organized and developed? Give reasons for your answer.

Computer Crime: A Modern Threat to Modern Banking

In 1973, a teller at the Union Dime savings bank in New York City made $1.2 million by removing money from newly opened accounts. He covered his tracks by making simple correction entries into the bank's computer. He was only discovered when police investigated the source of the money he used for his expensive gambling habit.

In 1978, Stanley Rifkin, a computer consultant at Security Pacific Bank, stole $10.3 million from the bank. He obtained the bank's "electronic funds transfer code," called up the bank from a public telephone, and used the code to have the money sent to his Swiss account. He then flew to Switzerland, converted the money into diamonds, and returned with them to the United States. He was found out, however, when he started boasting about how he beat the system.

These are just a couple of examples of how millions of dollars are being stolen annually from banks around the U.S. The criminals range from the amateur to the professional and computer systems are amazingly underprotected against them. Until recently computers were thought to be foolproof but current trends are dispelling that notion.

For instance, over the past decade the growth of computer technology was considered a boon that would create new markets and improve efficiency. However, protection for these systems received incredibly inadequate attention. As a result now, while the average embezzler takes home $19,000, computer related bank frauds average $450,000.* Computers have in fact opened up a whole new dimension to theft. Last year an estimated $3 billion was lost through reported and unreported crimes. This figure is roughly twenty times what it was in 1970.**

There are three major reasons for this sudden increase:

1. The increasing availability of low cost personal computers.
2. The increasing number of people, especially students, learning how to use computers.
3. The increasing number of bank employees with access to the computer systems.

In 1976, 1,500 personal computers were sold in the U.S. Today there are more than 500,000. By the mid-eighties the total is expected to exceed 3,000,000.*** Through the use of these personal computers many people can gain access to a bank's central computer and instruct it to transfer money into their accounts. However it is easier for amateurs to use personal computers to tap data transmission lines and steal information or feed in instructions to transfer money from one account to another. Banks use these data transmission lines to transfer more than $4 billion electronically each day. Motorola Inc. recently demonstrated how about $1,000 worth of equipment, including a $750 personal computer, can be used to program phony transactions in a bank's system. The modern thief, equipped in such a way, can make far more than the conventional armed bank robber with far fewer chances of being caught.

According to Donn Parker, a senior systems consultant with SRI International considered the nation's leading authority on computer fraud: "Most perpetrators are young, eighteen to thirty years old. They tend to be amateurs with no prior

* Omni. March 1981.
** Business Week. April 20, 1981.
*** International Data Corp.

criminal record. They love to play computer games and are fascinated by the challenge of trying to beat the system. Teachers like to show students how to crash the computer. Ostensibly this is done to familiarize them with the computer's inner workings. But things inevitably get out of hand—and the result is that universities are turning out a whole new generation of computer criminals."

A few years ago computers were protected from most people because most people knew very little about them. Today, computer programming is taught in most schools and stores like Radio Shack and Computerland offer a plethora of computer and electronics equipment. The result is that many teenagers are now ready to take on the large banking computers.

With the increase in size and complexity of computers used in banks the number of employees using them has increased too with the result that more and more people have direct access to a bank's computer system. Since most systems cannot identify users, these employees can easily make transactions with very slim chances of discovery.

A startling fact many people are unaware of is that Citibank is the only U.S. bank which has insurance coverage against third party wire tapping and consequent funds removal. In other words if money in a Citibank account is stolen in this way Citibank will get the same amount back. The other banks have no such coverage, and since wire tappers are so hard to trace, the chances that they will get their money back are extremely slim. Since banks have a reputation to maintain they quietly swallow losses incurred by electronic theft.

Many companies such as IBM and Motorola Inc. have started marketing sophisticated new devices designed to prevent electronic theft. They are confident that these will work. On the other hand the sophistication of equipment and methods used by thieves is bound to increase too. Whether the banks will ever manage to stop these criminals still remains to be seen. But both sides, banks and thieves, will certainly have to try hard to get ahead of the other.

Yusuf Mauladad

Suggested Writing Assignments

Theme 1

Purpose To give you practice in writing a clear and simple description that will be easy for an audience to read and understand.

Procedure Choose some job you currently have or recently have had and describe its chief features clearly and completely enough so that your reader would know whether he or she would want to take such a job. Before you start, write down what your audience would want to know about such a job and rough out some plan of organization to work from. Give enough specific information about the job—salary, hours, duties, good and bad points, and so on—to allow your reader to make an intelligent decision. Here are some of the kinds of jobs you might describe:

a. Working in an ice cream parlor or a doughnut shop
b. Delivering furniture for a furniture rental firm
c. Cooking in a franchised fast-food place; for example, Mc-Donald's or Kentucky Fried Chicken
d. Baby sitting
e. Modeling
f. Working as a hospital ward clerk
g. Working as a waterfront director at a camp

Theme 2

Purpose To give you practice in writing an anecdote or narrative that could serve as the basis for an informative paper by giving a specific and concrete illustration of a point you want to make. For example, you could illustrate the dangers of inexperienced and uninformed people going on a canoe or backpacking trip by narrating a story or incident that shows what can happen in such situations.

Procedure Drawing on your own experience or imagination, relate an anecdote or construct a credible narrative that would help you write a convincing paper on one of the topics below. The anecdote or narrative should probably be from two to four paragraphs long. Try to make your writing concrete and visual rather than depend on adjectives alone to carry your meaning.

Before you write your narrative, at the top of your paper identify your topic, describe in some detail the audience for whom you would be writing, and state the purpose you would have in writing.

Topics

a. The hazards of buying a used car
b. The unexpected spin-offs of hitchhiking
c. The disadvantages of being beautiful
d. Traveling alone in a foreign country
e. Riding a bicycle in city traffic
f. The folly of ignoring flood or tornado warnings

The 3 Components of Rhetoric

The introduction of this text defines *rhetoric* as the art of speaking or writing effectively and persuasively, and tries to convince you that the study of rhetoric would help you in many different ways when you need to communicate with someone. Your communication problem could range from writing directions for assembling a bicycle to giving a report on school desegregation in Atlanta to persuading a judge that your driver's license should not be revoked for a third speeding ticket to writing a campaign brochure for a candidate for the senate. Some people would claim that you do not need a command of rhetoric for the first two writing assignments because your purpose there would be primarily to explain and inform, that is, to do expository writing. They would argue that you need rhetoric only for the last two assignments because your purpose there would be primarily to persuade.

Knowledge of rhetoric is useful for all writing

In the broad sense, however, a person needs a command of rhetoric and an understanding of rhetorical principles just as much for expository or explanatory writing as for strictly persuasive or argumentative writing. To handle both tasks one must be aware of the four ingredients that are involved in the communication process and understand how they all work together. Those four ingredients are (1) the persuasive purpose, (2) the audience, (3) the speaker's or writer's role or persona, and (4) the content of the argument or the supporting material. Together these four components make up the *rhetorical square*.

The diagram of the square is useful for making an abstract concept a little more concrete, but we should realize immediately that in practice almost no writer or speaker gives a symmetrical presentation in which all the rhetorical elements have equal importance. Some writers are so dynamic and forceful that their per-

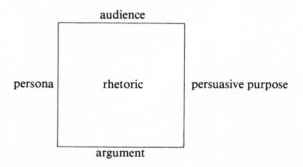

sonalities dominate the audience; others present such a clear and logical argument that we forget who is speaking. Still others present an audience-centered argument that seems to be more a sales talk than an expression of opinion. So the theoretical square sometimes turns out to be a lopsided quadrangle. Nevertheless, when we plan our rhetoric, we must take all the elements into consideration. The structure will be incomplete if any side of the square is omitted. Thus, the person who starts out to write a paper or a speech must start out by posing these questions:

Questions to ask when constructing rhetoric

1. What am I trying to do?
2. Who is my audience and what are its important characteristics?
3. How should I present myself to the audience?
4. What kinds of arguments or supporting material should I use?

When this same person becomes the reader or listener instead of the writer and wants to analyze and evaluate the rhetoric of others, the appropriate questions are these:

Questions to ask when evaluating rhetoric

1. What is the author's purpose?
2. Who is the audience? Does the author seem to be aware of and in tune with that audience?
3. What is the author's role or persona? Is it effective?
4. What are the arguments and how are they presented?

Only when you have considered each of these components of an essay or speech can you make a supported judgment about whether a piece is successful and why it does or does not work.

Purpose

The answer to the question "What is my purpose?" is often simple, even obvious. For some student papers, the rhetorical purpose may be stated in the assignment, as it is in some of the analytical writing assignments in this text. Or you may be asked to choose one side of a current issue and write an argument for or against it. In that case you establish your purpose as soon as you decide which view you want to support. But these kinds of writing exercises are really just that—exercises. They can provide useful practice in organizing and expressing your ideas, but they don't really require that you think carefully about your goals. To do that you need to move beyond the context of your composition class into real writing situations, either actual or simulated.

Finding your purpose in writing

Suppose, for example, that for your major paper in sociology you choose to write on some of the ways in which the women's movement seems to be affecting the marriages of young people. If you wanted to do an objective, analytical paper in which you simply list and describe such changes as more sharing of child care and housework, fewer children, more women continuing to work after marriage, and couples marrying later than they used to, your purpose is to inform rather than persuade. You should concentrate on presenting data and keep your language neutral. If, however, you feel strongly either that the women's movement has helped young people to make stronger and more rewarding marriages or that it has badly hurt the institution of marriage, your purpose will be primarily persuasive, and you should be aware of that before you start.

The purpose of your paper will control the kind of preliminary thinking and investigating you do, as well as the material that you include in your organizing outline, thesis sentence, or summary. For example, if you want to assert that the women's movement has improved marriage in this decade, your thesis sentence could look like this:

> The feminist movement has helped many of today's marriages by promoting more male participation in raising children, by encouraging women to become more interesting companions, by discouraging women from manipulating men through sex, and by encouraging women to become financially independent so that they don't feel trapped.

If, however, you want to argue that the new feminists are hurting today's marriages, your summary might look like this:

> The new feminists are hurting marriage and contributing to the rising divorce rate. They cause tension in households by

encouraging wives to compete with their husbands, and a wife's insistence that the husband help with the housework and children at times when he needs to be spending twelve hours a day on his job may seriously hurt his career. Liberated women also cause divorces when they decide that the marriage is stunting their personal development. Their new freedom and aggressiveness can also threaten a man sexually and thus hurt the physical side of the marriage. Also because more women can earn their own living, they sometimes just walk out when problems start rather than stay and try to work them through.

Either of these organizing tools will give you a solid foundation for your paper, help you cut out irrelevant material, and make it easier for you to control your writing because you know precisely where you are going.

This technique of articulating your purpose before you begin to write is useful whether you are writing papers or essay exams for one of your courses, writing a member of Congress to ask for support of a bill, drafting a statement of your personal goals in order to apply for a scholarship or admission to an honors program, or composing a campaign speech to be used in your race for the student senate. Knowing precisely what you want to do will help you shape your argument, eliminate unnecessary material, and make the most efficient use of the limited time and space you have.

Under some circumstances—writing an essay exam, for example—you may have to make a quick decision about purpose; at other times, you may have the leisure to think out your goals well ahead of the time you write. In either case, the time it takes to choose a purpose is well spent. Too often students will spend thirty minutes of a fifty-minute exam writing at random before they begin to focus on the real issues; their reasoning seems to be that showing the teacher they have a lot of information will bring rewards. Usually the reacher's response is, "This is all very interesting, but you haven't answered the questions." If you are writing an out-of-class paper, starting to write before deciding what you intend to do can produce a disaster like the paper from which the jargon paragraph on page 207 was taken.

Finally, you should learn to set reasonable goals for your writ-

Set reasonable goals in your writing

ing. You are, after all, not a professional writer or rhetorician, and no one expects you to produce brilliant arguments or profound judgments that will dazzle your audience. In a discussion you are accomplishing enough—indeed, a great deal—if you convince a skeptical audience that you have some good points and that they should think about them. When you are writing term papers, your philosophy professor will be satisfied with a paper that shows you have a decent grasp of a philosopher's theories; and your biology professor will be pleased with a report that is clear and accurate. If you set for yourself goals that are too ambitious and unrealistically high, you will defeat yourself before you start. The poet Robert Browning's suggestion that "a man's reach should exceed his grasp" is not necessarily good advice.

Audience

How to Analyze Your Audience

Once you have your purpose clearly in mind, your next task is to define and analyze your audience. A sure sense of your audience—knowing who it is and what assumptions you can reasonably make about it—is crucial to the success of rhetoric. In practice, you have probably been making sound inferences about audience for a long time and putting those inferences to good use in your personal rhetoric. Tailoring your appeal to suit your audience is, after all, primarily a matter of using everyday, common-sense psychology. Most young people know almost instinctively what tack to take when they want something from their parents. They know too that what may work with one parent may not succeed with the other; thus, they modify their arguments accordingly. They are equally skillful in varying their language, their tone, their modes of appeal to fit other audiences: teachers, friends, teammates, coaches, brothers and sisters, or prospective employers. By drawing on experience and information accumulated over a period of time they know, almost without thinking about it, how to approach a particular audience.

Start with common-sense psychology

The techniques you use to appeal to a larger, more remote, and less well known audience are no different from those you would

Catalogue the traits of your audience

use with a small group that you know intimately. You base your rhetoric on what you know about your audience. You must keep in mind the concerns and values of the people you want to reach; you should have some knowledge of their educational and social backgrounds, how old they are, what kind of work they do, and whether they are, on the whole, liberal or conservative about religion, sex, and politics.

Here are the key questions to ask yourself when you are analyzing your audience:

Key questions about your audience

1. Who are my readers? How well educated are they? How old are they?
2. What is important to my audience?
3. What economic and social class does most of my audience fit into?
4. What does my audience expect to get from reading my paper? Why will they be reading it?
5. What assumptions can I make about my audience's knowledge of my subject? Which terms will I have to explain? Do they have a general knowledge of my topic?
6. Is my audience going to take a positive or negative attitude toward my topic? How will that attitude affect my writing?

Once you realize who your audience is, however, your writing will begin to take on form and character, and you can start to fill in some of the unknowns.

Suppose, for example, that you are one of six students who have been chosen to meet with a board of professors and administrators to work out a new grading system for your college. You are the one who has been chosen to present the students' proposal that the college abolish pass/fail courses and go to a system of four grades: A, B, C, and Course in Progress. Under this program a student would be allowed to keep repeating a course until he or she had made at least a C in it.

What do you know about your audience? First, they are mostly middle aged, from thirty-five to fifty-five; they went to college under a no-nonsense grading system that punished poor students with F's. Second, they are intelligent, educated people who believe that they are open-minded, flexible, and willing to listen to reason. Third, they want to discourage dropouts and failures, but they are reluctant to do anything that will lower standards. Fourth, they are sensitive to the opinions of parents, alumni, and the board of trustees, and are aware that the school must have contributions from them. Armed with this kind of information, which is no more than an accumulation of common-sense observations, you would be able to choose the kind of argument that you think is best suited to your audience and purpose.

Advantages of Analyzing Your Audience

Even though drawing up this kind of description of your audience's principal traits requires little more than thinking about and writing down what you instinctively know about people, the analysis is nevertheless an extremely useful exercise. You should try to get in the habit of going through it before every writing task. For one thing, having to give your audience's pertinent character traits in writing forces you to think more specifically about what group or groups you want to reach and keeps your attention focused on that segment of the whole. In the situation just described, for instance, the students in your audience are comparatively unimportant, for they have no power to make the change you want. Your real audience is the faculty, who have to be persuaded that giving a student an F really doesn't help in the long run, and the administration, who must be convinced that the four-grade system is practical to administer and desirable because it will keep students in college.

Avoid writing for yourself

You should also try to keep your audience constantly in mind in order to avoid a habit that is all too easy to slip into—that of writing for yourself. Students who have strong opinions on social and political issues are particularly apt to do this. They want to show where they stand on a controversial issue and sometimes seem more concerned about showing the reader that they have admirable feelings than they are about convincing anyone.

Eliminate unnecessary material

A third reason for fixing your audience firmly in mind before you start writing is that by doing so you avoid wasting time with unnecessary explanations and definitions. If you are writing for your fellow students, you do not need to repeat what is common knowledge to all of you. If you are writing a paper or an exam for a course and your audience is just your professor, you will only cause irritation if you stop to define terms that are taken for granted as part of the working vocabulary of the course: for example, *ethical systems* in a philosophy course, *imagery* and *prosody*, in a poetry course, or *learning behavior* or *feedback* in an educational psychology course.

It is virtually impossible to frame an appeal that will work with large, undifferentiated masses of people, and you would do better not to try. The attempt to do so can produce little but bland and vapid generalities that would annoy any perceptive audience. The wiser course is to set the boundaries to your audience as precisely as you can, decide what major characteristics the members of that audience are apt to have in common, and keep those characteristics in mind when you frame your appeal. If you are addressing a group of medical doctors, you can reasonably assume that they are, as a whole, affluent, conservative, intelligent, and socially prominent. Some of them do not fit into these categories, of course, but reading the newspapers, knowing the legislative record of the American Medical Association, and drawing on your personal experience will support such a general judgment. Using the same process of reasoning, you can legitimately make comparable generalizations about farmers, teachers, blue-collar workers, military people, and other relatively homogeneous groups. In any group you characterize there will be numerous exceptions, but they are not the ones who set the patterns you must have to work from.

Legitimate appeals to your audience

The Importance of Sincerity

At this point, some of you are undoubtedly thinking: "But this is a sellout. You're suggesting that we compromise, that instead of saying what we think we should figure out what will please the audience and say that instead. That's dishonest." Such a reaction is understandable, but it misses the point. No one is recommending that you be insincere or pretend to agree with attitudes and beliefs in order to curry favor with your readers. In fact, that kind of approach will soon prove self-defeating because words have a way of catching up with one and because the writer or speaker who is strictly an opportunist may lose every segment of the audience.

There is a distinct difference between cynically playing on your audience's biases and prejudices and appealing to their legitimate interests and concerns. The rhetorician who does the first shows contempt for an audience by assuming that they can be easily manipulated through their emotions and do not have the intelligence to think for themselves. Chapter 11 on propaganda discusses this kind of approach. The writer or speaker who tries to appeal to an audience's legitimate concerns, however, can express opinions honestly, but in a way that shows genuine regard for the interests and sensitivities of the audience.

Suppose, for example, that you are helping with a fund-raising drive to add a new wing to your local library. If you have no scruples about how you do it, you might suggest to Mr. Jones, who you know is not interested in books and never goes near the library, that a large donation would get his name in the paper and make him look like a booklover and patron of culture. This approach is dishonest and exploitive. If, however, you point out to him that a good library is an asset to the town because it attracts young families who want to settle in a place with cultural advantages, you are making an honest appeal to his interests. But you don't have to start out by saying, "Mr. Jones, I know you don't care anything about books, but. . . . "

Keeping Your Audience in Mind

Probably the most common breakdowns in establishing communication with your audience come from neglecting to identify your audience before you start to write or from just forgetting to keep it in mind once you have begun. If you are going to argue that women should no longer settle for the secondary roles in the professions—nurse instead of doctor, bookkeeper instead of investment counselor, secretary instead of executive—you are not likely to make an effective argument unless you decide ahead of time whom you are going to address: women themselves, leaders in the professions, or the faculties of professional schools. Say you determine that your audience is predominantly conservative and practical; if you then allow yourself to go off into an idealistic and emotional argument—and this frequently happens with issues on which people have strong feelings—you are defeating your own rhetorical purpose.

At the worst, the failure to consider your audience and its characteristics can twist attempts at persuasion into what is actually a

*Watch out for
anti-rhetoric*

form of *anti-rhetoric*. Take, for instance, an ardent champion of civil rights who says she wants to improve job opportunities for blacks in her community. In a speech to a local civic service club she berates local employers for their exploitation of blacks and their discriminatory hiring practices while pointing out that she was putting blacks into key positions ten years ago and, in addition, was financing scholarships to help them. This speaker may be sincere about wanting to open more jobs for blacks, but she is not likely to do it by attacking those who could help and then further alienating her audience by holding herself up as a model of noble behavior. This kind of rhetoric does more to boost the speaker's ego than to persuade anyone. Her audience will become defensive and hostile and is likely to reject anything she suggests. Sociologists call the reaction *backlash*. The student radicals of the late 1960s, with their obscenities and "nonnegotiable demands," were really practicing anti-rhetoric.

There is, of course, a need for rhetoric that attacks, accuses, and agitates for change. You cannot and should not always try to be pleasant. But the best time to be militant and hostile in your speech or writing is when your real audience is not another person or group that you really hope to persuade, but a third audience whom you are trying to influence to be for you and against your opponent. For instance, suppose you were participating in a television debate about gun control laws; you are against them, your opponent is for them. Your real audience is the television audience, not the person who favors gun control laws. Under these circumstances you can attack gun control laws as an infringement on constitutional rights and interference with free enterprise. You are certainly not going to convince your opponent by such arguments, but you might influence many people in the viewing audience. So when you begin to compose an angry attack on some person or issue, stop to think who your real audience is. If, for instance, it is a legislator or administrator whom you really hope to influence, don't attack, reason. You simply do not convince people by antagonizing them.

*You do not convince
an audience by
making it angry*

Audiences for Student Writing

Students may go about finding their audiences in several ways. Often they have no problem because the audience is explicitly or implicitly designated in the assignment. You may be asked to prepare for a class a particular report, or to submit to a committee a statement of your reasons for wanting to participate in an honors seminar in history. If you are writing an essay exam or a term paper, obviously the audience is your professor or the grader; if possible, it may be a good idea to find out which. If, however, your only instructions are to write a paper about your views on credit cards or an argument for or against abolishing the English requirement in your college, you need to find your audience before you begin. One question you might ask yourself is, "Who would be interested in these topics?" That will give you a starting place. From there, you can narrow your audience further by concentrating on a group of people about the same age or of a certain educational level. In most cases, it is probably easier and more natural for you to write to other young people.

Identifying your audience for student papers

The simplest device for finding your audience for papers, and one that many teachers recommend, is to address your paper to your class. Doing this solves your problem about vocabulary and terminology and gives you a basis of common assumptions and experience from which to work. It also eliminates the artificial and intimidating situation of writing solely for your teacher. Whatever audience you decide on, you will produce a better paper if you write in capital letters at the top of your rough draft "AUDIENCE:_____" and specify your readers and their characteristics.

Persona

Once you have defined your audience, your next task is to decide the role that you, as rhetorician, are going to play for your audience. The term *persona* best describes that role because it is a comparatively neutral term. *Persona* derives from the Latin word for the masks worn by the actors in ancient classical drama, masks that immediately classified their roles for the audience: a smiling mask for a comic character, a sorrowful one for a tragic character. Thus, *persona* is an apt word to describe the identity assumed by a writer or speaker.

Now, only one paragraph into this section, I know I am already in trouble with my audience. For rather complicated psychological reasons that I will not try to go into here, almost all of you put a premium on "naturalness" and "being yourself," even though you may not have a precise idea of what you mean by those concepts. Thus, the words *masks, role playing,* and *assuming an identity* may have bad connotations for you. Once more, you may suspect that you are being advised to be insincere and artificial in order to persuade people. And once more, I will try to convince you that the techniques we use in rhetoric are really natural ways of behaving that all of us employ constantly without even thinking about it.

Role playing is natural

Psychologists have long known that the normal person plays many roles.[1] As a person who lives in a complex and sophisticated culture, you find yourself in a variety of different situations during the course of a day, and you adjust your behavior accordingly. You wear no mask when you are grousing at the alarm clock in the privacy of your room, but you assume one when you get to the breakfast table and want to be at least civil to your companions. In class you assume the role of student; you pay attention, take notes, ask questions. Your instructor is playing the role of teacher, acting quite differently in the classroom than in an office talking to a colleague ten minutes before. Late in the afternoon you may shift to the role of son or daughter when you are talking over the phone with your parents and that evening show another facet of your personality when you are drinking beer with your friends. All this behavior is unaffected and sincere; you are being yourself, but in a flexible way that allows you to choose responses appropriate to your situation and your audience.

How to Decide on Your Persona

Such flexibility is precisely what is involved in establishing your persona in a rhetorical situation. The only difference is that when you are not familiar with your audience, you need to think ahead about your purpose, the make-up of your audience, and the image of yourself that you want to project. In face-to-face situations, you can still rely largely on instinct; common sense tells you that it is all right to act casually at a meeting of student advisers but foolish to do so at a hearing before the dean of students. When

[1] See Kenneth J. Gergen, "The Healthy, Happy Human Being Wears Many Masks," *Psychology Today*, May 1972, pp. 31 ff.

you are writing, however, you have fewer clues to guide you; therefore, it is a good idea to think about your persona before you frame an appeal on an important issue.

Purpose and audience

For example, suppose you are writing to the city council to request that the city elections be held when college is in session in order that more students can participate. Before you start, ask yourself how you want to appear to the council members. Your answer will probably be something like this: young voter—responsible, mature, eager to participate in civic affairs. If, however, you are writing to set up a job interview the line after "PERSONA" might be: environmental engineer—intelligent, serious, hardworking, optimistic about opportunities in the field. For a rhetorical situation in which your purpose is to protest college plans to build a new swimming pool when the campus needs more classrooms, you could take on the role of the angry young person who is concerned about the quality of education and distressed about misplaced priorities in spending. There is no reason why all these roles cannot be quite honestly assumed by one person; a variety of roles does not necessarily reflect any conflict, deceit, or insincerity.

The Ethical Appeal

Your ability to establish a believable persona who is worthy of the respect and trust of the audience is the basis of the *ethical appeal*, the appeal that convinces because of the writer's or speaker's reputation for honesty, reliability, and competence. Now obviously proving that one is honest, reliable, and competent takes many years; in the long run you can establish good ethical appeal only by consistently behaving in ways that give people reason to trust you. In writing, however, there are certain things you can do that will make your audience feel that you are honest and reliable. For

Establishing credibility

one thing, don't make extreme statements that will suggest that you are either naive or careless about the facts. Also, write in a straightforward, unpretentious, and clear style that suggests that you are not trying to cover up anything. Cite examples and evidence to support your positions, and, whenever possible, briefly mention what experience or training you have that gives you the qualifications to write on that topic. Finally, do your homework on any issue you are going to write on, and don't be afraid to admit your limitations.

So remember to be yourself and don't try to fake it. Be aware, however, that you can assume many different roles and be genuine in them all. You can be a compassionate volunteer who is working with retarded children; you can be an angry critic of the school system's failure to teach 20 percent of our population to read; you can be an amused observer of the latest dress fad on your campus; or you can be a neutral investigator of the way in which traffic violations are handled on your campus. Each role is sincere and legitimate; you have just assumed different personas according to your purpose.

The Damaging Effects of Carelessness

Avoid making a bad impression

Writers who have obviously neglected to do sufficient homework before starting to write demonstrate one kind of carelessness, and a serious kind. Readers will turn them off with a contemptuous, "They just don't know what they're talking about." But there are also other kinds of carelessness that can seriously damage the image you want to present to your audience.

Suppose, for instance, that you are applying for a scholarship. You can demonstrate your financial need, show that you are both bright and ambitious, and produce excellent letters of recommendation. You put a lot of thought into the letter of application, but you do not take the time to check the spelling of Optimist Club; so you address the letter to the President of the Jonesville Optomist Club. You will make a bad impression even before the envelope is opened. In the body of the letter, you use *except* when you mean *accept*; you speak of your ambition to be a veterinarian, but spell it as most people pronounce it, *vetinarian*; when you mention a college's fine reputation, you write *it's* instead of *its*; you conclude the letter by saying, "I appreciate your consideration irregardless of your decision."

This letter may well ruin your chance of getting a scholarship because, without your being aware of it, you have established a persona quite different from the one you intended. By careless spelling and grammar you have created the image of someone who is too lazy to look up words and too sloppy to check a letter for errors. You have characterized yourself just as surely as you would by appearing for a formal interview with mud on your shoes, a button off your shirt, and grease stains on your coat. You may be an admirable person in spite of your dirty clothes and a promising student in spite of your bad spelling and faulty diction; but if you start off by establishing an image that annoys people, you will probably never have the chance to demonstrate your real abilities.

There are also other important ways in which you can damage your persona in a letter. If your writing is inflated and pretentious, and the reader has to dig through a layer of abstract phrases and vague terms to find your meaning, you are certain to make a bad impression. The kind of practical and knowledgeable people who make the important decisions of the world have little tolerance for pompous platitudes and no time to waste on writing that is hard to understand. They assume that the person writing the letter is also pompous and confused, not worth their time. People in responsible positions also judge a person's ability to write on the basis of their letters or applications. Editors have told me that they reject over half of the manuscripts that come across their desks simply because the covering letter is badly written. They reason that the person who cannot write a decent letter certainly cannot write an article or book worth considering.

You may protest that people who make judgments on the basis of spelling, punctuation, and writing style are being shortsighted and unfair. You may have a point. An inability to spell is scarcely an indication of bad character, and a fondness for clichés may not mean that a person is stupid. Nevertheless, the people who decide who will be accepted for law school or the foreign service, who will get scholarships or grants, and who will be chosen for an in-service training program or the position of district supervisor do judge people partially on the basis of their writing. The piece of paper with your words on it and your name at the bottom represents *you*. You cannot change that. And when an administrator or firm receives a flood of applications from well-qualified people, those who have written poor letters will not survive the first screening.

In other kinds of writing situations, getting all your commas and apostrophes in the right place may not be as important as adapting your vocabulary to your audience or finding the kinds of examples that your audience can understand. In the end, all such decisions have to be made with your audience in mind. You need to decide what tone you want to establish between you and your audience, and out of that tone the right persona will develop. All

People base judgments on writing

this is complex business that will be covered at length in the section on tone in Chapter 8.

The Content of the Argument

The ingredients of rhetoric that we have been discussing so far—persuasive purpose, audience, and persona—are essential parts of the rhetorical square. Without them, any argument exists in isolation, sealed off from the real world. But those ingredients, in turn, are totally dependent on the arguments; without it, they comprise a flimsy framework with nothing to support it. Finally, then, the argument itself is the most important part of the rhetorical square, for it must provide a substantial and well-constructed base on which to build.

This last side of the rhetorical square is too complex to explain in a few pages at the end of a chapter. In fact, the rest of this text concentrates on the analysis and evaluation of arguments, on the ways in which people seek to persuade, and on suggestions that will help you incorporate those techniques of persuasion into your own writing. Thus, the brief discussion here will be no more than general definitions and a description of the two categories into which argumentative techniques fall.

Logical and Nonlogical

Two categories of argument: logical and nonlogical

The simplest way to describe these categories is to label them *logical* and *nonlogical*. The logical modes of argument are those that appeal to the intellect, that try to persuade by setting in motion thought processes that will culminate in the audience's reaching the desired conclusion. The chief forms of logical argument, or what Aristotle called the "appeal to reason," are deduction, induction, cause and effect, definition, arguments from comparison, and the use of evidence and testimony. The nonlogical methods most commonly used in persuasion are connotation, figurative language, tone, and diction. The classical rhetoricians classified these techniques under the "appeal to emotion."

This classification looks attractively neat, but like most pigeonholing it oversimplifies and distorts the real article. In practice, almost any rhetorical appeal combines the logical and the nonlog-

Rhetoric combines the two categories

ical; sometimes it is nearly impossible to separate the two elements. For example, a sociologist making an inductive argument may have a respectable number of samples but may describe them in connotative language. Is this logical or nonlogical? A philosopher may build an impressive argument on analogy, but that analogy may be a persuasive metaphor. On close analysis we usually find that the skeleton or frame of any argument will be logical; that is, it will be built on induction, evidence, definition, or some combination of logical devices. The substance or body of the argument, however, will contain substantial amounts of nonlogical material, such as figurative language or connotative adjectives. To understand and evaluate the complete argument we need to analyze the parts. We shall do that when we study the language of rhetoric and how it works.

You are most likely to make use of the rhetorical principles outlined in this chapter if, for every paper you write, you fill out the form given below. Do it *before* you begin to write, check your paper against it when you have finished your first draft, and make any necessary adjustments. Making yourself follow this routine will be a nuisance at first, but gradually it will become a habit and one that will pay off.

You must be careful, however, to make your entries on the form specific and detailed. Simply putting down general categories will not help you focus your writing. Probably the item to which you should give the most thought is purpose, because almost no one can write an effective paper or speech without knowing from the start what the purpose of that paper is. And when you do know in advance just what you are trying to do, the writing job itself becomes easier.

Rhetorical Guidelines for Writing a Paper

I. Audience for paper:_____

Specific characteristics of the audience to keep in mind:

1. _____

2. _____

3. _____

4. _____

II. Persona of writer:_____

Important characteristics to convey to the audience:

1. _____

2. _____

3. _____

4. _____

III. Purpose of Paper:_____

_____

_____

IV. Arguments to be used:

1. _____

2. _____

3. _____

4. _____

V. Chief method of appeal (check one):
1. ethical
2. emotional
3. logical

Exercises

1. Write sample thesis sentences or summaries that could serve as statements of purpose for the following writing assignments:

   a. An essay on the benefits (or disadvantages) of living in a mobile home.

   b. An essay for (or against) Zero Population Growth.

   c. A report on the results of an experiment that you have recently done in your psychology class.

   d. A letter to the editor of the student newspaper suggesting that study facilities be improved in the college library.

   e. A letter to the board of regents asking for more subsidized housing for married students.

2. State briefly what your main purposes would be in the following writing assignments:

   a. A statement of personal goals to accompany your application to law school (or to a theological seminary).

   b. An application for a grant from a foundation in order that you may spend part of your sophomore year in field work doing an independent study in a subject of your choice (for example, nutrition for welfare clients, conditions in a mental hospital near your home, voting patterns within the eighteen to twenty-one-year-old age group, or racial attitudes among junior high school students in your town).

   c. A letter to the dean of your college asking for reinstatement in school after you have been expelled for getting drunk and taking a midnight swim in the Memorial Fountain.

3. In the fourth century B.C. Aristotle wrote what is probably the most famous of all rhetoric texts. In it he counseled his readers to adapt their rhetoric to the character of their audience and gave them the following guidelines to help them. What do you think of his analysis? Are his assumptions about the young and the old still valid? Would you use them if you were addressing audiences in that category? What specific criticisms would you make of his generalizations?

Young men have strong desires, and whatever they desire they are prone to do. Of the bodily desires the one they let govern them most is sexual desire; here they lack self-control. . . . The young are passionate, quick to anger, and apt to give way to it. . . . Fond of honor, they are even fonder of victory, for youth likes to be superior, and winning evinces superiority. They love both honor and victory more than they care for money. Indeed, they care next to nothing about money, for they have not yet learned what the want of it means. . . . The young think no evil, but believe in human goodness, for as yet they have not seen many examples of vice. They are trustful, for as yet they have not often been deceived. . . . They are high-minded; first, because they have not yet been humbled by life, nor come to know the force of circumstances; and secondly, because high-mindedness means thinking oneself fitted for great things. In their actions they prefer honor to expediency; for their lives are rather lives of good impulse than of calculation. . . . They carry everything too far; they love to excess, they hate to excess—and so in all else. They think they know everything, and are positive about everything.[2]

Of the elderly, Aristotle says,

The Old have lived long, have been often deceived, have made many mistakes of their own; they see that more often than not the affairs of men turn out badly. And so they are positive about nothing; in all things they err by an extreme moderation. . . . They think evil; that is, they are disposed to put the worse construction on everything. Further, they are suspicious because they are distrustful and distrustful from sad experience. As a result, they have no strong likings or hates. . . . They are mean-souled, because they have been humbled by life. Thus they aspire to nothing great or exalted, but crave the mere necessities and comforts of existence. And they are not generous. Property, as they know, is one of the necessities, and they have learned by experience how hard it is to acquire, how easy to lose. They are cowards, apprehen-

[2] Lane Cooper, *The Rhetoric of Aristotle*, © 1932, renewed 1960, pp. 132–133, 134–135. Adapted by permission of Prentice-Hall, Inc., Englewood Cliffs, N.J.

sive about everything . . . the old are not characterized by passion, and their actions are governed not by impulse, but by love of gain. . . . Their lives are rather lives of calculation than of moral bias.[p. 135]

4. Imagine that you have been asked to write articles for any three of these publications. Examine a copy of each of the three you choose, and in a sentence of no more than twenty-five words, specify who your audience would be in each case and what important characteristics that audience would have.

Seventeen	*Reader's Digest*
New York Times	*Christian Science Monitor*
Glamour	*U.S. News & World Report*
Playboy	*Family Circle*
Ebony	*Psychology Today*
Time	

5. What assumptions about the audience is the writer of each of the following advertisements making?

a. THE DURABLE ONE Our car may not be the prettiest and shiniest on the market, but it's the toughest. We built it to last. And not to cost you a fortune.

We start with a simple car that doesn't have an ounce of wasted space. Then we refuse to put on any frills. Instead, we make a tight car that doesn't rattle, doesn't rust, doesn't gobble gas.

And we test every car before it leaves the factory. No lemons allowed.

If you care more about durability than you do about decor, Bulldog is the car for you.

b. BAHAMA ADVENTURE Guided tours you don't want—they're stuffy and dull. But how about an adventure, a real ADVENTURE? A fun tour of the Bahamas with exciting nights and leisurely, sun-baked days?

Discover new people, new places, new things to do. You'll find the excitement of extraordinary places, off-the-beaten-path nightclubs and restaurants.

Only a few lucky souls find ways to put zest in their lives.

You can be one of them if you join this fabulous Cruise of Adventure that only Bahamas Unlimited offers you.

c. MINDPOWER: YOUR KEY TO SUCCESS! Most people drudge along in life using only a fraction of their real capacities. They feel—know—that they have potential that has never come to the surface. Buried in them somewhere is power, the power to do the things they dreamed of once. Are you one of these unhappy ones? Do you want to find the key that will release those vital forces?

Our new, scientifically based course in MINDPOWER will show you the way. By learning ten simple rules for awakening the hidden dynamics of your brain, you can throw off that inertia that has kept you from being the man you deserve to be. Write today!

6. Clip one of the columns of a well-known journalist—for example, Russell Baker, Meg Greenfield, William F. Buckley, Ellen Goodman, Marianne Means, William Raspberry—and tape it to a sheet of paper. Under it write a short description of the persona the writer is assuming and give some evidence to support your analysis. Keep it short, not more than one hundred words in all.

7. Describe very briefly the persona you would want to adopt in each of the following rhetorical situations:

a. You are participating in Operation Outreach, a project in which students and faculty visit high schools throughout the state to encourage members of minority groups to enroll in your college.

b. You have decided to get married next semester and want to continue your education, but really need to have some continuing support from your parents. Write a letter that gives them good reasons why they should not cut off your allowance.

c. You are trying to borrow fifty dollars from your roommate so that you can impress your date by taking her to Trader Vic's for dinner.

8. Read and evaluate the following student paper written in re-

sponse to an assignment that asked the writer to write an article for elementary school children who are from ten to twelve year old. Read the writer's statements of audience and purpose carefully and think about them when you are reading the paper. How well does the writer keep audience and purpose in mind? Are the topic, the word choice, and the style suitable for the audience?

Audience   Eleven and twelve year olds. They are beginning to develop spending habits which will last a lifetime. This brochure will accompany a classroom unit about money.

Purpose   To teach why we save money and to explain how to open a savings account at a bank. Since budgeting or planning is valuable for saving money, a budget should be included. New vocabulary should be defined.

Why Save Money?

Most people get money by earning it. Many students earn weekly allowances for doing work around the house. Another good way to earn money is by doing special jobs for others like cutting the grass, baby sitting, washing cars and pet sitting. These jobs are known as services. Money can also be earned by selling products which we find or make. Examples of products are arrowheads, aluminum cans and homemade crafts and foods.

Some people spend their money as soon as they get it. Others save part of it. One reason why we save money is to pay for something that is expensive, such as a bicycle, gift or vacation trip. By saving money regularly, it is possible to buy the expensive item.

Another reason why people save money is that there is nothing they really need at the moment. They save their money until it is needed for something special.

Finally, many people feel that it is important to save money for an emergency. We never know when an emergency will happen or what it will be. If, for example, you deliver newspapers every day on your bicycle and the bicycle chain breaks, you have an emergency. If you spent all your money, you may not be able to deliver the next day's newspaper. But, if you have emergency money saved, you can replace the chain right away.

We have probably all saved money by putting it in a piggy bank or a jar or a secret hiding place. The best place to save money is at a bank. Your money is safe at a bank. And, the bank pays you for keeping your money there. The money that the bank pays you is called interest.

If you are under 18 years old, a parent must accompany you to open a savings account at a bank. A bank employee, called a teller, will ask you to fill out an application form. The teller will also ask you to sign your name. Each time you go to the bank, the teller identifies you by your signature. Since nobody writes your signature exactly the way you do, only you can take money out of your account.

When you open a savings account, you receive an account book. The account book shows when money goes in and comes out of your account. The account book has five columns. The first column shows the date when money enters or leaves your account. The second shows when you add money to your savings. This is called a deposit. The third column shows the amount of interest which the bank pays you. The next column shows when money is taken out of the account. This is called a withdrawal. Finally, the last column shows the total amount of money in your savings account. This amount is known as the balance.

Account Book

Date	Deposit	Interest	Withdrawal	Balance
2/5/80	$50.00	$	$	$50.00
3/1/80	10.00			60.00
4/2/80	10.00	3.00		73.00
4/9/80			5.00	68.00

Each time you go to the bank to make a deposit or withdrawal, you must have your account book with you. A computer will print a new line of information in your book.

We each decide how to spend and save our own money. Each person is different. Making a budget helps us keep track of how we use our money. A budget shows how much money a person earns or receives and how the money is used.

The budget below is for a week. It consists of two lists. One list is for money coming in from an allowance and babysitting. The other list is for money going out. Notice that the totals of the two lists are the same.

Weekly Budget

Money Coming In		*Money Going Out*	
Weekly allowance	$3.00	Food	$3.00
Babysitting money	6.00	Bus fare	2.00
		School supplies	1.00
		Savings	3.00
Total	$9.00	*Total*	$9.00

A budget helps us plan how to spend money. Let's say you want to buy a new radio that costs $30.00. You plan to save $3.00 for ten weeks in order to pay for the radio. It takes self-discipline to stick to your budget. But, when you buy that radio, you can feel proud that you did a good job of planning and saving to get it.

Beverly Cotton

Suggested Writing Assignments

Theme 1

Purpose To make you aware of the importance of analyzing your rhetorical stance before you begin an argument and give you training in thinking about your audience and persona as you write.

Procedure Choose one of the topics given below or a similar one that your instructor approves. As part of your prewriting process, consider and make notes on these questions: (1) Who is your audience? What important characteristics—age, level of education, work habits, social attitudes, and so on—does it have that you should keep in mind as you write? (2) What is your persona or role? What kinds of habits, attitudes, goals, and values do you want to convince your audience that you have? On a separate sheet at the beginning of your paper, write two one-paragraph summaries of the most important points for each item.

Topics

a. You are applying to veterinary, medical, or dental school. One of the requirements is that you write a short—no more than five hundred words—autobiography to submit along with your college transcript and letters of recommendation. Your audience is a board of doctors who receive about three times as many qualified applicants as they can admit. Assume that your grades and letters of recommendation are good.

b. You would like to work next summer in some federally financed project in your field (nursing, environmental biology, forestry, social welfare, child development, or something similar). Such jobs are usually given on the recommendation of congresspersons or senators, so you are writing to your representative for support. Compose a letter that you think would help you get a job.

c. You want to become an apprentice to one of the top race horse trainers in the country. You have some experience and are knowledgeable about horses. Write to the trainer giving your qualifications and reasons for wanting the job.

d. You cannot return to school next year unless you receive a substantial scholarship. Possible sources are one of the service clubs in your home town, such as the Lions, Optimists, Rotary, or a church scholarship that has been set up to help deserving young people. Assume that you have a good high school record. Compose a letter that you think would help you to receive such a scholarship.

Theme 2

Purpose To develop your awareness of audience and rhetorical purpose in writing.

Procedure Choose one of the topics given below and write a paper of appropriate length (this will vary with the assignment). On a separate sheet at the beginning of the paper, do these things: (1) Write a one-paragraph summary of your audience in which you describe them and list the important traits and qualities you must keep in mind as you present your information. (2) Write a one-paragraph statement of your rhetorical purpose. Be specific about what information you want to convey to your audience or what changes you hope to bring about in their attitudes.

Topics
a. Write a press release to be sent to your local newspaper announcing the organization of a new local chapter of one of these groups:
1. Young Republicans or Democrats
2. National Organization of Women
3. Sierra Club
4. Farmers' Union or the Farm Bureau
5. Right-to-Life League (anti-abortion group)
b. Write a press release announcing the candidacy of your brother or sister (whose press secretary you are) for a seat in the state senate.
c. Write a statement for the college newspaper responding to the college president's proposal that the student counseling service be closed in order to save funds.
d. Write an informative, brief handout explaining the services of the local child and family counseling program or those of the Pregnancy Counseling Center to potential clients.
e. Write a letter to the general sales manager of one of the major car manufacturers complaining about your local dealer's failure to give the service you were guaranteed when you bought your new car.

4

Sentences

Sentences are amazing creations. One might say that they are the containers in which we package our thoughts in order to transmit them to other people; as such, they are our basic means of communication. The number of surprisingly different, yet predictable, ways in which we can put sentences together—that is, the wide variety of packages available to us—keeps grammarians and linguists speculating about the thought processes that underlie language. It also keeps them inventing new theories and terms with which to analyze and describe the process of making sentences, an ability that apparently comes naturally to native speakers, even if they are totally illiterate.

As a native speaker (or a non-native who is well trained in English) you already know how to make almost all the sentences you need to communicate with other people, and you are using them constantly as you talk. These same skills will serve you well in your writing. Probably your chief task now is to polish your skills with sentences and to learn how to adapt them to written communication.

Although most people who talk well can also learn to write well, writing is more difficult because readers do expect written prose to be more precise, economical, and better organized than conversation. One of the chief ways that writers achieve that precision, economy, and tighter structure is by tinkering with their sentences. That is, we redesign our packages to make them more efficient and, we hope, more attractive. This section will deal with various sentence designs that you can use.

Before moving to those options, however, it is important to point out what should be, but sometimes isn't, absolutely obvious to both students and teachers: *The content of the sentence is far more important than the way it is written.* Trivial observations and dubious assertions remain trivial and dubious no matter how they are tricked out in a fancy package. No amount of inverting, embedding, subordinating, balancing, or combining can compensate for careless or trite thinking.

Unfortunately, from time to time teachers put so much stress on style and mechanics that they unintentionally seem to give them higher priority than ideas. If that is the message they transmit to their students, the result may be smooth but empty writing that does more to annoy than to impress professors, admission boards, scholarship committees, and future employers and clients.

Kinds of Sentences

Although the sections coming up will talk about how you can use simple, complex, and compound sentences, it seems unlikely that most writers think consciously about the kinds of sentences they are going to write.[1] Rather, they must begin to write, unconsciously constructing the kinds of sentences that best suit their audience and their purpose. When they are writing for general audiences of limited education, they tend to use a high proportion of simple and fairly short sentences because they do not want to present too much information at one time. Unfortunately, a prose style with too many sentences of this kind, unrelieved by longer complex sentences or by comparatively long simple sentences into which a good deal of information has been compressed, often resembles what we call a *primer style*, particularly if it lacks transitions. (Notice how often advertising copy fits this description.) Inexperienced writers who feel insecure about handling complicated sentence structures frequently fall into this kind of writing. However, this choppy, primer style is comparatively easy to overcome, as we shall see, and ambitious students should not despise the simple sentence just because it is a favorite of beginners. It is also a favorite of professional writers because it has great possibilities.

Simple Sentences

The *simple sentence* is the natural choice for plain statements of fact, simple assertions, and definitions. When you want to draw attention to characteristics or a proposal, say "This has this quality" or "That ought to be done," the simple sentence works best. For example:

Federal desegregation of schools began in 1954.

Dancing is one of the seven lively arts.

Snowmobiles ought to be prohibited.

Expansion Simple sentences do not have to be short. They can be modified, expanded, enriched, and clarified by inserting ap-

[1] See the Index to Grammatical Terms in the Appendix for definitions of simple, complex, and compound sentences.

positives and phrases. In fact, the writer with a sense of possibilities can make a simple sentence do a great deal in relatively few words. For example, notice what can be done by starting out with a simple skeleton and expanding on it:

San Francisco is a fascinating city.

San Francisco, a center of culture and fashion, is a fascinating city.

San Francisco, simultaneously a center of culture and fashion and a bawdy international port, is a fascinating city.

Probably this is about as far as you should go with this particular sentence; to add more modifiers just to see if it could be done—and it could—would be adding superfluous decoration that might detract from the main idea. But notice that the second and third versions of the sentence are more concrete and more specific than the first and give the reader an idea of *why* San Francisco is a fascinating city.

One can also add introductory phrases to simple sentences to make them more specific, to qualify them, or to set a particular tone.

To me, San Francisco is a fascinating city.

Ironically, the size of the grain crop in Russia affects the price of bread in the United States.

In the boom years of the 1960s, every American city resounded to the din of construction.

In the last analysis, a public figure has no private life.

You can also increase the interest and concreteness of a simple sentence by adding adjectives, phrases, or other modifying terms. This process of increasing the amount of information in a sentence is sometimes called *embedding*. It will be discussed at more length later in this chapter. You should not, however, get into the habit of puffing out all your simple sentences with adjectives and phrases. The lean and direct simple sentence can be an important rhetorical tool (more on that later in this chapter).

Economy for emphasis Perhaps what the short simple sentence does best is emphasize. For instance, notice how Joan Didion uses a simple sentence for stark effect in this essay about a woman who murdered her husband in California when the "hot dry Santa Ana wind" was blowing:

> There has been no rain since April. Every voice seems a scream.[2]

Because of their attention-getting qualities, simple sentences also make good openers. For example, here are two opening sentences from columns by the *Boston Globe* writer, Ellen Goodman:

> They tell me apathy is in this year.[3]
>
> I have always been suspicious of nostalgia.[4]

You can imitate this technique by starting your papers (or paragraphs) with the plainest of assertions. For instance, "I hate shopping malls"; "Funerals are big business"; or "Money has its disadvantages." You would then go on to qualify, explain, and expand such an assertion.

When used primarily for emphasis, simple sentences like these are best kept bare. Qualifiers and modifiers will weaken rather than enrich them, and though you may incorporate more information, you will lose impact. For example, think how much would have been lost if the originators of these famous one-liners had tried to improve on them with adjectives:

> Texas is hell on women and horses.
>
> Make love, not war.
>
> We have not yet begun to fight.

Finally, clear and simple sentences are essential in most technical and business reports that stress facts and findings. One should never sacrifice accuracy and objectivity for elegance or color in that kind of writing. As a major text on technical writing puts it,

[2] Joan Didion, "Some Dreamers of the Golden Dream," *Slouching Towards Bethlehem* (New York: Dell Publishing Co., Inc., 1968), p.3.
[3] Ellen Goodman, "Forgive Me for Being Gauche, But I'm Voting," *Close to Home* (New York: Simon & Schuster, Inc., 1979), p. 110.
[4] Ellen Goodman, "Nostalgia in Small Doses, Please," *Close to Home*, p. 122.

In general, simple sentences should outnumber the other kinds: complex, compound, and complex-compound.[5]

Complex Sentences

The *complex sentence*, one which contains one or more dependent clauses in addition to a basic simple sentence, provides the best design for packaging complex thoughts.[6] By using complex sentences, you can show all kinds of complicated relationships between ideas. For example, you can indicate the comparative importance of statements, show that one thing happened because of or in spite of another thing, express contradictions and ironies, reservations and qualifications. And since mature people recognize how complicated good thinking must be—as some wise person said, "The truth is seldom plain and never simple"—we badly need the kind of writing tool that the complex sentence gives us.

Complex sentences show relationships

Here is a rather typical example in which a student used simple sentences when a complex one was needed. Writing on exercise 2 at the end of Chapter 6, the student began:

A good education is not essential for economic success in our society. Today many people believe that a good education is essential for economic success in our society.

By beginning with two contradictory statements written in such a way that they seem to be of equal value, the student confuses the reader from the start. One's first reaction is to ask, "Well, which way are we going to go?" If the student had realized the need to show the contradiction between points, he or she could have begun the first sentence with "Although . . ." and avoided the confusion, for example:

Although many people still believe that a good education is essential for economics success in our society, it really isn't.

[5] Gordon H. Mills and John A. Walter, *Technical Writing*, 3d ed. (New York: Holt, Rinehart & Winston, 1970), p. 48.
[6] A *dependent* or *subordinate clause* is a group of words that contains a subject and a verb but cannot stand as a sentence by itself.

Or it could have been written:

> In spite of what most people believe, a good education is really not necessary for economic success in our society.

Another student writing on the same assignment got off to a bad start as a result of not knowing how to use a complex sentence to show the desired cause-and-effect relationship. The paper began like this:

> The statement "You can achieve anything you set your mind to if you work hard enough" is a product of our American heritage. The idea was formed when the country was first settled. People came here to escape the caste systems of Europe.

Redoing this with a complex sentence would not only bring out the relationship and comparative importance of the ideas, but it would also get rid of the choppiness. For example:

> Because most of the people who settled America came here to escape the caste system of Europe, they believed strongly that an individual could do anything he wanted to if he just worked hard enough. Most of us still believe this. (*Notice the prudent addition of "most" here; not all settlers came to escape the caste system.*)

Rearrangements like this really are not hard to make when a writer becomes conscious of the need to tie ideas together.

Complex sentences use signal words

Complex sentences typically employ one or more *signal words*. Among the most common are *although*, *in spite of*, *however*, *unless*, *if*, *when*, *because*, *as*, *while*, *during*, *since*, and *instead*. There are, of course, many others; whatever serves as a conjunction or relative pronoun in making a clause dependent is a subordinating signal. Such clauses are flexible and variable. They can be lengthened or shortened; put at the beginning, end, or middle; and can be used as introductions, explainers, or just modifiers. For example, let's take this student paragraph and see how it could be rewritten to clarify and tighten the relationship between the student's points, which are in themselves sound and pertinent to the topic.

Original Advertising persuades people by making foods appear to be nutritionally good when they are not. Money is wasted on these foods. We should buy food that would be beneficial for us. The poor waste their food stamps frequently. Their grocery baskets are filled halfway with junk. The high cost of them is startling. Even bubble gum has gone up to two cents now. Money could also be saved from the dentist and doctor bills.

Revision Because so many of us are influenced by advertising that makes worthless food seem nutritious, we waste a shocking proportion of our food dollars. The poor, who spend their precious cash on food stamps, waste money when they spend those stamps on expensive junk like bubble gum. What we are buying is not only worthless; it actually damages our bodies and our teeth.

This revision could have been done several different ways, all quite acceptable.

Compound Sentences

The compound sentence is so similar to the complex one in the way it works and looks that there is no need to worry a great deal about the distinction. Simply, it is this: the complex sentence contains one simple sentence and one or more dependent clauses, and the *compound sentence* combines two or more simple sentences, connected with a coordinating conjunction or semicolon. We use it to join independent statements and ideas, and the kind of joining signal we use frequently tells us what the relationship of those statements is. The section on transitions in the previous chapter and the next one list many of those joining words and give their functions.

Here are some typical compound sentences:

The candidate must find new sources of money, or she will have to give up her campaign.

The combination of sedatives and alcohol is deadly; yet people looking for a thrill continue to mix them.

The first function of scientists is research; they are teachers only incidentally.

Ways of constructing compound sentences **Balanced sentences** The balanced sentence is a particularly useful variation of the compound sentence because it provides the ideal package for emphasizing similarities or differences, usually the latter. For instance:

Weak leaders crave love; strong ones prefer respect.

Football and basketball provide recreation for the young, but tennis and golf provide recreation for a lifetime.

Minorities must first win elections, and then they can win their rights.

Winning isn't everything; it's the only thing.

Parallel sentences Parallel sentences are much like balanced sentences in that they achieve an effect by repeating a pattern, but they are more flexible in form. You can set up simple parallels in a rather short sentence, or you can carry a parallel structure along for several sentences, for example:

We hope to attract new students by increasing our scholarships, by improving our faculty, by expanding our course offerings, and by promoting our graduate programs.

And from President John F. Kennedy's inaugural address, which depends heavily on balance and parallelism to achieve its effects:

Let every nation know, whether it wishes us well or ill, that we shall pay any price, bear any burden, meet any hardship, support any friend, oppose any foe to assure the survival and the success of liberty.

And from a student theme:

New York City is failing. It has overextended its resources for too long, true. It has given in to pressure groups for too long, true. It has allowed itself to be taken advantage of for too long, true. But the city is failing while the President and Congress debate.

Parallel structure can be especially useful when you are writing a thesis sentence that will act as an organizing tool for your paper. Some of the examples in the previous chapter fall into this pattern; others you might use could read,

> The advantages of buying a mobile home are that it is comparatively inexpensive, it can be moved out of an urban area, and it can be sold quickly if necessary; the disadvantages are that it is easily damaged by wind and hail and it is usually not attractive.

> I have decided to choose a career in nursing because it is a profession that will allow me to help people, to move around the country, and to earn a decent salary.

You can find more information about the guidelines for setting up parallel sentences in the handbook.

Ways of Improving Your Sentences

Choosing Concrete Subjects

Advantages of choosing concrete subjects

You will make your writing easier to read and to follow if you try to choose a concrete word, a personal one if possible, as the subject of your sentences.[7] Because we can visualize the things and people that concrete words refer to, we comprehend them more quickly. Of course frequently writers must use abstract subjects—if you skim over this text, you will find an abundance of them—but probably they don't need them as often as they think they do. What seems to happen is that often we begin with an abstract term without thinking of some other way to start. For example, if the assignment is to write about some of the consequences of cheating, our first impulse is to make cheating the subject of the opening sentence. Such a beginning is grammatically acceptable but immediately puts the writer at a disadvantage.

[7] See the beginning of Chapter 7 for more information on concrete language.

For one thing, the writer will almost certainly have to use some abstract generalization to complete the sentence, such as "Cheating is widespread" or "Cheating is a national scandal." Statements like this force the writer to begin supporting the assertion immediately, perhaps before the assertion is adequately developed. Also, the writer who starts with an abstract subject is more apt to use passive verbs that deaden and slow the writing. For example, "Cheating is found everywhere" or "Cheating is indulged in by many students" (more on this problem of passives in later sections). Furthermore, a writer cannot use vigorous or colorful verbs with this kind of subject. "Cheating" cannot plunge, strike, hesitate, or demand—it cannot logically *do* anything, but a concrete subject usually can.

Last, the writer who uses abstract subjects has a better chance of creating sentences with predication knots than the writer who starts out with people or things as the subject.[8] Here, for example, are some tangled sentences from a student theme on cheating:

> Cheating in college is attainable by someone else taking the test, looking on another's paper, or having a cheat sheet.
> Cheating often forfeits the student of learning and friends.
> Cheating also robs fairness to fellow students.

This student could hardly have gotten into this kind of trouble if the sentences had started with "Cheaters" or "Students who cheat."

Here are some more unfortunate sentences from a student who seems to have gone out of the way to use abstract terms for subjects and everything else:

> Absolute liberation can have no restrictions of specific dress, a certain community, or any material possessions that would contain him because of their ownership.
> This total independence is qualified by the individual having

---

[8] Predication errors occur when the writer completes a verb with a complement or adjective that does not fit logically with that verb.

no controlling motivations such as money, job, friend, or spiritual goal.

A completely necessary condition for total liberation is the independence from love.

This writer could so easily have begun the sentences with "The free person . . ." or "A person who wants to be free . . ." and avoided this stilted and confusing sentence structure.

Students who write like this are probably motivated partly by the desire to sound mature and learned and partly by a fear of using the pronoun *I* in their writing (more on that in Chapter 7). These students are victims of the "unfounded fear of simplicity" mentioned earlier. One of the first ways to start getting over that fear is to cultivate the habit of choosing concrete subjects for one's sentences. And better verbs will almost certainly follow.

Choosing Effective Verbs

Use verbs that show action

More than any other single sentence element, verbs give a piece of writing its color and vigor. Whether your writing drags along, perhaps boring your reader as it goes, or moves smoothly and surely toward your objective depends largely on the kinds of verbs you choose. For instance, the habitual use of *is* makes many sentences unnecessarily dull. Compare these two versions of the same idea:

There *is* a real need for free, tax-supported doctors and hospitals in the United States. Currently there *is* a movement toward such a program. It *is* called HMO or Health Maintenance Organizations.

Many Americans badly need free, tax-supported doctors and hospitals. The new HMO or Health Maintenance Organization program would fill this need.

Other problems caused by the verb *to be* are discussed in Hints for Polishing Your Writing in the Appendix.

You can also improve your writing by searching for verbs that make your readers think of actions; for example, "Inflation is *crushing* the poor" or "The candidates are *hugging* and *kissing* their way across the country." Notice for instance how skillfully Gordon Parks uses verbs to convey his admiration for Duke Ellington in this passage:

> For me, and many other black young people then, his importance as a human being *transcended* his importance as a musician. We had been assaulted by Hollywood's grinning darky types all of our young lives. It was refreshing to be a part of Duke Ellington's audience. Ellington never *grinned*. He *smiled*. Ellington never *shuffled*. He *strode*. It was "Good afternoon, ladies and gentlemen," never "How y'all doin'?" We wanted to be seen by the whites in the audience. We wanted them to know that this elegant, handsome and awe-inspiring man playing that ever-so-fine music on that golden stage dressed in those fine clothes before that big beautiful black band was black—like us [italics added].[9]

Notice that Parks uses only a few strong verbs, strategically placed, to achieve his effects. Too many action words jammed into a short passage can give one the impression of reading poorly crafted fiction, which overflows with words like *exploded, hurled, slashed, careened, screeched*, and so on. And action verbs that are connotative, as so many are, have little place in technical writing or other kinds of professional reports.

Passive verbs For some of the same reasons that they overuse abstract subjects, student writers are frequently addicted to using passive verbs. Passive verb forms (those in which the subject does not act, but is acted upon) hamper good communication for several reasons, many of which we will take up in the section on jargon. For now, I will just point out that writers who consistently use passive rather than active verbs will almost certainly produce

Avoid using passive verbs

plodding and dull prose. For example, "The change in the administration *was thought* by many people to be beneficial" drags, but "Many people *favored* the change in the administration" moves briskly to the point. "The conclusion that pigs are more intelligent than cows *was arrived* at from laboratory experiments

---

[9] Gordon Parks, "Jazz," *Esquire*, December 1975, p. 140.

that *had been conducted* over a period of five years" is a drab tedious sentence. "Five years of laboratory experiments *show* that pigs are smarter than cows" says the same thing better and faster. Notice that both the longer sentences also have abstract subjects.

Occasionally you must use the passive construction, and sometimes it is desirable. Technical writers, for example, use passives frequently; not only is it difficult to describe experiments or mechanical operations without them, but in most cases the technical writer wants to focus on the experiment or operation, not on the person doing it. People writing plain expository prose may sometimes want to use the passive for the same reason. For instance, "Chairs were overturned, books were thrown on the floor, and dresser drawers had been yanked out and emptied" focuses attention on the objects, not the actor; thus the passive is appropriate. Sentences like "Ralph was awarded the Navy Cross" and "Hundreds of people were turned away at the door" make good use of passive verbs because the actor is either unknown or unimportant.

But students who are trying to sound mature and judicious, or who are unconsciously imitating bad models, too frequently make a habit of using passive verbs. The results can be unfortunate; for instance:

> Three levels of interest *are considered* in developing an effective advertisement. The first level is the rational level which *is thought* of as the logical appeal of the ad. Rationality *is* easily *achieved* by using very simple topics which need little or no thought.

> Men's pride *would be injured* if women *were awarded* rights, recognition, and responsibility. The saying that men are smarter than women *would have to be recognized* as an untruth. Intelligence *is based* on the individual and not on sex. Women *would be taken* into certain fields of education that *were* previously *dominated* by men. Men would no longer *be chosen* for medical school and law school because they are men.

Dull, isn't it? Notice the improvement if we change to active verbs and more concrete subjects.

> If women *succeed* in *winning* the rights, responsibilities, and recognition they are *working* for, male pride will certainly

suffer. Men will have to *admit* that any claim that men are smarter than women is simply not true; intelligence *varies* by individuals, not by sex. Worse, women *will begin breaking* into fields that men have traditionally *dominated*. No longer will male applicants for medical and law school have an advantage simply because they are men.

Choosing active verbs and then rearranging the sentences accordingly make the paragraph tighter and more vigorous. Such changes are fairly easy to make on the second draft, although, of course, it is better if you can choose good verbs the first time through. Like most habits, an addiction to the passive voice is hard to overcome, but it really is important that you try. More about the reasons in a later section of the book.

Sentence Combining

One way you can learn to write different kinds of sentences to suit different purposes is to practice *sentence combining*. When you do sentence-combining exercises, you experiment with putting the elements of a sentence together in different ways.

Example A:

The highway department is being hurt by inflation.
It is being hurt by the increased cost of labor.
It is being hurt by the increased cost of road repairs.
It is being hurt by the drop in revenue from gasoline taxes.

Combined version 1:

As the cost of labor and road repairs increases and the revenue from gasoline taxes drops, the highway department is beginning to feel the pinch of inflation.

Combined version 2:

The highway department is being hurt by inflation as gasoline tax revenues drop and the cost of labor and repairs increases.

Example B:

Professional football players are folk heroes.
Professional football players are famous.
Professional football players are well paid.
Professional football players attract groupies.
This attraction is inevitable.

Combined version 1:

Famous and well paid, professional football heroes are folk heroes who inevitably attract groupies.

Combined version 2:

Groupies inevitably follow professional football players who are well paid and famous folk heroes.

Example C:

Women can pursue new professions today.
They can be engineers.
They can be doctors.
They can be business executives.
They can earn as much as males.
They can hold responsible positions.

Combined version 1:

Today women can pursue new professions, becoming engineers, doctors, or business executives and holding responsible positions in which they earn as much as males.

Combined version 2:

Today women cannot only hold responsible positions and earn as much as males, but they can also pursue new professions such as engineering, medicine, or business.

At the end of this chapter you will find several exercises that will allow you to practice sentence combining. By working with them, you will find out how you can achieve different effects by joining, combining, or rearranging elements. You should remember, however, that there is no one "right" answer when you combine sentences; there may be several good ways of arranging a sentence.

Sentence combining is like practicing scales

One well-known writing teacher has said the student who practices sentence combining can benefit from it in the same way that a piano student benefits by practicing scales.[10] Both kinds of exercises help the practicer develop the skills that are useful when he or she begins to work with a larger unit: writing a paper or playing a piece of music. As a result, after you have practiced sentence-combining exercises by themselves, you will become more conscious of ways in which you can combine sentences in your papers to produce smoother, tighter, and more economical sentences.

Probably the two strategies you will use most are *embedding* and *transforming*.

Embedding Incorporating information from one sentence unit into another one by means of inserting adjectives, appositives, or modifying phrases is known as *embedding*. For example:

Original Darrell Royal was head football coach at the University of Texas for twenty years. Royal is a former Oklahoma football star.

Revision 1 Darrell Royal, former Oklahoma football star, was head coach at the University of Texas for twenty years.

Revision 2 Former Oklahoma football star Darrell Royal was head coach at the University of Texas for twenty years.

Revision 3 Long-time University of Texas football coach Darrell Royal was once a star at the University of Oklahoma.

You can see the possibilities. Embedding is rather like splitting open the seam of a garment or slipcover and adding more material

[10] Mina Shaughnessy, *Errors and Expectations* (New York: Oxford University Press, 1977), p. 73.

to make the original cover more. By using the process skillfully, you can work a substantial amount of information into one sentence. For instance:

> *Original* Feminist fiction has come into fashion recently. Most of the authors are women. They usually write about a woman's battle to be a person in her own right. Some of the books are militant.
>
> *Revision 1* Almost all the authors of the feminist fiction that has become so popular recently are women who are writing, often in a militant fashion, about women who are battling to become individuals in their own right.
>
> *Revision 2* The newly popular feminist novels, some of which are very militant, are almost always written by women and deal with the problem of women struggling to become individuals in their own right.

Don't try to include too much in one sentence

You can see that the process is not really difficult to master although it can get complicated if you try to rearrange the content of four or five sentences at one time. The more information you try to include in one sentence, the harder it becomes to control. For that reason, you would probably be better off to limit the amount of material you try to embed (more on sentence length in a later section).

Transforming The other principal method of combining sentences is *transforming*, rewriting sentences by joining several elements and rearranging them in new ways to make more efficient and usually more graceful sentences. For example:

> *Original* Streetsweepers in San Francisco make more than $17,000 a year with little education. Many college graduates apply for the streetsweeping jobs in San Francisco.
>
> *Revision* Many college graduates apply for the $17,000-a-year streetsweeping jobs in San Francisco, positions that scarcely require a degree.
>
> *Original* One way in which *All in the Family* has a beneficial effect on social attitudes is through its ability to make people

laugh at themselves. By making people laugh at themselves it shows them the naivety of their prejudices.

Revision One way in which *All in the Family* has a beneficial effect on social attitudes is by making people laugh at themselves, thus showing them the naivety of their prejudices.

Original Argentinians are meat-and-potato eaters like Americans. However, their reason is that beef is less expensive than chicken. Beef is the prevalent meat dish because of the abundance of cattle ranching in the provinces.

Revision Like Americans, Argentinians are big meat-and-potato eaters; however, there beef is popular mainly because the abundance of cattle ranching in the provinces makes beef cheaper than chicken.

One advantage of sentence combining is that it allows you to merge the common elements of two or more sentences and eliminate choppiness and repetition. For example, notice the difference between the original and the revised versions of two paragraphs:

Original Tall buildings or large shops do not dot the skyline of Carmel [California]. As a person walks down the street, no large shopping centers are visible. Instead, there are a number of small specialty shops. Each shop is built in a different and unique fashion. There seems to exist a shop for every imaginable need. There are sweater shops and sweet shops, tea and tie shops, clothes and candy shops. Not all the stores are visible from the street. Many stores are hidden behind buildings and down paths. It is not unusual to follow a path and find a fountain and a number of shops tucked away in a small corner. Many enjoyable hours can be spent browsing through old shops and discovering new shops.

Revision that combines sentences As shoppers walk down the streets of Carmel, they will see not tall buildings or shopping centers, but a variety of small shops, each built in a different and unique fashion. They would find a shop to meet every imaginable need—sweater shops and sweet shops, tea and tie shops, clothes and cutlery shops. Some of them, however, are hidden behind buildings or tucked away down a path marked by a little fountain. Shoppers can spend many delightful hours browsing through old shops and discovering new ones.

Of course this is just one of several possible revisions; the sentences of the original could have been put together in a variety of ways.

> *Original* Society has traditionally treated the alcoholic as an outcast. Now more people realize that alcoholism is a disease. The disease is often caused by society. We must not shame those who are victims of the disease. We should accept them for what they are—human beings suffering from a social disease. We all are possible victims of alcoholism.
> *Revision that combines sentences* Traditionally, society has treated the alcoholic as an outcast, but today more people realize that alcoholism is a disease caused by society. Instead of shaming the victims of this disease, we should accept them for what they are—human beings suffering from a disease to which we all could fall victim.

Probably the best time to think about how you can use embedding and transforming in your sentences is when you are making on-the-spot revisions on the first draft. Combine some elements in your mind before you ever put them on paper; combine others after you have read over a paragraph and realize that you have been repetitious or that one sentence should really be a subordinate clause. After you have finished making changes on the first draft and have reread it, you will probably find several other places where you can combine phrases or whole sentences. Pencil in those changes and incorporate them when you write the final draft.

Length and Scope

Although sentence combining will help you to package more information in fewer sentences, still you should not try to do too much in one sentence. A long and very complex sentence is not

Remember that long sentences are not necessarily good ones

necessarily a good one, even though at one time a writing teacher who had you do combining exercises in order to write more "mature" sentences may have given you that impression. Unfortunately, some highly complex sentences come out disastrously because inexperienced writers are trying to juggle too many things at one time. Frequently, inexperienced writers cannot handle the demands of grammar, mechanics, and structure and simultaneously cope with three or four ideas. If they try, they turn out the kinds of confused messages illustrated by the following sentences taken from student themes (each is followed by a suggested revision):

Original Therefore, understanding the idea that all taxpayers should be allowed to attend a state-supported institution, and all citizens are taxpayers by the mere fact that they are consumers, it is reasonable to state that all citizens should be allowed to attend the state university.

Revision All taxpayers should have the right to use state-supported facilities. Obviously, then, anyone in the state should be able to attend the state university because everyone who buys anything pays sales taxes.

Original Therefore, the pressure of grading should be replaced with the practice of commenting and evaluation as is necessary so as to encourage the student to learn to write well, rather than force him.

Revision Writing teachers should put comments and evaluations on papers instead of grades. Such a system would encourage rather than force the student to learn to write.

Original As far as the council's right to act for the people goes, however, you must understand that although representative government is a fine idea, its use to deal with specific issues is not warranted when a significant number of the governed is vocally against its use, as it is on the question of appropriations.

Revision Although the council has the right to act for the people on many matters, it should not take actions to which a significant number of voters object. Appropriating money is that kind of action.

Sentences like the originals lose readers before they ever get to the end. Some of the difficulty, of course, comes from the excessive number of abstract words, including the subject. The last example is particularly bad on that score. But mainly these writers have confused their readers simply by trying to put too much into one package.

Very long sentences can cause problems with mechanics

Students who write long and excessively complicated sentences also risk getting tangled up in grammatical problems. Too much distance between the subject and verb frequently results in subject-verb disagreement, and too many clauses can lead to dangling modifiers. The kinds of predication problems mentioned earlier also crop up more frequently in long sentences. All these difficulties result from writers simply having taken on so much that they cannot keep track of the relationships between words.

More often than not, students don't really *intend* to write these kinds of sentences; they just happen. Working in a last-minute rush or without a clear idea of exactly what it is they want to say, inexperienced writers often just begin writing a sentence and trust that it will come out all right. If it's not a long sentence, it usually will, as the clarity of writing in personal letters and journals shows. But if the sentence is complicated, or the writer keeps adding words and clauses as new ideas come up, the result can be confusing.

Split your sentences if necessary

The best way to avoid producing such tangled sentences is to stop and check them over carefully before you write your second draft. If you are a person who writes quickly and does most of your revising as you do the second draft, you can wait until then to check over sentences to be sure you haven't put so much into one package that you have confused your reader. If you are a slow writer who frequently stops to reread as you work, check your sentences as they develop to see that they aren't getting out of control. In either case, don't hesitate to split up a long sentence if you think it will help your reader understand it more easily.

Cautions About Long Sentences

Even if you develop the ability to incorporate several ideas into a neatly constructed long and complex sentence, there are rhetorical reasons for using them sparingly in your writing. For one thing, a high proportion of rather complex sentences, packed with information, makes your writing *dense*, that is, fairly difficult for the average reader to understand, even if the writing is clear and well organized. The passage from Mill's *On Liberty* in Tips on Reading Expository Prose in the Appendix is a good example of that kind of density. For certain audiences, then, highly complex prose is not suitable. In addition, this kind of sentence structure seriously affects the *tone* of your writing (see Chapter 8). Dense sentences inevitably make your prose seem more solemn and serious. Thus if a casual tone seems best for your topic and your purpose, you will want to avoid long, complex sentences. If, on the other hand, you are writing on a serious topic for a well-informed audience and you can handle involved sentence structure without difficulty, a complex style is quite appropriate.

Vary sentence length according to audience

You should also be aware of the length of the sentences you are writing, whether they are simple or complex. Of course, most writers do not consciously start out by saying, "I'm going to write long sentences" or "I'm going to write short sentences"—they play it by ear according to their audience, their purpose, and the tone they want to establish. But practiced writers do realize that the trend in modern writing is toward shorter sentences, just as it is toward shorter paragraphs. By *shorter*, I mean sentences of from ten to twenty-five words. Comparatively short sentences are usually easier for a reader to follow; they also quicken the pace of the writing and help to create an informal tone. Obviously, advertising copywriters know all this and carry the practice to sometimes ridiculous extremes.

For the most part, student writers should not consciously try to write a majority of either long or short sentences. You will do much better to put your ideas down in what seems to you reasonable and normal sentence patterns, then take a look at them. When the sentences are choppy or repetitive, try combining them; when a sentence seems too long and poorly organized, try separating it. As you work, keep your audience in mind. If you think their education level is low or their attention span short, separate more sentences than you combine. If the material is difficult or rather technical, it is also better to keep your sentences short so the audience won't lose its way. If you're doing a breezy, casual article, use short sentences, perhaps even fragments (more on that later in this chapter).

When writing on an uncomplicated topic for a general audience, however, probably you would do best to try to vary the lengths of your sentences from reasonably long to medium to short and emphatic. For instance:

> You place a phone call and are put on hold. You wait. And then you wait some more. Should you hang up? Perhaps. After all, why waste another second of your valuable time? On the other hand, if you hang up, you'll only have to call again to accomplish whatever business put you on the phone in the first place. Anyway, you've already spent all this time on hold, so why give it up now? So you wait some more. At some point you finally resign yourself to the likelihood that you've been left on hold forever. Even as you hang up, though, your ear remains glued to the receiver, hoping to the bitter end that all the time spent waiting was not in vain.[11]

Notice that the writer uses very short sentences to make the most important points; they are also the sentences that especially catch the reader's attention. Working such short sentences into the text also improves the paragraph by varying the rhythm, and as a result the reader does not become bored by a repetitious, singsong effect.

Finally, you should remember that it is particularly important to limit the length and complexity of your sentences when you are writing something that will be read aloud. A listening audience will certainly have trouble following a rambling sentence that takes in several ideas, particularly if that sentence is heavy with abstractions. So for speeches or oral reports, edit your prose carefully. Write mostly simple sentences or complex and compound sentences with no more than two or three clauses in them. Use sentences of no more than six or eight words from time to time as a kind of punctuation. And be particularly careful to use concrete subjects and strong verbs when possible and to illustrate

Use shorter sentences for oral reports or speeches

[11] Jeffrey Z. Rubin, "Psychological Traps," *Psychology Today*, March 1981, p. 52.

your abstractions with concrete examples that help the audience's concentration by giving them visual images.

Common Grammatical Problems with Sentences

Fragments

Today composition teachers are finding it more and more difficult to explain to their students why they should not use sentence fragments in their papers when those students encounter fragments constantly in the messages they see and hear every day. Advertising copywriters seem to be particularly fond of the sentence fragment. If you are at all conscious of the commercials that daily assault you from all directions, you are familiar with the kind of ad that goes:

> The Different Look! The New Look! The *You* Look!
> Designed for discriminating people and available only at Felix's!

Presumably, people who write this way do so deliberately, and they have reasons for expressing themselves in sentence fragments rather than in traditional language units built around subjects and verbs. Usually those reasons are, first, that they want to catch the potential buyer's eye and, second, that they are really trying to convey an impression rather than an idea.

Some reasons for using fragments

If for some reason you have those same purposes in your expository writing, you could use the kinds of fragments that Tom Wolfe does in this passage:

> Thirty-nine years old! A recluse! Bonafide! Doesn't go out, doesn't see the light of day, doesn't put his hide out in God's own unconditioned Chicago air for months on end; *years*. Right this minute, one supposes, he is somewhere there in the innards of those forty-eight rooms, under layers and layers of white wall-to-wall, Count Basie-lounge leather, muffled, baffled, swaddled, shrouded, closed in, blacked out, shielded by curtains, drapes, wall-to-wall, blond wood, screens, cords,

doors, buzzers, dials, Nubians—he's down in there, the living Hugh Hefner, 150 pounds, like the tender-tympany green heart of an artichoke.[12]

Sentence fragments *are* attention getters, and used consciously in that way, they can be effective. But it is precisely because they are attention getters that a writer needs to be careful about using them (more about that shortly).

Experienced writers also use sentence fragments for emphasis and to provide contrast and variety in a passage of prose, for instance:

> Yeah, yeah, I know—speed kills, right? Safety freaks have been yapping about that for years and, wringing their hands with concern, they tell us that lower limits and tougher law enforcement will cut the death rate on the highways. A *simple solution but patent bullshit*. The fact of the matter is that pure speed on clear, uncongested roads has very little to do with fatal accidents [italics added].[13]

A student might make deliberate use of a fragment in the same way, for example:

> Most people believe that once a doctor or dentist has a degree in hand, he or she will break into the $100,000 a year bracket almost immediately. *Not necessarily.*

Almost no teacher is going to object to this kind of fragment.

Professional writers occasionally use fragments for at least two other reasons. First, they use them in dialogue or as answers to questions. Thus "Never!" or "Since noon" are workable fragments or, as some grammarians call them, minor sentences that are quite correct in context. And fragments are also useful in description, particularly when one wants to give the effect of stillness or separate distinct impressions. Conrad uses fragments this

---

[12] Tom Wolfe, "King of the Status Drop-outs," in *The Pump House Gang* (New York: Farrar, Straus & Giroux, Inc., 1968), p. 49.
[13] Brock Yates, "55 Be Damned!" *Playboy*, June 1976, p. 103.

way in his description of the Congo River in *Heart of Darkness*: "An empty stream, a great silence, an impenetrable forest."

So sentence fragments are by no means always ungrammatical or unacceptable in either student or amateur writing. There are, however, good reasons why *most* writers should not use sentence fragments in *most* things they write. One practical reason is that to almost all composition teachers—and other professors as well— a sentence fragment is a glaring grammatical error that indicates a student is either extremely careless or has such a poor grasp of the fundamentals of the language as not to recognize a sentence. A second reason for avoiding fragments is that they violate traditional sentence patterns and thus may confuse the reader and disrupt communication. A third reason, and probably the most important one, is that fragments make a bad impression on almost any audience. Average-to-well-educated readers are so conditioned to think of sentence fragments as serious mistakes that if they find one in a business letter, a report, or a proposal, they will almost automatically lower their opinion of the writer. For this reason, writers should be very careful about using fragments, even intentionally. In some situations, they risk alienating their audiences.

Guidelines for avoiding fragments Most students who do let sentence fragments slip into their writing do so quite unintentionally because they have forgotten certain conventions of standard English. Some of those conventions are:

1. Verbals, words derived from verbs but functioning in other capacities, *cannot* be the verb of a sentence. The three kinds of verbals are:
   a. Infinitives: to + the simple verb, for example, *to swim, to ride, to write*.
   b. Participles: adjectives made from verbs, for example, *running* horses, *sailing* ships, *condemned* prisoners, *recognized* experts.
   c. Gerunds: nouns made from verbs, for example, *running* the election, *seeing* people off at the plane, *preparing* a meal.

Undoubtedly much of the confusion caused by verbals results from the fact that *-ing* verb forms can be verbs in a sentence when they are used with *auxiliary verbs* (helping verbs). So *was running, are preparing, has been seeing* are verbs, but the *-ing* forms by themselves are not.

2. A dependent or subordinate clause cannot function as a sentence by itself unless it is phrased as a question or an answer to a question.
3. Phrases or clauses that are modifiers or appositives are not sentences and should not be separated off by a period.

Sentence fragments from verbals Infinitives are confusing because they often appear in a sentence with true verbs, and unless one thinks about it, they seem to be acting like verbs. For instance, in the sentences "We are going *to sail*" or "The coach wants us *to run* ten laps" the infinitives refer to people doing something; nevertheless they are acting as nouns. Therefore remember this rule: *An infinitive can* never *act as the main verb for a complete sentence.*

Here are some student examples of the kinds of fragments that occur if you ignore this rule.

Young people need to be on their own. To show their parents that they are reliable. (*Connecting the two word groups with "in order" would have solved the problem.*)

To stop waste of resources and pollution. This is the goal of the Sierra Club. (*Eliminating the period and "this" would solve the problem, but it might be better to just start out by saying, "The goal of the Sierra Club is. . . ."*)

Gerunds seem to cause more fragment problems than infinitives, particularly the word *being*, which students often use as a substitute for *is*. Perhaps they think *being* is more impressive or formal. Whatever the reason, the result is sentences like these:

The author makes surburbia seem inviting. One reason *being* the advantages children get from living there. (*Probably the student hesitated to say "reason is the advantages" but didn't want to take time to rephrase the whole sentence so "being" was stuck in.*)

The authorities did not approve of their acts. These acts being considered detrimental to society. (*The problem could be solved by putting a comma after "acts," adding "which were," and eliminating "these acts being."*)

Here are other kinds of fragments that result from confusion about *-ing* verb forms.

Knowing that the congressman once served in the Peace Corps. I think he will be interested in my proposal. (*Like many sentence fragments, this one could easily be fixed by joining the two parts with a comma.*)

Communication is a big problem. Parents forgetting that they were once twenty years old. (*This fragment results from the writer not realizing the connection between the two statements. They should be connected with "because," and the -ing from "forgetting" should be dropped.*)

Again, remembering one simple rule will eliminate almost all fragments caused by gerunds or participles: *An -ing verb form can never act as the main verb for a complete sentence unless it has an auxiliary verb with it.*

Sentence fragments from dependent clauses When writers use dependent or subordinate clauses as sentences, they probably do so because they don't recognize that certain words or constructions signal dependent or relative clauses. The following list contains the most common of those words:

If, although, while, even, when, in spite of, since, and *because* are often introductory words for dependent clauses.

That, thus, therefore, so, as, and *for* (and sometimes *because* and *since*) often mark the beginning of a subordinate clause.

Who, which, what, where, and sometimes *that* usually mark the beginning of a relative clause.

In most cases a separate group of words that is introduced by one of these words is not a complete sentence because it expresses only part of the author's full meaning.

Here are some typical examples from student papers:

If the legislature thought the standards of the university were going down. (*The student does not follow up with the "then" part of the sentence that we automatically expect when we read "if."*)

People assume they are dope addicts. When in reality they are only young people without much money. (*The problem could be easily fixed by using a comma instead of a period.*)

Trying to walk across the room, I accidentally fell over an ashtray. Which had been left in the middle of the floor. (*The "which" clause is a relative clause referring to "ashtray" and should be directly attached to it.*)

Sometimes writers allow relative clauses to get so long they forget about the sentences the clauses are part of. For example:

Your scholarship, which would help me start on my career in chemistry, a field that I believe will be very rewarding to me. (*There is no verb to go with "scholarship," the subject of the sentence.*)

Sentence fragments from disconnected phrases and causes Writers who construct this last kind of fragment sometimes seem to be imitating advertising copy, believing that setting off a part of a sentence helps emphasize it. Such separation can work, particularly if the phrase is short, but most inexperienced writers don't seem to be able to handle it successfully. The results turn out like this:

In his conclusion the author stresses another issue. A point that everyone today is concerned about—individuality. (*The student would have done better to omit "another issue" and add "a point that. . . ."*)

It has been a long and difficult fight. A fight mostly against people who find the rules restricting. Rules which limit what they can build, how they build it, and what they destroy in the process of building. (*This sample provides an almost classic example of prose that could be vastly improved by judicious sentence combining.*)

Thus, the college who grants him the scholarship gains national prestige. Prestige that was once limited to schools such as those in the Ivy League. (*Substituting a comma for the period solves the whole problem.*)

Certainly writers should not feel that they must always avoid sentence fragments in order to write good prose, but fragments are tricky. If you want to experiment with using fragments for emphasis or in a descriptive passage, and know what you are doing, by all means try them. Obviously some writers get good effects from fragments, and you may too. It might be prudent, however, if you are writing a paper to be graded, to add a footnote or marginal note that shows your instructor that you really do know the difference between a fragment and a sentence.

Run-on and Fused Sentences

For some reason, most students have much less difficulty with run-on and fused sentences than they do with fragments. Nevertheless, a reminder about sentence division is probably in order.

Run-on sentences A *run-on sentence* is one in which several ideas that really should be separated into independent sentences are tacked together with conjunctions. A reader is apt to get lost in one of these rambling creations, particularly because the conjunctions are not chosen carefully enough to reflect the desired relationship between the parts of the sentence. Here are some examples of run-ons and some suggested revisions:

Why to avoid run-on sentences

Run-on We came around the corner and saw that a crowd had gathered and there was some kind of trouble and the police were trying to stop it.

Revision As we came around the corner, we saw a crowd gathered. Apparently there was some kind of trouble that the police were trying to stop.

Run-on The person who wants to persuade an audience must remember who they are and she has to think about what kind of arguments they will respond to for if she does not they will not listen to her and she will have wasted her time.

Revision The person who wants to persuade an audience must remember what kind of people they are and the kind of arguments they will respond to. If she does not, she will have wasted her time because they will not listen to her.

Fused sentences Fused sentences are very similar to run-ons. The difference is that the writer has not even used conjunctions to connect the independent clauses. Rather, they are just run together without benefit of conjunction or punctuation; for example:

Revising fused sentences

> *Fused sentence* The great interest in professional football has inspired several football novels among them are *North Dallas Forty* and *Semi-Tough.*
>
> *Revision* The great interest in professional football has inspired several football novels. Among them are *North Dallas Forty* and *Semi-Tough.*
>
> *Fused Sentence* Some experts on nutrition accuse the American food industry of lying about health in this country by saying that we are the best-fed country in the world they are making us think we get good nutrition for our money but it isn't true.
>
> *Revision* Some nutrition experts accuse the American food industry of lying about health in this country. By saying that we are the best-fed nation in the world, they are making us think we get good nutrition for our money, but it isn't true.

Obviously, run-on and fused sentences are not only poorly constructed and thus difficult to read, but they can be confusing. Careful proofreading should eliminate them.

Comma Splices

Avoiding comma splices

Connecting sentences or independent clauses with a comma rather than separating them into two sentences or joining them with a conjunction or a semicolon is called a *comma splice*, a *comma fault*, or a *comma blunder*. Although, like sentence fragments, this kind of construction seems to be appearing more and more in advertising and popular writing, the careful expository writer should avoid it for several reasons. First, using a comma splice usually indicates indifference or uncertainty about the relationship of the ideas you are connecting. Second, when you join what should be two sentences with a comma, which should be only an *internal* mark of punctuation, you risk misinterpretation of your statements. Third, and this is important, most English teachers object to comma splices in student writing; therefore using them is definitely bad rhetoric.

Here are some typical examples of comma splices taken from student themes:

> Laughter is a form of release just like anger, a good laugh often relieves tension. (*It is not clear whether the phrase "just like anger" should go with "release" or "a good laugh."*)
>
> Congress is going to lose this battle with the President, they will win the next one if they are better prepared. (*The idea of subordination is lost here. The two parts could have been connected with "but," or the sentence could have begun "Although Congress is going to lose. . . ."*)
>
> James Joyce seems to be detached from his characters, they reveal themselves through their actions. (*The reader wonders what the connection between these two statements is. A good guess is that the writer intended to show cause and effect.* Suggested revision: *"Because the characters are revealed entirely by their actions, Joyce gives the impression of being detached from them."*)
>
> The hotel is ugly and old fashioned, it is the fashionable place to stay. (*The reader cannot tell if the writer means the hotel is fashionable because it is old fashioned and ugly or in spite of its being so. A conjunction of "but" or "because" would resolve the confusion.*)

Unfortunately, if you are in the habit of using comma splices frequently, you probably don't even realize that you are doing it. Once the bad habit is drawn to your attention, however, you should make a point of thinking twice about what sentences are and how you should join them. It will help you avoid both fragments and comma blunders.

Dangling Modifiers

Another mistake that crops up regularly in student papers year after year is *dangling modifiers*. Usually a dangling modifier is the introductory clause in a sentence. Because English is a language in which word order controls meaning, we read the beginning clause anticipating that the subject of the sentence is coming right after it and expecting the clause to tell us something about that subject. When the clause doesn't go with the subject but dangles independently, we are surprised, annoyed, and often amused. But most important, our thought processes are interrupted so that we do not—at first, at least—get the message that the writer intends us to get.

Here are some fairly typical examples of dangling modifiers from student themes:

> *When leaving high school,* clothes become the least important of matters.
>
> *Watching television before lunch,* a soda pop commercial encourages Sally to drink Coke with her meal instead of milk.

Notice that with both these sentences if the writers had used a personal subject for their sentences, they could scarcely have gotten into trouble. You are much less likely to attach an unsuitable modifier to a person than to a thing—although it does happen.

In these next examples, notice that the student's use of abstract subjects increases the likelihood of dangling modifiers.

> *Being a freshman student at the University of Texas,* finances are an essential need if I am to continue my education.
>
> *When hiring employees,* their appearance and attitude are an employer's main concern.

Students who have the habit of using the passive voice may also find that it leads them into dangling modifiers. For instance:

> *After having argued all morning,* a decision was reached.
>
> *By forcing students to conform to rules,* creativity is stifled and discouraged.

In each of these cases if the student had started out naming the person who was acting, she or he probably would not have gotten into the dangling modifier confusion.

Sometimes a dangling modifier appears at the end of a sentence, tacked onto an object or complement that it doesn't fit very well; for example:

> The conservatives are unhappy about the vice-presidential nominee, expecting a less controversial choice.
>
> The gun control laws will never make it out of Congress, being opposed by the National Rifle Association.

Writers need to try to clean dangling modifiers out of their writing because they make a writer seem careless and because the comic effect they sometimes create may lose them their audience's respect. The two best ways to get rid of them follow.

First, remember that in English, words usually modify the word or phrase that comes next to them. Be sure, then, that your opening phrase fits with your subject. Second, begin your main clause with a concrete sentence subject whenever you can. You are less apt to get phrases in the wrong place when you do this. An occasional dangling modifier is the price we all pay for trying to write more interesting and compact sentences, and it is really a small price. You can change them in the first draft without too much trouble, and usually you will have a better sentence because you have introduced a qualifying or explanatory clause into it.

One can spend a lot of time tinkering with individual sentences to produce gratifying results. Good sentences are not an end in themselves, however; actual writing requires that you combine sentences into paragraphs. In order to do this, you have to think about the relationships between sentences just as you have previously been thinking about the relationships between the parts of the sentence. The next chapter will deal with some of the ways to work out these relationships to produce good paragraphs.

Exercises

1. *Working with simple and complex sentences* Join the following simple sentences into one compound or complex sentence in a way that shows a relationship between the ideas being expressed. There is not any one right way to do each example.

You can show different relationships by using different linking words, and several options may work for each example.

a. The senator was forced to resign. He will probably never run for office again.

b. Several people have applied for the job. It will not be easy to fill.

c. Educators are alarmed about the steady decline in SAT scores. Legislators keep demanding an explanation.

d. Parents have been crusading against violence on television for more than a decade. We now have almost no westerns. We have detective shows instead.

e. Some physicians say that expensive yearly physical examinations are pointless. Other physicians, particularly gynecologists, think regular checkups are essential.

f. According to sociologists, even small children make class distinctions. They reflect their parents' biases.

2. *Getting rid of abstract subjects in sentences* Try to find a concrete subject, a personal one if possible, to replace the abstract subjects in the following sentences. If necessary, you can change the word order or substitute different words.

a. Being academically prepared was the first thing I realized I lacked.

b. Choice of clothes are a combination of personal tastes, fads, and practicality.

c. A common finance concept would control all hospitals under a government system.

d. Consideration of a multitude of problems must be made by any candidate who wants to be elected.

e. The availability of openings for girls in dental school was a major factor in my decision.

f. The stopping of the encroachment of new building along the sea shore has been a long-time objective of the Sierra Club.

3. *Selecting better verbs* Try to improve these sentences by substi-

tuting a more vigorous verb for those which are underlined. There may be several good choices in some instances.

a. The danger of explosion *remains* a continuing threat in the oil fields.

b. The rating of our football team *is* at a lower level than last week.

c. Geese *are* often *present* in this neighborhood in the winter.

d. Pornographic material *has* no constructive use in our society.

e. I *am* of the opinion that the interference *is* not *warranted.*

4. *Changing passive verbs to active verbs* Change the italicized passive verb constructions in these sentences to the active voice. You may alter the word order if you wish.

a. To make the program work, participation *was needed* by a large number of volunteers.

b. Acupuncture *is believed* to be better than drugs because it has instant effects.

c. The kinds of experiences that *are encountered* in the inner city leave a lasting impression on the young people who *are raised* there.

d. The demands that *were made* by the auto workers *were considered* excessive by the company.

e. It *is* easily *grasped* by the reader that the basis on which this opinion *was formed* is shaky.

5. *Sentence fragments* Rewrite the following sentence fragments to make complete sentences. Join two groups of words if necessary.

a. The author criticizes Texans for the amount of money they bet on high school football. And the things that school boards do to make prospects eligible for their teams.

b. Men have been considered strong and intellectually powerful. Whereas women are considered passive and emotional.

c. When both the husband and wife are working, each feels needed. He in a financial way and she in an emotional way.

d. More people should learn about the benefits of exercise. To stay well and look better.

e. The author makes his home town seem inviting. One reason being that the people are easygoing.

6. *Dangling modifiers* Rewrite the following sentences to get rid of the dangling modifiers.

a. When leaving for college, a car becomes a major problem.

b. Coming from a lower-income family of five children, our bank account allows only enough for one year of college for each child.

c. When hiring employees, their appearance and attitude is an employer's main concern.

d. By learning about genetics, many children with birth defects could be avoided.

e. When given all the relevant information, problems of this kind can be solved.

7. *Comma splices or blunders* Rewrite these sentences with correct punctuation to avoid comma splices.

a. The thought of a comedian like Bob Hope using a canned laugh track is appalling, comedians like him are good enough to be appreciated without trickery.

b. Living close to campus saves money, it is also easier to go to laboratories at night.

c. After getting my passport, the obstacles were gone, all I had to do was borrow the money to go.

d. Parents always put pressure on their children to make good grades, this is due partly to the high cost of education.

e. We will deal with the problem tomorrow, we will be better prepared then.

8. *Exercises on sentence combining*

1. Combine all the sentences in each of the following groups to make one sentence that is tighter and more efficient:

Group A:

   a. Mainland U.S. companies have invested money in Puerto Rico.

   b. They have invested very heavily.

   c. They have encouraged a single-crop economy.

   d. A single-crop economy ultimately hurts a country.

Group B:

   a. The grand jury system originated in England.

   b. It began eight hundred years ago.

   c. It was designed to protect the common people.

   d. The common people often suffered injustice from the nobility.

Group C:

   a. Bicycling is not always healthy recreation.

   b. Bicycling on city streets can be dangerous.

   c. There is danger from heavy traffic.

   d. There is danger from air pollution.

   e. There is danger from reckless drivers.

Group D:

   a. I started college at eighteen.

   b. My goals were simple.

   c. I wanted to get a degree.

   d. I wanted to become a writer.

   e. I wanted to earn lots of money.

Group E:

   a. Americans treasure their privacy.

   b. They do not want others watching their movements.

    c. They do not want others listening to their conversations.

    d. Americans dislike the CIA.

    e. They do not believe in spying on American citizens.

Group F:

    a. The counseling center was started in 1960.

    b. It has grown each year.

    c. It is popular with students.

    d. It is popular with faculty.

    e. It serves more people every year.

Group G:

    a. The instructional program is unique.

    b. It was developed in 1972.

    c. The influence of the program spreads beyond this campus.

    d. It reaches teachers in other universities.

    e. It reaches teachers in high schools and community colleges.

Group H:

    a. Alan Alda is a popular actor.

    b. He is an ardent feminist.

    c. He is one of the top-earning entertainers in the country.

    d. He writes the scripts for many of his own movies.

    e. He directs many of his own movies.

Group I:

    a. The charms of New Orleans are varied.

    b. The city has good jazz.

    c. The city has good food.

d. The city has preserved its distinctive architecture.

e. The city maintains its Creole traditions.

2. Combine all the sentences in each of the following groups into a single sentence; then arrange those sentences into an effective paragraph:

Group A:

a. Many new hotels are being built in America.

b. Most of these hotels are luxury hotels.

c. They are designed for conventions.

d. They are designed for business people.

Group B:

a. These hotels are very large.

b. Many of them have more than one thousand rooms.

c. Some of them have several restaurants.

d. Some have indoor, heated swimming pools.

e. Some have health clubs.

f. Some have tennis courts.

Group C:

a. These new hotels are elaborately decorated.

b. They have enormous lobbies.

c. Some lobbies have trees and flowers growing in them.

d. Some lobbies have waterfalls and terraces.

e. Some lobbies feature ornate crystal chandeliers.

f. Many hotels have glass elevators that look onto the lobby.

Group D:

a. One can find these hotels in many major cities.

b. One such hotel is Loew's Anatole in Dallas.

c. Another such hotel is the Peachtree Plaza in Atlanta.

d. Another such hotel is the Hyatt Regency in San Francisco.

Group E:

a. Prices in these hotels are expensive.

b. Rooms often cost one hundred dollars a night.

c. Drinks in the hotel bar may cost five or six dollars.

d. Breakfast in the hotel café often costs ten dollars.

Group F:

a. These luxury hotels show how the role of hotels has changed.

b. The main purpose of these hotels is not to furnish weary travelers a room for the night.

c. These hotels provide lavish entertainment.

d. These hotels provide facilities for conventions.

e. These hotels provide elegant vacation weekends.

Group G:

a. These hotels are not supported by tourist dollars.

b. They are supported by expense account money.

c. They are supported by tax-deductible entertainment funds.

d. They are supported by giant national conventions.

3. Combine the sentences in these student paragraphs to make them read more smoothly:

A. There are only a few sports at the university which receive the honor of varsity status. Along with these eight or ten varsity sports, there are some thirty other sports at the university which are only given the status of "club sports." These club sports consist mainly of minor sports or sports which are not big crowd drawers. The university treats these sports poorly. The majority of the club sports receive little if any funding from the university. This lack of funding is one of the major hindrances to the further development of these sports.

B. Buying a used car is a tricky business. A good place to start looking is the classified section of the newspaper. Look for personal ads from individuals who want to sell a car. They are your best bet. Ads cover a wide variety of cars in all sizes and prices. If you look hard enough, you can usually find a good machine for a reasonable price. Buying from an individual instead of a dealer takes more time. Nevertheless, it is worth it.

Suggested Writing Assignment

Theme

Purpose To give you practice in some types of writing you may have to do in everyday life.

Procedure Read the directions that a person receives who opens a charge account or takes out a credit card, or find out what rights you are guaranteed by the Equal Employment Opportunities Act. Gather all the necessary information for any one of the writing tasks listed below, and write a letter that gives the evidence the company or bureau needs to act.

Topics

a. Write a concise and specific letter to an oil company or credit card company explaining how and when you lost your credit card and requesting that no charges be made on it from now on. Give all the necessary information to cancel the card.

b. Write a department store explaining an error that has been made in sending you merchandise you did not order. Give the specific details that will enable the store to correct the error and credit your account for the amount of the merchandise.

c. File a complaint with the local office of the Fair Employment Practices Commission specifying how you think you have been unfairly discriminated against by a company who refused to hire you because of your race or sex. Request an investigation of the company.

Writers can look at paragraphs from two perspectives. First, they can look at them from the *outside;* that is, a writer can ask herself, "How are my paragraphs going to look to the reader? What kind of paragraph arrangement does my reader expect to find in my paper, and how long should my paragraphs be?" These are important questions because one major purpose of paragraphs is to divide a long unit of writing into smaller units so that readers can get short breaks between units and thus process and absorb more easily what they are reading.

Writers can also consider paragraphs from the *inside;* that is, a writer can ask himself, "What is the nature of a paragraph? What is a paragraph supposed to do, and what should I keep in mind as I write one?" These are also important questions because the second major purpose of a paragraph is to develop an idea.

Paragraph Unity

Looked at from the inside, a good paragraph's essential quality is unity. The well-written paragraph has one point to make and every sentence in the paragraph relates to that point. It flows smoothly from one sentence to the next, each seeming to fit naturally with the ones that come before and after it. It doesn't sag with unnecessary detail, nor does it veer off in unexpected directions. The paragraph does what it started out to do and neither surprises nor disappoints the reader. It is under control.

Beginning with a Commitment

Probably the best way to control your writing in a paragraph is to begin by stating a commitment in an opening topic sentence and then to be sure that everything else in the paragraph relates to and develops that sentence. There are, of course, other workable approaches to paragraph writing, but the traditional method of making your assertion in the first or second sentence of a paragraph and following it immediately with expansion or supporting information seems to work best for inexperienced writers. They are less apt to wander off the track or lapse into generalities if they start off with a commitment they have to respond to. Here, for instance, is a paragraph that is an almost perfect model of this kind of development.

> If I could name but one thing that beer joints provide, greater than all their many other gifts, it would be music. Jukebox music, preferably country and western. Hell, *got* to be country and western! I am not comfortable or happy in a beer joint, cannot give it a star rating, unless the guitars are jangling and the fiddles whining behind the voices of such as Ernest Tubbs, Willie Nelson, Tom T. Hall, or Merle Haggard, and they sing of walking the floor over you, blue eyes crying in the rain, old five and dimers, making it through December. Never do good-hurtin' old memories come flooding back quite as effectively, never are concerts quite so personal, as when that beer drankin' music floods the soul and the beer is cold enough to ache your teeth almost as much as the music aches your innards. It is no less—as Thomas Jefferson said of the presidency—than a spendid misery; it can almost make you glad that the Taddy Joes and the Linda Lous once took pains to break your heart.[1]

Notice that every sentence that follows King's commitment to show why music is an important attribute of beer joints vividly describes that music and its effects. He makes the general specific and the abstract concrete.

Here is another typical paragraph using the general commitment/specific response pattern.

> In the last 12 years, the Scholastic Aptitude Test scores (SATs) of high school seniors have declined. In 1962 the average score was 490; in 1974 it was below 460. A few years ago, some 54,000 seniors got verbal SATs over 650, which is outstanding; one year later, average scores had dropped eight points and only 40,000 seniors scored that high. Even at prestigious schools, such as Harvard and Brown, average verbal SAT scores are down.[2]

[1] Larry L. King, "The Beer Joint," *Texas Monthly*, March 1976, p. 80.
[2] Carol Tavris, "The End of the IQ Slump," *Psychology Today*, April 1976, p. 69.

This opening paragraph from a student theme does the same thing:

> Both animals and people respond positively to rewards. As experiments have shown, rats in a Skinner box will systematically press a lever in order to obtain food. Dogs will perform tricks in response to verbal praise. People, like those who practice and practice in order to reach the Olympics, also work for rewards. English teachers should be aware of this motivational principle and incorporate it into their teaching methods.

On the other hand, here is a student paragraph that falls apart because the writer does not seem to realize that in the first sentence a commitment has been made that must be followed through on in the rest of the paragraph.

> Give careful consideration to the courses you want to take in your first semester at college. Keep in mind that college is a different institution with new things to experience and new situations to adapt to. I had always been told that college isn't hard and that it's just a matter of keeping up in your classes. This is true, but I have found it to be very difficult and time consuming. My advice to the freshman is that he be sure that the number and kind of courses he takes are those he can handle. In college there is a vast number of courses one can take.

Sentences should not be in random patterns

Although punctuation, grammar, and spelling are all correct, this is a wretched paragraph. One reason is that all the sentences that follow the opening assertion are hackneyed generalities—ten minutes of reading this kind of writing would put anyone to sleep. Another reason is that the paragraph has no thesis, no clear topic sentence that would allow the reader to get a grasp on what the writer intends to say. Instead it is made up of a series of statements that can be moved around like dominoes on a board and put together in several ways. And anytime you can do that to the sentences in a paragraph, or the paragraphs in a theme, you're in trouble. A piece of writing in which the parts can be assembled at random is poorly organized and hard to follow.

Notice too that the writer never fulfills the commitment to explain why first-semester freshmen should give careful consideration to the courses they take. Instead the writer makes three more commitments but does not meet those either; at one point the commitments even contradict one another. Another serious fault in the paragraph is the writer's failure to use specific and concrete language. The writer gives no examples and appeals to no senses but rather stays on the top level of abstraction throughout the paragraph (see Chapter 7 on abstraction levels). Now notice the change if we retain the topic sentence but expand and support it with concrete details:

> New students should give careful consideration to the courses they take their first semester in college. For one thing, they should balance science and nonscience courses so they do not have too many time-consuming labs. They should also try to get a mixture between subjects they find fairly easy and those that are difficult for them. For instance, the student who does well in history but expects to have a terrible time with calculus might plan on taking both in the same semester to balance the work load. The student who does not plan carefully and takes five tough courses the first term may wind up on scholastic probation.

Downshifting A paragraph like this not only gives several specific examples that explain the assertion of the first sentence, but it also illustrates a useful writing technique that Professor Francis Christensen calls *downshifting*. Christensen notes that one develops a paragraph by addition, just as one expands a sentence by embedding modifying words and phrases. He points out, moreover, that "when sentences are added to develop a topic or subtopic, they are usually at a lower *level of generality*."[3] Thus the term *downshifting* is used to suggest that one clarifies a point by moving down the ladder of language abstraction. The most effective paragraphs, Christensen points out, are those which have several levels of generality. Using his method of diagramming

Writing on various levels of generality

[3] Francis Christensen, *Notes Toward a New Rhetoric* (New York: Harper & Row, Publishers, Inc., 1967), p. 56.

the different levels in a paragraph, we could analyze the levels in the preceding paragraph like this:

1. Students should give careful consideration to the courses they take in their first semester in college.
  2. For one thing, they should balance science and nonscience courses so they do not have too many time-consuming labs.
  2. They should also try to get a mixture between subjects they find fairly easy and those that are difficult for them.
    3. For instance, the student who does well in history but expects to have a terrible time in calculus might plan on taking both in the same semester to balance the work load.
    3. The student who does not plan carefully and takes five tough courses the first term may wind up on scholastic probation.

Employed in conjunction with other unifying devices, downshifting is effective in holding a paragraph together because it keeps reinforcing the main idea in the reader's mind. For example:

. The most memorable Wyeth holiday, and the one Andrew refers to most often, was Christmas. Everyone contributed to the house decorating, a sumptuous and extravagant affair which induced particular smells and colors that still stimulate Andrew's mind with memories of the excitement and innocence of his childhood. The climactic moment in the celebration came early Christmas morning when N. C. [Wyeth], charading as Old Chris, would thump his way across the roof, crying out, ringing his sleighbells, and then quickly descend a ladder into the house to deliver presents to the ecstatic and terrified children. "I used to wet my bed, I was so excited on Christmas Eve," recalls Andrew Wyeth,—"and then move to the other side of the bed to let it dry out. Pa used to scare the hell out of me, those big feet stamping on the stairs. Old Chris was always to me a giant, plus a marvelous, magic merry spirit—but a man who terrified me." Even N. C. would become so moved on these occasions that he cried from pleasure and excitement.[4]

In the first sentence the author makes a commitment to show the reader what was memorable about Christmas at the Wyeth's and she does it by downshifting to four levels, each more specific than the last.

Adding transitions Writers who work at giving enough examples and concrete details to develop the main idea of their paragraphs can usually turn out unified paragraphs without too much difficulty. The parts seem to fit together with natural links or hooks. Sometimes, however, the separate sentences in a paragraph can be clear and pertinent to the topic, but the reader gets the impression that there are awkward gaps or rough spots between them. In that case the writer needs to find ways to work conventional transitional words and phrases into the sentences.

Need to link sentences together

Most of the transitional hooks and signposts recommended in the second chapter for tying the parts of a paper together work equally well in constructing paragraphs. As you develop your main point, words like *also, moreover, therefore, however, nevertheless, consequently,* and *furthermore* will probably come to mind almost automatically as you expand or qualify your supporting material. However when you are working *within* paragraphs, probably the most useful connective words you can use are the pronouns, both relative and demonstrative (for definitions of these terms, see the Handbook). By pointing back to the main topic of the paragraph, they keep the reader's attention focused on the thread of the argument. Here is a professional example that uses this technique:

> To the men who shop in *them, they* feel like private clubs. *They're* sanctuaries that spare a man's having to walk through the toy department or an acre of furniture displays when he has better things to do.

[4] Wanda M. Corn, *The Art of Andrew Wyeth* (Boston: New York Graphic Society, 1973), p. 121.

If you're already known in *them*, you'll be greeted by name and engaged in conversation before being shown the items known to suit your taste. If you are a new face, chances are you'll be treated like visiting royalty. Some are equipped with a private bar where you'll be offered a complimentary drink. In none of *them* will you be greeted with that salesclerk's cliché, "Can I help you?"

What *they* are called depends on where you live or the circles you travel in. Some people call *them* boutiques. Others call *them* specialty stores. In plain, simple English, *they're* men's stores—and there are more than 21,400 of them from coast to coast [italics added].[5]

Here is a theme from a student who uses the same device:

Today's military is often managed by men *who* either cheated on exams and got away with *it*, or knew *it* was going on but ignored *it*. What the former learned at the academy was that duty and honor are pretty much optional. *They* play plenty of lip service to *these* two ideas, but *their* only uncompromisable responsibility is to *their* own welfare. These are the men *who* disobey unpleasant orders; *who* falsify records, stretch the truth in reports, or pass the blame on to someone else when convenient. *They* get away with *it* because the only ones to blow the whistle on *them* are the same men *who* refused to do *it* in the academy. *These* professional cynics have found that it's much easier to move up the ladder if *they* remain inconspicuous. [italics added]

Good transitions are not noticeable

No matter how many rules and tricks one knows, achieving smooth transitions between sentences and between paragraphs never becomes automatic, even for professional writers. On the second or third draft, they still find gaps that must be bridged and loose ends that must be tied. But good transitions are so essential to effective writing that it is worth your while to work at them. You will have succeeded only when the reader is not even aware of the links in your prose.

[5] Rita Johnson, "The Stores Behind the Man," *Esquire*, October 1979, p. 68.

Ways of Developing Paragraphs

Mastering the techniques of developing paragraphs is much like mastering the techniques of smoothing out connections between sentences and paragraphs. Although there are no sure-fire formulas or easy solutions, there are some traditional ways to approach paragraph development that seem to work for many writers. These approaches probably sound familiar: illustration and examples, comparison and contrast, cause and effect, narration, question and answer, and analogy. You can also use the six modes of argument explained in Chapter 9 just as effectively for paragraph development as for theme development.

You have many options, a variety of methods available to you. You should not, however, think that they are the only ones or even the best ones for you. You may be better off just to follow your own organizational instincts, as many writers obviously do. Certainly an analysis of the structure of paragraphs in a wide sampling of magazines reveals that there are so many good ways to put a paragraph together that we can't begin to classify them. If, however, you have trouble getting started, some of the following approaches could be helpful.

Illustration and Examples

One can handle the illustration-and-examples approach in at least three ways. The first is the straightforward one mentioned earlier in the section on topic sentences. You make an assertion, usually *How to use examples* a generalization, in the first sentence, and then you give the concrete examples on which it is based. For example:

The future lies before Russell Francis, voluptuously waiting to be had. At twenty-two, he is strong, graceful, poised, and six-and-a-half feet tall. He owns a Maserati, a condominium town house, and a Beechcraft Sierra with much of the instrumentation of an airliner. He has a quick, analytical mind, a warm, open manner, and a contract to play football with the New England Patriots that is said to be in excess of $200,000. He is a superb surfer, a first-rate student, a competition rodeo rider, and, in the words of Paul Brown, a sage of football sages, "the best tight-end prospect I've seen in the last ten years."[6]

The most common variation of this kind of generalization-with-support pattern is a simple reversal, putting the general statement at the end of a list of particulars rather than at the beginning. For example:

Manuel Gregorio Moreno and his wife Magdalena are *campesinos,* the rural people who make up about half of Mexico's 60 million people. Neither Manuel nor his wife Magdalena can read or write. Nor can their children. The chances of their attending school even to the third grade are slim. They are into—and die in—a life of labor and deprivation. Despite efforts by the Mexican government to improve their depressed standard of living and provide them with work, the life of the campesinos in the country or in the city is one of abject misery.[7]

Another, slightly more subtle variation of the same pattern appears in this paragraph from *Newsweek:*

In Gills Rock, Wis., diving students last week knifed 45 feet into the 38-degree water of Racine Quarry to qualify for the certification card that would enable them to dive anywhere in the world. In northern California's Sierra Nevadas, underwater forty-niners are dredging river bottoms for gold. At the Florida Institute of Technology at Jensen Beach, 170 people have applied for the 100 places available next fall in a two-year-old underwater technology program that qualifies students as commercial divers. And in the unpredictable water off Cape Hatteras, one group is attempting to raise the Civil War ironclad, the U.S.S. Monitor, while another is trying to recover Cornwallis's fleet in Yorktown, Va. This week, Columbia Pictures will begin filming Peter Benchley's best-selling book, "The Deep," about a honeymoon couple who discover a sunken treasure of narcotics in Bermuda.[8]

[6] Russel Kahn, "Russell Francis, Patriot," *Esquire,* December 1976, p. 51.
[7] George Natanson, "Wetback," *Texas Monthly,* September 1975, p. 83.
[8] "Life Under Water," *Newsweek,* July 12, 1976, p. 44.

Here the writers give you the particulars, and the generalization is implied (see Using Inductive Arguments, Chapter 10). Obviously, however, even though they don't directly state the commitment they have made to the reader, they are very much aware of it. Everything in the paragraph illustrates the growing popularity of underwater exploration.

Comparison/Contrast

Uses of comparison and contrast

Another kind of paragraph development that seems to come naturally to most writers is the *comparison/contrast technique*. Useful as a tool of definition (see Chapter 9), it also works well when one wants to discuss both the good and bad points of something in one paragraph; for example:

> The credit card can be a wonderful device for instant purchasing power without wads of cash or batches of checks. Cards can be an easy means of identification and of establishing one's credit worthiness for bank loans or mortgages. But at the same time, these plastic rectangles helped many people become deadbeats for the first time in their lives. Both BankAmericard and Master Charge reported that the number of delinquent accounts rose to more than 5 percent of their total membership rolls, up almost one percentage point from the year before.[9]

This pattern of organization can also be used as the basis for an entire theme.

Another way this method works is by setting up a contrast in the topic sentence of a paragraph and then carrying the pattern through in the other sentences; for instance:

> For generations textbooks and readers and children's books used in our school have depicted girls as passive observers, boys as bold achievers. Boys have been playing baseball or football while girls watched admiringly, hands clasped behind their backs. Girls were easily frightened; brave boys saved them from danger. Boys made rockets and peered through

---

[9] "Plastic Power: Credit Card Primer," *Ms.*, August 1975, p. 22.

microscopes; girls played with their dolls and tea cups. Boys have been portrayed as tousled and dirty from boisterous contact with life; girls as starched and pinafored, made of sugar and spice and everything nice.[10]

Cause and Effect

Writing about cause and effect is another kind of development that seems to occur to us almost spontaneously because the urge to explain and give reasons is strong in most of us. This way of handling paragraphs is particularly appropriate for expository writing in which one is trying to analyze a situation or philosophy and speculate about consequences. For example:

> The slaves were powerless for two major reasons. Their legal status was that of chattel without rights in court and without the protection of any institution. The master was all-powerful and had the right to control every aspect of slave life from birth to death, from sex to settling disputes. His power was enhanced by additional factors. Black slaves in a predominantly white controlled land were readily identifiable. The slaves were not of a single tribe origin with a long group history and a resultant cohesive bond. They were far from home and generally unwanted except for economic exploitation. They were not able to maintain the organizational elements of their respective previous cultures—kinship ties, family organizations, religion, government, courts, etc. Thus they were not able to run away en masse; to turn in on their own culture for psychological support or to effectively organize to attack their oppressors.[11]

Cause-and-effect paragraphs may well form the backbone of an argumentative paper. For example, a student arguing for approval of a legislative proposal to increase teachers' pay by 40 percent based his appeal on the belief that the quality of teachers in the

[10] Dan Lacy, "Men's Words; Women's Roles," *Saturday Review*, June 14, 1975, p. 25.
[11] Hugh Davis and Ted Gurr, *The History of Violence in America* (New York: Bantam Books, Inc., 1969), p. 451.

state was going to decline if they did not receive the raise. The opening paragraph went like this:

> If the state legislature does not pass a major pay increase for our public school teachers soon, within a few years all our best college graduates will be going into other jobs. Right now an accountant graduating from the university can start work at $20,000 a year. A dietitian working for the state will begin at $16,000. A pharmacist can make from $17,000 to $24,000, depending on where he or she is willing to live. Even technicians with only two years of training earn more in most jobs than the $11,000 that we pay our beginning school teachers. Under these circumstances we can hardly expect able young people to go into teaching.

The pattern is easily reversed; for example:

> They are often called Caspar Milquetoasts by the psychiatrists who try to treat them. They are so timid and fearful of rejection that they find it impossible to cope with many of the ordinary social situations that occur in life. They cannot send back a steak that arrives carbonized when they have ordered it rare; they lack the will to dispute an obvious overcharge on their grocery bills; some are even afraid to ask a stranger what time it is. Not surprisingly, this kind of repressive timidity takes a heavy toll in mental anguish and psychosomatic symptoms, including stomach ulcers, loss of appetite, alcohol and drug dependence, stuttering, high blood pressure and sexual impotence.[12]

Narration

Uses of narration

Writers use narrative paragraphs when they want to recount an event or an experience or when they want to tell a miniature story or an anecdote. Usually they include people in their narration, and they relate the events in straight chronological order. For example:

[12] "The Timid Souls," *Newsweek*, March 26, 1973, p. 48.

Once in a long while, four times so far for me, my mother brings out the mental tube that holds her medical diploma. On the tube are gold circles crossed with seven red lines each—"joy" ideographs in abstract. There are also little flowers that look like gears for a gold machine. According to the scraps of labels with Chinese and American addresses, stamps, and postmarks, the family airmailed the can from Hong Kong in 1950. It got crushed in the middle, and whoever tried to peel the labels off stopped because the red and gold paint came off too, leaving silver scratches that rust. Somebody tried to pry the end off before discovering that the tube pulls apart. When I open it, the smell of China flies out, a thousand-year-old bat flying heavy-headed out of the Chinese caverns where bats are as white as dust, a smell that comes from long ago, far back in the brain. Crates from Canton, Hong Kong, Singapore, and Taiwan have that smell too, only stronger because they are more recently come from the Chinese.[13]

Here is another kind of narrative paragraph:

They lined up facing the silhouetted targets on a makeshift practice range set up at the Holiday Inn in Santa Monica. Then 50 women and three men took turns firing: ready, aim—spray. "Killed that sucker flat," shouted one woman. "Got him," yelled another. When the two-hour, $35 class at the California Tear Gas School ended, the graduates received official state permits allowing them to carry and use tear gas for self-defense. Most of them departed clutching small gas canisters. "I've had my purse snatched three times," said one middle-aged woman. "If I had this gas I would have used it. I'm getting on a bus right now—and I feel better already."[14]

This kind of paragraph can work especially well as an opening paragraph because its personal tone and concrete language help

[13] Maxine Hong Kingston, *The Woman Warrior: Memoirs of a Girlhood Among Ghosts* (New York: Alfred A. Knopf, Inc., 1975), p. 57.
[14] "Capitalizing on Crime," *Newsweek*, March 9, 1981, p. 66.

catch the reader's interest. Narrative paragraphs are also useful when you want to bring in a specific example to illustrate a theoretical point.

Question and Answer

Introducing your topic with a question

Another direct and effective way to get into a paragraph—or a paper—is to ask a question that sets up the topic to be discussed. For example, "Why is it so hard to quit smoking?" or "What is the fascination of television soap operas?" can lead you into a cause-and-effect paragraph. "What is so bad about junk foods?" or "What kind of people are attracted to drugs?" are good ways to work into a paragraph of definition. Questions can also act as good transitions into paragraphs. For instance, you might start a paragraph of explanation by asking, "How can we meet these problems?" Or you could introduce a paragraph of support by asking, "What is the evidence for such a statement?" A question can also work well in a lead-in to the conclusion of a paper. For example, in an article on the declining popularity of history courses in college, the author introduces the last section by saying, "So what does the future hold for the field of history?"

Question-and-answer paragraphs are useful in expository writing because they allow the writer to focus the reader's attention on the specific issue and thus make it less likely that the reader will get lost. For example:

> What is the information content of the brain? Let us consider two opposite and extreme poles of opinion on brain function. In one view, the brain, or at least its outer layers, the cerebral cortex, is equipotent; any part of it may substitute for any other part, and there is no localization of function. In the other view, the brain is completely hardwired: specific cognitive functions are localized in particular places in the brain. Computer design suggests that the truth lies somewhere between these two extremes. On the one hand, any nonmystical view of brain function must connect physiology with anatomy; particular brain functions must be tied to particular neural patterns or other brain architecture. On the other hand, to assure accuracy and protect against

accident, we would expect natural selection to have evolved substantial redundancy in brain function. This is also to be expected from the evolutionary path that it is most likely the brain followed.[15]

Analogy

A more sophisticated, but potentially very useful, kind of paragraph that writers can employ for a variety of purposes is one built on an *analogy.* This device, which is covered at some length in Chapter 9, clarifies or expands on an idea or theory by comparing it to something with which the reader is familiar. For example, a student writing about the psychological stresses that astronaut crews undergo might compare a journey abroad a space capsule to a month-long trip for four in a camper mounted on a pickup, with dehydrated food of the kind carried by backpackers.

Ways of using analogies

Game analogies can also work well. For example, in a magazine published by medical students, the lead article began like this:

> It's turning into one of the roughest games around. The stakes are high—admission not only to medical school but to perhaps the only profession that still carries some guarantee of financial security and personal prestige. The players—some 43,000 applicants scrambling for 15,000 places last year—are becoming more and more ruthless in their desperation to win acceptance. And the irony of winning is blatant—those who do succeed often are the ones least likely to become the kind of doctors our society needs and wants.[16]

Analogies from everyday experience

Drawing analogies requires some reflection and imagination, but many of us have good material for comparison in our own experiences if we just learn how to look for it. The most ordinary events can furnish references that will help to make ideas concrete. For example, a person who has grown up on a ranch knows that fixing fences is a tedious, grueling, and never-ending job. That knowledge might be worked into a paragraph in this way:

[15] Carl Sagan, *The Dragons of Eden* (New York: Ballantine Books, Inc., 1977) p. 29.
[16] Dianne Rafalik, "Getting In: Games Applicants Play," *The New Physician* (publication of the Student American Medical Association), March 1976, p. 21.

Anyone who is planning to go into radio and television because he thinks he will have a glamorous and exciting job that will allow him to travel and talk to interesting people should talk to a news reporter at a local station. He will find that being a TV reporter is about as exciting as being a cowboy; making the rounds of the police stations, club meetings, city council meetings, and justice of the peace courts is no more glamorous than going out every day to fix the sags and breaks in a barbed-wire fence.

Drawing analogies from your own experience

Almost everyone has an area of expertise; it may be bicycling, cooking, golf, horses, anything. Students who have played football and follow professional and college ball can draw from their store of information to set up comparisons. People who have worked in the construction business or waited on table or helped in a political campaign or taught swimming have special knowledge to draw on for both examples and analogies. Certainly you have the same kind of knowledge about something—perhaps several things—and when you learn to use these resources to illustrate points you want to make in a paper, your writing will become more concrete and more interesting. For example:

The first week on a new job that you want desperately to succeed at can be terrifying. You're sure everyone in the office knows more than you do and is just waiting to laugh at you if you make a mistake. You feel ignorant and awkward and confused. But jobs really aren't that different and if you've ever waited table in a restaurant—and done it right—you can handle most other jobs the same way. Start out by listening to the orders people give you. If you're not sure what they want, ask—twice if necessary. Write it down so you won't forget anything, then check off the items as you take care of them. After you've filled the order, don't disappear, but stay close enough to get any new instructions. In a few days you'll find out that coping with the new job is a lot easier than you thought it would be.

Training yourself to think in analogies takes some practice, but if you are going to do much writing, you should try to cultivate the habit. A good analogy is invaluable for clarifying a difficult point.

Remember though, that when you do suddenly think of a good comparison, write it down. You'll forget it if you don't.

The Length of Paragraphs

Now let's shift perspectives and look at paragraphs from the outside; that is, let's look at paragraphing from the reader's point of view. When we do that, the first question that arises is "How long should a paragraph be?" As with so many other questions about writing, the answer to that has to be, That depends. It depends on the purpose, the audience, and the tone you are trying to convey in your writing. And the old rule about one idea to one paragraph really doesn't help much when you get down to actual writing situations.

Reasons for dividing writing into paragraphs

Nevertheless, the two basic principles of paragraphing can give us some guidance. The first of those principles is that writers break their writing into units—sentences, sections, chapters, and parts, as well as paragraphs—in order to help their readers follow their ideas more easily. The second principle—and it also applies to all of the other units except the sentence—is that the function of a paragraph is to develop an idea.

Deciding about Paragraph Length

The first principle suggests that in informal writing for the general reader, paragraphs should not be overly long. That vague suggestion means something like not over seven or eight sentences to a paragraph unless good unity really demands extending it beyond that length. In formal, scholarly, or scientific writing, paragraphs may run much longer, but even there the trend is certainly toward the shorter paragraph. A long block of unbroken print does look rather intimidating, after all, and many of us are more inclined to read an article if we see breaks on the page.

Bad effects of one-sentence paragraphs

The problem is that some newspaper editors and advertising copywriters who worry about the way print will appear in a long column have taken to breaking their articles and ads into one- or two-sentence paragraphs with almost no regard for the continuity of their material. The effect is choppy, distracting, and hard to follow. For example:

> Thousands of people every year trade the helter-skelter pace of urban living for the more relaxed schedule of rural life in central Texas.
>
> Most have few regrets, but some find unexpected differences between the two lifestyles more than they bargained for.
>
> Big city residents who wanted to escape the crowded conditions, the rush and high taxes of urban living find they also have left behind a number of services taken for granted in the city.
>
> Lower taxes pay for a lower level of service and the relatively vast areas to be covered make it difficult, if not impossible, to provide high quality service.[17]

This kind of writing jerks the reader from one point to another without benefit of connectors or transitions to tie them together. It also violates the rock-bottom fundamental of paragraphs: the ideas in them must be developed.

Since students, consciously or not, tend to model their own writing on the kind of writing they are frequently exposed to, many of them have gotten into the habit of writing one-sentence paragraphs without really thinking about what they are doing. To make matters worse, in some journalism classes students are actually being taught to write like this. Unfortunately the result is often a series of unsupported assertions, because when students construct one-sentence paragraphs they are no longer thinking in terms of developing an idea.

Paragraphs should be long enough to meet commitment

So one answer to the question "How long should a paragraph be?" is that it should be long enough to allow the writer to make some response to the commitment made or implied in the topic sentence. The writer who is listing evidence in order to build up to that topic sentence should collect enough data in the paragraph to warrant the conclusion. If the point is being developed by restatement and examples, the writer needs to have enough examples to strengthen the topic sentence and lead to clear rephrasing at the end. One cannot carry out that task in a single sentence and probably not in two.

[17] Steve Hultman, "Home on the Range," *Austin (Texas) American-Statesman*, July 18, 1976, p. B1.

This is not to say that one should never write a one-sentence paragraph. Occasionally you need them to emphasize a single point that you want to stand out. John F. Kennedy's inaugural address, for instance, has several one-sentence paragraphs listing the gains he expected to make in his administration. In a long narrative essay about the effects of the atom bomb that was dropped on Hiroshima, Alexander Leighton highlights the central event in this one-sentence paragraph:

One-sentence paragraphs used for emphasis

> The bomb exploded several hundred feet above their heads.

And he drives home his conclusion with two one-sentence paragraphs:

> There was one woman in Hiroshima who said, "If there are such things as ghosts, why don't they haunt the Americans?"
> Perhaps they do.[18]

Inexperienced writers, however, should use the one-sentence paragraph *very* sparingly, and only when they have a clear idea of why they are using it.

Deciding Where to Break Paragraphs

Finally, how does one know where to break one's writing up into paragraphs? Obviously the answer to that must be that even professionals don't know precisely where divisions should come. The old rule of thumb is to start a new paragraph when you start discussing a new idea, but often adequate development of even one idea can require several paragraphs, so we need a more specific guideline. Perhaps the only useful one is that you can break a paragraph when you are introducing a new idea or when you find a time or space separation or a slight shift in direction.

Guidelines for breaking paragraphs

Notice, for instance, that the following paragraph could be broken at two places without violating the unity of the ideas. One

---

[18] Alexander Leighton, "That Day at Hiroshima," *Atlantic Monthly*, October 1946, p. 90.

break could come after the third sentence, and a new paragraph could start with "Everyone likes the way he looks, though: magnetic, exotic." Another break could come after the following five sentences, starting a new paragraph with "There is no player with faster reflexes or greater speed." In the rest of the passage, however, the sentences seem so closely tied to each other that it would be difficult to find a logical division point.

> But the fans love him [Ilie Natase]—and those who don't, love to hate him. Which is part of his draw but much of his trouble. They hooted and hollered at him during the Pohmann match like drunks at a bearbaiting; even many of the players felt sorry for him. Everyone likes the way he looks, though: magnetic, exotic. He walks like a jaguar, has the eyes of a gypsy, the body of Apollo. And his game is an amalgam of all that is spectacular in tennis. He has Manuel Santana's top-spin lob and is at times a mirror image of Rod Laver—he has a strong first serve, a good volley and two or three ground strokes to follow them up. He has, of course, all of Pancho Gonzalez' chair-throwing, ball-slamming anger. He plays closer to the net and with greater effectiveness than almost any other player on the tour; his attacks from the base line are devastating. There is no player with faster reflexes or greater speed. He has an exquisite touch with a racket, a feel for the ball that cannot be learned. It is how Gordie Howe caresses a hockey puck. He can break his wrist in ways that would fracture another player's, masking his top spin until the last instant. He plays against the movement of his opponent. He is simply breathtaking to watch.[19]

Certainly current writers are showing more and more inclination to favor the short paragraph. It seems easier to read and is probably also easier to write because one does not have to concentrate for as long at a time. But don't just arbitrarily chop your writing into little segments that may look like paragraphs but are really only groups of sentences put together without unity or develop-

[19] Eric Lax, "Nasty!" *Esquire*, March 1977, p. 98.

ment. Be sure each paragraph acts as a small unit of thought, a discernible block in the larger structure of the essay.

Opening Paragraphs

Opening paragraphs bear a heavy load because a reader expects so much from them. Most readers want the first paragraphs of an essay to do three things:

The functions of opening paragraphs

1. Catch the reader's attention.
2. Make a promise or a commitment that tells the reader what to expect from the rest of the essay.
3. Show the reader why he or she should continue to read.

As one British language expert puts it, we get started in both writing and reading by moving along tracks that have already been laid down,[20] and a key function of opening paragraphs is to lay those tracks.

But even though readers know what they want from opening paragraphs, it's hard to generalize about what kind of paragraph best meets those needs. For, once more, you can't really make intelligent decisions about what kind of opening paragraph you need until you have defined your audience and your purpose. (Later in this chapter there will be suggestions about adapting your introductions to your audience and your purpose.) Good opening paragraphs, however, nearly always share one characteristic: they make a commitment to the reader. They raise expectations, either directly or subtly, and establish a contract with the reader. For the rest of the essay, the writer's chief concern should be to meet that commitment, to carry out that contract.

Most opening paragraphs make commitments

Your Commitment to the Reader

The need for you as a writer to realize that you have an obligation to live up to the commitment you make your audience is so cru-

---

[20] James Britton, "The Functions of Writing," *Research in Composing*, ed., Charles Cooper and Lee Odell (Urbana, Ill.: NCTE, 1978), p. 24.

cial to good writing that it is worth explaining more fully. When you begin to write a paper or an article you make—or very strongly imply—a promise to the readers. Usually, but not always, you make that promise in the first sentence of a paragraph or the first paragraph of a paper. By that promise you bind yourself to explain and support a statement or to give more information on a topic. By reading your promise, readers learn what to expect. If they are not interested, they don't read any further. If they do read beyond the first sentence or paragraph, they expect you to do what you said you would do. If you disappoint them, you have not lived up to your part of the bargain.

Next time you read an article in a magazine or a newspaper, notice the opening paragraph. Almost always it—or the second paragraph—will tell you what is going to be discussed and even give you some idea of the author's attitude toward the topic. To illustrate the point, here are three short examples from magazines that usually feature good writing:

> John Kennedy's unfathomable death created in many Americans a terrifying expectancy. If that could happen, anything was possible. We sense that the potential for political murder had been only partially discharged with Kennedy. Somehow it was still suspended above the nation, a nearly palpable menace awaiting its next moment. Who would be next, we wondered.[21]

The readers anticipate instantly that the article is going to be about the political assassinations in this country that followed John Kennedy's death. And it is.

> Many critics worry about violence on television, most out of fear that it stimulates viewers to violent or aggressive acts. Our research, however, indicates that the consequences of experiencing TV's symbolic world of violence may be much more far-reaching.[22]

---

[21] James McKinley, "Death Crosses the Color Line," *Playboy*, June 1976, p. 127.
[22] George Gerbner and Larry Gross, "The Scary World of TV's Heavy Viewer," *Psychology Today*, April 1976, p. 41.

The readers assume immediately that the authors are going to report on a research project they have done with people who watch television and tell you what conclusions they have come to. And they do.

> Mexico City has its faults; its residents live under the constant threat of earthquakes, and the city regularly experiences tremors and occasional minor quakes. But it is the man-made disasters, rather than the natural ones, that threaten to destroy the city which has been called the Paris of the Western Hemisphere.[23]

The readers who start this article expect to learn how Mexico City has deteriorated in the past years. And they do.

Although these writers have the professional polish that no one expects from a student, it is the method, not the style, that is crucial here. And it is as important for you to let your reader know what you are going to do, and then do it, as it is for professional journalists. Well, almost as important—if they don't do it, they will soon be out of a job.

Follow through on your commitment

Making a commitment to your audience and then following through on that commitment with explanation and details are so basic to day-to-day communication that usually we don't even think about the process. When we open a conversation with "San Francisco is a great city" or "Inflation will be a crucial issue in the next election," our audience expects us to follow through with supporting details, and ordinarily we have no trouble doing so because we already know what our reasons are for making the assertion. And if we forget to give our reasons, our audience will remind us of the lapse by saying, "Why do you say that?" or "What do you mean?" In writing, however, we often have to remind ourselves that we need to follow up on our commitment.

Varieties of Opening Paragraphs

Opening paragraphs that announce the writer's purpose

The straightforward announcement Anyone writing a technical or business report should begin with a direct, clear, carefully

---

[23] George Natanson, "Mexico City Is the Most Uninhabitable City in the World," *Texas Monthly*, September 1975, p. 79.

organized statement that lets the reader know exactly what to expect:

> The primary purposes of an introduction to a technical report are to state the subject, the purpose, the scope, and the plan of development of the report. In addition, it is sometimes necessary to explain the value or importance of the subject. Often it is desirable to summarize principal findings or conclusions.[24]

Of course such a statement might take much more than a paragraph; the point is that any writing whose principal purpose is to communicate facts and straight information should do so without delays or digressions. No tricks, gimmicks, anecdotes, or unnecessary preliminaries. And in general this rule applies to letters of application for scholarships and fellowships, grant proposals, reports of experiments or surveys, and autobiographies or statements of goals written to send with applications. The audience for these kinds of documents wants facts, stated quickly and economically; it does not want opinions or generalities. So with any writing that is strictly informative, the best introduction is one that goes straight to the point, for example:

> I am writing to apply for the position of shop foreman that you advertised in Sunday's *Times-Herald*.

> I would like to be considered for the four-year scholarship in tax law and accounting that your firm offers to an Illinois high school graduate every year.

> My name is Joanna Benson. As a native Georgian and recent honors graduate of Emory University, I meet the requirements for a graduate fellowship.

> This paper is a preliminary report of the findings of the Minnesota Council on Child Abuse, appointed by the governor in 1975 to do a two-year study of child abuse in the Minneapolis-St. Paul area.

> This report will be an analysis of the data collected in

[24] Gordon Mills and John Walter, *Technical Writing*, 3d ed. (New York: Holt, Rinehart & Winston, 1970), p. 253.

twenty-four experiments conducted with rats from September 10 through September 17, 1976, in Skinner boxes in the psychology laboratories of Purdue University.

Notice that there are no adjectives in any of these sentences. The sentences that make up the rest of these opening paragraphs should follow the same pattern of giving pertinent information in an objective tone, and each should carry out the commitment to give supporting information that the opening sentence implies.

There is nothing wrong with using a direct and simple introductory paragraph for nontechnical papers written for a variety of audiences and purposes. It can frequently do well the two things that any opening paragraph should do: get the readers' attention and give them a reason to continue reading. For example:

Last year there were fifty million unwanted dogs and cats in the United States and despite the efforts of humane societies to dispose of strays and persuade people to neuter their pets, this animal population continues to grow. The results are pathetic and sometimes frightening. In many cities, one often sees big dogs wandering in packs searching for food. Bought for protection but abandoned when they proved too costly or troublesome to keep, they pose a menace to tame animals and even to small children.

The cheating scandal that erupted at West Point in the spring of 1976 raised once more the question of whether the United States service academies can continue to hold their cadets to strict honor codes. Lawyers for the West Point cadets who have been charged allege that cheating is far more widespread than the academy authorities will admit. They maintain that up to half of the graduating class is involved and that all of them should be dismissed from the service if that penalty is imposed on those who have admitted their guilt.

Explicit, no-nonsense opening paragraphs like these get the reader's attention by pointing out a problem; anyone who is interested in that problem will continue reading for more information and suggestions about ways to solve it. Not only are such introductions courteous to the reader in that they don't waste time, but also they are fairly easy to write. Once you have made up your mind to just say it like it is, you can usually break through that barrier of inertia that stymies all efforts to get started.

Using a narrative in your opening paragraph

The anecdote or narrative Often you can catch your reader's interest and establish a commitment to hold it by starting with a narrative paragraph that creates a picture or sketches out a situation. For example.:

> While waiting in a particularly long checkout line at the supermarket the other day, it occurred to me that a discernible pecking order exists among mothers. I was idly sizing up the woman in front of me on the basis of her grocery cart contents. Freakies and Pop Tarts. Hmmm, probably sleeps late and watches the soaps and sends her son to school with a lunchbox full of Hostess Twinkies, which he trades for my son's fresh banana. But glancing over my shoulder, I couldn't help noticing that my Morton's frozen doughnuts were being smugly regarded by a woman whose cart contained a bag of whole grain flour, six cartons of yogurt, and four packages of yeast.[25]

Here an observant person has taken a commonplace experience that her readers will easily recognize and used it as a hook to catch their attention.

Another example is from a student paper:

> You have donned all of your equipment and are ready to go overboard. Taking a few short puffs of air from your regulator to make sure your equipment is working properly, you enter the sea by taking a giant stride off the boat. As the bubbles clear you find yourself suspended weightlessly above a beautiful tropical reef. Below, you might see basket sponges as large as an oil drum and a sea fan as wide as you are tall. Brightly colored corals are everywhere. From under a coral head a spiny lobster waves his long antennae at you much like

[25] Prudence Macintosh, "Tube or Not Tube," *Texas Monthly*, September 1975, p. 37.

a swordsman might threaten his opponent. And all around you are multicolored fish moving about totally undisturbed by your presence in their watery realm.

This writer draws his reader into his essay on scuba diving by beginning with a colorful narrative of descending into the water.

Other kinds of openers Another standard way of leading into an expository or persuasive essay is to ask a question in your first paragraph. For example:

> Is public broadcasting nearly dead? The casual PBS viewer, who has seen the quality and variety of public TV programs improve over the years, may be stunned to learn that right now this is an urgent question. In the corridors of local public stations everywhere and in the system's seats of power in Washington, there's talk of a rapidly approaching doomsday for public television. The suddenly looming villain: cable TV.[26]

Notice that this opener focuses the reader's attention on the issue to be discussed, and it also makes a strong commitment to explain how cable TV is threatening public television.

Another frequently used opener is the appropriate quotation or reference to a news item, but for a student, unless you happen to know where to lay your hand on the news item or actually know the quotation well enough so that you only have to check the source, it is probably not worth taking the time to dig something out. Searching for a reference to fit your idea usually isn't practical.

Common faults in opening paragraphs

Poor opening paragraphs Two problems often mark opening paragraphs that don't work well. One is that the writer strings together a series of generalities that do little more than state the obvious. The reader quickly becomes bored and impatient; if possible, he or she probably quits reading. Here is a student paragraph that illustrates this problem:

---

[26] Peter Caranicas, "Can PBS Survive Cable?" *Saturday Review*, January 1981, p. 36.

There are many things about college which are much different than high school. It is really hard to put in words. You would need to be part of it to really know what I am talking about exactly. There is so much difference between such things as study habits, clothes, people, athletics, and other things also.

A second major fault of opening paragraphs is that they fail to make a commitment, fail to let the reader know what to expect. Here is a fairly typical example of such a failure, which also incorporates the first fault, rambling generalities:

America is the best-fed nation in the world. Our country is, after all, a very prosperous nation. Our food supply is sufficient, even abundant. Our farmers utilize the most modern, efficient techniques to increase harvests. Our educators and physicians are top-notch and our technology is superior. Our dilemma is that the advanced techniques that furnish us with quick, convenient, time-saving, instant foods also allow nutrients to be lost and discarded during this food processing. The refining and processing of almost every food cause the loss of much or all of its nutritive value. However, highly refined foods keep better than do natural foods; they are easier to store and to ship. On the other hand, being fed with refined foods does not make a nation "best-fed."

These paragraphs have much in common: both are repetitious and vague; they give the reader no facts or concrete details; and they don't tell the reader what to expect from the rest of the paper. The authors are really just warming up, getting ready for the real thing, like golfers practicing their swings or a football team doing jumping jacks and knee bends before the first play is called. This kind of writing might also be likened to a dog turning round and round several times getting ready to lie down. Such exercises may be useful as a part of prewriting—they are at least preferable to staring at a piece of blank paper—but they should be cut out of the final paper. They bore the reader, and they contribute nothing to the development of your idea.

Two other kinds of introductions that students would do well to avoid are the overworked leadoff with a dictionary definition or obvious fact—"Lyndon Johnson was the thirty-seventh president of the United States"—and starting off with a summary of background material that is either trivial or irrelevant. For example, avoid an autobiography that begins like this:

> My birth took place in St. Paul's hospital in Dallas, Texas. I have been told that I was a happy, healthy baby whose greatest feats were walking at seven months old and talking at an early age. The childhood memories I still retain are mostly happy. They consist mainly of my family and the carefree moments of play I enjoyed with my younger brothers and sisters as well as with the other children of the neighborhood.

It is painful to think how an admissions board would react to this application.

Writing your introduction last

Finally, remember that there is not a thing wrong with writing your introduction last. Professional writers frequently work that way, because after they have finished an article they know better how they want to introduce it. An added bonus of waiting until last to write the introductory paragraph is that you may find you really don't need one. Rereading may show that you have said everything you want to say and the paper doesn't need any opening ruffles and flourishes. This is particularly true of short papers. For them, beginning with a single sentence that gives your main assertion often does the job quite well. Don't feel compelled to add any trimmings.

Concluding Paragraphs

After reading through scores of closing paragraphs in a wide variety of essays, both amateur and professional, I can only conclude that one cannot safely generalize about what makes a good conclusion. Again, it depends on whom you are writing for and what your purpose is. If you are doing a report, particularly a long one for a business group or a class, you should summarize your main points in the conclusion. If you are trying to persuade your audience to accept an idea or an opinion, you should probably restate

Wide variety of concluding paragraphs

your thesis at the end, just as a trial lawyer would sum up a case for a jury. Sometimes signal transition phrases such as *Finally, Thus, In conclusion,* or *We can then* are good openers for a last paragraph. And remember that for short papers, you may not even need a last paragraph. One sentence that seems to tie up loose ends will frequently do the job.

Although it is difficult to give any positive guidelines for writing those painful last paragraphs, two warnings about what *not* to do in conclusions may be useful. First, don't keep on writing after you have actually finished what you have to say. When you are through, stop. It is better to be a little abrupt than to risk boring your audience with mere repetition or a statement of the obvious. Remember how many times you have thought, "If the speaker had just quit ten minutes earlier, it would have been a much better speech." So stop while you still have your audience's attention.

Kinds of conclusions to avoid

Second, resist the temptation to indulge in platitudes or nice-sounding generalities at the end. For some reason—perhaps because conclusions *are* hard to write or because theme outlines always call for conclusions—inexperienced writers often end up with what might be called *pious-platitude* or *noble-sentiment endings.* They don't really have any more to say, but they want to add something that sounds good. Feeling reasonably sure that no one could object to what is obviously "right thinking," they tack on paragraphs like these, the first written for an assignment about the generation gap.

> Today the generation gap still goes on; there will probably always be one. Nevertheless, steps have been taken to bridge that gap. If we cannot close it, we must work harder, both young and old, to make the gap as small as possible. Only in that way can we make this a better world to live in.

This closing paragraph came at the end of a paper about the role of the American business person abroad:

> The American businessman must realize that he can protect our American heritage. He is the only one who can preserve capitalism and free enterprise. America possesses a great

society and economic woes must not destroy it. By having a government of the people and for the people, America can remain a world power and not fall in to being a second rate country.

Conclusions like these, which sound as if they could have been manufactured by a computer stocked with clichés, make their authors sound embarrassingly naive.

Good conclusions give a sense of closure

Finally, all one can really say about concluding paragraphs, whether for essays, stories, or books, is that they should give the reader a sense of closure, a feeling that the writer has finished saying what he or she started out to say. The best conclusions, like the best transitions, grow out of the structure of the writing, and ideally you shouldn't have to point out to the reader that you are stopping. But ideals are hard to achieve, and conclusions remain hard to write. My only advice is to keep tinkering until they look right.

Exercises

1. What kind of commitment are the authors of these opening paragraphs from magazine articles making to their readers?

a. Shrimping in the Gulf has never been a calling men pursued for the fun of it—or for the easy money. Oh, there was plenty of money to be made once: the lowliest deckhand could return from a fifteen-day trip with $3000 in his pocket. But the work was brutal and, most of all, lonely: two or four or six weeks on a pitching boat in the middle of the hostile ocean. Shrimp are elusive creatures, apt to change their feeding grounds from year to year, and some years the shrimpers never quite figured out where they were. Those were the years of frustrating summers and lean winters. And then in the good years the crew could work themselves near to death, hauling up the writhing beasts by the ton, working around the clock to get them decapitated and iced down before the sun had a chance to make them spoil.[27]

[27] Victoria Loe, "Shrimpers," *Texas Monthly*, April 1981, pp. 128–129.

b. Despite all the current fuss and bother about the extraordinary number of ordinary illiterates who overpopulate our schools, small attention has been given to another kind of illiterate, an illiterate whose plight is, in many ways, more important, because he is more influential. This illiterate may, as often as not, be a university president, but he is typically a Ph.D., a successful professor and textbook author. The person to whom I refer is the straight-A illiterate, and the following is written in an attempt to give him equal time with his widely publicized counterparts.[28]

c. Many observers have concluded from the news coverage of the past year—the Reagan sweep, the disarray of political liberalism, the tighter constraints of our economy, the emergence of fundamentalist groups opposed to the ERA, abortion, and sex education—that the United States is swinging back to the disciplined, self-sacrificing habits that ruled American life before the heyday of affluence. But that inference is incorrect. Tomorrow is not going to look like yesterday. In fact, tomorrow—to the extent that research data can yield clues about it—is being shaped by a cultural revolution that is transforming the rules of American life and moving us into a wholly uncharted territory, not back into the lifestyles of the past. Irreversible in its effects, this cultural revolution is as fateful to our future as any changes in the economy or politics.[29]

2. Write from three to five sentences that would adequately fulfill the commitment made in one of these opening sentences for paragraphs:

a. Swimming is a particularly good form of exercise.

b. Television commercials seem to be at their worst during the evening news programs.

c. In my opinion, we must defeat the incumbent senator.

d. Some critics feel that a college education is not necessarily a good investment.

---

[28] James P. Degnan, "Masters of Babble," *Harper's*, September 1976, p. 37.
[29] Daniel Yankelovich, "New Rules in American Life: Searching for Self-Fulfillment in a World Turned Upside Down," *Psychology Today*, April 1981, pp. 35–36.

3. Rewrite the following two paragraphs to make them smoother and more coherent. Begin each one with a topic sentence that will serve as a guideline for developing the rest of the paragraph.

a. All too often young people enter into the bond of marriage without considering the future financial situations that can arise. One such problem is self-supported education. College educations are expensive and one or both partners may have to work. This results in separation of the couple. Further separation is caused by the many hours that have to be spent studying and doing homework. Working eight hours a day, going to school, and studying leave very little time for the couple to spend together. Most jobs require the student to devote his full attention to the work being done. Little time is left, therefore, for his studies.

b. "I did not know I was eligible to enter the university." This is what Eddie Jones said to his high school counselor when he was told his grades met the university entrance requirements. Eddie is an average student who believed the myth that our university is only for smart people. Many students fail to apply simply because they are uninformed about its requirements. Minority students are the most uninformed about their opportunities. I think all minority students would be able to attend the university. At other colleges drives to enlarge enrollments always succeed in increasing the number of students. Therefore, concerted drives should be made to bring more minority students to this university.

4. Evaluate the following opening paragraphs from student themes. What are your reasons for thinking they are successful or not successful?

a. You have hardly stepped out of your building, and what do you see? Runners. Spread a picnic in the park and there they are again. Their races are televised, their faces sell credit cards and cereal. Can you even cross the street without being trampled? Maybe you once thought running was all a quirky fad that would pack its bags and fade away one night. But now that over 25 million Americans run regularly, how much longer can you ignore the tiny little voice inside that nags, "Shouldn't I join them?"

b. Pornography should not be banned because people are basically curious. Almost every animal is curious, and people are not any exception. A child that has recently reached puberty will be increasingly curious about the opposite sex. Curiosity is the basis for human progression. Humans must be curious in order to search into the truth of the unknown.

c. In the United States, education is considered a right and thus is tax supported so that all children in this country can have the opportunity to go to school. Our children's education is not neglected because parents do not have enough money. Education is even more than a right, for children are required by law to attend school to a certain age. But is health care a right? No, good health care is the privilege of those who have the money to pay the bills.

d. Nearly 250 years ago on the green and brown slopes of the volcano, Vesuvius, on the west coast of Italy, a young peasant farmer plowed in his field. The sun's early morning rays cast his long shadow on the dark moist soil and white clouds covered the dark, wide mouth of Vesuvius. Below, the blue sea sparkled and shivered in the Bay of Naples. The peasant was plodding along in his usual morning routine, when suddenly his plow scraped against a solid object. He bent to remove what he thought was only a rock, and jumped in surprise when he saw bright and vivid colors glaring at him through the black fertile dirt. Brushing aside the soil, he pulled from the ground a beautiful vase of very fine quality. He stared in amazement and awe at the scene he saw painted so delicately on the vase.

5. Analyze the commitment the writer has made in the opening paragraph of this student paper. What is it, and how does she meet it? Then analyze the way the writer develops her paragraphs, paying particular attention to the strategy of *downshifting*.

Causes of Declining Feminist Activism

Have you ever identified yourself as a feminist and been promptly rewarded with a look that screamed "heretic"? These looks and the attitudes behind them usually mark a person who misunderstands feminist principles and goals. Their misconceptions cause them to respond in a negative, emotional, reactionary manner.

Opponents of the movement often believe that it wants to destroy their lifestyle which is based on traditional values and beliefs. For example, they may oppose feminism because they feel that it threatens the traditional family roles they have chosen. Homemakers often feel that their role is demeaned by a movement that pushes hard to get women into the workforce. And men frequently see their safe, assured, breadwinner role imperiled by aggressive, successful women who do not need or want their support. In both cases, a source of identity is endangered, arousing a defensive response.

The same reasoning causes many religious groups to oppose feminism; they feel that their established beliefs and values, a source of stability and security, are being attacked. They seem to forget or ignore the fact that others have the right and the will to practice differing beliefs. Consequently, they often use their religious doctrines to "prove" that feminist positions are wrong. For instance, several groups contradict the feminist stand that women should receive equal pay for equal work by maintaining that women should not work in the first place. This assertion avoids the issue. Over fifty per cent of United States women *do* work, and the issue is fair treatment. Logic does not reign, however, and emotional side issues such as this have mushroomed into a boiling cloud of controversy, obscuring the main thrust of the movement.

Opponents of feminism often try to rationalize their position, but the reactionary terms they use indicate the real emotional foundation of their opposition. They often label it, at best, as a misguided effort led by abnormal females and, at worst, as the advancement of deviancy by perverts. This degradation of the enemy is a common tactic used to rationalize opposition to or suppression of another group. By giving feminists labels with derogatory connotations, by establishing them as strange or bad, feminism's opponents can justify their position. They can reach this end by labeling feminists unfeminine, lesbian, anti-men, and so forth.

In addition to these stigmas, people often attribute the same moral and political beliefs to all feminists. The movement's extremist minority seems to receive special attention, probably because it makes better news, so the resulting labels are often derogatory in nature. Also, people tend to add feminism to a conglomerate of causes, assuming that each shares the beliefs and goals of the others. For example, a feminist may also be considered an anti-nuclear energy activist. Many times men and women find these labels and assumptions unflattering and inaccurate. Some feel that connection with such stigmas damages their reputations and careers.

When you consider the widespread misunderstanding of feminism, its negative, anti everything image, and the derogatory connotations connected to the movement, it is no wonder that many refuse to actively support feminism or identify themselves as feminists. The lack of involved, visible supporters has weakened the movement, causing it to lose momentum and slip toward ineffectiveness. This in turn further discourages participation. We can take the initiative and break the cycle by informing the public and emphasizing the pros of feminism. With your participation, the feminist movement can become better understood and develop a new, positive image. You can help begin a new, progressive movement.

Connie Willer

Suggested Writing Assignment

Theme

Purpose To give you practice in writing tight, unified, and adequately developed paragraphs.

Procedure Reread the section on commitment and response and topic sentences. Then choose two of the topic sentences from the list below, and write for each one a paragraph of four to six sentences that responds to the commitment made in the topic sentence and gives concrete or specific points in development of the topic sentence. You might want to review the section on ways to develop a paragraph before you start. Remember to downshift into your levels of generality for at least two or three of your sentences.

Topics
a. Most car dealers promote installment buying.
b. I think the city tax assessor has overvalued my home.
c. A good secretary is an invaluable asset in any office.
d. Shopping malls are giant energy consumers.
e. Being a computer programmer is hardly a glamorous job.

Where Rhetoric Starts— and Stops

6

We are now ready to begin the study of the language of rhetoric and various kinds of rhetorical strategies. Before we proceed, however, we need to decide when rhetoric is relevant and when it is not, and what limitations we must work under. For however much we may enjoy arguing and exercising our wits, there are times when it is pointless. Thus in order to avoid wasting our time and intellectual energies, we ought to know what kinds of issues it is useful to discuss.

Assertions

Consider, for example, the following statements:

1. Chocolate cake is a wonderful dessert.
2. Democracy is a good form of government.
3. The Pittsburgh Steelers won the Superbowl game in 1979.

Strictly speaking, all three statements are what the logicians call *propositions*, that is, they are statements that can be affirmed or denied. Only one of them, however, is really arguable and, therefore, a proper topic for the exercise of rhetoric; that is the second one, "Democracy is a good form of government." It alone is a *legitimate assertion*: a statement of belief or judgment that can be logically supported with reasons.

How to recognize a legitimate assertion

Proposition 1 is simply an expression of taste; the writer is saying, "I like chocolate cake." The statement is not debatable because there is no point in arguing about taste, a subjective, non-rational reaction to an experience. You cannot persuade people through reasoning that they like what they are convinced they do not like. Thus if you like slapstick movies, but your friends hate them, don't waste time trying to persuade them that they will enjoy a double feature of *Blazing Saddles* and *Silent Movie*.

Don't argue about subjective reactions

Nor can emotional reactions be reasoned away with facts and logic. For example, if your father is afraid to fly and refuses to travel by plane, you are not likely to change his mind by pointing out to him that flying is less dangerous than traveling in a car and that it is a convenient and efficient way to travel. Your pattern of reasoning might look like this:

No rational person fears flying because it is convenient, efficient, and comparatively safe. You are a rational person. Therefore you do not fear flying.

The syllogism is perfect, but the person with whom you are arguing simply does not agree emotionally with the major premise; therefore the logic is irrelevant. (The *syllogism*, a logical device for deriving a conclusion from two premises, is discussed in Chapter 10.)

Similarly, it is pointless to use rhetoric to determine whether water-skiing is a better sport than surfing if by *better* you mean more enjoyable. People do or do not like raw oysters; they love, hate, or are indifferent to cats; they prefer sports cars to station wagons, and science fiction to mystery stories. It would be silly to challenge such preferences. On such matters we ought to relax and enjoy human differences. There is really no reason why everyone should like the same things we do, and the sensible course is simply to agree to disagree. Although it is true that people often do change their tastes over a period of time, they usually do so because of experience, not because someone logically demonstrates that one taste is better than another.

Don't argue about verifiable facts

Proposition 3, "The Pittsburgh Steelers won the Superbowl game in 1979," may or may not be true, but it is not a matter of opinion or judgment. It is a matter of fact that can be checked in a sports almanac, and no amount of argument or discussion will alter the truth. Only small children or naive adults would waste their time debating such a point.

The situation becomes more complicated, however, when someone makes a statement that must be either true or false, but we have no means of checking it. On such occasions, many people argue furiously without realizing that they are wasting their breath because the answer is unknowable. This kind of argument may involve questions such as "Do some people actually have extrasensory perception?" and "Is astrology a valid science?" Although it may be entertaining to speculate about matters of this kind and listen to people advance their opinions, allowing yourself to become involved in rhetoric about them is about as pointless as engaging in the old theological dispute about how many angels could dance on the head of a pin.

There are, however, certain kinds of disputes about factual matters that can be investigated and reasoned about. For example, one might argue about what kind of civilization existed in Mexico in prehistoric times and use archeological evidence as the basis for speculation. Or one could exchange theories and opinions about which presidential candidate is most likely to win an election or whether biologists are close to being able to create life in a laboratory. In cases like these, one attempts to draw conclusions from available data.

When rhetoric is worthwhile

Engaging in rhetoric is worthwhile only when there is a possibility of throwing new light on a topic, bringing people into closer agreement, persuading them to alter their attitudes, or getting them to take action. Discussing proposition 2, "Democracy is a good form of government," offers such possibilities. So does arguing about such statements as "Journalism is a more rewarding career than advertising," "The future of farming in this country is in serious jeopardy," "The study of poetry is a waste of time," or "All high school graduates should spend two years working or in the service before they decide whether they want to go to college." All these declarations—and it would be easy to think up dozens of similar propositions—have elements in common. First,

Characteristics of assertions

they are assertions, that is, judgments and/or expressions of opinion. Second, although they reveal preferences, they do more than simply express likes and dislikes; the concept of *ought* or *should* is implicit in the way they are stated. Third, they require support because as they stand they have little force. The immediate reaction of a listener, even a sympathetic one, is "Why do you say that? I want to hear your reasons." Because such assertions can be supported with concrete evidence and examples, fruitful discussion is possible.

Thus, assertions, statements that can and must be supported, form the basic framework of expository and rhetorical writing. You need to construct your own assertions carefully and cautiously because once you have made one you have the responsibility of supporting it. Don't, in a fit of enthusiasm or outrage, set out to prove far more than you can manage in one paper, or make statements that you cannot possibly support. "Democracy is a good form of government" is a reasonable declaration, one for which you can find evidence; but "Democracy is the best form of government that the world has ever devised" is unsupportable even in a five hundred-page book. To make a convincing argument for that sweeping generalization, you would have to compare democracy with all the other forms of government that have ever existed. Only an expert would have enough information even to attempt such a comparison. You would make yourself look foolish if you tackled such an enormous task.

Assert only what you can support

Equally foolish are such extreme assertions as "People on welfare are parasites who want something for nothing" or "In these days a person without a college degree cannot hope to make a decent living or be respected in society." Both statements put a nearly impossible burden of proof on the arguer. More has been claimed than the evidence will support, and if the reader thinks of even a few exceptions to the assertion, the arguer's case is irreparably damaged. Such statements mark the rhetorician as naive or irresponsible—or both.

Watch for support in the rhetoric of others

When you are analyzing the rhetoric of others, you need to be equally alert to the way in which the author's main assertions are stated. What claims are made, and what positions does the author undertake to support? Writers who make a greater commitment than they can handle weaken their rhetorical position from the beginning. One of the chief flaws in the arguments of extremist groups in this country has been their unbelievable assertions. Militant blacks, for example, sometimes assert that the United States is the most racist country in the world. Anyone who is aware of the apartheid policies in the Union of South Africa knows that such a statement is an exaggeration. Thus, the writer immediately loses credibility with a large portion of the audience. In general, you should be skeptical of rhetoricians who load their assertions with superlatives such as *most, best, worst,* and *greatest*; their tactics are likely to be as shaky as their claims, because such statements can rarely be supported with legitimate and sensible arguments.

Assumptions

If assertions form the framework of rhetoric, assumptions are its foundation. An *assumption* is the supposition that something is true, the taking for granted that a statement or belief is so obvious that there is no need to explain it or support it.

Necessary Assumptions

In discourse we all make two kinds of assumptions: first, that our audience shares with us certain knowledge and experience and, second, that it shares certain values, beliefs, and attitudes. We must make such assumptions, or we could not begin to communicate; we would spend so much time laying the basis for an argument that we would never get to the main point.

Assumptions about shared knowledge

The first class of assumptions causes relatively few problems for anyone who is reasonably alert and sensitive. We know without actually thinking about it that most of the people we come in contact with in the United States share our experience of living in a complex industrial society and going to public schools. We assume that they know the principles of Christianity, that they are familiar with American history and traditions, and that because they are exposed to radio, television, and newspapers, they have some idea about current happenings. Although we are conscious of some differences in the common experiences of old and young, black and white, women and men, northerners and southerners, on ·the whole we have a large area of common ground with most people we meet. If we did not have this broad base of shared experiences and information, communication would be difficult and persuasion almost impossible.

Assumptions about shared values

Making assumptions about what people feel and believe is considerably more hazardous than making assumptions about what they know; yet we must do it, even at the risk of occasionally oversimplifying. If we refuse to generalize about the attitudes of people because we are afraid of falling into stereotyping—and that is a real danger—we cannot draw the kinds of inferences about our audience that we must draw in order to write effectively. So we must draw reasonable and prudent generalizations about groups of people. For instance, we assume that young college women are more interested in the feminist movement than are their mothers; we assume that people in the higher income brackets are likely to be more politically conservative than those in the lower brackets; we assume that the residents of Detroit and

Chicago are more sympathetic to labor unions than those in the rural areas of Michigan and Illinois. If we try to think carefully about our assumptions and be specific about the grounds upon which we base them, we will probably be right a good percentage of the time. And when we make sound assumptions, our audience is likely to respond sympathetically; if we make faulty ones, however, whatever we say or write will have little effect.

Unwarranted Assumptions

Danger of attributing one's own values to others

Making faulty assumptions has many causes—carelessness, bad judgment, and laziness are a few—but the primary source of unwarranted assumptions is the common habit of attributing our own values to other people. We all have our biases, and we forget that others do not share them. Undoubtedly you have had the experience of being present when someone told a joke or story that you found offensive. If you think about it, you will realize that the reason you were offended was that the narrator had made unwarranted assumptions about you. If the person told a derogatory joke about blacks, women, Jews—particularly if words like *nigger*, *broad*, or *kike* are used—that person is assuming you are an admitted bigot. The person who tells dirty jokes or uses obscene language assumes that you are not offended by it. The person who tells anecdotes that suggest that all politicians are crooks, that everyone cheats on his or her income tax, and that all people in positions of power got there either by bribes or pulling strings assumes that you share this cynical view of the world.

Sometimes we may choose to argue with people who make assumptions that we don't agree with, but more often most of us just walk off or end the conversation as soon as we can. We feel that it's not worth trying to communicate with people who are so unperceptive about their audience. And writers who are unthinking and careless about the assumptions they make also risk losing their audiences.

Faulty assumptions lead to oversimplified judgments

For instance, a person might argue quite forcefully that it is not worthwhile for most married women to hold jobs; because of the added money spent for clothes, the cost of transportation, the higher expense for lunches and eating out frequently, and the elevation into a higher tax bracket, the average woman's net profit is so small that it is pointless for her to work. The person who reasons along these lines reveals assumptions that a woman's only reason for working would be to make money and that women do not take pride in their work or get a sense of accomplishment from it in the same way that men do.

Our assumptions can also lead us into hasty judgments about other people. As the psychiatrist Robert Coles points out, "The assumptions we make about a person's social and political behavior have to do with the kinds of lives we ourselves live." Thus, the person who remarks that it is a pity that a woman of thirty-five isn't married reveals an assumption that all women need a husband; the individual who labels people who criticize the government as "malcontents," "un-American," or "antisocial" reveals the assumption that all "normal" people endorse the status quo.

The way we view certain problems is also controlled by our assumptions. You have probably heard the argument that we are unduly alarmed about air and water pollution or the depletion of our natural resources; by the time the lakes are stagnant, we will have found a way to purify them. A similar claim is that if our energy sources run out, we will find new ones. This kind of thinking is based on the assumption that there are technological solutions to every problem. A closely related assumption is the common belief that spending more money will cure our social ills: poor education, slums and ghettos, lack of adequate medical care, and juvenile crime.

The tricky thing about these kinds of assumptions is not that they are necessarily wrong—some of them prove to be sound—but that so often we are not aware that we are making them. We are not aware of the foundations upon which we are building our arguments because our opinions are so deeply entrenched that we do not see our own biases. Such blindness makes it easy for other to poke holes in our neatly constructed arguments. For example, in recent years, some older people who have complained that too many of today's students cannot spell have assumed that the spelling contests they had when they went to school produced a whole generation of good spellers. If they were to insist that schools must go back to spelling contests in order to produce students who can spell, researchers in English education could quickly tell them that (1) spelling contests reward only those who are already good spellers, and (2) there is no evidence that members of the older generation are better spellers than the members of the new one. Their argument would be demolished because it was based on an unexamined and unwarranted assumption.

Of course, one cannot always be sure that the assumptions on which an argument is based are totally warranted. The most we can do is to recognize that assumptions we are making and be prepared to defend them if necessary. And we can get into the habit of looking for the assumptions that underlie our own speech and writing, as well as the speech and writing of others. We all will be better thinkers as a result.

A priori Premises

A priori premises reflect our deepest convictions

Many arguments, especially deductive arguments, as we shall see in Chapter 10, are based on a special kind of assumption that has an even stronger emotional and cultural basis than the kinds of cultural beliefs and attitudes discussed in the previous section. We call these particular kinds of assumptions *a priori premises*; the term *a priori* means "based on a hypothesis or theory rather than on experiment or experience; made before or without examination; not supported by factual study."[1] The phrases, "made *before* or *without* examination" and "not supported by factual study" are the key parts of this definition. Thus people who believe something a priori believe it at a gut level; they just *know* it is true, even though they haven't examined any evidence on the matter or seen any supporting data. They don't need evidence because they believe so strongly. As you can see, most patriotic, religious, and moral beliefs fall into this category, and so do many cultural, social, and racial convictions.

It is not always possible to distinguish between common and widely held assumptions, such as "Southerners are naturally hospitable" or "City dwellers are more cautious and suspicious than people who live in the country" and a priori premises like "People are basically lazy" or "Slavery is wrong." The two categories

---

[1] ©1981 by Houghton Mifflin Company. Reprinted by permission from *The American Heritage Dictionary of the English Language.*

are going to merge and overlap from time to time, and inevitably students will sometimes disagree on how a particular statement should be classified. In general, however, we can say that a priori premises are beliefs that are so deeply and fervently held that they take on the force of facts or eternal truths. By their nature they *cannot* be proved, but by their nature they cannot be *disproved* either. People can, however, usually find some evidence to support their assumptions. The evidence may be skimpy or slanted, but they can give some examples. And although the statement may surprise you, it is easier to support the contention that city dwellers are suspicious than it is the assertion that slavery is wrong. For the last statement, you would have to fall back on another a priori premise, and then another, and another.

One of the most famous a priori statements comes in the introduction to our Declaration of Independence: "We hold these truths to be self-evident: that all men are created equal, that they are endowed by their Creator with certain inalienable rights, that among these are Life, Liberty, and the Pursuit of Happiness." The crucial words here are *truths* and *self-evident*; they suggest that the authors are positive that everyone agrees with their claim about inalienable rights; they have neither the need nor the obligation to support their assertion. But are these "truths" really universal and eternal? An Indian who had been reared in a caste society would probably claim that it is self-evident that all people are *not* created equal, that a tightly stratified society is natural and right. Members of other societies, ancient and modern, would call the statement that any person has inalienable rights absolute nonsense. The state or the church, not the individual, decides what a person's rights are.

A priori premises are often cultural

So a priori premises are often cultural or national, and most of them are certainly not eternal. But that qualification does not diminish their force for the people who hold them. To nearly all Americans, the original statement still stands as an article of faith, unshaken by the most vigorous challenge. We don't have to prove it; we *know* it.

Premises about Human Nature

One of the chief classes of a priori premises are statements about human nature. Romanticists such as Rousseau, Emerson, and

*They often concern
human nature*

Wordsworth held that people are naturally good; the Calvinists held that they are naturally sinful. Both sides based their entire philosophical systems on a priori premises, which are unproved and unprovable. In modern times, one school of psychology argues that people behave as they do because of sexual drives and frustrations, and another claims that people are motivated chiefly by drives for power and dominance. Both schools can construct theories and cite dozens of case histories, but they cannot actually prove their premises.

Among the oldest of our a priori assumptions are those concerning the nature of women. For centuries, theologians, psychologists, and anthropologists have been claiming that there are basic and radical differences between the "natural" personalities of each sex and that certain traits are inherently "feminine," others inherently "masculine." Now, people like Betty Friedan, Germaine Greer, Gloria Steinem, and many women novelists are challenging these long-held beliefs by claiming that what is thought of as the "feminine nature" is really the product of cultural conditioning and expectations, not natural at all. As a result, a new set of a priori premises about women is emerging and gaining strength in many circles.

Premises about Morality

*A priori premises
often concern
morality*

Another important class of a priori premises are those that deal with morality. Assertions that define what is right and wrong, good and bad, are the foundation of all ethical discussion and pronouncements. We—and all cultures—have so many moral premises that it would be impossible to list even a representative sample, but typically they deal with such matters as honesty, loyalty, trustworthiness, fairness, kindness, and so on. When we take a moral position, we inevitably base our argument on an a priori premise that we feel sure our audience shares. For example, the senator who launches an investigation into corporate bribes is saying that honesty is a virtue. The people who condemn the killings by terrorists are saying that human life is valuable; those who call for an investigation of brutal practices in prisons are saying that cruelty is wrong.

Such moral feelings are so strongly rooted in us that we forget they cannot be proved or tested without falling back on other convictions that are also held a priori. Take, for example, the statement "Slavery is wrong." If someone were to ask you to prove that it is, what would you say? Perhaps, "Human liberty is a basic right." The next questions might be "Basic to whom? Did the ancient Greeks think so?" Your answer: "No, but today everybody knows that slavery is wrong." The reply might follow, "*I* don't think it's wrong—in fact I wish my family still owned slaves." And so it could go, round and round. You could not *prove* your point.

But you don't have to prove it. The fact that some or even many other people do not share our basic convictions need not in any way weaken the force of those convictions. All people have the right to say that because of training, experience, reflection, or intuition, they hold certain principles, that these principles are true and valid, and that they will serve as the basis of actions. Such an attitude is, and must be, the basis of morality.

Many a priori premises gradually change

In time, of course, many a priori premises change, or they wither away and are replaced by others. Gradually, as our culture and our circumstances alter, so does our thinking. For example, some of the basic premises about thrift and work that were so strong in this country a few generations ago have today lost much of their force. They are being replaced by other less stern opinions, such as encouragement of people's attempt to realize their potential and more relaxed standards for sexual behavior. Such changes are confusing. What is often termed "culture shock" or "the generation gap" occurs precisely because groups no longer agree on a priori premises. But the tensions may be easier to handle if at least one side understands the nature of the problem.

The point to keep in mind is that wise rhetoricians recognize when they and their opponents have irreconcilable a priori premises and say simply, "We cannot have a productive discussion because we have no basis from which to start." Too many arguments proceed in parallel lines because both opponents are so busy expounding their views that they have not stopped to articulate their primary assumptions. If they did, they would find that agreement is impossible. A person who believes that people are naturally peaceful and cooperative is wasting time arguing for disarmament with someone who thinks that people are basically aggressive and acquisitive. If you are a sensualist, a person who holds that physical pleasure is the chief good, you would be naive to discuss the good life with one who believes that people get the most out of life by developing the powers of the intellect. When you find yourself at an impasse in a discussion, you should stop and examine the a priori premises that you are bringing to it. If on reflection you find them sound but radically different from your opponent's, you might as well desist and start talking about the latest movie you've seen.

Realize that at times useful discussion is impossible

Exercises

1. Which of these statements are arguable assertions? Give your reasons for rejecting those you do not find arguable.

   a. Helen of Troy was the most beautiful woman the world has ever known.

   b. Football is my favorite game.

   c. Food manufacturers are largely responsible for the poor diet of many Americans.

   d. Mt. Everest is the highest mountain in the world.

   e. The Basic Books should be a part of everyone's education.

   f. Chocolate ice cream is better than strawberry ice cream.

   g. Fifty percent of teen-age marriages end in divorce within five years.

   h. Political dirty tricks are never justified.

   i. All women drivers should take a course in defensive driving.

   j. The Washington Redskins won the Eastern division championship in the National Football League last year.

   k. College is a waste of time.

   l. More money is bet on football than on horse races.

2. Rephrase the following assertions into more reasonable statements that you could probably support in a paper of about one thousand words.

   a. Too much television watching is the cause of the continuing decline in students' ability to read and write.

    b. A woman cannot be elected president of the United States.

    c. Dope addiction is the cause of the growing crime rate in our cities.

    d. Fast-food restaurants all serve terrible foods.

    e. Multiple-choice tests are the worst kind of examination.

    f. William Faulkner is the South's best writer.

3. What assumptions underlie the following statements? Do they seem warranted?

    a. We should stop spending billions on defense so that we can clean up the environment, build hospitals, and eradicate the slums and traffic congestion that plague our cities.

    b. Oh, you're an English teacher. I'll have to watch my grammar.

    c. Joe and Harriet must be getting a divorce. Yesterday I saw her having lunch with George Williams.

    d. With the kind of grades Stanley gets, he'll never amount to much.

    e. Of course, you'll prefer this painting. It's an original.

    f. Vivian is thirty five and starting back to college. It's certainly going to be hard for her to keep up with those young kids.

    g. Those doctors in public health can't be very good or they'd be out in private practice where the real money is.

    h. Well, Jack's nervous breakdown doesn't surprise me. He has such a high IQ.

4. It is both useful and enlightening to examine one's own assumptions from time to time. After trying to examine your thought processes as closely as you can, jot down the assumptions that you find you have about one or two of these issues. Try to be honest with yourself. What effect do these assumptions have on your thinking?

    a. The effect of money on people's political affiliations

    b. The single most important asset that a woman can have

    c. The single most important asset that a man can have

    d. The intellectual capacities of plumbers

e. The cultural preferences of farmers

f. The business ability of professors

5. Try to work out an a priori premise that might be the basis for a person making each of the following statements. To do so, think about what each statement might imply about the speaker's view of right or wrong or what he or she thinks is basic to human nature; for example, that most people are lazy. Of course, there could be more than one right answer to each.

a. What's good is what you feel good after.

b. If people cease to believe in God, there will be a collapse of morality in this country.

c. Under a system of socialized medicine, doctors would lose their incentive to practice.

d. An administration that has permitted twenty million people in this country to live in poverty does not deserve another four years in office.

e. If the voters have all the facts, they will invariably choose the best person.

f. With his upbringing, Charles was bound to get in trouble sooner or later.

g. Government sponsorship of birth control clinics is an unwarranted interference in the lives of private citizens.

h. If we established a guaranteed annual income in this country, millions of people would just quit working.

i. Don't make a thief out of this young person. Lock your car!

j. A person who would plagiarize a term paper should not be allowed to teach in this school.

Suggested Writing Assignments

Theme 1

Purpose To make you aware of your own a priori premises and to help you see how they control the stands you take on controversial issues.

Procedure Pick one of the topics listed below, and write a short paper in which you argue for one side of the issue. Before you begin to write, think carefully about what a priori belief or beliefs you hold that determine the position you are going to take in your argument. Write those beliefs in a separate section at the beginning of your paper. Remember that your a priori premises will almost certainly be statements about the nature of people or moral pronouncements about right and wrong, such as "people are basically selfish" or "people are basically kind"; "the government should ensure the basic needs of all its citizens" or "government handouts damage people's character."

Suppose you are asked to take a stand on one side or the other of the controversial antiabortion amendment to the Constitution. If you are strongly in favor of it, the a priori premises on which you would base your argument would probably include these: (1) A fetus is a human being from the moment of conception. (2) The deliberate taking of a human life is immoral. If you are against the amendment, your premises would probably include these: (1) No unwanted children should be brought into the world. (2) A woman has the right to decide whether she wants children. If your audience accepted one or more of your premises, you would have a good chance to influence them. Using this procedure, write on one of the following topics. Remember to define your audience and purpose.

Topics

a. We should (should not) have free, tax-supported hospitals, just as we have free, tax-supported schools.

b. The Federal Communications Commission should (should not) ban the advertising of nonnutritious foods from television programs that are produced especially for children.

c. Unwed mothers should (should not) receive government subsidies to pay for prenatal care, delivery, and subsistence for six months.

d. A marriage contract specifying the obligations and privileges of husband and wife should (should not) be a standard feature of modern marriage.

e. Bribes are (are not) necessary and legitimate expenses in doing international business.

Theme 2

Purpose To help you recognize and state the a priori premises that underlie someone else's expository or persuasive prose.

Procedure Read very carefully the following excerpt from a magazine article. Then write a short paper in which you do the following: First, in one paragraph explain what seems to you to be the author's rhetorical purpose in this selection. What attitudes or reactions does the author hope to produce in the reader? Then, in two or three more paragraphs, pick out and state what seem to you to be the chief a priori premises on this subject that the author has and seems to assume that the audience shares. That is, what strong beliefs or moral values does the author seem to hold and to use as the basis for comments? Write out each premise and then explain how you deduced that premise from the evidence in the passage; that is, what statements, observations, or comments led you to your conclusion?

Admittedly, this is a difficult assignment that asks you to draw conclusions that may be shaky, but remember that there is no one right answer. There are really several good answers that you could choose from, all of them defensible.

A year or two at Woodway [a singles apartment complex] can be great therapy for a man who's gone through a painful divorce, or been sealed off in a high-rise apartment where the only chance for achieving close contact with tenants of the opposite sex is to be stuck overnight in a crowded elevator or to hit the laundry room while the redhead from 18N is still in her spin-dry cycle. But let him settle into this sexual Disneyland on a long term basis and he may find sophomorism becoming a way of life.

Mickey "Flash" Gordon, for example, is well into his 41st year and his second chin. But he nonetheless keeps a neo-seraglio apartment at Woodway, outfitted with harem cushions, a hyper hi-fi set, ha-ha candles made to look like penises, and colored strobe lights over the satin-sheeted king-size bed. Scattered on a bathroom shelf are half a dozen little beauty aids, including a jar labeled "nightcap facial massage,"

(neo=new)

(youth vs. age)

a 60-second bronzer, and a wrinkle-stick. For him, not for his guests.

Apart from a *Playboy* calendar, the only work of art in Mickey's apartment is a wallful of record albums, proudly displayed on special slanting racks. (The afternoon I stopped by for a visit, Mickey's display consisted of two Herb Alperts and an Aretha Franklin flanked by a Peter, Paul and Mary and some romantic-looking Percy Faiths.) Mickey can't remember the last book he's read all the way through (very few Woodwayites I talked to could), but his conversation revealed a vague acquaintance with *Jonathan Livingston Seagull* and *Every Woman Can!* His coffee table offers further evidence of (?) literacy with a pile of back issues of *Playboy*, *Penthouse*, and *Gallery.*

eclectic wine, records ↓ not well-rounded for its own sake, but to please people instead

Mickey's proudest possessions are wedged into his tiny pullman kitchen: two giant refrigerators—one provided by Woodway, the other brought in at Mickey's own expense. Open one and you see seven six-packs of beer, ten bottles of Spanish Chablis, five plastic (to take to the pool) bottles of red wine, two bottles of Rhine wine, five bottles of Lancers' rosé, four magnums of domestic champagne. So you figure the other refrigerator must be stocked with food. Wrong. Except for a few lonely Swanson pies huddled in the back of the freezer, the contents are more bottles of wine and champagne, plus tonic, bitter lemon, soda water, and Dr. Pepper. And that's by no means all Mickey has in store for his guests. In a nearby cabinet are exactly 15 fifths and 11 half gallons of assorted hard liquor, plus three bottles of Strega.

"You just never know when a really big blastaroo is gonna break loose around here, and I hate to be caught short," Mickey explains.[2]

---

[2] Cynthia Proulx, "Sex as Athletics in the Singles Complex," *Saturday Review of the Society*, May 1973, p. 65. Copyright © 1973 by *Saturday Review*.

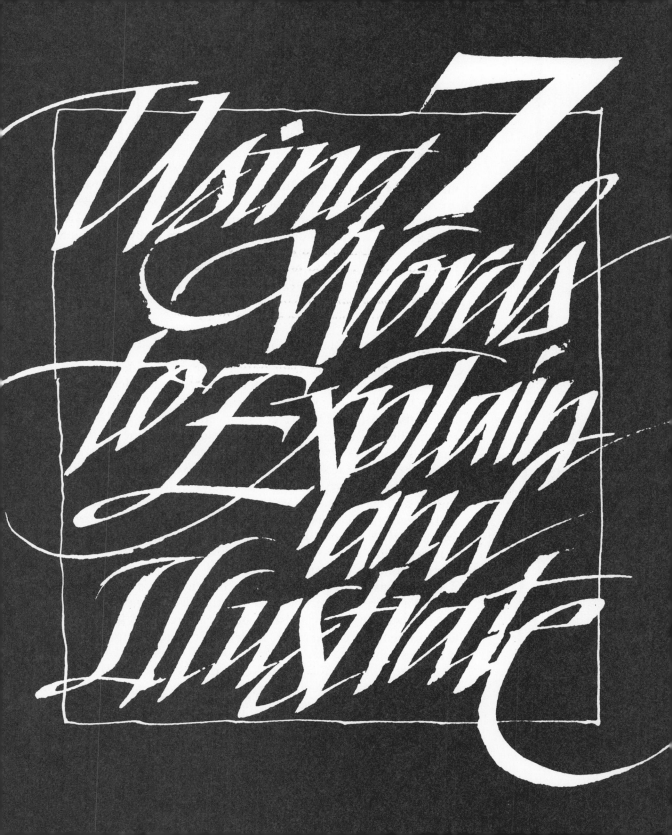

Using Words to Explain and Illustrate

7

In the two previous chapters you have been learning something about rhetorical theory and the various concerns you must keep in mind if you want to communicate effectively with other people. Such knowledge is a useful psychological base for your writing, but the actual act of writing always comes back to those basic units of human communication: *words*. How do writers choose the words that will best convey the meaning and impression they want to leave with their audience? No one can really give you the answer to that question because there are no formulas for creativity. There are, however, some guidelines that should help you choose words that will serve your rhetorical purposes.

Abstract/Concrete and General/Specific Language

A convenient way to begin talking about the vocabulary we use in rhetoric is to distinguish between abstract and concrete words. *Abstract* words are those that describe ideas, qualities, attitudes, and characteristics. They refer to concepts that we know only intellectually, not through any of our senses. The term *loyalty* is abstract; so are *love, tolerance, misery, dissatisfaction, philosophy,* and any other word that stands for something we cannot see or experience. *Concrete* words, on the other hand, refer to objects, living things, and activities that we know through our senses. *Swimming* and *running* are concrete terms; so are *kitten, girl,* and *tree,* or, *shiny, rough, blue, pink,* and other image-producing words. In general, we *perceive* the concrete through our senses; we *conceive* the abstract through our minds.

The difference between abstract and concrete words

Definitions like these are useful, but they are also oversimplified. We cannot just call a word "abstract" or "concrete" and be finished with it; we must also recognize degrees and levels within each category. For example, *house* is a concrete term, but it is much less concrete than *two-story red-brick Colonial home; illness* is a concrete word, but it is not as concrete as *typhoid fever* or *pneumonia. Philosophy* is more abstract than *existentialism,* and *literature* is more abstract than *poetry* or *drama.* In his book *Language in Thought and Action,* the semanticist S. I. Hayakawa illustrates the concept of word levels by setting up a ladder of abstraction with steps moving from the most concrete to the least concrete and simultaneously from the least specific to the most specific. Such a ladder looks like this:

> 6. ethical philosophies
> 5. religion
> 4. Christianity
> 3. Protestantism
> 2. the Baptist Church
> 1. the First Baptist Church of Canton, Ohio

Distinguishing between general and specific words

In talking about language, it is also important to distinguish between *general* and *specific* words. General words refer to large groups or broad categories; for example, "people" and "country" are general words. Specific words refer to individuals, items, particular groups, or particular cases; for example, Maya Angelou refers to a specific individual, and Guatemala refers to a specific country. And just as there are levels of abstraction, there are levels of generality, and words can be arranged on a scale. For instance:

> 7. Creative people
> 6. Artists
> 5. Authors
> 4. English writers
> 3. Sixteenth-century dramatists
> 2. Elizabethan playwrights
> 1. William Shakespeare

"Creative people" represents the broadest class, and as we move down the scale of generality, we encounter words that represent smaller and more specific groups. At the bottom is a single individual of the class.

Generally, but not always, abstract and general words overlap; for example, the word "government" is both general and abstract, and so is the word "housing." Concrete and specific words also overlap frequently; for example, the word "snowmobile" is both specific and concrete, and so is the word "sandwich."

Using Abstract and General Words

Despite the repeated advice to writers to "Be concrete" and "Try to be more specific," obviously we must often use abstract language if we are to talk about anything weightier than the weather or the price of groceries. To discuss values, beliefs, and theories we have to employ conceptual language. Thus, sentences like "An unshakable belief that private enterprise leads to the exploitation of the working classes is fundamental to Marxist theory" and "Some ethical philosophers hold that all moral values are merely expressions of cultural preferences" are necessary kinds of statements. Furthermore, it is broadly true that the more knowledge we have and the more complex our thinking becomes, the more we have to depend on abstract words to express ourselves. We must expect, therefore, that much of our communication about ideas will use words taken from the upper levels of the abstraction ladder.

Using Concrete and Specific Words

The problem is, however, as pointed out in Chapter 4 that a number of writers, both amateur and professional, have come to equate abstract language with wisdom and the circles of higher learning. They forget that to hold their reader's attention they must work through the senses as well as the intellect.

In the following passage, the poet and critic John Ciardi illustrates how effectively a writer can communicate an abstract concept by supporting it with a vivid, concrete example:

> It is certain that man has put an enormous amount of his psychic energy into shaping language, and that language has, in turn, powerfully affected his behavior. In most primitive languages, for example, . . . the same word does for both "stranger" and "enemy." If I have separate words for these two ideas, I can look at an unknown person without an alarm signal. If I have one for them, I will be less ready to let the man pass unmolested. I am already in Oedipus' chariot en route to Thebes and half-cocked to kill my unknown father when his chariot blocks mine on the road. The language my fathers made, made me my father's killer.[1]

On the other hand, this paragraph from a book by a contemporary economist demonstrates the shortcomings of writing that is completely abstract.

[1] John Ciardi, "Tongues," *World,* February 27, 1973, p. 6.

There may be no realistic hope of the present underdeveloped countries reaching the standard of living demonstrated by the present industrialized nations. . . . Noting the destruction that has already occurred on land, in the air, and especially in the oceans, capability appears not to exist for handling such a rise in standard of living. In fact, the present disparity between the developed and underdeveloped nations may be equalized as much by a decline in the developed countries as by an improvement in the underdeveloped countries. A society with a high level of industrialization may be nonsustainable.[2]

The paragraph is by no means incomprehensible to an intelligent reader who is willing to work at it, but it is difficult and dull, primarily because there are no concrete examples in it. As you read it, your mind wanders because nothing in the passage appeals to the senses or calls up an image. Writing like this is not merely dull, it is literally lifeless.

Fortunately, student writing seldom reaches an extreme level of impersonality and dryness. Too many students, however, succumb to the notion that college writers should use stiff, abstract language. Thus, in their effort to be formal and rise to new expectations, they produce sentences like these:

It is required that regular school attendance be observed by everyone.

Compulsory school attendance is a general law that is nationally observed.

The concept of compulsory school attendance is accepted throughout the educational system.

Grammatically, the sentences are acceptable; rhetorically, they are a flop. They are lifeless; they bring to mind no images, not even a school. Moreover, there is no point in their being written so abstractly, since the idea expressed in them is not complex or difficult. To say, "In most states everyone has to go to school un-

[2] Jay W. Forrester, *World Dynamics* (Cambridge, Mass.: Wright-Allen Press, 1971), p. 12. Quoted in Arthur Herzog's *The B. S. Factor* (New York: Simon & Schuster, Inc., 1973), p. 44.

til he or she is seventeen" would do the job simply and effectively.

Concrete Sentence Subjects

The sample sentences above also illustrate a problem mentioned in Chapter 4: the difficulties that writers create for themselves when they habitually use abstract rather than concrete subjects for their sentences. By choosing abstract rather than concrete words as the subjects of their sentences, these writers have sharply limited the kinds of verbs they can combine with them. Abstractions such as "attendance" and "concept" cannot, logically, *do* anything; therefore a writer almost instinctively puts with them some form of the weak verb *to be*. Although you can sometimes overcome this tendency if you use imagination (for example, "loyalty" may "demand" and "tyranny" may "crush"), it is easier to avoid boxing yourself in in the first place. Make a habit of trying to choose concrete subjects and active verbs. Notice how much difference such choices could have made in these sentences from student papers:

Concrete subjects help writers to avoid weak verbs

> *Original* In federally financed hospitals the abilities and facilities of all could be easily brought together to conquer the problems in medicine.
>
> *Concrete revision* In federally financed hospitals, doctors and scientists could come together in laboratories to solve medical problems.
>
> *Original* Achievement in sports trains a person to be able to work hard and under pressure.
>
> *Concrete revision* The young boy or girl athlete who competes in sports events learns to work hard under pressure.
>
> *Original* The corruption of youth appears to be a more common topic of discussion with adults than the assets of youth.
>
> *Concrete revision* Adults seem to enjoy talking about what's wrong with youth more than they do discussing what's right about them.

Combining the Abstract and the Concrete

Outline with abstract main points and concrete subdivisions

Since all writers must deal with abstract concepts from time to time, they all face the problem of finding ways to use concrete language to clarify their writing. One good way to approach the problem is to begin the execution stage of your writing process by roughing out an outline or summary in which you use general statements to express the main points and then make notes about concrete examples to use as second- or third-level supporting material. Suppose you are going to write a paper to argue that your college should give full scholarships to students who excel in the sciences, as well as those who excel in athletics. Your main points will be value statements that you must express in abstract terms; your supporting evidence, however, should be concrete, vivid, and specific. An outline for your paper might be:

I. The present practice discriminates among students on the basis of physical ability and sex.
    A. Thousands of high school athletes receive full scholarships.
    B. Few women athletes receive scholarships.
    C. Bright science students must compete for only a few National Science Foundation grants, grants often quite small.
    D. College athletes get extras: tutoring, fraternity dues, summer jobs.
II. Present practice discourages scholastic achievement among high school students.
    A. High school athletes work hard to develop talents because rewards are substantial.
    B. Science students have little incentive to spend extra hours and effort on developing abilities because there is no tangible reward.
    C. Scholarships reinforce high school value system: worship of athletes, indifference to studies.
III. Over a long period of time the present practices will prove shortsighted.
    A. Subsidized college athletes usually become professional football players. Earning years are relatively short; contribution to society relatively minor.

  B. Subsidized students in science would become doctors, biologists, research scientists, or teachers. Earning years long; contributions to society potentially great.

When you have an outline like this, you are not likely to write a theme that is simply a collection of generalities. Moreover, in the process of writing, you will probably think of actual incidents that illustrate your points and thus can add a personal note to the paper.

To summarize: in order to make your writing as clear and as forceful as possible, keep in mind these four guidelines.

1. Use abstract language to express ideas, but whenever possible reinforce and clarify it with concrete and specific examples.

2. When you are writing try to avoid those vague and overworked adjectives I call *fuzzy intensifiers*, words like "fantastic," "horrible," "incredible," "marvelous," "unbelievable," "wonderful," and "awful," to name just a few. Although such words can add emphasis in casual conversation, in writing they are so trite and imprecise that they really tell the reader nothing. They only take up space without creating images or adding to information. Rather than cluttering your writing with such nonwords, you are better off to leave out the modifier altogether.

3. Try to avoid using abstractions as sentence subjects, particularly those overworked words *aspect, factor, element,* and *concept.*

4. Keep in mind the excellent advice Hayakawa gives in his book: "The interesting writer, the informative speaker, the accurate thinker, and the sane individual operate on all levels of the abstraction ladder, moving quickly and gracefully and in orderly fashion from higher to lower, from lower to higher, with minds as lithe and deft and beautiful as monkeys in a tree."

Four guidelines for using abstract and concrete language

Jargon

Jargon is a style of writing characterized by wordiness, a preponderance of abstract terms, excessive and irresponsible use of the passive voice, euphemisms, weak verbs, pretentious diction, and clichés, excessive caution, and the absence of strong words and

Characteristics of jargon

statements. A piece of writing does not have to have all these qualities to be labeled as jargon. Even a few jargon phrases, if overused, can turn decent prose into gobbledygook. Writing that is weighted down with jargon is, at its best, dull and confusing. At its worst, it is pretentious, evasive, and incomprehensible. Any level of jargon is a nuisance to the reader, who must unwrap a cocoon of words to extract the meaning. Take, for example, this paragraph from a student theme on *Brave New World*:

> Through sex, pleasure achieves its maximum capabilities. Without reproduction, man would fail to exist. Reproduction is creation and creation is reproduction. Man is the instrument of reproduction and what man reproduces determines what man is. In creating attitudes about sex, man also creates attitudes about himself. The attitude man takes toward sex takes a part in determining how much man cares about himself. Sex can teach man to care about existence. However, when other values are added to sex, then sex can be used to control desire and ambition. . . . If a man wants to remain free, then he must retain his desires and ambitions. If we use sex to care about life, then we are able to keep desire and ambition as qualities of life.

Jargon may be free of mechanical errors

Although the quoted paragraph represents, in my opinion, almost the worst kind of writing, the author has committed none of what the average student thinks of as mistakes in composition. There are no spelling, punctuation, or grammar errors; the predication error, "pleasure achieves capabilities," is a lapse, but a sophisticated one. Subjects and verbs agree, the sentences are properly constructed, words are used correctly, and on the surface at least, the writer seems to have no trouble with expression. The organization is poor, but all the sentences do, more or less, focus on sex, reproduction, and morality. Yet the paragraph is a disaster because it is a collection of glib and meaningless generalities, and of statements so obvious they are not worth putting on paper—for example, "Reproduction is creation and creation is reproduction." Other statements look as if they are saying something but are actually incomprehensible, for example, "However, when other values are added to sex, then sex can be used to control desire and

"... to have and to hold in counterproductive as well as productive time frames, so long as you are bilaterally capable of maintaining a viable life-style. ..."

ambition." There is not a concrete word in the paragraph and not a single example to illustrate any of the concepts.

Causes of Jargon

The student who wrote the preceding theme and several others like it was a bright young man who liked to write and thought that the papers he was doing were not just acceptable but really quite good. He wanted to write well, as nearly all students do. Why, then, did he write so badly? The answer has to be that he learned to write this kind of pretentious and empty prose, not by being directly told to do so, but by being rewarded for doing so. At some time he impressed someone with his ability to string abstract words together in grammatical and properly punctuated sentences. So he abandoned the plain, straightforward style in which he probably talks and began writing his papers in a style that he would never use in a letter or private journal. He started operating from at least three unspoken assumptions about what constitutes good writing.

Three false assumptions that may lead to jargon

False Assumptions The first assumption is that the grade on a composition will vary in direct proprotion to the length; if two pages merit a C, then four pages will bring an A. A corollary to this assumption says that the best students are those who have the most to say. If you apply this standard to writing themes, the natural result is that the ambitious people will pad their writing with inflated phrases rather than trying to make it crisp and concise. The common practice of requiring a minimum number of words reinforces the idea that quantity equals quality.

False assumption 1: quantity = quality

The second assumption is that big words are necessarily better than little ones and that long sentences, especially complex ones, are better than short ones. Students may draw this conclusion because they have been urged to expand their vocabulary and to practice writing several different kinds of sentences, but probably they are most influenced by the examples of inflated writing they encounter in the kinds of models discussed in Chapter 1. Such imitation is understandable, but unfortunately it sometimes produces sentences like this:

False assumption 2: big words and long sentence = quality

> In my opinion lowering the drinking age to eighteen would increase imbibage and satisfy none of the need for social jurisprudence.

A third assumption is that writing that is hard to understand but somehow sounds official and authoritative must be good writing, and therefore is what students should try to imitate. Thus they try to impress their readers by using important-sounding terms like "discontinuation of membership" and "availability of viable options," and they pad their writing with words they have read but only vaguely understand, words like "parameter," "actualize," and "interface." This is the kind of writing Russell Baker is spoofing in the Little Red Riding Hood parody on page 462.

False assumption 3: hard to understand = quality

Passive verbs Some students have also unconsciously developed a pompous style because they overload their sentences with passive verbs. This habit probably stems from three common assumptions: first, passive verbs sound more dignified and scholarly than active ones (they also take up more space); second, a writer must avoid at all costs using *I* in a paper; and third, a passive verb is safer than an active one. The writer who chooses verbs on the basis of these assumptions increases the chances of writing jargon.

The following example from a student theme illustrates some of the hazards of using passive verbs in order to sound dignified:

> An agreement *is* also *felt* by the two dictators that people *can be made* happy if their frustrations *are stopped*. This happiness *is brought about* by the leaders. The people *are* told that sin *will be allowed* and they *are conditioned* not to feel guilty.
> [italics added]

Although one can understand the passage, it is tedious and dull. None of the subjects acts; all are acted upon. The writing has no force, no vigor, no motion. Notice the improvement if we substitute active verbs:

> Both dictators agree that people will be happy if they have no frustrations. The leaders promote this happiness by allowing sin and eliminating guilt.

The second version is shorter, clearer, and more vigorous.

Overly cautious writers often use passive verbs to avoid making a firm and direct statement about a controversial or complex topic. The person who writes "Cocaine is not considered by some people to be habit forming" or "IQ tests are thought to be an inadequate measure of real intelligence" may take comfort in thinking he or she has not really made a commitment on what may turn out to be a disputed matter. What the writer has done, however, is run the risk of being called irresponsible by an audience who wants to know on what grounds such statements are made.

Lazy writers may also slide into the passive voice in order to avoid taking the trouble to track down the source of a statement. Writing "Claims have been made" or "Objections are being raised" is easier than doing the homework of finding out who claims and who objects, but it is also irresponsible. Most irresponsible, though, is the writer who deliberately hides behind the passive voice so as to avoid specifying who is doing an action; for instance, "Rocks were thrown at the busses" or "Charges of immoral conduct have been brought against the candidate."

As pointed out in Chapter 4, there are times when passive verb forms are both acceptable and necessary. Technical writers must use them frequently, and they often work well in reports, summaries, or abstracts when the repeated use of *I* would cause the tone to be inappropriately personal. But careful writers who want to keep their prose vigorous and crisp should systematically clean passive constructions out of their writing whenever possible. You should use them only after you have made a conscious decision that they best serve your purposes; otherwise you risk having your writing seem flat, stodgy, and evasive, like bureaucratic jargon.

Passive verbs also contribute to jargon

Taboo on "I" A surprising number of students come to college with the firm conviction that they must never use *I* when they are writing a paper. This taboo, along with the equally groundless one that they must never put a preposition at the end of a sentence, can lead writers into some awkward passive verb constructions. For example:

False assumption: passive verbs sound dignified

> This experience was obtained by me two years ago.
>
> My situation is felt to be one of hopelessness. Training will be given to me in order for a decision to be made about the kind of work into which to go.

All these sentences are needlessly wordy and confusing; they are also dull because the writers have had to start with abstract subjects in order to get rid of the *I* they were naturally inclined to start off with.

You may have trouble shaking the conviction that using *I* in a paper is one of the seven deadly sins of composition, but noticing how often professional writers use it should ease your guilt. The pronoun comes to a writer naturally when she or he is expressing personal opinions or conclusions or referring to personal experience. The first person is certainly appropriate in most informal writing in which there is little distance between the writer and the audience, although you would probably want to use it sparingly in reports or objective accounts. But whatever you do, don't try to get rid of *I* by substituting *we* when there is only one of you.

Timid qualifiers Like bureaucrats, students are often understandably anxious to avoid penalties for expressing what may be an unpopular or erroneous opinion. In order to do so, they not

Platitudes and timid qualifiers contribute to jargon

only take refuge in passive verbs and abstract phrases, but they also pad their writing with timid qualifiers and disclaimers like "It is somewhat the case that," "The author rather tends to," "It is not unlikely that," and "It might sometimes be thought." As one writer puts it,

> For the writer who is afraid of his own direct, aggressive impulses and of what people might think, jargon provides protection in muffling anonymity. . . . In jargon nobody ever does anything, feels anything, or causes anything; nobody has an opinion. Opinions are had, causes result in, factors affect. Everything is reduced to vague abstraction. The writer can even abolish himself, for jargon never sounds as though somebody had written it. . . .[3]

Platitudes The ultimate form of self-protection is to fall back on safe platitudes, to write something so trivial and obvious that no one could take strong objection to it. For example, "Man will always have anxieties and trials in his everyday affairs, and when man can challenge these trials and anxieties he is striving for the complete happiness which can only come by overcoming troublesome obstacles as he goes through life." The person who writes like this makes the reader wonder if the writer could really be that naïve or is just catering to the perceived biases of the audience.

How to Avoid Jargon in Your Writing

To eliminate jargon from your writing completely would be as difficult as always staying on a diet or never wasting time when you study. All of us lapse occasionally; we get careless or lazy or in a hurry and let phrases slip into our writing that we know we should revise or eliminate. So don't expect perfection of yourself or get discouraged because clichés and euphemisms keep popping into your mind as you write. Just keep crossing out the jargon, and gradually your writing will become clearer and stronger.

Many jargon problems will disappear if you observe the general

[3] Robert Waddell, *Grammar and Style* (New York: Holt, Rinehart & Winston, 1951).

rules for improving your writing: try to be concrete and specific; use active verbs whenever possible; remember that writing simply is a virtue, not a defect; be as brief as you can be and still cover your topic adequately. More specific guidelines to keep in mind are these:

Six guidelines for avoiding jargon

1. Be wary of overloading your writing with abstractions; you will need some, of course, but they should be reinforced and clarified with concrete language.
2. Whenever you use the passive voice, ask yourself if it conceals the agent that is acting, slows down the sentence, or makes the sentence stiff and flat. If it does, replace it with an active verb.
3. Use straightforward (though not vulgar) diction instead of genteel expressions or euphemisms. *Under the influence of alcohol* instead of *drunk*, *relieved of the position* instead of *fired*, or *passed away* instead of *died* weaken your writing and irritate your reader.
4. Try to find simple substitutes for pretentious words. *Student* is better than *scholastic* and *building* is better than *edifice*. There is seldom a real need for foreign words and phrases such as *vis-à-vis* or *Zeitgeist*, and business terms like *finalize* and *maximize* are not appropriate for most writing.
5. Avoid inflated expressions such as *at this point in time* instead of *now*, or *it is not without a certain amount of hesitation that* instead of *I hesitate*. Plain prepositions are better than stretched-out phrases; for example, use *about* instead of *in regard to* or *on the subject of*.
6. Keep in mind the distinction between using needless qualifiers and making sensible reservations. Phrases such as *most students* or *many people* and words such as *often, usually,* and *frequently* put limits on what otherwise would be sweeping generalizations. *Somewhat, to a great extent, rather,* and *to a certain degree* are phrases that usually hedge rather than clarify.

Coping with Jargon in Your Reading

Winning the war on jargon is difficult because students continually encounter jargon and other forms of cumbersome, flabby

Don't be intimidated by jargon you may encounter

writing in essays, magazines, and textbooks. What is a student to think of this paragraph by socialist Herbert Marcuse?

> A comfortable, smooth, reasonable, democratic unfreedom prevails in advanced industrial civilization, a token of technical progress. Indeed, what could be more rational than the suppression of individuality in the mechanization of socially necessary but painful performances; the concentration of individual enterprises in more effective, more productive corporation; the regulation of free competition among unequally equipped economic subjects; the curtailment of prerogatives and national sovereignties which impede the international organization of resources. That this technological order also involves a political and intellectual coordination may be a regrettable and yet promising development.[4]

Well, one reaction the reader might have is that if Marcuse wrote all the campaign literature for socialism, the movement would not be likely to get many converts. The paragraph (it is by no means the only example in the essay) is jargon. It is almost impossible to understand, not because the vocabulary is difficult—it isn't— but because it contains few concrete words and no illustrative examples. The individual phrases sound as if they make sense, but when you try to pin down the meaning, it simply eludes you.

Here is a paragraph from the writings of John Dewey, an eminent educational philosopher whose influence on American schools has been substantial:

> The successful activities of the organism, those within which environmental assistance is incorporated, react upon the environment to bring about modifications favorable to their own future. The human being has upon his hands the problem of responding to what is going on around him so that these changes will take one turn rather than another, namely, that required by its own further functioning. While backed in part by the environment, its life is anything but a peaceful exhalation of the environment. It is obliged to struggle—that

---

[4] Herbert Marcuse, *One Dimensional Man* (Boston: Beacon Press, 1964), p. 1.

is to say, to employ the direct support given by the environment in order indirectly to effect changes that would not otherwise occur. In this sense, life goes on by controlling the environment. Its activities must change the changes going on around it; they must neutralize hostile occurrences; they must transform neutral events into cooperative factors or into an efflorescence of new features.[5]

In Dewey's paragraph too, the chief communication problem is caused by abstract language. As soon as you insert explanatory examples, the passage begins to make more sense. Phrases like "react upon the environment to bring about modifications favorable to their own future" and "employ the direct support given by the environment in order indirectly to effect changes" are wordy and clumsy, and "efflorescence of new features" instead of "advantages" is pretentious. The effect of the entire paragraph is to make the eyes glaze and the mind go numb.

To say that writers like Marcuse and Dewey can get away with jargon but that you should not use it may suggest we require more from amateur writers than we do from professionals, that we have in fact a double standard. This is not so. Those philosophers and other major thinkers who write jargon do not really get away with bad writing; rather, their ideas, if they survive, survive in spite of it. Who knows how many thinkers have ruined their chances to be understood because they let their ideas be smothered by abstract, skull-cracking prose?

However maddening this kind of jargon may be, there is a lot of it around, particularly in the fields of education, philosophy, sociology, psychology, and literary criticism. What is necessary is that you learn to cope with jargon: assimilate the ideas being expressed, recognize it as bad writing, and avoid using it yourself. Every piece of writing, exposition or fiction, should be judged on its own merits; having a famous name attached to it does not automatically mean that it is good. You should, however, remember that if you have difficulty with certain kinds of reading, the author is not necessarily at fault. The concepts the author is ex-

Remember that not all difficult prose is jargon

[5] John Dewey, *On Experience, Nature, and Freedom* (Indianapolis: The Bobbs-Merrill Co., Inc., 1960), pp. 24–25.

pressing may be hard for anyone to grasp at the first reading. A dialogue by Plato or a treatise by John Stuart Mill, for example, will tax the powers of most students because the ideas in it are complex and the vocabulary unfamiliar; those qualities alone, however, do not make it bad writing.

Weasel Words

We have been analyzing a kind of writing that is fuzzy, obscure, and sometimes pretentious, but usually not deliberately deceptive. Jargon written by most students falls into that class, and so does that of authors like Marcuse and Dewey. Such writers want their audiences to understand what they are saying, but they seem unable to simplify their writing or unwilling to take the time and trouble to write more clearly. There are, however, some kinds of jargon that writers use to confuse or deceive their audiences. In so doing they use not only clichés and vague, fuzzy language, but also what the semanticist Mario Pei called "weasel words," the language of whitewash and evasion.

Some jargon is deliberately deceptive

Sometimes these terms are simply euphemisms coined to disguise or soften unpleasant labels: *previously owned auto* for *used car, career apparel* for *uniforms, budget level* for *bargain basement, underachiever* for *slow learner,* or *cremains* for *human ashes.* Such attempts to disguise reality are more amusing and pitiful than they are vicious or dangerous although to label a department store charge plate a "happiness card" perhaps borders on the irresponsible.

There is, however, a kind of jargon that officials and administrators use deliberately to disguise unpleasant facts and harsh truths. No one has described this kind of weaseling better than George Orwell in his famous essay, "Politics and the English Language":

In our time, political speech and writing are largely the defense of the indefensible. Things like the continuance of British rule in India, the Russian purges . . . and the dropping of atom bombs can indeed be defended, but only by arguments which are too brutal for most people to face, and which do not square with the professed aims of political parties. Thus political language has to consist largely of euphemism, question-begging, and sheer cloudy vagueness. Defenseless villages are bombarded from the air, the inhabitants driven out into the countryside, the huts set on fire with incendiary bullets, and this is called *pacification*. Millions of peasants are robbed of their farms and sent trudging along the roads with no more than they can carry; this is called *rectification of frontiers*. People are imprisoned for years without trial, or shot in the back of the neck or sent to die of scurvy in Arctic lumber camps; this is called *elimination of unreliable elements*. Such phraseology is needed if one wants to name things without calling up mental pictures.[6]

Although Orwell wrote this essay more than thirty years ago, his comments are far from dated. Although governments may sometimes feel that war is necessary, no one seems to want to talk about it in straightforward language. Apparently, some officials feel that they must protect the general public from the harsh truth that people are being killed. Mario Pei calls the jargon such officials use "the language of annihilation."

In the field of mass destruction, [there is] a tendency to understand and minimize the implications of the concepts involved. This is natural. Total war means total annihilation and no one likes the prospect of being annihilated. Those who deal in annihilation must therefore undersell, not oversell, their commodity, which in the final analysis is death. Can death's pill be sugar coated? Apparently some think it can.[7]

Jargon as sugar coating

Those in charge of the sugar-coating depersonalize their language as much as possible. In an ironic reversal of the guidelines that state that you should use vigorous and concrete language whenever possible, they deliberately use bland and abstract terms. The "language of annihilation" never mentions people; it talks of "personnel deterrents," "protective reaction strikes," "consoli-

[6] George Orwell, "Politics and the English Language," in *Shooting an Elephant and Other Essays* (New York: Harcourt, Brace & World, 1945), p. 88.
[7] Mario Pei, *Words in Sheep's Clothing* (New York: Hawthorn Books, Inc., 1969), p. 12.

dating territorial acquisitions" and "damage inflicted on ground forces." These phrases suggest a conflict in some unpopulated area between robots and machines—no blood ever flowing. Such weaseling should fool nobody, but unfortunately, it probably does, perhaps even the writers who concoct the jargon.

Other kinds of political jargon

But Pentagon officials are not the only ones trying to disguise the truth under a blanket of vague terms. In recent years so many other public figures have taken to twisting the language that the National Council of Teachers of English has formed a Committee on Public Doublespeak to point out and try to correct confused and confusing political language. Here is an example of the kind of thing they object to, taken from a talk by Alan Greenspan, chairman of President Ford's Council of Economic Advisers in 1975.

> Thus, once the inflation genie has been let out of the bottle, it is a very tricky problem to find the particular calibration and timing that would be appropriate to stem the acceleration in risk premiums created by falling income without prematurely aborting the decline in the inflation-generated risk premiums. This is clearly not an easy policy path to traverse, but it is the path that we must follow.[8]

The official who can talk like this and convince an audience that something has been said avoids the discomfort of being forced to make specific recommendations for dealing with a concrete problem.

Learn to recognize and avoid jargon

Students who are trying to learn to handle language effectively, both their own language and that which is directed to them, face two challenges. First, they must learn to recognize jargon and doublespeak when they encounter it and learn to reject it as meaningless, ridiculous, or in some cases, outright dishonest. They should be neither impressed nor intimidated. Second, they need to form the habit of keeping a sharp eye on their own prose in order to keep out the fuzzy, pretentious, pseudointellectual phrases that are so often dangled before them as models. Proba-

[8] Quoted by Edwin Newman in "Viable Solutions," *Esquire*, December 1975, p. 147.

bly the surest way of doing that is to ask, "Can I really explain just what this phrase means?" If the answer is "No," don't use it.

Don't allow jargon to dull your critical abilities

What you need to guard against most, however, is the effect that jargon has on your thinking. As Orwell points out in "Politics and the English Language," it is actually easier to write pretentiously and tritely than it is to write clearly. "By using stale metaphors, similes, and idioms, you save yourself much mental effort at the cost of leaving your meaning vague, not only for your reader but for yourself." Just as (to use John Stuart Mill's words) society provides molds to save people the trouble of forming their own characters, every culture also provides platitudes, canned sentiments, and ready-made expressions to save people the trouble of doing their own thinking. If you habitually allow yourself to tack together a series of conventional responses and overworked arguments and call it a paper—and even worse, if you get rewarded for doing so—you will eventually kill your own ability to think a problem through and come up with realistic and usable solutions. As the section on propaganda (p. 376) points out, demagogues know that a good way to keep people from thinking for themselves is to provide them with enough slogans and clichés to take the place of original ideas. Don't anesthetize your own brain by doing that to yourself.

Exercises

1. Which of the following words are abstract, and which concrete? Notice that you may have to settle on a limited definition for some of these words before you can classify them accurately.

science	expressway	tone
machine	safety	barrier
identity	recognition	son-in-law
dormitory	character	deed
condominium	treaty	abortion
duty	yellow	integrity

2. Arrange the following three lists of words into ladders of abstraction:

gasoline-propelled conveyance	three-month-old Great Dane	the poems of T. S. Eliot
product of the Ford Motor Company	dog	academic subjects
mode of transportation	domesticated animal	twentieth-century literature
two-door automobile	canine species	English
Mustang	mammal	"The Love Song of J. Alfred Prufrock"
Mach II fastback	puppy	

3. Write short paragraphs that develop concretely these two opening sentences:

a. A brief tour of the campus reveals an urgent need for modernization.

b. The candidate's record on ecology issues will hurt her with young voters.

4. Bring to class a paragraph from an essay or magazine article that you think is particularly well written. What parts of the writing are concrete and what parts abstract?

5. Study the following sentences from student themes; then, rewrite them to make them more concrete and effective. Use different words if necessary.

a. The behavior of the residents is also a factor of annoyance.

b. The author tends to have a negative attitude toward the values of youth.

c. Social and economic conflicts will arise if the student takes any involvement in college affairs.

d. The author's words produce feelings of unfavorable reaction in the reader.

e. The writer uses phrases that negate the idea of sexual freedom in our culture.

f. The first consideration that should be taken is what particular interests the person has in the areas of job preference.

6. Analyze the example of student jargon on page 209. What specific faults do you find in it? How would you rewrite to improve it?

7. In "Politics and the English Language," George Orwell rewrote a famous passage from Ecclesiastes 9:11 as a modern author might have phrased it. Here are the original and Orwell's jargon version:

I returned, and saw under the sun, that the race is not to the swift, nor the battle to the strong, neither yet bread to the wise, nor yet riches to men of understanding, nor yet favor to men of skill; but time and chance happeneth to them all.

Objective consideration of contemporary phenomena compels the conclusion that success or failure in competitive activities exhibits no tendency to be commensurate with innate capacity, but that a considerable element of the unpredictable must invariably be taken into account. [p. 84]

What particular qualities of the original passage make it good writing? What specific characteristics of jargon has Orwell incorporated into his version? The first version has more words than the second, but the second one seems much longer. Why? If you read the two versions aloud, what striking differences do you notice in the way they sound?

8. Here are two student papers written in class on the following topic: Women who are raped and do not report it to the police (should, should not) be subject to misdemeanor charges and possible fines. In three or four paragraphs, argue on one side or the other.

Read, analyze, and evaluate the two papers. In your opinion, which writer uses words more effectively? Which paper is the more concrete and specific? Give examples from the paper to illustrate your analyses.

a. The number of rapes occurring annually in the United States is rapidly on the increase. However, in comparison to the large number of rapes, few of the rapists are ever tried and convicted. One reason why few of these rapists are ever convicted is the fact that many rapes go unreported. Therefore, women who do not report rape cases to the police should be subject to misconduct charges because they are obstructing justice.

Fear stalks the rape victim. The horrible memories of the crime, the fear of facing public ridicule, and the fact that she will have to recount the crime to the jury all result in her desire to remain silent. But it is this very silence that is the crime. If more women would report their rapes, then the public would awaken to the harsh reality that rape is a common occurrence in today's society. This in turn would help erase the myth that women purposely entice men to rape them. Then with the change in public attitude and the increase in the amount of evidence, it would be possible to try and convict more rapists.

These actions will not likely occur unless the "silence" is broken. Therefore, in order to increase the number of rapes reported and rapists convicted, women who do not report rape cases to the police should be subject to misconduct charges and fines.

b. Susan Sampson was raped last night. This morning when she woke up, the awful memory flooded over her—the humiliation, the pain, the anger. And the confusion. Susan is a nineteen-year-old university student living in a co-op not far from campus. Away from home for the first time in her life, she has become very self-sufficient—the kids who know her describe her as a "loner." Now Susan has reached a crisis but, instead of reaching out for help, she has turned to herself, choosing not to disclose her horrible secret. She considered going to a rape crisis center or to the police but talked herself out of it, saying, "If I went to them, I'd become just another statistic. What happened to me cannot be categorized and filed away. Besides, there would probably be legal hassles . . . I can take care of myself."

Susan shares this attitude with many women—they can "take care of themselves." Not everyone needs to go outside for help—many people have developed their own personal problem solving resources. For this reason, it is wrong to require that all rape victims report to the police. And to suggest that those who do not report be fined or charged with misconduct is a direct violation of freedom of choice.

If a woman (or man) can cope with a crisis such as rape without going to the police, why not let them be? The anguish they have already suffered would most likely be provoked by questions, examinations and impersonal treatment. If we force people into doing what is basically wrong to them, we will be creating more harm than good.

Six months from now, Susan Sampson will be back into her old routine. Having been allowed to handle her situation in her own way, she learned to cope and is now "recovered" mentally. Shouldn't other victims be given this choice?

Suggested Writing Assignment

Theme

Purposes (1) To sharpen your awareness of problems created by jargon by having you write a specific criticism of a passage of jargon. (2) To give you practice in translating jargon. (3) To have you practice your own writing skills by rewriting the passage in acceptable prose.

Procedures (1) By using the guidelines given on page 213 supplemented by what you have learned in class discussion, write a criticism of the defects in the following passage. You cannot, and should not, try to discuss all the faults in the passage. Focus your criticism on a few that seem most offensive to you, and organize your theme around those points. Give examples to support your criticism. (2) Rewrite the passage in language that is more colorful and concrete and easier to understand. You may write a free translation that makes use of your own examples and words, but it should express approximately the same idea. Your version need not be as long as the original. One tight paragraph should be enough.

Contemporary Conjugal Lifestyle Problems

Marriage roles in our current cultural context are now being seen by many participants as interpersonal commitments of a nonpermanent nature rather than assumptions of traditional provider/supporter functions. Both men and women undertake the marriage experience with the anticipation that they will be able to relate to each other in a meaningful way that will hopefully culminate in a viable *modus vivendi.* Conventional expectations about male fiscal responsibility obligations and female house-centered activities are seen as inoperative. Attitudes of this kind are most in evidence on the part of college-educated young people who have cohabited together during their educational phase.

Examination of available data on marriages contracted in this frame of reference indicates that most of the parties to these marital arrangements have not been able to effectuate their goals. Neither men nor women are able to function in a completely rational manner vis-à-vis nonsexist distribution of domestic obligations. Because of different kinds of growth patterns experienced in adolescence, males and females have divergent attitudes toward the propriety of the husband making a contribution to doing the cooking and the laundry. The average young American male has been so conditioned by excessive maternal solicitousness to assume gratification of all personal needs that he responds negatively to his wife's expectations of sharing responsibilities. The average young American college-educated female, however, at this point in time, is conditioned by exposure to the neofeminist movement to be antipathetic to the servant/caretaker role that the woman assumes in the traditionally structured domestic picture.

Thus affective factors become the dominant force in what had been cognitively perceived as a situation subject to intellectualization and rational regulation. It is not unlikely that young people will continue to experience disappointment in this regard for the foreseeable future of the next ten or fifteen years because learned behavior tends not to supersede early childhood orientation in areas in which the id rather than the ego is the more dynamic value. Changes may be brought about when the majority of male marriage partners are the offspring of mothers who have integrated and maximized women's liberation tenets. Timewise, we may anticipate a substantive delay.

Using Words to Convince and Persuade

8

In many writing situations, a writer's chief purpose is to persuade readers, to get them to accept an argument or respond to an appeal. Writers can use several different methods to achieve this purpose, but one of the most common and most successful is to use language that appeals to the emotions. They usually make that kind of appeal by using one or more of these strategies: connotation, metaphor, and tone.

Connotation

In June of 1940 the British prime minister, Winston Churchill, faced the task of telling his country that with the defeat of the French and British armies at Dunkirk, the British people must prepare themselves for a possible invasion of their island by German troops. After explaining the hard facts of the situation in a comparatively restrained and objective manner, Churchill concluded with an emotional appeal calculated to stir his audience to push their courage, patriotism, and determination to such a point that they could face any odds. Even now, at a distance of more than forty years, that portion of the speech is tremendously moving:

> I have, myself, full confidence that if all do their duty, if nothing is neglected, and if the best arrangements are made, as they are being made, we shall prove ourselves once again able to defend our Island home, to ride out the storm of war, and to outlive the menace of tyranny, if necessary for years, if necessary alone. . . . The British Empire and the French Republic, linked together in their cause and in their need, will defend to the death their native soil, aiding each other like good comrades to the utmost of their strength. Even though large tracts of Europe and many old and famous States have fallen or may fall into the grip of the Gestapo and all the odious apparatus of Nazi rule, we shall not flag or fail. We shall go on to the end, we shall fight in France, we shall fight on the seas and the oceans, we shall fight with growing confidence and growing strength in the air, we shall defend our Island, whatever the cost may be, we shall fight on the beaches, we shall fight on the landing grounds, we shall fight

in the fields and in the streets, we shall fight in the hills; we shall never surrender, and even if, which I do not for a moment believe, this Island or a large part of it were subjugated and starving, then our Empire beyond the seas, armed and guarded by the British Fleet, would carry on the struggle, until, in God's good time, the New World, with all its power and might, steps forth to the rescue and the liberation of the old.[1]

Churchill's concluding appeal is a classic example of persuasion based on emotion. He depends heavily on the connotative force of words and phrases such as "the menace of tyranny," "defend to the death their native soil," "grip of the Gestapo," and "odious apparatus of Nazi rule." Then, with an unerring rhetorical instinct for the impact of repeating the simple dramatic phrase "we shall fight," he builds to the climax, "we shall never surrender" and brings in the vision of the "New World, with all its power and might," coming to the "rescue and the liberation of the old."

The example is an extreme one—seldom does one face a situation that calls for such a gut-level, all-out emotional appeal—but the principle it illustrates is sound. That principle is that in most rhetorical situations one of the most effective tools that any writer can use is connotation. It is true that usually one cannot use *only* connotation; most audiences require some evidence, and the more alert and astute the audience, the more evidence it demands. Nevertheless, without some use of connotation, some words or allusions that touch the sympathies of the reader or listener, arguments have limited appeal.

How Connotation Works

We can understand better how connotation works if we define it precisely and look at some of its sources. The *connotation* of a word is the emotional baggage that it carries in addition to its

[1]Winston Churchill, "Dunkirk," *Blood, Sweat, and Tears* (New York: G. P. Putnam's Sons, 1941), pp. 296–297. Reprinted by permission of G. P. Putnam's Sons and Cassell Ltd. from *Blood, Sweat, and Tears* by Winston Churchill. Copyright © 1941 by Winston S. Churchill.

Connotation appeals to the emotions

denotative, or strictly dictionary, definition. The term *socialism* readily illustrates the point. Denotatively, stripped of its emotional baggage, it means a system or condition of society in which the means of production are owned and controlled by the state. The definition is descriptive and neutral; it passes no judgments. The connotation of the word is quite another matter. Now, the emotional baggage added by the reader alters the word for better or worse. United States citizens associate socialism with communism, communism with totalitarianism, totalitarianism with the horrors of George Orwell's *1984*. Because of this chain of associations, they distrust and fear any proposal that has been labeled *socialist*. That their view of socialism may be grossly inaccurate—there are, after all, socialist democracies, such as Sweden and England—is not relevant. On the other hand, Russian citizens, who have grown up under a socialist government and heard it praised from childhood, carry emotional baggage that predisposes them to favor any measure called *socialist*. As a result of their conditioning, neither group is likely to use the word objectively.

By the time we are young adults, all of us have added to our vocabularies an astonishing collection of emotional baggage. Those of you who studied Latin may remember that the Latin word for baggage is *impedimenta*. For our purposes, that definition is singularly appropriate because the connotative baggage we have piled on our language actually acts as an impediment to clear thinking. Obviously, we cannot purify our thought processes simply by jettisoning our emotional baggage. Nor would we really want to eliminate connotation. Language purged of all color would be fit only for conversing with a computer. What we can do, however, is minimize the extent to which we are unwittingly controlled by language by developing an acute sensitivity to connotation and by bringing the way in which it works out into the open.

Appeals to the senses. Connotation functions by the process of association. At the simplest level, it does little more than trigger reactions. We hear or see the word *silky*, and without actually thinking about it, we remember the sensation of feeling silk. For most people, the memory is pleasant, and the good vibrations transfer to whatever the word *silky* is describing. This is the kind of response a company depends on when it advertises, "Your hair

Connotation works by triggering associations

will turn out silkier, more lustrous, glossier than it was when you started." All direct appeals to our senses work in this way. *Smooth, soft, shining, shimmering* set off good reactions; *gritty, harsh, slimy, mushy* set off bad ones. In the following passage, Philip Wylie depends on the reader's sensuous response to put over his point:

> Most foods, cooked or uncooked, are destroyed in the deep freeze for all persons of sensibility. Vegetables with crisp and crackling texture emerge as mush, slippery and stringy as hair nets simmered in Vaseline. The essential oils that make peas peas—and cabbage cabbage—must undergo fission and fusion in freezers. Anyhow, they vanish. Some meats turn to leather. Others to wood pulp. Everything, pretty much, tastes like the mosses of tundra, dug up in midwinter. Even the appearance changes, oftentimes. Handsome comestibles you put down in summer come out looking very much like the corpses of wooly mammoths recovered from the last Ice Age.[2]

Wylie borrows two of the advertiser's favorite terms, "crisp" and "crackling," to get the reader's approval for fresh foods, and he condemns the frozen product by the words "slippery" and "stringy." He then reinforces his point with a series of unpleasant visual images: "wood pulp," "mosses," "corpses of wolly mammoths."

Connotation often appeals to stereotypes

Appeals to prejudice Other kinds of connotation work in a more complex way by reminding us of the stereotypes that we all carry around in our heads, images that include racial types, policemen, DAR matrons, small-town girls, politicians, pot parties, admirals, professors, the Mafia, and dozens of others. A single reference to one of these stereotypes can evoke a mass of associations, both positive and negative. Writers are depending on this kind of nonlogical reaction when they use terms like *hippie, hard-hat, cop, communist, bureaucrat,* or other loaded labels.

For any thoughtful reader, such labels should be a signal to stop and ask: What images do these words evoke? Are they accurate and warranted? Or, as S. I. Hayakawa puts it, do they

[2] Philip Wylie, from "Science Has Spoiled My Supper," *Atlantic Monthly*, April 1954, reprinted by permission of Harold Ober Associates, Incorporated. Copyright © 1954 by the Atlantic Monthly Company, Boston, Massachusetts.

place an imaginary map in the mind, a map that does not really describe the territory it is supposed to?

Appeals to beliefs To attempt to track down and identify the sources of all our emotional responses to language would be an impossible task, so I shall limit myself to setting up a broad and sketchy third general category of association, that of attitudes and beliefs. Because most of us believe in the traditional virtues of honesty, courage, loyalty, self-reliance, hard work, and fair play, there is little doubt about the way we will respond to words such as *indolent, shifty, craven,* or *freeloader.* We Americans conventionally believe in independence and individualism, in freedom and dignity, in progress and prosperity (all concepts we have absorbed with our education), and we nod our approval to any term that reminds us of them. We prefer—or think we do—the natural to the artificial, and so *real, genuine, original,* and *authentic* are good words; *synthetic, imitation, substitute,* and *pseudo* are bad ones.

Connotation appeals to popular attitudes

Appeals to insecurity We have other attitudes that we are not quite so proud of but that influence us as much as, or more than, our traditional beliefs. We crave approval. We want to be thought of as young, sexually attractive, intelligent, and successful. No one wants to be classified as a mediocre person: dull, conventional, and timid. Notice how a magazine ad can play on these apprehensions in a positive way.

Connotation appeals to personal needs

> Are you the kind of man who wants *more* from life? Wants that new adventure, that special kind of vacation that others don't know about? Do you want to set the pace, not follow? If you're a leader, have that special knack for taking charge, our magazine is for you. Read *Paladin* to find out where to go for the best and the brightest. The last word in life-styles is at your nearest newsstand.

In the same way, our desire for status makes us susceptible to snob appeal ads, which encourage us to buy expensive cars that will make our neighbors envious. Brewers promote our continual pursuit of happiness by coining slogans such as, "You only live once—why not enjoy the finest beer brewed?"

Appeals to fear Probably the most insidious kind of connotation is that which attempts to sway us by touching our deepest, instinctive fears. Phrases such as "communist conspiracy" and "fascist plot," with their innuendoes of secrecy and mysterious machinations, may immediately put us on our guard. Labels such as "outside agitators," "alien influences," and "foreign elements" appeal to the distrust and suspicion of outsiders that are difficult for even open-minded people to overcome. An inclination to panic at the prospect of injury or death assures a response to mottoes like "Insure your safety" or "Protect your loved ones," phrases that can serve equally well to sell burglar alarms, insurance, a politician's position on law and order, or an intercontinental missile system.

Using Connotation

Strengths and weaknesses of general connotation

General connotation The kinds of connotation discussed so far—and the examples are intended to be representative, not exhaustive—are broadly based and general; that is, their emotional appeal rests on warranted assumptions about the majority of the people in our society. The sum of generally shared attitudes is the conventional wisdom of our society, the prevailing opinion of that mythical person in the street. Writers at both ends of the political spectrum depend, and with good reason, on their audience's responding to words that have general connotation.

The rhetorician who addresses a large, heterogeneous audience must rely on these kinds of words, but the broad, unfocused emotional appeal can have serious weaknesses. For one thing, many words and phrases have been used so often that they have lost their impact and degenerated into clichés. We are so accustomed to hearing about "good government," "individual freedom," "democratic processes," and "human rights" that the terms simply roll off our minds; at best they evoke mild approval and little action. Another problem is that the more alert portion of an audience refuses to be impressed by what they view as "push-button" techniques aimed at people totally governed by their emotions. The writer who tries to sway everyone may alienate rather than persuade this last group.

Learning to use selective connotation

Selective connotation Thus, connotative language works best when it is selective, chosen with a specific audience in mind. Writers who decide to tailor their appeals to particular groups are taking a risk, of course; they must make assumptions about their audiences that may be wrong. But for the person who makes a careful and rational analysis of an audience, using the methods discussed in Chapter 3, the gamble will probably pay off. For instance, a candidate who is promoting tax-supported day-care centers for preschool children might speak of "more freedom for mothers" and "equal opportunity for career women" if she were addressing a group of young women. If she were advocating the same measure to a men's club, she would avoid those phrases and instead talk about the ways in which day-care centers could improve the efficiency of women workers and about the advantages to the children of being in the care of licensed, professional people. By varying her approach, the speaker is not compromising her principles; since both her arguments are legitimate, neither contradicts the other, and both promote the same purpose. Rather, she is showing sensitivity to the concerns of her audiences and is adapting her diction to the rhetorical situations.

In the same way, astute writers sense when words like *intellectual, liberal,* and *idealist* will antagonize their audiences and find acceptable substitutes for them. Other words with strong selective connotations are *capitalist, businessperson, artist, student,* or *Texan;* some abstract terms that trigger mixed reactions are *law and order, civil liberties,* or *right-to-work laws.* Such lists of words with controversial connotations could go on almost indefinitely, but the point should be clear. Rhetoricians who are unaware of how their audience will respond to their language will fail.

Risks of Connotation

Don't overuse connotation

Rhetoricians risk defeating their own purpose when they overuse connotation. The writer or speaker who expects to persuade mainly through slanted language is assuming that the audience, like a laboratory animal, is totally conditioned and has no critical faculties. Such tactics may work when the audience is already in full agreement with the speaker; in that case the speaker is doing little more than leading a cheering section anyway. In a genuine rhetorical situation, however, the audience is likely to be more insulted than convinced by a barrage of connotative words and phrases, whether the phrases are political slogans or advertising clichés.

Except on those few occasions that are unabashedly emotional, such as Winston Churchill's Dunkirk address, connotation is most effective when it is used with restraint. Like the plaster, paint, and trimming on a building, it adds interest and appeal, but it cannot sustain much weight. The solid framework of an argument must be constructed out of evidence, logic, rational processes, and supporting examples, or it will not stand up to pressure. On the other hand, just as we would not want to live in a completely utilitarian house, stripped of all but essentials, we would find it unrewarding either to construct or to read a totally logical piece of persuasion. For this reason, the added ingredient, connotation, is appropriate and useful, but unless the arguer applies judgment and restraint in adding it to the main structure, it will mar rather than enhance the whole.

The Ethics of Connotation

Connotation has a valid place in discourse

Inevitably, the study of connotative language leaves some students with the impression that connotation is bad and should be purged from the language. The reaction is understandable. You've been warned to be sensitive to connotation, to sift through the emotional terminology and get to the facts, and to be aware of how some politicians and advertisers seek to manipulate you through language. Nevertheless, to eliminate connotation altogether would be semantic overkill; it would leave us with a drab and sterile language fit for little but communicating data and reports. We would rob our language of much of its richness and ourselves of an indispensable tool for persuasion and expression. What we need, then, is not to do away with connotation but to find guidelines by which to evaluate the way others use it and to control it in our own writing. Such guidelines must, of course, be applied impartially; it is intellectually dishonest to endorse slanted language when we approve of its purpose but condemn it when we disagree with the writer's purpose.

One area of writing in which one can say without qualification that connotation has no place is that of news stories and reports. People who read newspapers and news magazines for information have a right to a straightforward account uncolored by the opinions of the writer. An article about socialists running for office should identify the candidates as socialists, not as left-wingers or radicals. A reporter should not call an accident tragic or a victory glorious.

Connotation does not have a place in factual reports

Similarly, value terms do not belong in a report you are making for a class or a committee. If your assignment is to present evidence, you are meeting it when you say, "Thirty percent of the residents of South Chicago live in dwellings classified as substandard by the local housing commissioner"; you are not if you write, "One-third of the people exist in intolerable, filthy conditions." The latter kind of language has its place in editorials, in persuasive feature articles, or in syndicated columns appearing beneath a writer's name, but not in any writing that is supposed to be giving only facts. Thus Rachel Carson, in her book *The Silent Spring*, is justified in writing,

> The most *alarming* of man's *assaults* upon the environment is the *contamination* of air, earth, rivers, and sea with *dangerous* and even lethal materials. This *pollution* is for the most part irrecoverable; the *chain of evil* it initiates not only on the world that must support life, but in living tissues, is for the most part irreversible. [italics added; p.6]

In an ecology textbook, however, a scrupulous author would avoid biased language and strive to give only verifiable facts.

Much of what we read and write is, like Carson's book, frankly persuasive. We are, after all, as interested in exchanging ideas and opinions as we are in gaining or giving information. But how do we set limits on the kind of emotional language that an author may properly use to influence the audience? The answer is necessarily less than exact, but it is possible to set at least minimum standards.

Trying to win an argument by clobbering your opponent with derogatory labels such as *quack, bleeding heart, fascist pig,* or *fuzzy-minded idealist* is both immature and foolish. This kind of unrestrained emotional outpouring has no place in responsible writing. The responsible and skillful writer is the one who uses connotation sparingly, and with judgment and good taste, and who does not depend on it as the only, or even principal, method of persuasion. And the more knowledgeable and sophisticated the audience is, the more likely it is that restrained and careful rhetoric will work.

Metaphor

Metaphors draw comparisons

As used here, the terms *metaphor* and *metaphorical language* mean figures of speech that draw comparisons between unlike things. Technically, a comparison containing *like* or *as* is a simile, and one *equating* different things is a metaphor, but in practice "He plays like a demon" and "He's a regular demon on the basketball court" say the same thing. (Remember, though, that not all comparisons are metaphors. When you say "She is just like her mother" or "Washington is a cleaner city than Chicago," you are making comparisons, but you are not using metaphorical language.)

The inclination to express ourselves in metaphor must be as old as speech itself. Our desire to communicate with others makes us instinctively draw comparisons, search for a reference to the familiar to explain the unknown. Imagine, for instance, an Indian who has been scouting new hunting grounds for the tribe. He comes back to tell them of the vast herds of buffalo he has seen beyond the river. How can he best convey this information graphically and impressively? Rather than talk of dozens or hundreds, he says, "There are as many animals as there are trees in the forest around us" or "The buffalo are as thick as ants swarming on the carcass of a dead dog." He would get his point across, particularly if the metaphor he chose were new to his audience.

Familiar metaphors in everyday discourse

Our own everyday language abounds in metaphorical expressions, but too often we do not get our point across because our figures of speech are so familiar they have lost their impact on people. Expressions such as "sleep like a log," "eat like a horse," "cry like a baby," "feel fit as a fiddle," and "work like a trooper" have lost the power to enlighten or impress. We have an inexhaustible supply of worn-out metaphors that make casual conversation almost effortless. Without thinking we refer to "being caught in the rat race," "fighting tooth and nail," "blowing a fuse," "playing the game," or "being driven up the wall." Certainly no real harm is done by our resorting to such clichés when we are only making small talk with friends. If we had to think constantly of new and vigorous ways to express ourselves in everyday talk, conversation would become a terrible chore. But when we are speaking or writing seriously with the desire to explain, to clarify, or to persuade, it is essential that we get rid of metaphors that anesthetize rather than stimulate the audience. In those situations, if you cannot find a fresh metaphor that will serve your purposes, it is probably better not to use one at all.

How Metaphor Works

We can understand the benefits of figurative language as a rhetorical tool if we examine how it works and what some of its uses are. Like connotation, metaphor works by setting up associations, but it operates more directly and specifically. For example, a book written in 1893 by the American novelist Frank Norris has as its theme the railroad's exploitation of the people and lands of the western United States in the late nineteenth century; the title of the book is *The Octopus*. For most readers the word *octopus* raises an unpleasant image; they see a frightening creature with tentacles that stretch out to grab anything within its reach and strangle it to death. Because Norris has equated the railroad with the octopus, readers transfer their impressions of the creature to the railroad and think of it as a grasping and destructive live thing that preys upon people.

A passage from the literary critic Alfred Kazin's autobiography, *A Walker in the City*, provides another example. He writes, "When I passed the school, I went sick with all my old fear of it. . . . It looks like a factory over which has been imposed the facade of a castle." Here Kazin wants his readers to attribute the characteristics of a factory to the school. Our picture of a factory is that of a place in which a uniform product is turned out by assembly-line techniques. The atmosphere seems mechanized, regimented, and impersonal; any item that does not meet the specifications set by the management is rejected. When the readers envision a school that operates this way, they react in a surge of pity for students caught in such a system. Notice too the phrase "the facade of the castle," another metaphor that illustrates the school administration's pretensions about the institution. The method employed by Norris and Kazin is simple: A = B; therefore, B has the characteristics of A. The effect is illumination; the readers see a thing

The metaphorical equation

that is ordinary and familiar to them in a new light. For convenience, we shall call this kind of comparison *straight metaphor*, a simple equation of unlike objects. We need also to consider three other categories, the submerged metaphor, the extended metaphor, and allusion.

Submerged Metaphor

The *submerged metaphor* is the simplest, commonest, and easiest to incorporate into your writing. It consists of implied comparisons made in one or two words, usually verbs, nouns, or adjectives. Take the sentence "The vice president of the firm had clawed his way to the top." The word "clawed" is metaphorical, not literal; people do not have claws. The verb implies the ruthlessness and ferocity associated with a wild animal; the writer has gotten a lot of mileage (notice the submerged metaphor in the noun "mileage") out of a single word. The phrases "He cut down the opposition's case" and "She tortured her hair into the latest style" use the same verbal technique. Although this kind of metaphor is sometimes deliberatively connotative, frequently a writer uses submerged comparisons to give the language vigor and color. For example, "The speech *triggered* immediate repercussions"; "Jim *erupted* into a stream of profanity"; "The author was *deluged* with requests for interviews." Reading just a few pages of a newspaper or a magazine like *Time* or *Newsweek* reveals how heavily reporters depend on figurative language. "The company recently *launched* a new advertising campaign"; "The movie has *spawned* a host of imitations"; "Today the police chief said they had *dealt a knock-out blow* to drug pushers in the city." Of course, the device can get out of hand. Tabloid writers' efforts to find a sensational adjective become comic at times, and many authors of mystery and adventure stories overload their fiction with fast-action verbs and shocking metaphors.

Using metaphorical verbs for vigor and color

Most student writing, however, is not likely to be marred by too much flashy language. More often, the desire to play it safe, to be correct, and to sound weighty overcomes natural speech habits. The color fades from writing as the proportion of abstractions, passive constructions, and linking verbs increases. The result is dull to write and dull to read. If you are adventuresome enough to try a metaphor now and then, either straight or submerged, you can put some life into your prose. Instead of writing "It is my opinion that drastic changes must be made if we are to solve this problem," try "The problem calls for a full-scale overhaul of the system." Whenever possible use verbs that call to mind some kind of physical action. Occasionally, your imaginative efforts may misfire, but with practice you will learn to write with a livelier style. The gamble is worth it.

Extended Metaphor

Working with *extended metaphor*, one that carries a comparison through several sentences or even paragraphs, is more complex, but certainly not beyond the abilities of many inexperienced writers. Here is an example by a person known for colorful and effective language:

> "I figured when my legislative program passed the Congress," Johnson said in 1971, "that the Great Society had a real chance to grow into a beautiful woman. And I figured her growth and development would be as natural and inevitable as any small child's. In the first year, as we got the law on the books, she'd begin to crawl. Then in the second year, as we got more laws on the books, she'd begin to walk, and the year after that, she'd be off and running, all the time growing bigger and healthier and fatter. And when she grew up, I figured she'd be so big and beautiful that the American people couldn't help but fall in love with her, and once they did, they'd want to keep her around forever, making her a permanent part of American life, more permanent even than the New Deal. . . . It's a terrible thing for me to sit by and watch someone else starve my Great Society to death. She's getting thinner and thinner and uglier and uglier all the time; now her bones are beginning to stick out and her wrinkles are beginning to show. Soon she'll be so ugly that the American people will refuse to look at her; they'll stick her in a closet to hide her away and there she'll die. And when she dies, I too will die."[3]

[3] Quoted by Doris Kearns in "Who *Was* Lyndon Baines Johnson?" *Atlantic*, June 1976, p. 73.

Allusion

Allusion adds extra meaning to writing

A final kind of metaphor is *allusion*, a reference to events or characters from an outside source, usually literary or historical. The device acts as a rhetorical shorthand, which enables writers to compress extra meaning into a few words when they use short phrases that bring associations to mind. For example, the phrases *sour grapes* and *cry wolf* describe certain kinds of human behavior with a minimum of words because we know the Aesop's fables to which the writer refers. The terms *Good Samaritan* and *kiss of death* describe by evoking our memories of Bible stories, and references like *Achilles' heel* and *Trojan horse* say a great deal in a few words if we have read *The Iliad*.

Although myth, legend, classical literature, and the Bible are the most common sources of allusion, a writer can also use contemporary references with good effect. You might characterize a prejudiced but likable person as "an Archie Bunker"; a quick and effective way to describe a reformer would be through a comparison with Ralph Nader. Such references not only add vigor and concreteness to your writing but also increase your rapport with your audience by drawing on a stock of shared experiences and common knowledge. Sports, television, movies, popular songs, books, current events, magazines—almost everything around us can furnish material for allusions that will help us to communicate.

Effect of allusions depends on knowing audience

When you are using allusions, you should stop to ask yourself if they are general enough for an educated reader to grasp; if not, you should omit them. On the other hand, part of your own educational responsibility is to increase your stock of general information so that you can learn from the writings of others. Students who know nothing of Greek myths, Arthurian legend, Shakespeare, or biblical history are handicapped whether they are reading The Great Books or *Newsweek*. Serious authors assume they are writing for educated audiences; your obligation is to rise to their expectations by looking up allusions in a dictionary or encyclopedia.

Using Metaphor

Understandably, student writers may despair of achieving professional eloquence in their writing, but actually they may be able to do something comparable on a modest scale. The key is to find

Learn to equate knowns with unknowns in metaphor

a well-known process or object to use as one part of your metaphorical equation and then to show how the concept you want to clarify resembles what is already familiar. For example, one student compared the frustration of trying to decipher a passage of jargon to the frustration of trying to see through frosted glass. A football player on scholarship equated his way of life with that of a prize fighter, who entertains the public for a living.

Use metaphors
1. To add vigor
2. To add concreteness

The varieties of metaphor serve several rhetorical purposes. First, as already discussed, they give color and vigor to writing, bring it to life, make it move. That result alone helps to win your audience. Second, using metaphor is one way to make the abstract concrete. Philosophers and psychologists frequently employ metaphor to help their readers grasp difficult concepts. In one of the most dramatic passages in philosophy, Plato illustrates the function of the soul by saying that it is like a team of two horses with its charioteer; the charioteer is the guiding force for the horses, one of which represents good instincts and the other, bad instincts.

> The horse that holds the nobler position is upright and clean-limbed; it carries its head high, its nose is aquiline, its color white, its eyes dark; it is a lover of honor . . . temperance, and decency. . . . It needs no whip, but is driven by word of command alone. The other horse, however, is huge, but crooked, a great jumble of a creature with a short, thick neck, a flat nose, dark color, grey bloodshot eyes, the mate of insolence and knavery, shaggy-eared and deaf, hardly heeding whip or spur.[4]

Plato extends the figure of speech for several paragraphs, vividly dramatizing the struggle that reason, the charioteer, has in finally bringing the black horse, or the soul's sensual desires, under control.

3. To explain theory

Writers often use metaphor to clarify or explain a theory. The sociologist David Riesman elucidates his classification of people as "inner-directed" and "other-directed" by saying that inner-directed people have what he calls a "psychological gyroscope."

[4] Plato, *Phaedrus*, trans. W. C. Helmbold and W. B. Rabinowitz (Indianapolis: The Bobbs-Merrill Co., Inc., 1956), p. 38.

"This instrument, once it is set by the parents and other authorities, keeps the inner-directed person . . . 'on course' even when
tradition . . . no longer dictates his moves." In contrast, other-directed people pattern their behavior according to the responses
they receive from those around them. "What [is] internalized is
not a code of behavior but the elaborate equipment needed to attend to . . . messages. . . . This control equipment, instead of
being like a gyroscope, is like a radar."[5] This kind of vivid clari-
fication we find too seldom in the writing of social scientists,
many of whom seem addicted to writing in wordy and weighty
abstractions. When we do encounter such striking figures, they
stick in our memories.

4. To explain the
unknown

Another example of a metaphorical explanation is one used by
a psychologist to make a normal person comprehend the agony
felt by a person who is the victim of irrational fears. The psychologist dramatized the psychotic's fears of the most routine
things, such as sleep, by comparing the psychotic's feelings to
those a normal person would have toward sleeping in a bed located at the edge of a precipice.

5. To persuade

A final rhetorical function of metaphor is that of persuasion. By
drawing comparisons, not only can writers make you see things
more clearly, but also very often they can influence you to see
them their way. Some persuasive metaphors are obvious: "Television is a giant wasteland" or "Lake Michigan is the sewer of
Chicago." Others, however, are so subtle that readers may not realize they are being influenced. Let us take an example from
James Baldwin's *Notes of a Native Son*.

That year in New Jersey lives in my mind as though it were
the year during which, having an unsuspected predilection for
it, I first contracted some dread, chronic disease, the unfailing
symptom of which is a kind of blind fever, a pounding in the
skull, a fire in the bowels. Once this disease is contracted,
one can never be really carefree again, for the fever, without
an instant's warning, can recur at any moment. It can wreck
more important things than race relations. There is not a
Negro alive who does not have this rage in his blood—one has

[5] David Riesman, *The Lonely Crowd* (New Haven, Conn.: Yale University Press, 1950), pp.
31–32, 37.

the choice, merely, of living with it consciously or surrendering to it. As for me this fever has recurred in me, and does, and will until the day I die.[6]

Baldwin equates his resentment and anger and hatred—his rage in the blood—with a disease. Think for a minute of the characteristics of a disease. First, it infects a person without the person knowing it; one does not deliberately choose to have a disease. Thus, Baldwin cannot be held responsible for his "rage in the blood." Second, a disease, and particularly a fever (notice that he repeats the word three times) affects a person's ability to act rationally. Again, we cannot hold Baldwin responsible for what he does while he is in its grip. Third, a disease is painful ("a pounding in the skull, a fire in the bowels"), and so we feel sympathy, not anger, for the person afflicted with it. If we make the transfer of characteristics that Baldwin wants us to make, we will view some of the problems of black people from a new perspective.

In this passage, written a hundred years earlier, John Stuart Mill also used persuasive metaphors to make a plea for understanding:

> Persons of genius are more individual than any other people—less capable, consequently, of fitting themselves, without hurtful compression, into any of the small number of molds which society provides them in order to save its members the trouble of forming their own character. If from timidity they consent to be forced into one of these molds, and to let all that part of themselves which cannot expand under the pressure remain unexpanded, society will be the little better for their genius. If they are of strong character, and break their fetters, they become a mark for the society, which has not succeeded in reducing them to commonplace, to point at with solemn warning as "wild," "erratic," and the like; much as if one should complain of the Niagara River for not flowing smoothly between its banks like a Dutch canal.[7]

The imagery of people being forced into molds is worth noting here, but more interesting and subtle is the comparision of per-

[6] James Baldwin, *Notes of a Native Son* (Boston: Beacon Press, 1955), p. 94.
[7] John Stuart Mill, *On Liberty* (Indianapolis: The Bobbs-Merrill Co., Inc., 1956), pp. 77–78.

sons of genius to the Niagara River. We associate the Niagara with energy and power; we are awed by its magnificence and repelled by the thought that someone might want to tame and subdue it. By getting readers to transfer their attitudes toward the river to people of genius, Mill succeeds in persuading them that genius is not only necessary to society but also an actual asset.

You may protest that the power of metaphor is exaggerated, that you do not make all these associations when you read and therefore are not particularly affected by an author's clever comparisions. It is true, of course, that because few of us pause in our reading to make a close analysis of figurative language, many of the author's nuances escape us; nevertheless, if we accept the metaphors an author creates, we also, without really thinking about it, are inclined to accept his or her point of view. A particularly apt comparison, such as Kazin's identification of the elementary school with a factory, can be more persuasive than an elaborate explanation.

Tone

Tone conveys a writer's attitude

The *tone* of a piece of writing is the frame of mind and mood that it conveys to readers. Analogous to a speaker's tone of voice, it reveals the writer's attitude toward audience and material. It is an extension of the persona, an essential part of the image of oneself that is projected to the audience. Thus if writers want to seem confident, their words must not seem hesitant or apologetic; and if they want to seem tactful and conciliatory, their words should not sound as if they are issuing orders. For these reasons, writers who want to make a favorable impression on their audiences will carefully edit their writing and take out any words that might jar the tone they want.

A passage from Benjamin Franklin's *Autobiography* illustrates how important one's manner of speaking or writing is. As a young man, Franklin worked out a plan of self-improvement; he made a list of twelve character traits that he wanted to acquire and outlined a plan for achieving them. In writing about his program, he comments:

> My list of virtues contain'd at first but twelve; but a Quaker
> friend having kindly informed me that I was generally thought

proud; that my pride show'd itself frequently in conversation; that I was not content with being in the right when discussing any point, but was overbearing, and rather insolent, of which he convinc'd me by mentioning several instances; I determined endeavouring to cure myself, if I could, of this vice or folly among the rest, and I added *Humility* to my list. . . .

I cannot boast of much success in acquiring the *reality* of this virtue, but I had a good deal with regard to the *appearance* of it. I made it a rule to forbear all direct contradition to the sentiments of others, and all positive assertion of my own. I even forbid myself . . . the use of everyword or expression in the language that imported a fix'd opinion; such as *certainly, undoubtedly*, etc., and I adopted, instead of them, *I conceive, I apprehend*, or *I imagine* a thing to be so or so; it so *appears to me at the present*. When another asserted something that I thought an error, I deny'd myself the pleasure of contradicting him abruptly, and of showing him immediately some absurdity in his proposition; and in answering I began by observing that in certain cases or circumstance his opinion would be right, but in the present case there *appear'd* or *seem'd* to me some difference, etc. I soon found the advantage of this change in my manner; the conversations I engag'd in went on more pleasantly. The modest way in which I propos'd my opinions procur'd them a readier reception and less contradiction; I had less mortification when I was found to be in the wrong, and I more easily prevail'd with others to give up their mistakes and join me when I happened to be in the right.

And this mode, which I first put on with some violence to natural inclination, became at length easy, and so habitual to me, that perhaps for fifty years past no one has ever heard a dogmatical expression escape me. And to this habit (after my character of integrity) I think it principally owing that I had early so much weight with my fellow-citizens when I proposed new institutions, or alterations in the old, and so much influence in public councils when I became a member; for I was but a bad speaker, never eloquent, subject to much hesitation in my choice of words, hardly correct in language, and yet I generally carried my points.[8]

[8] Benjamin Franklin, *The Works of Benjamin Franklin*, ed. and comp. John Bigelow (New York: G. P. Putnam's Sons, 1904).

What Franklin changed, of course, was his tone. By doing so he induced his audience to accept him as a reasonable and moderate man. Hypocritical? Not at all. He gave up no principles and did nothing dishonest. He simply adjusted his diction and delivery to show respect rather than contempt for his audience.

There is, of course, much writing that is essentially "toneless" because the author has no purpose other than to convey information as accurately and objectively as possible. For example, in the following passage Isaac Asimov explains acceleration to the layperson:

> When something moves, it has kinetic energy. The quantity of kinetic energy possessed by a moving object depends upon its velocity and its mass. Velocity is a straightforward property that is easy to grasp. To be told something is moving at a high or low velocity brings a clear picture to mind. Mass, however, is a little more subtle.[9]

Informational writing should be toneless

You are no more aware of tone in this writing than you would be of tone of voice in a weather report or the stock market quotations. Writing that is strictly informational—and that includes newspaper reports—should have a neutral and unemotional tone; if writers allow their biases to show, they are violating their persona of the objective and impersonal observer.

Word choice also determines tone. The list of words for describing the kinds of tones or attitudes that writers can project includes almost all the words we use to talk about our emotions: angry, proud, ironic, amused, sorrowful, disgusted, indignant, pitying, bitter, amused—the list could go on for half a page. We also need to be thinking about what kinds of people the writers seem to be. What do we think we can tell about the character of writers from the way they write?

Casual Tone

Characteristics: 1. Contractions and slang

Writers achieve a casual, easygoing, conversational style and tone by using language suited to talking intimately with a few people. They make free use of contractions such as *it's, don't, wouldn't,*

[9] Isaac Asimov, "The Ultimate Speed Limit," *Saturday Review of Science,* July 8, 1972, p. 53.

2. First person pronouns
3. Simple diction
4. No distance between writer and reader

and *can't.* They may inject a few slang words and phrases such as *swinging* or *cool* and occasionally lapse into one of the minor grammatical errors that people often make in conversation: *It's me* or *It runs good.* The pronouns *I, you, we,* and *our* appear frequently, and bits of conversations are quoted directly. Most of the words are concrete rather than abstract, and the sentences are comparatively short and simple. In writing with this kind of tone there is virtually no distance between writer and reader; it is as if two or three people were chatting over a cup of coffee or a beer.

Some writing assignments may warrant your using this casual, colloquial tone, but they are apt to be few. Unless you are writing a personal narrative or doing a satiric description of a person or a group, extreme casualness is inappropriate. One problem is that advertisers have so overused the casual tone that it often sounds insincere. The fake friendliness of many ads has made it difficult for the amateur writer to write in a colloquial tone without running the risk of sounding cute, coy, and phony.

Informal Tone

The style and tone that will best meet most of your writing needs is that of informality. The term *informal tone* is about as broad and inclusive as the phrase *informal clothing,* and there are parallels between the two classifications. The notation *informal attire* on an invitation, loosely interpreted, means "Don't wear a nightgown or a swim suit, and don't wear a tuxedo or white tie and tails, but almost anything else will do." Similarly, informal tone excludes the intimate or the ceremonial, but almost any other kind of writing qualifies.

Characteristics
1. Short distance between reader and writer
2. First and second person pronouns
3. Standard usage

Writers who use an informal tone establish a comfortable distance between them and their readers, one at which speakers do not have to raise their voices or use a public address system. The writer's imaginary setting might be a classroom, a club meeting, or a gathering of colleagues at a dinner. Authors who are writing for this kind of situation probably make free use of the personal pronouns *I* and *you,* assuming that they and the audience have mutual concerns and interests. They write carefully and employ standard English usage although they might use a few contractions; if they bring in a slang term, they probably put it in quotation marks. Their vocabulary is that of educated people, and their language is a mixture of the abstract and concrete.

The advantage of choosing the informal tone is that within it you can develop topics ranging from the humorous to the serious, the simple to the complex. Furthermore, it will stretch to accommodate a wide range of emotions: sympathy, amusement, outrage, cynicism—almost any feeling a writer wants to express.

Multiple uses of informal tone

Formal Tone

The uses of formal style and tone, on the other hand, are limited, mainly because of the distance writers put between themselves and their readers. People who write in a consistently formal tone give the impression of addressing a large audience they do not know. The imaginary scene could be one in which they are addressing a crowd from a speaker's podium; the occasion would be dignified, the topic serious. In formal writing, writers use an elevated vocabulary and an abundance of abstract terms; their sentences are relatively long, probably complex. They may use the pronoun *I* but do not address their audiences as *you*. The grammar is meticulously correct, and there is no slang or use of popular idiom. The uses for formal tone are almost as limited as those for a cutaway coat; after all, you do not joke or get angry or show deep emotion when you have put yourself at such a distance that there is little sense of identity between you and your audience.

Characteristics
1. Great distance between reader and writer
2. High-level vocabulary, abstract words
3. Long sentences
4. Few first or second person pronouns

In our time, so few people speak or write formally that it is almost impossible to find examples. John F. Kennedy's inaugural address comes close to it:

Few uses for formal tone

> We dare not forget today that we are the heirs of that first revolution. Let the word go forth from this time and place, to friend and foe alike, that the torch has been passed to a new generation of Americans—born in this century, tempered by war, disciplined by a hard and bitter peace, proud of our ancient heritage—and unwilling to witness or permit the slow undoing of those human rights to which this nation has always been committed, and to which we are committed today at home and around the world.

The balanced and complex sentence structure, the abstract language, and the lofty sentiments expressed qualify the passage as formal writing, although Kennedy does not seem completely remote from his audience.

In earlier, less hurried times, there was an abundance of formal writing. You will encounter it now mainly in reading nineteenth-century writers like Matthew Arnold or John Stuart Mill or in our own Federalist papers. It can be eloquent and elegant, but neither statesmen nor the public seem any longer to have the temperament or the patience for it.

Although students should learn to read formal writing and to appreciate its dignity, they should avoid it in their own writing. On the few occasions when your topic might seem weighty and lofty enough to call for it, it would be better to stay with serious informal writing. If not handled with great skill, formal writing can be dull, pretentious, and difficult to follow. At its worst, it degenerates into jargon.

Keeping your audience in mind will help you decide on tone

If you can manage to keep the elements of rhetoric constantly in mind as you write, and always be aware of how you want to come across to your audience, you should not have too much trouble setting and maintaining the right tone for your rhetorical purpose. Try simply to observe the rules dictated by ordinary good sense. One rule is to avoid accusations and name calling that will mark you as ill-tempered and vindictive. Another is to eliminate from your writing the standard kinds of "nice" sentiments or routine moralistic comments that are so conventional that they strike the reader as trivial and superfluous. A third is to avoid heavy-handed attempts to be witty or sarcastic.

Keep your tone consistent and appropriate

Finally, remember that your tone should be consistent; not serious in one part of the paper and casual or colloquial in another. And do try to strike a tone that is appropriate to your topic. Comparatively minor issues, such as campus parking problems or the troubles of the baseball team, do not warrant the same seriousness of tone as do crucial ones, like poverty programs or inadequate psychiatric facilities in your city. Similarly, you should avoid an emotional or light tone when the occasion calls for straightforward writing, as a report, petition, or grant proposal does. In those cases your best approach is that of sincerity and candor.

Irony

One particular kind of tone deserves special attention both because one encounters it so often in newspaper features and mag-

Writers use irony to
point out
inconsistencies

azine articles and because it causes inexperienced readers so
many problems. That variation is *irony*, a rhetorical device that
writers use frequently to point out the discrepancy between the
way things are and the way they think they ought to be; through
irony one can emphasize the inconsistencies between word and
deed, between the ideal and the real, and between myth and
fact.

Ironic writers, though frequently social critics, try to avoid any
show of emotion. They attack indirectly, seeming to maintain distance and detachment from the target of criticism. Probably the
most famous example of this kind of writing is Jonathan Swift's
"A Modest Proposal," in which the author makes the apparently
calm and objective suggestion that the Irish solve their problems
of starvation, poverty, and overpopulation by allowing the poor to
sell their babies for food. Although Swift was actually very emotional about the Irish crisis, he drew more attention by pretending
to be callous than he would have by venting his anger openly.

Irony is often
difficult to spot

This kind of straight-faced "put-on" by a writer may sometimes confuse readers because many people are inclined to assume that any article that appears in a newspaper, magazine, or
book of essays is serious. An article that deals ironically with a
major political or social issue is especially apt to be misjudged because we approach it expecting a straightforward discussion. Occasionally, we realize immediately that a writer is being heavily
sarcastic, saying precisely the opposite of what is meant. We may,
however, fail to grasp the purpose of a writer who slips in an occasional ironic phrase, or we may miss the subtle innuendoes of
a writer who is writing tongue in cheek. Unfortunately, readers
who are consistently insensitive to irony not only deprive themselves of much pleasure in reading but also run the risk of being
thought naive.

Techniques of irony
1. Exaggeration

An ability to recognize irony cannot be developed overnight
with only the help of five easy rules for recognizing irony; even
the practiced and perceptive reader occasionally has to ask, "Is
this writer really serious, or is this a joke?" Nevertheless, authors
writing in an ironic tone employ certain techniques often enough
for us to come up with some guidelines. One such device is *exaggeration*. A short example from Tom Wolfe, a consistent critic of
pretentiousness, should make the point. He is describing the San
Francisco city hall:

The lobby is officially known as the great central court and it's like some Central American opera house, marble, arches, domes, acanthus leaves and Indian sandstone, quirks and galleries, and gilt filigrees, like Bourbon Louis curlicues of gold in every corner, along every molding, every flute, every cuspy, every waterleaf and cartouche, a veritable angels' choir of gold . . . and all kept polished as if the commemoration of the Generalissimo's birthday . . . and busts of great and glorious mayors of San Francisco, perched on top of pedestals in their business suits with their bald marble skulls reflecting the lacy gold of the place.[10]

2. Understatement

A very different kind of ironic technique is *drastic understatement.* Jonathan Swift was also responsible for one of the classics of that kind when he said, "Last week I saw a woman flayed [skinned], and you will hardly believe how much it altered her person for the worse." Mark Twain often expressed his deep loathing for slavery and slave holders by the same method, which shocks the reader into awareness by treating abuses in an apparently indifferent manner. Another of Twain's favorite ironic techniques was the *unexpected joining of opposites.* For example, in his

3. Unexpected joining of opposites

book *A Connecticut Yankee in King Arthur's Court* he has a scene in which Queen Morgan le Fay is interrupted in her torturing and killing of prisoners by the call to prayers. The narrator's comment is, "I will say this much for the nobility: that, tyrannical, murderous, rapacious, and morally rotten as they were, they were deeply and enthusiastically religious."

4. Irreverent twist

Catching the reader's attention by emphasizing the unexpected and incongruous is also the basis of an ironic device called the *irreverent twist* or *deflating anticlimax.* Here the writer begins with what promises to be a routine comment, then suddenly changes direction. The comedian Dick Gregory employed this technique when he remarked that he sat in at a lunch counter for a week during the civil rights demonstrations, and when they finally agreed to serve him, there wasn't anything on the menu that he liked. And one of the most famous examples appears in Mark

[10] Tom Wolfe, *Radical Chic and Mau-mauing the Flak Catchers* (New York: Bantam Books, Inc., 1971); p. 176.

Twain's *Puddinhead Wilson's Calendar:* "The holy passion of Friendship is of so sweet and steady a nature that it will last through a whole lifetime, if not asked to lend money."

Finally, there is the standard ironic device of flatly saying the opposite of what is actually meant. When John Stuart Mill talks about people being upset by "dissentients afflicted with the malady of thought," he certainly does not mean that thought is an illness or an affliction; by inversion, he is criticizing those who do not think. When a magazine refers to a man's mistress as his "great and good friend" or to a congressperson who has been convicted of fraud as "that distinguished representative of the people," the editors expect the reader to infer their real meaning. Used sparingly, this kind of irony is effective, but the writer who overdoes it runs the risk of letting the criticism deteriorate into heavy-handed sarcasm.

Suggestions for using irony

Although few of us will ever be able to handle irony with the deft touch of Tom Wolfe or Mark Twain, the technique is certainly suitable for many student writers. Though you may not want to write a full-length satire, a touch of irony here and there can make your writing more interesting to both you and your audience. For example, some students have used the technique to highlight the differences between the way their home town really looks and the way it is portrayed in a chamber-of-commerce brochure. You could use the same method to compare the promises made by the coach who wants to recruit athletes and the reality those athletes encounter on campus. And straight-faced understatement might give you a new approach to writing about chronic and much-discussed problems like traffic congestion, air pollution, or sex discrimination. The advantage of treating such topics ironically is that you can make your points without seeming to preach. If, however, you think that irony is not your style, you will probably do better to avoid it. If you are willing to take a risk, though, it can be fun.

Exercises on Connotation

1. Analyze the connotations of the terms in each of these groups. Are the words negative, positive, or neutral?

club woman, joiner, civic leader

playboy, hedonist, good-time Charlie

moralistic, straight-laced, ethical

do-gooder, crusader, volunteer worker

athlete, sportsman, jock

pious, sanctimonious, devout

nonconformist, individualist, eccentric

reactionary, conservative, prudent

2. What associations do you think automobile manufacturers wanted to establish when they chose these names for their cars?

Cougar

Imperial

Skylark

Toronado

Cutlass

Tempest

Mustang

Jaguar

Charger

Firebird

3. What stereotypes do these labels evoke?

red neck

cowboy

freak

quack

brass hat

egghead

bleeding heart

banker

frat rat

homemaker

bureaucrat

women's libber

4. Rewrite the following paragraph, first with unfavorable connotation, then with favorable connotation. Which rewriting do you find easier to do? Why?

In 1970 the President's Commission on Obscenity and Pornography concluded that the sale and distribution of pornographic material to adults in the United States should

not be restricted. The report asserts that no one has
established a connection between exposure to pornography
and sexual offenses, that legislation to ban pornography is
ambiguous, unenforceable, and potentially repressive, and
that a nationwide sex education program would do more to
solve sex-related problems than the banning of pornography
would.

5. Identify the connotative words in the following passage, then
   rewrite the passage without them. Is the meaning of the rewritten passage substantially different from the original?

   "McDonald's Hamburger Stand is right in your
   neighborhood," says the company's annual report. It is no
   idle boast, for the firm has some 3,000 stores located almost
   everywhere. This $1.5 billion giant has a greater impact than
   merely intruding into America's diverse neighborhoods with
   its neon uniformity and trash-strewn presence. Its unerring
   sameness alters our perception of food. Mimi Sheraton,
   writing for *New York* magazine, reported that the fish caught
   for McDonald's Filet O'Fish sandwiches is treated on factory
   ships to stay white and be odorless and tasteless. It is then
   frozen and shipped to a central plant, where it is cut into
   shape, thawed, breaded, refrozen, and shipped to golden
   arches throughout the world. . . .

   The McDonald's standard is conformity. Their buildings
   look the same, their food tastes the same, their people act
   the same. They even operate a training center in Illinois,
   called Hamburger University, to make sure that their
   management and hamburgers in Toledo *are* the same as those
   in Phoenix. It is that conformity that they are selling—
   wherever you are, you can be sure that a meal at McDonald's
   will be uniformly clean. There is not much chance of your
   getting food poisoning at these places, but neither will you
   get excited.[11]

---

[11] Jim Hightower, *Eat Your Heart Out* (New York: Vintage Books, 1975), pp. 291–292.

Suggested Writing Assignments

Theme 1

Purpose To have you evaluate the effects that a writer can achieve through the use of connotation.

Procedure Read carefully the following passage by Malcolm X and decide what his specific persuasive purposes are, both positive and negative. Jot these down as part of your prewriting process. Then, go through the passage and underline the connotative words.

Begin your paper with a short paragraph in which you summarize the persuasive purpose in your words. Do not try to include all the points; mainly, just answer the question "What does Malcolm X want the reader to believe after he reads this passage?" Then, using as many paragraphs as you need, analyze the way in which Malcolm X has used connotation to achieve his purpose. Illustrate your analysis with specific examples from the passage and show *how* the connotative words and phrases work.

Conclude your paper by evaluating the effect of the passage on a reasonably well informed and educated audience. Review the standards for proper use of connotation given in the text (page 233 before you do your evaluation, and support your opinion with concrete reasons for thinking the passage is or is not effective.

Be careful to avoid the two most common mistakes in rhetorical analysis. Do not make your theme primarily a summary of the passage, and do not either argue or agree with the author's ideas.

Not even in the *Bible* is there such a crime! God in His wrath struck down with *fire* the perpetrators of *lesser* crimes! *One hundred million* of us black people! Your grandparents! Mine! *Murdered* by this white man. To get fifteen million of us here to make us his slaves, on the way he murdered one hundred million! I wish it was possible for me to show you the sea bottom in those days—the black bodies, the blood, the bones broken by boots and clubs! The pregnant black women who were thrown overboard if they got too sick! Thrown overboard to the sharks that had learned that following the slave ships was the way to grow fat!

Why the white man's raping of the black race's women began right on those slave ships! The blue-eyed devil could not even wait until he got them here! Why, brothers and sisters, civilized mankind has never known such an orgy of greed and lust and murder.[12]

Theme 2

Purpose To make you aware of the ways in which critics of contemporary culture use connotation as a tool.

Procedure Begin with a short paragraph in which you summarize the author's main purpose in the passage; that is, answer the question "What specific attitude does Kroll want the reader to have toward the particular type of movies and movie stars he is writing about?" Then discuss, giving examples, the connotative words and phrases he uses to achieve his purpose. Naturally, you cannot include them all; pick out those which seem the strongest to you and discuss *how* they work.

Conclude by stating what you think the rhetorical effect of the passage would be on a fairly intelligent and perceptive reader, and support your evaluation with reasons. Be specific in your conclusions; such comments as "The article is interesting to read" and "He holds the reader's attention" do not constitute specific judgments.

Again, be sure to avoid the two common errors in rhetorical analysis. Do not simply summarize the content of the passage, and do not waste your time either agreeing or disagreeing with Kroll's opinion.

Erb-man

Together, Clint Eastwood, Burt Reynolds, and Charles Bronson make almost enough money to relieve the states of the burden of welfare. And in some ways they're lucky not to be on it. In a better world, guys like this were consigned to B

---

[12] Malcolm X and Alex Haley, *The Autobiography of Malcolm X* (New York: Grove Press, Inc., 1964), p. 202. Reprinted by permission of Grove Press, Inc. Copyright © 1964 by Alex Haley and Malcolm X. Copyright © 1965 by Alex Haley and Betty Shabazz.

movies, a useful metaphysical category for the cheaper dreams of modern Western man. That category has been taken over largely by television, which by routinizing our cheap dreams has deprived them of their ceremoniousness and cheesy glory. What we have now are B movies disguised as A movies. . . .

The real B movie hero was someone like Chester Morris or Richard Dix, types who lacked the size and splendor of the Cagneys or Coopers but had a compact energy and appeal of their own. There was an honesty and sincerity about them that helped to make the B movie a kind of industrialized folk art. Even a figure like Jeff Chandler, who was a walking collage of big-star giblets—the swaying walk of Wayne, the sexy smirk of Gable, the clenched larynx of Douglas—had a kind of hand-me-down charm. But ERB—Eastwood, Reynolds and Bronson—are dispiriting signs of the confusion in contemporary masculinity.

Erb-man is cool. In matters of love and sex his passivity is positively catatonic. Reynolds's Gator McCluskey, the Robin Hood moonshiner, is shocked by the brothel girls who pop pills and do dirty things with men, and Lauren Hutton has to seduce him. . . .Bronson's St. Ives, crime novelist and soldier of fortune, needs his beauty sleep and has to be seduced by Jacqueline Bisset. . . .Eastwood's Josey Wales, the Missouri sodbuster who becomes a confederate guerrilla after Union irregulars massacre his family, briefly eyes an Indian wench, but while he ponders, a septuagenarian redskin beats him to the punch.

. . . Only Reynolds, the former stunt man, has any real zest for action. . . . Bronson and Eastwood specialize in potential energy, only with Bronson the explosion never really comes, just poofs of violence, a gunshot here and a groin-kick there. Eastwood uses his rangy body as a machine to detonate firearms, above which he grimaces with ferocious reluctance.

In fact, indecisive violence is the hallmark of Erb-man. Gator is reluctantly dragged from his swampy Arcadia . . . St. Ives would rather hide with his unfinished novel under the sheets in his cheap Los Angeles hotel room than to fight; Josey Wales has been pulled from his plow by the lawlessness of a dislocated nation. Erbism is an oddly abashed form of machismo, a far cry from the seedy but stern moral codes of

Sam Spade, Philip Marlowe, or Wyatt Earp. With Erb-man the icky icons of advertising have taken over the magic image of the male star. Reynolds's face has a weird pasted-on look; he's become a living centerfold with cutout clothes. Bronson's marinated mustached mug and soberly sharp suits reflect the Mad Ave. Man who wants to be Genghis Khan after hours. Eastwood, whose facial apertures open to the minimum for speech and vision, is the Marlboro man with chaps.[13]

Exercises on Metaphor

1. Analyze the persuasive purpose of the following metaphors:

   a. "Television is the opiate of the white middle classes and the agent provocateur of the black masses" [John Hersey, *The Algiers Motel Incident*].

   b. "The socialists and the Communists strive with all their might to strap humanity to an operating table, and the truth is now abroad that these social surgeons are maniacal quacks who would operate on us with an ax" [Eric Hoffer, "No Redemption via Socialism"].

   c. "And if a beachhead of cooperation may push back the jungles of suspicion, let both sides join in creating a new endeavor" [John F. Kennedy's inaugural address].

2. Identify the submerged metaphors in the following sentences:

   a. The lobbyists carefully cultivate members of Congress with favors and reap their rewards when the votes are taken.

   b. Trapped in a white-dominated world, blacks have learned to live with trouble.

   c. The methods of psychoanalysis remain shrouded in half truths.

   d. Professionals steeped in jargon are bound to ooze it out in their writing.

   e. Contemporary people are free, but often rudderless.

[13] Jack Kroll, "Erb-man," *Newsweek*, September 13, 1976, p. 89. Copyright 1976 by Newsweek, Inc. All rights reserved. Reprinted by permission.

f. Office holders are besieged by requests for special favors.

g. He is a hard-boiled character.

h. Marxism carries the seeds of its own destruction.

i. One of the main planks of their platform is a pledge to close tax loopholes.

j. The program has too many strings attached to it.

3. Study the front-page stories and the editorials in your daily newspaper to find examples of metaphorical language. Which ones seem to be chosen deliberately, and which are little more than clichés? In your opinion, do those which appear to be chosen. deliberately help the writer's persuasive purpose? How?

4. Write out the meaning suggested by each of the following allusions. For example, you might explain the phrase "the Midas touch" as the ability to make money from any business venture. If necessary, consult an unabridged dictionary or a desk encyclopedia.

Procrustean bed	Pyrrhic victory
Achilles' heel	Gordian knot
Socratic method	Rabelaisian humor
Machiavellian tactics	Panglossian optimism

5. Think of ways in which these contemporary references could be used as allusions in your writing.

Ralph Nader	Disneyland
Hugh Hefner	Earl Campbell
Gloria Steinem	Charlie Brown

Suggested Writing Assignment

Theme

Purpose To sharpen your awareness of the rhetorical function of figurative language by having you do a careful analysis and evaluation of an extended metaphor.

Procedure Read the following passage carefully at least twice. Decide what the author's persuasive purpose is and what associations he wants his reader to draw from the extended metaphor he creates. Begin your paper with a short paragraph that states specifically the main idea that Bellamy is trying to convey to his audience. Then, using as many paragraphs as you need, analyze the important parts of the metaphor and show how they work to achieve the desired effects. Conclude your theme with a short evaluation of the author's rhetoric: does he, through the use of his figurative language, succeed in convincing his reader of his point of view? why or why not?

By way of attempting to give the reader some general impression of the way people lived together in those days, and especially of the relations of the rich and poor to one another, perhaps I cannot do better than to compare society as it then was to a prodigious coach which the masses of humanity were harnessed to and dragged toilsomely along a very hilly and sandy road. The driver was hunger and permitted no lagging, though the pace was necessarily very slow. Despite the difficulties of drawing the coach at all along so hard a road, the top was covered with passengers who never got down, even at the steepest ascents. These seats on top were very breezy and comfortable. Well up out of the dust, their occupants could enjoy the scenery at their leisure, or critically discuss the merits of the straining team. Naturally such places were in great demand and the competition for them was keen, everyone seeking as the first end in life to secure a seat on the coach for himself and to leave it to his child after him. By the rule of the coach a man could leave his seat to whom he wished, but on the other hand there were so many accidents by which it might at any time be lost. For all that they were so easy, the seats were very insecure, and at every sudden jolt of the coach persons were slipping out of them and falling to the ground, where they were instantly compelled to take hold of the rope and help to drag the coach on which they had before ridden so pleasantly.

. . . had they no compassion for fellow beings from whom fortune alone distinguished them? Oh, yes, commiseration was frequently expressed by those who rode for those who had to pull the coach, especially when the vehicle came to a bad place in the road, or to a particularly steep hill. . . . At such times the passengers would call down encouragingly to the toilers of the rope, exhorting them to patience, and holding out hopes of possible compensation in another world for the hardness of their lot, while others contributed to buy salves and liniments for the crippled and injured. It was agreed that it was a great pity that the coach should be so hard to pull, and there was a sense of general relief when the specially bad piece of road was gotten over. This relief was not, indeed, wholly on account of the team, for there was always some danger at these bad places of a general overturn in which all would lose their seats.[14]

Exercises on Tone

1. Analyze the tone of the following passages. Ask yourself these questions: What reactions do the authors seek to evoke from their audience? How do the authors present themselves? What word or words describe the tone? What specific elements in the passages contribute to that tone?

   a. "Main Street is the climax of civilization. That this Ford car might stand in front of the Bon Ton Store, Hannibal invaded Rome and Erasmus wrote in Oxford cloisters. What Ole Jenson the grocer says to Ezra Stowbody the banker is the new law for London, Prague, and the unprofitable isles of the sea; whatsoever Ezra does not know and sanction, that thing is heresy, worthless for knowing and wicked to consider.

   "Our railway station is the final aspiration of architecture. Sam Clark's annual hardware turnover is the envy of the four counties which constitute God's Country. In the sensitive art of the Rosebud Movie Palace there is a Message, and humor strictly moral.

   "Such is our comfortable tradition and sure faith. Would he not betray himself an alien cynic who should otherwise portray Main Street, or distress the citizens by speculating whether there may not be other faiths?"[15]

[14] Edward Bellamy, *Looking Backward* (Boston: Houghton Mifflin Company, 1966; originally published in 1888), pp. 6–8.
[15] Sinclair Lewis, *Main Street* (New York: Harcourt, Brace & World, 1920), preface.

b. "Whether it's polyester, boutiques, or what-have-you, for syrupy excursions into the never-never land of domestic fantasy you cannot beat the manufacturers of woman's products. You get men going mad with lust over somebody's bra, people being swept off piano stools, emaciated women standing precariously on six-inch pedestals with pasty-faced homosexual mannequins mooning at them from the base, and so on in an endless phantasmagoria. The terrible thing is, and this in answer to those who wonder who pays any attention to advertising, that no matter how much or to what extent Madison Avenue is criticized, satirized, and generally taken over the coals, they keep right at it; obviously it works, and if the advertisers are made to cry because nobody likes them, they must, like Liberace, cry all the way to the bank."[16]

2. Bring to class two advertisements with contrasting tone. Some pairs of magazines that could be useful are *Saturday Review* and *Seventeen*, *Playboy* and *Ebony*, *Cosmopolitan* and *Reader's Digest*, or *Psychology Today* and *Ladies' Home Journal*.

3. Analyze the tone of this student paper. What elements in the paper create the tone?

American Business Interests Kill Cupid

What has America made of Valentine's Day? Business Profits. Valentine's Day is defined as one day in which a sweetheart is "chosen or complimented." Well, a compliment is one thing, but an inundation of candies, cards, and carnations is something else! American business interests have brainwashed us into feeling obligated to buy our friends', family's, and lovers' love annually on February 14th with such products as candy, greeting cards, and flowers. Instead of a day complimenting our loved ones, Valentine's Day has become a profit-making occasion for certain money-hungry American business interests.

Red Hots. Sugar Hearts. Heart-shaped boxes of chocolate.

---

[16] Edith de Rham, *The Love Fraud* (New York: Pegasus, a Division of Western Publishing Company, 1965), pp. 71–72.

Who needs a bunch of red-mouthed Americans running around? And what about those silly little sugar hearts you buy in little boxes? Have you ever read the sayings on them? "Hot Shot." "O.U. Kid." "Red Hot Mama." These outdated slogans are written on candies that don't even taste that good. And, aah, the infamous heart-shaped boxes of chocolate by Whitman's, Pangburns, and Russell Stover, to name a few of the designer candy companies. These are the epitome of the valentine cliches. So many thousands of them are packaged each year, they can hardly be considered a special compliment. And did you ever wonder how long the chocolates have been sitting in those pink and red-cellophaned parcels? Since we know how overweight America is, it would only do us good to forego all of this Valentine candy.

Rack after rack of cards, cards, and more cards. The greeting card industry further exemplifies how American business interests have blown Valentine's Day way out of proportion. You know that Hallmark and the others have stretched the limit when they begin to print Valentine's cards for moms, dads, sisters, brothers, and Toto, too. Sure a card complimenting your sweetheart is appropriate, but a "Grandma and Grandpa, Be My Valentine card" is a little ridiculous.

Carnations. Red roses. The American flower industry definitely makes a killing on February 14th each year. That golden man must really wear out his little wings making all those deliveries. And poor (literally) boyfriends. They either buy their sweethearts a dozen long-stemmed red roses or their name is mud. And if it's not enough that the guys feel obligated to buy flowers in the first place, the florists also hike up their prices in honor of this one-day occasion. Thus, Valentine's Day is not only a day in which we are made to feel coerced and guilty by American business interests, it is also a giant rip-off!

Candy, cards, carnations. All have been used by American business interests to make Valentine's Day one of the most commercial holidays. Instead of expressing our love and affection 365 days a year, we have been taught that February 14th is *the* day set aside each year to show our love with material, store-bought goods. Romanticists unite. Let us kill the commercial features of Valentine's Day and enable Cupid to live!

Elizabeth Ann Black

Suggested Writing Assignments

Theme I

Purpose To give you practice in writing a short talk and establishing a tone that will be effective for the particular audience.

Procedure Imagine that you have been asked to come back to the homecoming assembly in your small high school and give a talk entitled "Things I Wish I Had Known Before I Went to College." The invitation makes you nervous, of course, but you are willing to do it because you think that your high school promotes some attitudes that can cause a college freshman problems. Remember that your real audience is the students although it may be that the teachers need enlightenment too. The first step in your prewriting should be to narrow your topic to a manageable size by choosing some particular area in which false ideas are common. Possibilities could be grading standards, study habits, clothes, relative importance of athletics and other activities, or anything else you have found caused you problems. Decide on the main points you want to make and what examples you will use to illustrate them. Your tone could be serious, humorous, ironic, or, if you think the situation warrants it, even bitter, but decide ahead of time what tone you think will best suit your purpose and try to be consistent throughout your paper.

Theme 2

Purpose To give you practice in developing a method and tone that could be useful for writing a paper in sociology, government, history or a general studies course.

Procedure One of the rhetorical techniques used by social critics who want to illustrate the need for change is to show the difference between commonly held beliefs, or conventional wisdom, and the actual situation. Choose one of the beliefs listed below and refute it using the comparison/contrast method; that is, give an example or examples that illustrate the myth and one that illustrates the reality as you see it. Remember that you should be as specific as possible; a few concrete cases or situations are more impressive than generalities. Again, be sure to narrow your topic to a manageable size.

Topics
a. Thrift is a trait that is highly valued in our culture.
b. Anyone who has ability and persistence can go to college.
c. You can achieve anything you set your mind to if you work hard enough.
d. A good education is essential to success in our society.
e. Choose a similar topic suggested to you by your own experience. (It would be prudent to check it out with your instructor ahead of time.)

9

Modes of Argument

Arguments are beliefs supported by reason

In this text, the term *argument* does not necessarily mean a controversial exchange of opinions or an attempt to convince someone that he or she is wrong. It is used in a much broader sense to mean "a unit of discourse in which beliefs are supported by reasons."[1] By this definition, arguments include expository as well as persuasive prose, and any discussion or persuasion that seeks to enlighten or instruct can legitimately be called an argument.

The starting point of any argument is an assertion, which states the belief, position, or point of view that the arguer is going to expand and support. As pointed out in Chapter 6, the proposition that you undertake to support should be a moderate one, limited by reasonable qualifications that keep you from committing yourself to more than you can handle. For when you state the proposition, you take on an obligation to develop that proposition by rational and logical methods. You have said, in effect, "Here is what I believe and I shall show why I believe it." You have made a commitment and you are responsible for following it up with supporting arguments. The purpose of this chapter is to help you discover where and how to find arguments to meet your commitment.[2]

The Argument from Definition

Writers who want to argue intelligently and effectively must learn how to construct good definitions because often the first thing readers demand of a writer is that he or she explain key terms and define the issues to be discussed. And if readers don't understand those definitions, they are likely to quit in disgust. Thus the competent writer should understand what kinds of definitions he or

[1] Lionel Ruby, *The Art of Making Sense* (Philadelphia: J. B. Lippincott Company, 1954), p. 104. Reprinted by permission of Harper and Row Publishers, Inc.

[2] In his *Rhetoric*, Aristotle described several different kinds of arguments and called them "the topics," a term he derived from the Greek word *topoi* meaning "places or regions." His intent was to show that there are specific areas of experience or knowledge in which people can find arguments to support their assertions. Thus, the term *rhetorical topics* designates various kinds of arguments. Since we are accustomed, however, to using the word *topic* in other contexts, the modes of argument will be discussed here in terms that are simply descriptive.

she can use, which kind works best for specific situations, and how one goes about constructing them.

Traditionally, definitions fall into three categories: logical definitions, figurative definitions, and extended definitions.

Categories of Definitions

Logical definition sets precise limits to a word

Logical definition Logical definition works by describing the thing to be defined briefly, explicitly, and objectively. For example, "A slave is a person who belongs to another"; "A book is a collection of printed pages bound together"; "Education is the training of the mind." Introducing a logical definition that sets precise limits to a word is often helpful in avoiding confusion in expository writing. For instance, in writing about the problems of narcotics, you would need to know the exact definition of *narcotic*. You look in the dictionary and find it defined as a drug that, taken moderately, dulls the senses, relieves pain, and induces profound sleep but that in excessive doses causes stupor, coma, or convulsions. Given these specifics, you would not be justified in calling tobacco a narcotic, but you might well classify alcohol as one. Similarly, you should know precisely what terms such as *capital crime* and *corporal punishment* mean when you use them in a paper.

Standards:

1. Reversible

2. Not circular

Usually you will be able to find a clear logical definition by going to the dictionary, but it is well to remember that logical definitions must meet two standards. First, they must be reversible; that is, the order of the word being defined and its definition can be reversed without affecting the meaning. Second, they must not be circular. A reversible definition of *narcotic* is: "a drug that dulls the senses, produces sleep, and with prolonged use becomes addictive."[3] It would not, however, be reversible if it defined *narcotic* as "anything that induces sleep." That description could fit an anesthetic, warm milk, or even a dull teacher. The circular definition that describes a narcotic as something that induces narcosis has little value because it simply repeats the key word in another form. Not quite so obvious but equally circular is a defi-

[3] © 1981 by Houghton Mifflin Company. Reprinted by permission of *The American Heritage Dictionary of the English Language.*

nition that defines feminine traits as characteristics typical of women.

Figurative definition defines through metaphor

Figurative definition Figurative definitions are those that define by using a figure of speech, principally metaphor. A figurative definition may be striking and colorful, but because its purpose is usually to persuade rather than to clarify, it should not be used when you are honestly trying to explain or identify. Here are some famous figurative definitions.

> Religion is the opiate of the people [Karl Marx].
>
> A cauliflower is only a cabbage with a college education [Mark Twain].
>
> War is hell [General Sherman].
>
> Man is but a reed, the weakest in nature, but he is a thinking reed [Pascal].

Notice that the real purpose of all these definitions is to express an opinion. Used as a nonlogical rhetorical device, the figurative definition may be effective, but it is an inadequate reply to someone who asks you to define your terms.

Extended definition An extended definition is, in a sense, an expanded logical definition that gives more information or details about a particular term or phrase. It can range in length from a paragraph to an entire essay or even a whole book. A literary handbook, for example, could define *satire* in one paragraph, but a teacher giving a course in satirical literature might take two or three lectures and many examples to give an adequate definition.

Purpose of extended definition is often persuasive

Frequently writers who are making extended definitions are trying to persuade as well as enlighten. By writing at length to show how they would define a term, they are really trying to convince their audience to share their beliefs. So Cardinal Newman wrote *The Idea of a University* to promote his beliefs about education, Thoreau wrote *Walden* to promote the simple life, and Sartre wrote *Existentialism and Human Emotions* to promote the philosophy of existentialism. And many writers have defined their ideal society in books: Plato's *Republic*, More's *Utopia*, and Skinner's *Walden II* are famous examples of such utopian literature.

How to Define

Writers define by using a variety of techniques, singly or in combination. The most common ones are these attributing characteristics, analyzing or enumerating parts, comparing and contrasting, giving examples, and stating functions. These categories overlap, or even merge occasionally, but it does not matter if the categories cannot always be identified distinctly. Knowing how a process works is more important than giving it exactly the right name.

Give distinctive characteristics

Attributing characteristics Defining by attributing characteristics requires that you concentrate on characteristics distinctive to the thing being defined. For example, if you were listing the characteristics of democracy, it would not be sufficient to say that in a democracy the rulers have the support of the majority of the people and are responsive to their will, because other kinds of government, monarchies or dictatorships, can also have those characteristics. The necessary and distinguishing characteristic of a democracy is that the rulers are chosen by the people in free and regular elections.

Similarly, if you were giving the defining characteristics of alcoholics, you would have to do more than say that they are people who drink too much. Alcoholics have other distinctive characteristics, such as drinking secretly and drinking compulsively. Notice that in the following passage Susan Sontag defines woman (or the role that she thinks our culture has assigned women) by listing what she identifies as uniquely feminine characteristics:

> To be a woman is to be an actress. Being feminine is a kind of theater, with its appropriate costumes, decor, lighting, and stylized gestures. From early childhood on, girls are trained to care in a pathologically exaggerated way about their appearance and are profoundly mutilated (to the extent of being unfitted for first-class adulthood) by the extent of the stress put on presenting themselves as physically attractive objects. Women look in the mirror more frequently than men do. It is, virtually, their duty to look at themselves—to look often. Indeed, a woman who is not narcissistic is considered unfeminine. And a woman who spends literally *most* of her time caring for, and making purchases to flatter, her physical

appearance is not regarded in this society as what she is: a kind of moral idiot.[4]

Listing important qualities

Analyzing parts Defining by analysis or enumeration of parts is a similar device in that it lists features that are peculiar to and typical of the thing being defined. For example, the definition of *jargon* on page 206 gives a list of the various writing defects that typically appear in jargon. A definition of *beef stroganoff* would list the ingredients: strips of beef, onions, mushrooms, beef bouillon, and sour cream. A person who is defining the comparatively new term *inner city* needs to specify the particular conditions that make an area qualify for that term. Some of them are traffic congestion, dilapidated housing units, a comparatively high rate of unemployment, a relatively high proportion of residents with low income or on welfare, substandard schools, few recreation areas, and inadequate public services such as garbage collection and maintenance of streets.

In the following passage an author defines by analyzing the component parts of the topic:

Unscathed by women's liberation, couples "living in sin," gay liberation, recession and inflation, social change or sexual revolution, the American way with weddings remains a constant—with the expense of it CONSTANTLY on the increase. . . .

For many families (his and hers combined), that means engraved invitations and announcements; personal stationery for the bride; wedding attire and personal trousseau for the bride, wedding attire for the bridegroom and parents; engagement and wedding photographs; aisle carpet and canopy; banks (literally and figuratively) of flowers for the church and reception; flowers for the mothers; bride's bouquet and going-away corsage; bouquets, a luncheon and gifts for bridesmaids; boutonnieres for the men in the wedding and bachelor dinner and gifts for the ushers and best man; organ

---

[4] Susan Sontag, "The Double Standard of Aging," *Saturday Review of the Society*, October 1972, p. 34. Copyright © by Saturday Review, Inc. First appeared in *Saturday Review of the Society*, October 1972. Used with permission.

music and orchestras; ornate cakes, coffee, nuts and mints; seated dinners, receiving lines, champagne toasts and bartenders; garters and bride's books; clergymen, rented halls, clubs or hotel accommodations; engagement and wedding rings; medical examinations and/or blood tests; accommodations for out-of-town attendants; marriage license and honeymoon.[5]

Showing likenesses and differences

Comparing and contrasting One of the most popular defining techniques is that of comparison and contrast. For example, you can define good writing by comparing it with bad writing. Good writing is clear, vigorous, precise, and original; bad writing is confusing, dull vague, and hackneyed. The comparison/contrast technique is particularly useful in writing extended definitions of concepts or beliefs, for example, Riesman's "inner-direction" and "other-direction" mentioned on page 241; the literary movements of "realism" and "romanticism"; the notions of what is "masculine" and what is "feminine."

The device can also be useful for defining personalities. For example:

Tom Heggen and Ross Lockridge were similar in that neither had any previous notoriety, and they came from obscure, middle-class, Midwest backgrounds. Yet as men they could not have been more different.

Ross was an oak of prudence and industry. He rarely drank and he never smoked. He excelled at everything he did. He had married his hometown sweetheart, was proudly faithful to her and produced four fine children. After a sampling of success on both coasts he had gone home to the Indiana of his parents and childhood friends.

Tom Heggen had a taste for low life. He had been divorced, had no children and shared bachelor quarters with an ex-actor and screenwriter, Dorothy Parker's estranged husband, Alan Campbell. Tom was a drinker and a pill addict. He turned up regularly at the fashionable restaurant

---

[5] Jane Ulrich, "I now pronounce you married and bankrupt," *Austin (Texas) American-Statesman*, January 9, 1977, p. D1.

"21," usually bringing along a new girl, a dancer or an actress.[6]

Dick Reavis defines two kinds of motorcycles and the people who ride them in "You Are What You Ride," an extended comparison/contrast essay in the Samples for Rhetorical Analysis section of the Appendix (p. 460).

Showing specific examples

Giving examples Probably the simplest and most concrete way to define is by giving examples. At the most elementary level, this technique amounts to pointing to an object that a word stands for; for instance, the easiest way for an architect to define a mansard roof would be to show you one. In writing, however, we usually use examples to supplement and expand other kinds of definitions. If you were defining *antiutopian writing,* you would probably first specify that in this kind of literature authors depict planned and controlled societies that they want readers to reject. To support and expand the definition, you could then give Aldous Huxley's *Brave New World* and George Orwell's *1984* as examples of this kind of writing. Such examples are often invaluable in clarifying a definition. The term *natural sciences,* for example, can be defined as studies that deal with physical matter and phenomena. This definition seems vague, but your reader will understand the meaning immediately if you list physics, chemistry, biology, and geology as natural sciences. Defining with examples is one of the chief ways in which you can put into practice a cardinal rule of explanation: whenever possible, refer to the concrete and familiar to explain the abstract and unfamiliar.

Stating the function Finally, we sometimes define by giving the function of a person or object; that is, we answer that key question, "What is it for?" Sometimes specifying function may be the most important part of a definition. For example, a psychiatrist is a doctor who is trained to treat mental disorders; the purpose of sociology is to study patterns and processes in society; a thesaurus is a book that lists synonyms. At other times, listing the function of something may be of secondary importance, or it may be in-

[6] John Leggett, *Ross and Tom* (New York: Simon & Schuster, Inc., 1974).

Listing use or purpose

applicable or even impossible. You might, for instance, define a commune as an experiment in a new style of living and extend your definition by listing features typical of communes, analyzing the economic and domestic arrangements, and giving examples. Saying precisely what the purpose of a commune is would be more difficult. For some residents it might be saving money; for others, it might be expressing protest, seeking friends, or just trying something new. And when it comes to defining certain abstractions such as loyalty, liberalism, wealth, or existentialism, the question of function simply does not arise.

In practice, most of us define by combining some or all of these methods, often without even thinking about what we are doing. But when you must define and are puzzled about how you should go about it, reviewing the commonly used techniques can help. Suppose, for example, that you are one of that great number of students classified as "undetermined major"; you are "undetermined" because you cannot decide what kind of job would suit you best. So you sit down to work out a definition of a good job for you. The process might go like this:

Characteristics Would involve a variety of activities; would not require that I live in a large city; would make a contribution to society; would be reasonably lucrative ($20,000 to $25,000 a year) and offer chances for advancement; would not require eight hours a day in an office; would involve taking responsibility and making decisions.

Analysis A job that allows me to make use of my talents in mathematics and physical sciences; one in which I could make use of my natural mechanical abilities; one that does not require study of a foreign language or literature, subjects in which I do poorly.

Comparison and Contrast A good job would be interesting, demanding, satisfying, and profitable; a bad job would be dull, frustrating, unrewarding and unprofitable.

Examples Some jobs that might fit my specifications are: civil engineer, veterinarian, airline pilot, rancher, or ecology consultant. Some occupations that certainly would not fit my standards are: law, advertising, accounting, or writing.

Function Furnish a comfortable living, give me a sense of

accomplishment and self-respect, and provide a satisfying outlet for my energies and talents.

In working out these techniques of definition, you have done more than simply seek a solution to a problem; you have also created an assertion by spelling out what, in your opinion, a job should be. You have set up an "ought" statement, the kind of statement that is the foundation of rhetoric. In this particular case, your audience is only yourself or perhaps your family, but the techniques of definition you have employed are the same kind that you might use in a variety of rhetorical situations.

Defining can help solve problems

Using the Argument from Definition

The argument from definition usually does one (or more) of three things: first, it may create a yardstick or standard of measurement and then evaluate something according to that yardstick; second, it may describe an ideal and seek to persuade the audience to adopt that ideal; and third, it may give the bad features of a person, institution, or theory and state or imply that the thing being defined ought *not* to be as it is. For example, a student employing the first form might outline the criteria for a good athletic program and then, by applying them to the program at the college, argue that officials need to make major changes. You could use the same method to argue that *Crime and Punishment* is a great novel, Anthropology 302 is a worthless course, or our welfare system is a failure. The process is simple: formulate a yardstick, apply it, and make a judgment.

1. Set a standard and evaluate

2. Set an ideal and persuade

3. Define the ideal by describing the real

Martin Luther King provides an example of the second form in this excerpt from his famous "Letter from Birmingham Jail":

One may well ask: "How can you advocate breaking some laws and obeying others?" The answer lies in the fact that there are two types of laws: just and unjust. I would be the first to advocate obeying just laws. One has not only a legal but a moral responsibility to obey just laws. Conversely, one has a moral responsibility to disobey unjust laws. I would agree with St. Augustine that "an unjust law is no law at all."
Now, what is the difference between the two? How does one determine whether a law is just or unjust? A just law is a man-made code that squares with the moral law or the law of

God. An unjust law is a code that is out of harmony with the moral law. To put it in the terms of St. Thomas Aquinas: An unjust law is a human law that is not rooted in eternal and natural law. Any law that uplifts human personality is just. Any law that degrades human personality is unjust. All segregation statutes are unjust because segregation distorts the soul and damages the personality. It gives the segregator a false sense of superiority and the segregated a false sense of inferiority. Segregation, to use the terminology of the Jewish philosopher Martin Buber, substitutes an "I-it" relationship for an "I-thou" relationship and ends up relegating persons to the status of things. Hence segregation is not only politically, economically and sociologically unsound, it is morally wrong and sinful. Paul Tillich has said that sin is separation. Is not segregation an existential expression of man's tragic separation, his awful estrangement, his terrible sinfulness? Thus it is that I can urge men to obey the 1954 decision of the Supreme Court, for it is morally right; and I can urge them to disobey segregation ordinances, for they are morally wrong.[7]

The next example, taken from an article urging radical changes in reform schools, illustrates the third form of the argument from definition, negative definition. By showing what reform schools are, the author argues for their abolition.

(1) They are expensive. Officials in a number of states have pointed out that it costs as much to keep one juvenile in an institution for one year as it would cost to send him to the most prestigious and costly prep school. . . .

(2) They are populated by children of the poor, generally blacks and Puerto Ricans in the East and blacks and Chicanos in the West . . . 89 per cent of the inmates came from homes where parents were on, or eligible for, public assistance. . . .

(3) They cannot be institutions of learning. The so-called industrial or training schools teach skills, not subjects, and the skills are generally those that are obsolete or designed to

[2]Martin Luther King, Jr., "Letter from Birmingham Jail—April 16, 1963" from *Why We Can't Wait* by Martin Luther King, Jr. Copyright © 1963 by Martin Luther King, Jr. Reprinted by permission of Harper & Row Publishers, Inc. and Joan Daves.

anchor the juveniles securely to the bottom of the social and financial scale.

(4) Their professional personnel are generally of low caliber. . . .

(5) Study after study has shown that the recidivism rate of young people is directly proportionate to the amount of time they spend in institutions. . . . A youth who spends several years in an institution is almost certain to spend most of his life behind bars.

(6) Finally, and perhaps most important, reform schools are prime devourers of the lard doled from the political pork barrel. Jobs in the school from top to bottom are political appointments, and local politicians are fighting tenaciously to retain this power to make appointments.[8]

Argument from definition is usually a moral argument

The argument from definition, then, is usually an ethical argument, calculated to appeal to the audience's sense of what is right and moral, what is desirable, what ought to be. Although you may not think of yourself as an idealist, when you begin to construct an argument on a matter that interests you, you are likely to find that you have strong opinions about the right course of action; you are, therefore, an idealist on at least that topic. You might, for example, think that a good education should include a study of Western civilization, and consequently courses in it should be required of anyone who receives a college degree. Or, you might argue that your college should not force all students to live in college-approved housing, basing your argument on your belief that everyone should have the right to choose where to live. In both these cases, you are arguing from your definition of what is good. If by extending and supporting your definition, you can persuade your audience to accept it, you have a good chance of achieving your rhetorical purpose.

The Argument from Cause and Effect

The attempt to persuade an audience that one event caused another or that certain effects will follow from certain actions must

[8] Brian Vachon, "Hey, Man, What Did You Learn in Reform School?" *Saturday Review of Education*, October 1972, p. 72.

be one of the oldest forms of argument. One can imagine rulers in ancient times trying to understand the causes of floods or earthquakes or plagues in order that they might explain such disasters to their subjects. Lacking the knowledge to make scientific explanations, they could make only erroneous ones: often they cited the anger of the gods as the cause and recommended that the people make some sacrifice or do penance to keep the effect from occurring again. So strongly does the human mind want to find causes for things it does not understand that everyone believed the explanations. Such naiveté strikes us as childish, but our responses to cause-and-effect arguments are often equally unsophisticated.

You can, however, improve your own arguments and better evaluate those of others by observing these elementary guidelines and cautions. First, when making a cause-and-effect argument, be willing to settle for establishing reasonable probability; don't overstate your case and force yourself into an indefensible position. You cannot really prove that the Supreme Court's abolishment of the death penalty will cause an increase in major crimes or that rising medical costs are going to bring about socialized medicine in this country. At best, you can only hypothesize and say that under the circumstances such results seem highly probable. And after you have made such a hypothesis, you have an obligation to support it by explaining how you arrived at your conclusion and by giving examples that reinforce your reasoning.

Second, avoid simplistic thinking about cause and effect. One kind of oversimplification is assuming that an event is the result of a single cause; for example, some social critics have asserted that the student riots of the sixties were the direct result of permissive child-raising practices in the forties. Others claim that increased juvenile crime is the result of children's watching violence on television. Both theories are attractively neat and simple, but they reveal their proponents' ignorance of the complexities of human behavior. If you want to make these kinds of hypotheses—and it is certainly possible that there is an element of truth in each of them—have the good judgment to limit yourself to saying "one of the causes of."

Another kind of simplistic causal reasoning confuses coincidence or simple sequence with cause and effect. This can be as primitive as saying that you had a wreck because a black cat ran

Guidelines:
1. Establish
reasonable
probability

2. Avoid
oversimplification

3. Do not confuse coincidence with causation

in front of your car, or it can be as sophisticated as Bertrand Russell's supporting his assertion that conventional living destroys creativity by pointing out that the quality of Wordsworth's poetry declined after he left his mistress and married. We will come back to this kind of erroneous thinking in the chapter on fallacies. For now, just remember to be wary of this oversimplification both in your arguments and those of others.

4. Avoid setting up scapegoats

Finally, be suspicious of cause-and-effect reasoning that brings in scapegoats or conjures up conspiracies to explain misfortune, and avoid it in your writing. Complex social problems have complex causes, and trying to solve them or to rationalize them away by blaming one group is naive or deceitful. A classic example of this tactic is Hitler's propaganda campaign against the Jews. By blaming them for the economic and social problems that followed World War I, he was able to divert the attention of the German people from their dissatisfactions and concentrate their hostility on a scapegoat. The same thing occurs in our country when people try to explain riots and demonstrations by blaming them on "foreign elements" and "outside agitators." Such simplistic rationalization prevents us from looking for the real causes of social unrest and postpones solutions. The critical thinker avoids this kind of thinking and rejects it in the writings of others.

The Argument from Circumstance

The argument from circumstance is a special kind of cause-and-effect argument in which the speaker or writer seeks to persuade the audience to approve or at least accept a certain course of action on the grounds that no other course is practical or possible. Certain phrases recur so frequently in the argument from circumstance that they signal it. Typical ones are: "It is inevitable"; "We have no choice but to"; "Under the circumstances, our only option is"; "We are forced to"; and "Whether we like it or not, we must." Sometimes the argument contains the appeal "our backs are to the wall" or "we are trapped by forces beyond our control." At other times it takes the fatalistic approach of "we might as well accept the inevitable." In any case, the task of the rhetorician is to convince the audience that the circumstances described as a cause are so pressing, so serious, that certain effects

Characteristic signals

must follow. This is usually done by giving a detailed analysis and description of the circumstances.

The rhetoric of the Declaration of Independence fits the pattern of the argument from circumstance well. To explain why they advocated revolution, the writers used these words:

> But when a long train of abuses and usurpations pursuing invariably the same object, evinces a design to reduce them [the people] under absolute despotism, it is their right, it is their *duty*, to throw off such government, and to provide new guards for their future security. Such has been the patient sufferance of these colonies; and such is now the *necessity* which *constrains* them to alter their former systems of government. The history of the present king of Great Britain is a history of repeated injuries and usurpations, all having in direct order the establishment of an absolute tyranny over these states. To prove this, let facts be submitted to a candid world. [italics added]

Fourteen paragraphs follow detailing the oppressive acts of George III. Apparently, the colonists agreed that the circumstances described were indeed intolerable and accepted revolution as the only solution.

In our own time, Martin Luther King's "Letter from Birminghan Jail" furnishes another example of the argument from circumstance:

> You deplore the demonstrations taking place in Birmingham. But your statement, I am sorry to say, fails to express a similar concern for the conditions that brought about the demonstrations. I am sure that none of you would want to rest content with the superficial kind of social analysis that deals merely with effects and does not grapple with underlying causes. It is unfortunate that demonstrations are taking place in Birmingham, but it is even more unfortunate that the city's white power structure left the Negro community *with no alternative.*
>
> ....
>
> As the weeks and months unfolded we realized that we were the victims of a broken promise. The signs remained. As in so

many experiences of the past we were confronted with blasted hopes, and the dark shadow of a deep disappointment settled upon us. *So we had no alternative* except that of preparing for direct action, whereby we would present our very bodies as a means of laying our case before the conscience of the local and national community. [italics added; pp. 79, 80]

Arguments that explain human behavior solely in terms of environment constitute another kind of circumstantial argument. To claim that a person became a criminal because of growing up in a slum is really saying that "under the circumstances, crime was inevitable." Novelists often use this kind of argument by creating a set of circumstances to account for their characters' behavior. In *The Grapes of Wrath,* for example, Steinbeck carefully sets up natural and economic events that drove the Joads to become migrants. By portraying them as a poverty-stricken tenant farm family in Oklahoma during a prolonged era of drought, he makes the reader feel that their trek to California is inevitable.

Typical arguments from circumstance

We encounter less dramatic forms of the argument from circumstance in our everyday lives. For instance, when someone uses that old cliché "If you can't lick 'em, join 'em," argument from circumstance is being used. People who reason that if they do not take advantage of an opportunity, someone else will, or who justify an action by saying that everyone else does it, are also arguing from circumstance. Anyone who argues that people can't help being the way they are is using the same reasoning.

The argument from circumstance can be extremely persuasive and difficult to refute. If a rhetorician can convince the audience that the circumstances are indeed compelling, so overwhelming that they lead to only one logical conclusion, probably she or he will win the point. In 1975, for instance, New York City authorities persuaded the administrators of City College of New York that students attending the college were finally going to have to start paying tuition even though such a move violated the traditions on which the college was based. They did so by simply pointing to the New York City budget and saying, "We can no longer pay the bills to run the college as it is." That claim was reinforced when the college closed its doors for several weeks and the faculty did not receive their paychecks. That kind of argument from circumstance is irrefutable. The crucial task in presenting a circumstantial argument is giving enough evidence to make a strong case for your side; merely hypothesizing about what *might* happen under certain circumstances will probably not convince a skeptical reader.

Weaknesses of the argument from circumstance

The weakness of the argument from circumstance is that often it is distorted into a justification for immoral or self-serving acts. People who are going to do something unethical, something that they are ashamed of, usually want to divert blame from themselves. Thus, they may try to avoid taking responsibility for their acts by pleading that they are victims of forces over which they have no control. For example, a scholarship athlete may justify his poor grades by pointing out that the four hours a day he has to devote to football practice make it impossible for him to study as much as he should; a politician may excuse broken campaign promises by saying that he had to make them in order to get elected; the owner of a business may claim that if she spends money to install pollution control devices, she will be forced out of business by her competitors. The argument from circumstance can easily degenerate into the argument from expediency. In evaluating both your own circumstantial arguments and those of others, you need to make careful distinctions between the inevitable and the merely probable, between consequences that are disastrous and those that are only inconvenient or unpleasant.

The Argument from Comparison

The Argument from Analogy

The person who argues from analogy tries to persuade by suggesting to an audience that things that are alike in some respects are probably alike in other respects. The logical process on which this kind of argument is based goes like this: if A and B share the qualities of X and Y, which we can observe, then they are likely to share the quality of Z, which we cannot observe. For example, *How analogy works* a person who thinks that Americans are extremely conforming people who are easily influenced and led, draws an analogy by calling them "sheep"; the suggestion is that they are also stupid and unthinking. A person who opposed nuclear power plants may call them "time-bombs," suggesting that not only do the two things have in common the quality of containing explosive materials and being dangerous, but that both are unpredictable and possibly lethal. (Notice, of course, that both these analogies use metaphorical language; a great many do, and the purpose of the metaphor is often persuasive.)

The argument from analogy is often striking and dramatic and for those reasons, it is frequently persuasive. You should remember, however, that at best it only enlightens and clarifies. Used as a reinforcement for other kinds of arguments, analogy can be very effective, but it never *proves* anything. The reason it does not is that rarely do you find two things that are alike in every major respect. Also, if the concepts or situations being compared are alike in one or two important ways, but not at all alike in other significant ways, the analogy will break down.

Analogy can clarify but it does not prove

Take for example the "lifeboat" analogy proposed in this article:

> If we divide the world crudely into rich nations and poor nations, two-thirds of them are desperately poor, and only one third comparatively rich, with the United States the wealthiest of all. Metaphorically, each rich nation can be seen as a lifeboat full of comparatively rich people. In the ocean outside each lifeboat swim the poor of the world, who would like to get in, or at least share some of the wealth. What should the lifeboat passengers do?
>
> First, we must recognize the limited capacity of any lifeboat. For example, a nation's land has a limited capacity to support a population, and as the current energy crisis has shown, in some ways we have already exceeded the carrying capacity of our land.
>
> *Adrift in a Moral Sea.* So here we sit, say 50 people in our lifeboat. To be generous, let us say it has room for 10 more, making a total capacity of 60. Suppose the 50 of us in the lifeboat see 100 others swimming in the water outside, begging for admission to our boat, or for handouts. We have several options: we may be tempted to try to live by the Christian rule of being "our brother's keeper," or by the Marxist ideal of "to each according to his needs." Since the

needs of all in the water are the same, and since they can all be seen as "our brothers" we could take them all into our boat making the total of 150 in a boat designed for 60. The boat swamps, everyone drowns. Complete justice, complete catastrophe.

Since the boat has an unused capacity of 10 more passengers, we could admit just 10 more to it. But which 10 do we let in? How do we choose? Do we pick the best 10, the neediest 10, "first come, first served?" And what do we say to the 90 we exclude? If we do let an extra 10 into our lifeboat, we will have lost our "safety factor," an engineering principle of critical importance. For example, if we don't leave room for excess capacity as a safety factor in our country's agriculture, a new plant disease or a bad change in the weather could have disastrous results.[9]

The analogy Hardin draws is appealingly simple and, as he intends it to be, alarming. But it is also weak. The prosperous countries of the world do not really have much in common with lifeboats filled with prosperous people afloat in a sea in which other struggling and hostile people are swimming. For one thing, there are no more resources to be found or developed in a lifeboat; everything that can be used is already there. This is not true in the world, especially not in vast areas like Russia, China, and Brazil. Also for the population of the world the choice is not simply float and survive, or sink and die. The people of the underdeveloped countries are, in most cases, surviving although sometimes not very well. And some of the countries, such as India, are taking drastic measures to see that they don't sink. There are also other major flaws in the analogy that any thoughtful person who questioned it would quickly see.

The following is an example of a more cogent and thought-provoking argument from analogy:

Public education is the nation's largest consumer industry. . . . In cases where quality of education is demonstrably poor, there is reason to believe that consumers

[9] Garrett Hardin, "Lifeboat Ethics: The Case Against Helping the Poor." Copyright © 1974 by Ziff-Davis Publishing Company. Reprinted from *Psychology Today*.

may legitimately take action in the courts. Students, parents, taxpayers, and, for that matter, Ralph Nader may well claim that the principles of law that govern business, industry, and some professions extend to education.

Do they? Here are some parallels that suggest possible lines of attack:

When a doctor or lawyer performs negligently, ignoring proper practice, he bears legal responsibility. When school boards, administrators, or teachers behave negligently in their instructional duties, do they bear major responsibility? Do they bear *any* responsibility?

When consumer products fail to work, the manufacturer or producer bears some legal responsibility for the failure. When teachers fail to teach, do the schools of education that produced those teachers bear responsibility for their failure? Similarly, when students fail to learn, are those responsible for their learning—schools, teachers, and publishers and purchasers of educational materials—legally responsible for student failure?

When a consumer purchases a car, there is an "implied warranty" from the manufacturer and his agent to the purchaser that the car will perform certain minimal functions; for example it will start, propel itself, turn, stop, give a warning signal. Is there an implied warranty to the customer of educational services from the state and its local agents that, as a result of schooling, graduates will perform certain minimal functions?[10]

The authors of this article prudently frame their analogies as questions, inviting the reader to consider if the reasoning is indeed valid. Such an approach actually strengthens their argument because, instead of annoying their audience by claiming more than they can prove, they simply say: Here is a new way to look at the responsibility of educators that has some profound implications. What do you think?

Also, don't forget that analogies are particularly useful for ex-

Do not push your analogy too far

[10] Gary Saretsky and James Mecklenburger, "See You in Court?" *Saturday Review of Education,* November 1972, p. 50.

plaining new concepts. The selection "The Chemistry of Brain Clocks," page 463 in the Appendix, effectively illustrates their value as teaching devices.

The *a fortiori* Argument

A special kind of argument from comparison

This Latin term (which is pronounced "ah-for-shee-ór-ee") literally means "all the stronger." It is used to describe a mode of argument that is based on probability. The argument works like this: you hypothesize about two possibilities, the second of which can happen more easily than the first; then, if you can show that the first possibility became a reality, you conclude that the second one should also materialize. In practice, this process is not nearly as complicated as this abstract description makes it sound; you have probably encountered it frequently and occasionally used it yourself. In its complete form the *a fortiori* argument looks like this:

> If we can have the technology to put a shuttle into space, we should be able to figure out how to feed the hungry people in the United States.
> We have the technology to put a shuttle into space.
> Therefore, we ought to utilize our technology to feed the hungry people in the United States.

Presumably, launching a space shuttle is a much more complicated and difficult task than finding ways to feed people; the implication, then, is that it is ridiculous for us to be able to do the first and not be able, or at least willing, to do the second. Reduced to the form in which we usually find it, this argument reads, "If we can launch a space shuttle, we ought to be able to feed people in this country."

Appeals to our sense of logic

Some *a fortiori* arguments are effective because they appeal to our sense of what seems logical. The argument that if an eighteen-year-old boy is old enough to fight for his country, he is old enough to be allowed to buy a beer is this kind of argument. An *a fortiori* argument that is sometimes advanced in favor of socialized medicine is this: if the state builds public schools and pays teachers in order that everyone may have the right to an education, why should it not build public hospitals and pay doctors in order that everyone might have the right to good health? It is a line of argument that is not easy to refute.

Another form of the *a fortiori* argument appeals to our conviction that people are consistent and predictable. Arguments based on that assumption might run like this: if a woman will cheat a member of her family, she will certain cheat a stranger; if a student will turn in a plagiarized paper, it is likely that he or she will cheat on an examination; if an army cadet panics in war games, he will go to pieces under enemy fire; the person who does well in difficult subjects like calculus ought to do well in comparatively easy ones such as Spanish. This kind of argument, which involves speculation about human behavior, is not as solidly grounded as those based on reason, but it can be forceful nevertheless.

Appeals to belief that people are predictable

The Argument from Evidence

From the moment that you began the study of rhetoric, you have been counseled: "Be concrete"; "Give examples"; "Support your assertions with evidence." Such advice was really little more than a reminder to do in writing what you do almost instinctively in speech. It seems to come naturally to all of us to draw on external sources when we argue because we realize that our opinions carry more weight when we give outside evidence to support them. We turn to what we have seen, read, or heard in order to corroborate and reinforce our own ideas. All information of this kind comes under the general category of evidence. That term, however, encompasses a variety of data that need to be described and analyzed. The five principal kinds of evidence are reports, statistics, personal testimony, factual references, and the appeal to authority. At times, of course, these categories will merge and overlap.

Purpose is to reinforce

Reports

In our mass-media culture, we have an unprecedented number of reports; television, radio, books, newspapers, and magazines keep us informed about a multitude of events and topics. The person who keeps up with current events through these channels has an impressive stock of resources with which to reinforce rhetoric. If you want to argue that this country should subsidize public hospitals, you can quote from an article in *Harper's* magazine that reveals what happens to the quality and cost of health care when business begins building hospitals for profit.[11] You can bolster arguments on defense spending, migrant labor, or political propaganda by quoting television documentaries on those topics. Both the news columns and feature articles in newspapers can furnish you with supporting evidence for papers on topics such as conditions in the local jails, the cheating problem in colleges, or the need for more medical schools in your state. When you are writing on almost any controversial topic, you can find reports that will give you usable information.

Two questions to ask about reports:

1. Is the source reliable?

2. What bias might the reporter have?

Reports are valuable when you are relying on evidence as one of your chief modes of argument, but they do present a problem because obviously all reports are not of equal value. How, then, do you evaluate them? There is no easy answer, but a good rule of thumb is to ask two questions about every report: (1) Is the source reliable?; (2) What is the bias of the person or group doing the reporting? In general, we can assume that major newspapers, national television and radio networks, and magazines of established reputation tell the truth. They may use loaded language and they may leave out certain important details, but what they print or broadcast is reasonably accurate. They cannot afford to have it otherwise. Less well known newspapers and magazines that specialize in sensationalism or cater to an uncritical and poorly informed audience are less apt to be reliable.

Answering the question about bias involves determining whose interest the report might serve. Often the answer is that it serves no special interest, and you should not be so suspicious or cynical that you assume most reports are distorted in favor of a particular group or party. But only a naive person would fail to realize that a report on the condition of the beef industry put out by the Cattleman's Association is going to differ in tone and emphasis from

[11] Roger Rapoport, "A Candle for St. Greed's," *Harper's*, December 1972, pp. 70–75.

one put out by the Consumers' Protection League, just as a report on the quality of health care in this country that is made by the American Medical Association is going to differ from one made by the World Health Organization. It is not that the people who make reports deliberately lie; it is rather that someone who has an investment, emotional or financial, in a particular area—education, business, defense, medicine—can scarcely avoid stressing some points and playing down others. The persons who receive and use those reports should at least be alert to possible bias.

Statistics

Problem of bias in statistics

The use of statistics can pose the same problem of bias. After all, whose statistics are they? A good rule here is to trust statistics and data that come from research organizations such as the Brookings Institution, from government bureaus and agencies, from national survey organizations such as the Gallup poll, from a nationally known encyclopedia or publications such as the *World Almanac,* and from research groups funded by universities or nonprofit foundations. But you should be at least slightly skeptical of polls financed by candidates or a lobby and about reports sponsored by individual companies, and very skeptical of any statistical data from unspecified sources. Phrases such as "reports show," "an independent research organization has found," and "statistics prove" do not constitute good evidence.

Personal Testimony

Personal testimony, their own and that of others, provides student writers with an easy and effective way to support many kinds of arguments. If you are working with a topic about which you have firsthand knowledge, you can use no better source of evidence than your own concrete experiences. What you have learned about race problems from incidents in your high school or what you have found out about graft in the construction business by helping to build an apartment house in which shoddy materials were used is impressive testimony, as good as an incident reported in the *New York Times* or *Playboy* magazine. When you recall the variety of experiences you have had in your life or know about in other people's lives, you will find that you have a surprising amount of testimony on which to draw. You should be careful, of course, not to overgeneralize from one or two incidents because the personal experiences of one individual are not enough to *prove* a general theory, but used as reinforcement and illustration, they add interest and concreteness to your papers.

Consult experience of others

Using the personal testimony of others can also be effective, but here you may encounter problems regarding reliability. When you cite the experiences of another person as evidence to support your point, be sure that you have direct knowledge about that experience or know the person well enough to vouch for his or her credibility. Anecdotes that you hear in casual conversation, particularly those for which no source is given, may be enlightening, but they do not provide substantial evidence with which to support a serious assertion. A critical audience will dismiss that kind of testimony as no more than "hearsay evidence," not admissible in any court and therefore not to be taken seriously. A statement

Avoid hearsay evidence

like the following sentence from Paul Goodman's *Growing Up Absurd* is an example of such hearsay evidence: "The pastor of a large church in an ordinary Midwestern town told me that, in his observation, not one marriage in twenty was worth-while." The reader is unlikely to accept a claim that the institution of marriage is disintegrating simply on the basis of this kind of extreme and completely unverifiable statement.

Factual References

The careful writer supplies the reader with solid evidence. For instance, in a column arguing that the United States is not a healthy country, Michael Killian compares the life expectancy in the United States with that of Iceland:

> The world's healthiest country is the one that would be my favorite even if it was the world's least healthy—Iceland. Life expectancy at birth in Iceland is now 73 years for men and 79.2 years for women—the highest expectancy on the planet.

This compares with an American life expectancy of 68.7 years for men and 76.5 for women.[12]

A student writing a paper arguing for nationally subsidized day-care centers used these facts:

The Soviet Union has poured over one billion into a new day care system in the past two years, and the system now serves more than 13 million children. The French have an extensive nursery system, a free kindergarten network for children over the age of three, state licensed agencies that place children with volunteer sitters, and some 200,000 professional nannies. The Swedish government not only provides a day care center for children through the ninth grade, but will also pay 90% of one parent's salary for a year so one parent can stay home.

Your references should be reasonably familiar to your audience

The supporting evidence used by both these authors is effective because it employs references that are familiar to a reasonably well informed person. If you search your memory when you are writing a paper, you will probably find that you have a stock of similar material readily available. You can draw on historical as well as contemporary material, or you can use what you are learning in other courses. If you are writing a paper in which you try to show that harsh repression of unpopular opinions is not only cruel but also shortsighted, you might cite the examples of the Romans' persecution of the Christians, the Church's persecution of Galileo, and the British government's treatment of Mahatma Gandhi. In a paper arguing for tighter controls on television advertising, you could support your claim that commercials are often misleading by bringing in two facts you learned in your nutrition course: rats fed for three weeks solely on so-called enriched bread died of starvation, and some cereals advertised as "nutritious and full of energy" really furnish the body nothing but calories. Once you develop the habit of looking for rhetorical material in your

---

[12] Michael Killian, "No Work to Longevity," *Austin (Texas) American-Statesman*, December 1, 1978, p. 14.

own experience, you will be surprised at how much information you have stored in your head.

The Appeal to Authority

The final kind of evidence that you can draw on in order to support your rhetoric or exposition is the appeal to authority. In an argument to support your assertion that there should be unity among the various factions on campus, you might quote Lincoln's warning: "A house divided against itself cannot stand." If you are trying to prove that riots and demonstrations are not phenomena of the twentieth century only, you could quote from the report of the presidential commission on the causes and prevention of violence. You could support a proposal to abolish the grading system by pointing out that low or failing grades have bad psychological effects on children, citing as your authority the famous behavioral psychologist B. F. Skinner, who claims that people learn best when they receive positive, not negative, reinforcement.

Ways of appealing to authority

If you argue against smoking, you would be making an appeal to authority by quoting the inscription on all cigarette packages, "Warning: The Surgeon General has determined that cigarette smoking is dangerous to your health." You are also using authority when you cite a dictionary definition; for example, "Prejudice is an adverse judgment or opinion formed beforehand or without knowledge or examination of the facts; a preconceived preference or idea; bias."[13] References to the Constitution, the Bible, or any other revered document to emphasize or strengthen a point constitute another kind of appeal to authority. You can see that the stock of authoritative sources available to you is vast and varied. Usually the difficulty is not finding an authority to quote, but deciding which one best suits your purposes.

Problems with the appeal to authority

Because most of us are awed by experts, especially those with advanced degrees, titles, and several impressive awards, the argument from authority can be a powerful one. It does, however, pose certain problems. First, does the authority cited have cre-

---

[13] © 1981 by Houghton Mifflin Company. Reprinted with permission from *The American Heritage Dictionary of the English Language.*

dentials that will command the respect of your audience? You are more likely to win assent to your claims if you give the title, position, and qualifications of the authority you quote. For example, if you want to cite evidence on the problems of college faculties, you may say, "Dr. Reece McGee, professor of sociology at Purdue University and the author of *The Academic Marketplace* and *Academic Janus*, says that"; in an argument against cutting defense spending, you could quote an opinion from the chief of naval operations. In both cases, you show that your authorities have the position, the qualifications, and the experience to make their testimony worth listening to. To rely on unverifiable and vague references such as "a well-known economist" or "the president of one of America's major universities" is an evasion of responsibility. And just as you should not rely on such devices yourself, you should not be impressed by them in the rhetoric of others. Remember also that you should not give much weight to the evidence of an authority who is operating outside of the field of expertise. If a Nobel Prize-winning geneticist criticizes the space program, he should be listened to as a private citizen, not as an authority; when Paul Newman endorses a political candidate or O. J. Simpson recommends a car rental agency, their opinions should be regarded as those of private citizens because their expertise in show business or in professional football does not carry over to politics or rental cars.

The other problem with using the argument from authority is that one can, without too much trouble, often find two qualified, reliable authorities who take opposite views on the same topic. Certainly you have heard biblical quotations brought in as support for both sides of an argument: "An eye for an eye, a tooth for a tooth" opposed to "Father, forgive them; they know not what they do." On the question of disarmament, you will find Senator William Proxmire on one side and Senator John Tower on the other, both experienced, knowledgeable men, but with radically differing opinions. Two well-known, highly trained, and well-thought-of psychologists, Carl Rogers and B. F. Skinner, disagree violently on the best ways to influence human behavior. And so it goes. In situations like these, you can conclude only that intelligent authorities of good will often view matters differently and that there may be no single right answer available. For your rhetorical purposes, it is perfectly legitimate to try to find qualified authorities who support your point of view. If you give their credentials and quote them both accurately and in context, you are arguing fairly.

Combining Arguments

In practice, of course, any rhetorician combines several modes of argument (including some we have not yet discussed) and a variety of persuasive techniques in order to make her or his arguments convincing. You will be doing the same. It should be easier now that you realize how many places there are where you can look for ways to develop and support your assertions. As an illustration of how many means are available to the arguer, let us analyze the kinds of arguments that one man put together in a short, persuasive essay.

Does the Devil Make Us Do It?

From evidence: personal testimony

New York—I was passing a sex shop on 42nd Street recently when the police were conducting a raid. The cops went in and the patrons came out. One customer, trying to duck the television cameras, exited quickly and then pretended he was merely a passer-by. He sidled up to me, to blend into the crowd, and watched.

"What's happening?" I asked him.

"A raid."

"What for?"

"Because," the man said, indignant now, "they got all that filth in there."

From definition: attributing characteristics; giving examples

The incident says a lot about the confusing American view of pornography. That view has always been a hypocritical one. As a nation we have never made up our mind, when handed a dirty picture on the corner, to smile, to call the cops, or both.

I vote we just smile. What's all the big sweat, anyway?

From definition: attributing characteristics

From definition: stating function
From evidence: factual reference

From evidence: factual reference

From cause and effect
From evidence: factual reference

From definition: stating function

From definition: giving examples

From definition: giving examples
From cause and effect

From cause and effect

From evidence: appeal to authority

We are a people titillated by sex. Increasingly so. Where once the smut business in this country was largely manufactured in France or at least made in Japan, it is now fully an American industry. It is big, big business. New York City has two dozen weekly sex newspapers selling from 50 cents to $1 an issue. Forty-second Street hawkers sell everything from phony stimulants to pathetic photos of "genuine schoolteachers from Ohio."

Silicone-breasted go-go dancers perform in the shadow of Washington's capitol, not rarely for nightclub-touring government officials. X-rated movies have become so common many drive-ins have begun offering them, along with customer anonymity. . . .

Indeed, pornography has gone socko. Why? Because the nation wants it (although the nation won't admit it). People now spend as much as $2 billion annually, by some industry estimates, to further the phenomenon.

Undeniably, much of what has happened has been unfortunate. Manhattan's 42nd Street, which used to be a tourist attraction, is now, with its bosom-boosting, a mean tourist trap. The sex clubs along Washington's 14th Street are, late at night, overly aggressive, with their loud music, their nude window photographs and their pimps at the door begging customers. Many people are genuinely offended that newspapers now advertise X-rated movies with their drippy titles ("The Midnight Plowboy"). This kind of aggressiveness is, perhaps, open to legislative restriction—if only because it foists pornography on that part of the population which is definitely not interested.

But beyond this protection of the innocent (including children), there seems to be no logical or even moral reason to call the cops on smut. You look or you don't look. You buy or you don't. If nobody forces you, what really is the crime? . . .

Two years ago, the President's Commission on Pornography and Obscenity released the results of a thorough, three-year, extremely objective study of smut in America. It was a blanket admission that the nation, the John Birchers, the J.

From evidence: testimony

From evidence: appeal to authority; testimony

From evidence: appeal to authority; testimony

From definition: attributing characteristics

From evidence: appeal to authority

From comparison: a fortiori

From definition: comparing and contrasting

From evidence: testimony

From evidence: personal testimony

From circumstance

Edgar Hoovers, had been worrying for naught for generations. The commission says that exposure to sexual material does not cause crime, emotional problems or lead to character deterioration. It said that it is "extremely unwise" for governments to attempt the legislation of morality beyond behavior. It said that all laws prohibiting or limiting sale or showings of sexual material should be repealed. And it said, moreover, that most Americans believe in sexual propaganda.

The commission's report, predictably, was buried under a blanket of condemnation. But its findings are, two years later, no less relevant and revealing. The First Amendment of the Constitution (free speech, free press) applies to all or it does not really apply to any. If we allow this newspaper to print, we have to also, constitutionally, even though we personally object, allow the beady-eyed peddlers to go to press too.

So smile. Smile! Is sex really so decadent?

O.K. So you don't like pornography. Stout fellow. But others do, a good many others, and hypocritical though some of them are, they are remarkably human. The fellow outside the 42nd Street shop, for example. When he started cheering the police raid, I told him to can it, that I had seen him slink out of the door, that even then he had a dirty book in his pocket.

"Oh," he said, turning colors, ending up in green, "well, ah, that is," he took out the book and grinned, "the devil made me do it."[14]

Exercises

1. Identify the mode or modes of argument appearing in the following examples:

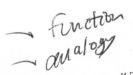
— function
— analogy

a. Running a university is like running a business, and therefore it is a good idea to have businesspeople for regents. The

[14] Tom Tiede, "Does the Devil Make Us Do It?" *Taylor (Texas) Daily Press,* November 24, 1972. Reprinted by permission. © 1972 NEA, Inc.

"a fortiori"

Cause/effect

Authority

Analogy

definition

purpose of a university, after all, is to turn out a reliable product.

b. If a person can find time to jog and play handball every day to keep in shape, you would think that he or she could find time now and then to read a book to keep the mind in shape.

c. I see nothing wrong with selling dirty books at the college book store. If it doesn't do it, the store next door will.

d. "A State which dwarfs its men in order that they may be more docile instruments in its hands even for beneficial purposes—will find that with small men no great thing can really be accomplished; and that the perfection of machinery to which it has sacrificed everything, will in the end avail it nothing. . . ." (John Stuart Mill)

e. The head of the psychology department at our university says that this country is on the brink of a sexual and social revolution.

f. "In all things that are purely social we [the black and white races] can be as separate as the fingers, yet one as the hand in all things essential to mutual progress." (Booker T. Washington)

g. A true liberal is one who believes in progress and is willing to listen to new ideas. Senator Paul Tsongas's voting record has convinced me that he fits the description.

h. Henry cannot really be blamed for stealing the car. His home life, the pressures of poverty, and our culture's stress on the automobile as a status symbol made it impossible for him to resist.

i. The Department of Labor recently put out a bulletin showing that there would be a 26 percent increase in the demand for nurses and other health workers in the next decade. Obviously these professions provide the ideal choice for an ambitious young person.

j. Professional football is now the king of sports in this country. When I try to visit my friends on Sunday afternoon or Monday night from August through December, I find them sprawled in their living rooms with their eyes glued to the television. Half the sports section each week is taken up with analyses of games past and games to come. Like well-paid gladiators who cannot last in the arena more than a few seasons, the battered but arrogant pros endure their weekly agony so that the citizenry may be entertained. Our new national heroes are violent and brutal men, and the effect on our young people is bound to be degrading.

2. Using at least three of the standard methods of defining, write an extended definition of one of the following:

   a. A slum
   b. An unscrupulous politician
   c. A successful athlete
   d. A bad environment for a child
   e. A foolish parent
   f. A racist
   g. A conservative

3. Analyze the various methods of defining that the author is using in the following selection:

   "Ghetto" was the name for the Jewish quarter in sixteenth-century Venice. Later, it came to mean any section of a city to which Jews are confined. America has contributed to the concept of the ghetto restriction of persons to a special area and the limiting of their freedom of choice on the basis of skin color. The dark ghetto's invisible walls have been erected by the white society, by those who have power, both to confine those who have *no* power and to confine their powerlessness. The dark ghettos are social, political, educational, and—above all—economic colonies. Their inhabitants are subject peoples, victims of the greed, cruelty, insensitivity, guilt, and fear of their masters. . . .

   The ghetto is ferment, paradox, conflict, and dilemma. Yet within its pervasive pathology exists a surprising human resilience. The ghetto is hope, it is despair, it is churches and bars. It is aspiration for change, and it is apathy. It is vibrancy, it is stagnation. It is courage, and it is defeatism. It is cooperation and concern, and it is suspicion, competitiveness and rejection. It is the surge toward assimilation, and it is alienation and withdrawal within the protective walls of the ghetto.[15]

4. How good are the following analogies?

a. "The House version of the bill gave the President the right arbitrarily to cut back [Congressional] spending in any area at all—including, theoretically, social security, or veterans' pensions, or interest on the national debt. . . . There is plenty of resistance in Congress, in part for the same reason that an extravagant wife resists when her husband proposes to take over sole control of a joint checking account. Senate Majority Leader Mike Mansfield has even said that if the House bill became law, 'you might as well abolish Congress,' which is the kind of exaggeration to which extravagant wives are prone."[16]

b. "What could become of such a child of the seventeenth and eighteenth centuries, when he should wake up to find himself required to play the game of the twentieth? Had he been consulted, would he have cared to play the game at all, holding such cards as he held, and suspecting that the game was to be one of which neither he nor anyone else back to the beginning of time knew the rules or the risks or the stakes? . . . Probably no child born in the year held better cards than he. Whether life was an honest game of chance or whether the cards were marked and forced, he could not refuse to play his excellent hand. . . .

"As it happened, he never got to the point of playing the game at all; he lost himself in the study of it, watching the errors of the players."[17]

---

[15] Kenneth Clark, *Dark Ghetto: Dilemmas of Social Power* (New York: Torchbooks, 1967), pp. 11–12.
[16] Stewart Alsop, "What Nixon Hears the Voters Saying," *Newsweek*, October 23, 1972, p. 120.
[17] Henry Adams, *The Education of Henry Adams* (New York: Modern Library, 1931), p. 4.

5. Carefully examine the analogies that are drawn in the passage from the article "See You in Court?" on page 283. What likenesses are the authors suggesting between the processes and products of an educational system and those of a corporation? What likenesses are there between the professional obligations of a doctor, lawyer, or engineer and those of a teacher? What major similarities do you see? What major differences do you see? What strengths and what weaknesses do you find in the analogies? If, as the authors imply by their title, the charge of the schools' turning out substandard products were taken into court, what do you think the decision would be?

6. Which of the following cause-and-effect arguments and arguments from circumstance do you find convincing? Why?

a. The high standard of living in the United States has brought about our energy crisis.

b. We must grant the Department of Justice the privilege of tapping phones and installing listening devices in homes or offices because if criminals make use of this modern technology, law enforcement agencies cannot afford to do without it.

c. Doing away with the grading system in college would put a stop to students' cheating.

d. Television advertising is responsible for the "revolution of rising expectations" in this country.

3. The power of the farm bloc in Congress has declined in the last twenty five years because the number of people living on and making a living from farms has dropped from 15 percent to 7 percent.

7. Analyze and evaluate the following student paper.

Ferrari Fever

Some people have no goals in life or are not sure about them. Not me. I have one very specific goal. Some day, I hope soon, I will own a Ferrari. Now that wouldn't seem like much of a goal except for the fact that the one I want costs about $125,000.

It wasn't until 1975 that I made up my mind on this. Before that I was like most anyone else in that I hadn't the faintest idea what I wanted from life. Sure, I liked fast cars before then, but not so much that I devoted my life's endeavors to owning one. The change occurred when I got a chance to drive one of the fastest cars ever made.

I was home on leave from the Navy at the time and was having a great time partying with my old high school friends. My best friend, Don, had recently met a guy named Jim with whom he'd go running quite often. Jim was an avid sports car fan and, knowing that I was too, he invited me up to a racetrack where he and other members of a club raced their cars. Everyone there has a nice car, but the one that stood out was a Ferrari Daytona. With sleek lines, flawless red paint, and a powerful exhaust note, it was, in my mind, the epitome of the exotic Italian racing machine.

I was in love with it as soon as I saw it. I had seen Ferraris before but never a Daytona. To actually drive this car would make the rest of my life anticlimactic. But I wasn't getting my hopes up. Anybody that owned a car like this wasn't about to let a stranger drive it around a track. So when Jim asked the owner if he would let me take it for a spin, I nearly fainted when he said yes. Later I learned that he's so rich that he lets almost anybody drive it.

To adequately describe the sensation of driving a Daytona would require writing skills far beyond mine. The car was better than anything I had imagined. However, not being an experienced racer, I wasn't about to throw it around at top speed. But even at moderate speeds it was a hell of a lot of fun to drive. It made my Datsun 240Z seem like a Sherman tank, which isn't easy to do. My ride was much too short, of course, and when I reluctantly turned the car back over to its owner, all I could manage to say was "Thanks, nice car." The rest of the day was a blur, and I think I spent most of it figuring how many banks I would have to knock over to buy my own Ferrari.

So as I have said, since then all I've wanted from life is a Ferrari. To you, that may seem a rather short-sighted goal. But I'm not like most people; I don't want a wife and three kids, a 16-room house, three cars, one boat, and a lifetime membership at the country club. Instead, give me an endless stretch of twisty road, a Ferrari, and enough money to keep both of us fed. Nothing more, nothing less.

Robin Smith

Suggested Writing Assignments

Theme 1

Purpose To make you aware of ways in which definition may be used for rhetorical purposes.

Procedure Using the argument from definition, write a theme that seeks to persuade your audience to share your attitude toward the subject you are defining. Remember, the paper must show your bias. First, review pages 269 to 274, on the methods of developing definition, for example, comparing and contrasting, giving examples, and enumerating parts. Then, pick one or two techniques with which to work. Choose a topic from the list below. Limit your topic to a manageable size; pick out a few main points you want to emphasize; be specific and concrete, and avoid broad generalities that do little more than repeat routine prejudices.

Topics
a. A liberated woman
b. A student leader
c. A male chauvinist
d. A member of the Establishment
e. An individual's character by describing that person's room or apartment

Decide before you begin what your attitude is and choose details to support it. In addition to your argument from definition, you may use connotation, figurative language, selected illustrations or whatever you need to persuade. Your thesis sentence, outline, or summary should show the main points you intend to include in your definition.

Theme 2

Purpose To make you aware of the modes of argument you may use to develop a thesis by having you write a paper in which you use two or more of the standard argumentative devices. The possibilities are the arguments from definition, cause and effect, circcomparison, and evidence.

Procedure Choose one of the topics listed below and write an argumentative paper. Before you start, think out the stand you want to take; then do some exploratory thinking about what kinds of arguments you can use to develop your paper. For example, if you were writing a paper supporting the assertion that the world should acheive Zero Population Growth, you might use these arguments as the main points in your paper:

Definition: attributing characteristics An overcrowded world will not be a decent one to live in.

Cause and effect Continued population growth will cause poverty, hunger, and war.

Comparison: analogy Experiments with rats have shown that overcrowding increases hostility.

Circumstance The present rate of population growth is so catastrophic that we have no choice except to legislate restrictions.

Comparison: a fortiori If we believe in controls on education and health, we should believe in controls on population even more.

Evidence: testimony Statistics or examples to support your points.

Evidence: authority Quotations from experts such as Paul Ehrlich.

Remember that you would not have to use all these kinds of arguments. (Of course, all points would have to be expanded.)

When you have finished your paper, go back and label your arguments in the left-hand margin opposite each paragraph. This is an important part of the assignment.

Please begin with a thesis sentence or summary of the main points you are going to make. It need not be a part of your actual theme.

Topics

a. This university should (should not) make a converted drive to bring larger numbers of minority students to this campus.

b. Every high school should (should not) require all students to take a course in home and family relations that would include the study of nutrition and credit management.

c. All papers that a student writes for an English course should (should not) be returned with comments but no grade, and the final grade in the course should (should not) be "Satisfactory" or "Unsatisfactory."

Theme 3

Purpose To give you experience in using evidence as the basis for a persuasive or informative essay.

Procedure Choose a topic in which you are interested and on which you have or know how you can get a substantial amount of information. Then think about who might be interested in reading a paper on such a topic and what your purpose might be in writing such a paper. For example, if you are interested in new developments in ski equipment, you might write an article for an outdoors club newsletter to let readers know the advantages of the latest equipment and persuade them that it is worth the added expense.

After you choose a topic, define your audience and specify your purpose in writing. Then assemble your evidence and from it write a paper in which you develop your main idea by using reports, factual references, personal testimony, statistics, and/or authority. You might get some ideas for a topic from the following list:

Local ice-cream parlors; for example, Baskin-Robbins, Swenson's, Häagen-Dazs, and so on.

Country-western dance halls

Pizza parlors

Camping and backpacking equipment

Restaurants with decent food and reasonable prices

Motorcycles (see "You Are What You Ride," p. 460)

Three 10 Approaches to Argument

In addition to using one or more of the modes of argument that we have just been discussing, writers who want to persuade with an appeal to reason frequently rely on one of the two traditional forms of logical discourse: *induction* and *deduction*. These terms are simply formal labels for reasoning processes that are familiar to all of us. This chapter will examine those reasoning processes and suggest ways in which we can use them most effectively and then explore a third, nontraditional method of reasoning that has been gaining popularity in recent years.

Induction

The person who argues inductively is using a variation of the argument from evidence; he or she gathers data, reports, testimony, or other evidence and, by examining that evidence, arrives at a conclusion. Another way of describing inductive reasoning is to say that it is a method of reasoning in which one moves from observations about specific cases to a generalization about all those cases; that is, one notes the characteristics of some of the parts of the whole and generalizes that what is true of the parts is true of the whole.

Induction moves from the specific to the general

All of us use inductive reasoning, but too often we do not even stop to think about whether we are being careful about the kinds of conclusions we draw or whether we are generalizing from too little evidence or from evidence that is biased or poorly chosen. Unfortunately, many people form strong opinions from inaccurate and inadequate data and, by doing so, brand themselves as sloppy thinkers. For example, suppose you are trying to convince your parents that you should change your major from business to psychology because you have decided you want to become a family and marriage counselor. They refuse even to talk about it because they once went to a counselor who had so many personal problems of her own that she finally committed suicide. They insist that all counselors are crazy themselves. You would be furious and frustrated because they were basing decisions about your career on just one example.

Yet an astounding number of people are too lazy or too attached to their biases to go to the trouble of looking at a number of samples before they make up their minds. And you may be in that class yourself if you conclude that all economics courses are a bore just because you took one you didn't enjoy, if you assume that all football players are stupid just because you knew three in high school who didn't graduate, or if you insist that all politicians are crooked because two members of the state legislature have been indicted for fraud. Thoughtful people don't jump to conclusions that easily. But breaking the habit is difficult because most of us are so quick to make judgments. As the logician Lionel Ruby points out,

Pitfalls of induction

> Hasty generalization is perhaps the most important of popular vices in thinking. It is interesting to speculate on some of the reasons for this kind of bad thinking. One important factor is prejudice. If we are already prejudiced against unions, or businessmen, or lawyers, or doctors, or Jews, or Negroes, then one or two instances of bad conduct by members of these groups will give us the unshakable conviction that "They're all like that." It is very difficult for a prejudiced person to say, "Some are, and some aren't." A prejudice is a judgment formed *before* examining the evidence.[1]

Generalizations are necessary

Nevertheless, as Ruby goes on to say, in spite of our knowing that generalizations are dangerous, we must generalize. If we did not, we could not learn from our experiences or make any inferences from information that we gather. What we must do, then, is to find guidelines for the legitimate use of the inductive method, guidelines to follow in constructing our own arguments and to use as a check in evaluating the inductive arguments of others.

Criteria for Valid Induction

As usual, we cannot expect perfection in any argument, but we can set up and apply reasonable criteria. The criteria for the

---

[1] Lionel Ruby, *The Art of Making Sense* (Philadelphia: J. B. Lippincott Company, 1954), p. 259. Reprinted by permission of Harper & Row Publishers, Inc.

proper use of evidence in an inductive argument are, briefly, as follows:

1. The evidence should be of sufficient quantity.
2. The evidence should be randomly selected.
3. The evidence should be accurate and objectively presented.
4. The evidence should be relevant to the conclusion drawn.

Choose a big enough sample

Sufficient evidence When you construct an inductive argument in this manner, the first question you should ask yourself is "How big should the sample be?" The answer, of course, depends on the size of the whole about which you are going to generalize. Although there are no hard and fast rules about proportion, common sense tells you that the larger the population (to use sociological terms) to be included, the larger your sample should be. Thus, if you are going to generalize about a student body of ten thousand, you should probably gather data on at least five hundred individuals in that body; to use fewer would be to run the risk of missing important evidence. Note, however, that in generalizing about a comparatively small group, you have to use a proportionately larger sample. It stands to reason that if you have an assortment of cards bearing ten different designs, you will not get a representative cross section of those designs by turning up only five cards out of one hundred; if you were to turn up five hundred cards out of a total of ten thousand, however, your chances of getting a fair sample are much better. Similarly, if you were polling a class of one hundred, you could not come to any supportable conclusions by interviewing only five people from that class.

In practice, few writers specify exactly how many individual items their sample includes or mention the size of the total population about which they are generalizing. Rather, they give several examples, and the reader must decide whether the examples are sufficient. The reader must also estimate the size of the total group, but in most cases that is not too difficult to do. Usually a reader can tell whether a writer is generalizing about a whole population or a comparatively small subgroup, such as factory workers, professors, or housewives. Since there are, after all, time and space limitations when presenting an argument, readers should not be too critical or always ready to reject an argument because the sample may not be as large as, ideally, it ought to be. They must be satisfied with what seems like a reasonable number of examples.

*Choose a
representative
sample*

Random samples When you are gathering evidence for an inductive argument, the amount of evidence you collect may be less important than the variety of evidence. For valid inductive arguments, you must have a *random sample*. Investigators can get a random sample in two ways: first, they can choose data strictly by chance, or second, they can choose data that reveal a true cross section or representative picture of the whole population. (The term *population* is used here to mean the group being investigated.)

This second kind of sample is exemplified by the voter profile analysis method the major television networks use in order to predict final results very early in the evening on election night. You may have been surprised (and a little irritated by the apparent wisdom of computers) to hear the news reporter say, "On the basis of 2 percent of the vote now in in our sample precincts, we predict that Senator Percy will win by a landslide in Illinois." And usually he turns out to be right, not because he or the computers possess any supernatural wisdom, but because the sample precincts have been carefully chosen to be as representative as possible of the state as a whole.

If Illinois has 39 percent Protestants, 13 percent Jews, 38 percent Catholics, and 10 percent other, so do the precincts; if the state has 12 percent of the population earning above $30,000, 27 percent earning between $20,000 and $29,000, 40 percent earning between $10,000 and $19,000, 22 percent earning between $5,000 and $9,000, and the remainder below $5,000, so do the precincts. Other relevant data, such as level of education, occupation, percentage of eligible voters going to the polls, and political party registration, also enter into the calculations. The tremendously complex process is made possible by sophisticated computers that can retain and analyze huge amounts of diverse information. The result is a nearly perfect piece of inductive reasoning.

In ordinary rhetoric you have neither the need nor the means to do such detailed and meticulous sampling, but you can learn much from the voter profile method. If you are generalizing about a group, you must have evidence from a representative cross sec-

Suggestions for choosing a random sample

tion of that group; if you do not, your sample will be warped or skewed. For instance, if you want to find out what the dominant political opinions are on your campus, you will need to get evidence from students in a variety of departments: engineering, business, fine arts, languages, English, pharmacy, and physics might make a representative sample. You will also need to include students from different income levels. The accurate distribution of your sample will be as important, or more important, as the number of students you poll, for people in certain occupations and income levels have a predisposition to think alike. If you take your sample from only one group—the group easiest to reach—you will not get a true cross section.

If you do not have enough information about the subdivisions of your total population to construct a "sample precinct," you can use the other technique that will ensure a random sample: selecting your evidence solely by chance. One way to do this would be to pick every tenth name out of the student directory; another would be to interview every tenth student who goes into the university book store at textbook-buying time or every twenty-fifth student who comes through the line to pay registration fees. If your sample is large enough it will be a reasonably accurate cross section. Professional pollsters like Gallup or Roper use both the representative and chance methods to ensure an unbiased, truly random sample of public opinion. They are also careful to frame their questions in neutral terms because loaded questions produce biased evidence. Asking people "Are you opposed to forced busing to achieve integrated schools?" will evoke quite different answers from "Are you in favor of busing as a tool to achieve racial balance in schools?"

A few examples will illustrate the dangers of generalizing from a skewed sample. The classic instance is the 1936 presidential poll conducted by the now defunct magazine *Literary Digest*. On the basis of responses from people chosen by chance from the telephone books of several cities, the editors predicted that Landon would defeat Roosevelt. They couldn't have been more wrong. What they failed to consider was that in 1936, when the Depression was still severe, only the relatively prosperous segment of the total electorate had telephones.

Examples of biased samples

In 1976 Shere Hite exhibited the same kind of bias when she chose the sample for her book *The Hite Report: A Nationwide Study of Female Sexuality* primarily from women's groups, including chapters of the National Organization for Women, abortion rights groups, university women's centers, and women's newsletters. She also solicited responses from readers of *The Village Voice, Mademoiselle, Brides,* and the paperback *Sexual Honesty by Women for Women.*[2] Women from most of these groups would probably be strong feminists and predisposed to look critically at male/female relationships. Furthermore, out of a mailing of 100,000 Hite received only 3,000 replies, not a large return. And since one can expect that women who willingly responded to a long questionnaire about their sexual relationships would be unusually outspoken, Hite's conclusions about the way women feel about sex probably do not accurately represent the opinions of the majority of American women.

Another example of a biased sample occurred in 1980 in a report that suggested that a high-fat and cholesterol diet may not be as harmful as earlier studies had indicated. The report drew angry criticism when it was revealed that "half of the 15 members of the nutrition panel have acknowledged that they have financial ties to the food industry."[3]

Why people go wrong in choosing samples

We all should keep in mind how easy it is to fall into the habit of basing conclusions on biased evidence. Most people prefer to spend their time with others who think as they do: businesspeople talk to other businesspeople, professors talk to professors, doctors to doctors, and students to other students. Occasionally, we may have a serious conversation with someone whose views differ from ours, but usually we seek out individuals whose opinions reinforce our own. It's more comfortable that way. The danger is, however, that we will take the small part of the world that we know best as representative of the larger whole. So doctors may find it difficult to believe that any substantial number of people are in favor of socialized medicine, and business people tend to think that everyone is satisfied with our economic system. Because we tend to believe what we want to believe, it is all too easy to interpret agreement from others like ourselves as broad-based support. Politicians, pollsters, and research scientists are

---

[2] Shere Hite, *The Hite Report* (New York: Macmillan, Inc., 1976), p. xix.
[3] Anne Roard, "Science Academy's Nutrition Report Arouses Congressional Ire," *The Chronicle of Higher Education,* June 30, 1980, p. 14.

among the few classes of people who make a conscious, consistent effort to take a truly random sample before they draw conclusions. The rest of us could learn from their methods.

Accurate evidence Judging the accuracy of inductive evidence may pose problems. In this age of specialization and experts, many of us are not qualified to decide which data are genuine and which spurious. Most of the time we have to rely on the integrity of the speaker or writer; we must assume that most people tell the truth and that they do not falsify reports that could easily be checked. If, for example, a government official says, in arguing for a continuation of our Intercontinental Ballistic Missile program that the Soviet Union has 1,712 intercontinental missiles, that person may be exaggerating but probably is not. The senator who opposes the program also has access to such information and would be quick to attack a false statement.

How to judge the integrity of the source

Use your common sense to test evidence. If you read a statement in some magazine or paper you suspect is biased, don't accept it unless the writer has included supporting statistics or facts and given the source of those facts. And be suspicious of the writer who makes extravagant claims on the basis of a small number of data.

Identify your sources

The student writer also has an obligation to identify sources when quoting material or opinions. If you use statistics, you should be sure they are reliable, and you should let the reader know where you found them. If you make a positive statement about a matter on which there are conflicting views, show in some way that you have significant information to back up your statement; you could, for example, quote a professor from whom you took a course, or you could cite a documentary film you saw. And you should, of course, as pointed out in Chapter 8, state your evidence in neutral language.

Relevant evidence, relevant conclusions Finally, we must ask whether the conclusion drawn from the evidence is relevant and whether the facts given actually do point to the conclusion that we or a writer or speaker have drawn. Although it is true, for example, that Americans spend more of their personal income for medical care than the people of any other nation, we are not justified in concluding that consequently we get the best health

Be sure evidence is relevant to the conclusion

care. Doctors' fees, drug prices, and hospital charges are significantly higher in the United States than in other countries, but there is no provable correlation between cost and quality. Similarly, concluding that today's farmers are lazy because most of them no longer keep a milk cow or raise chickens would not be warranted, for it ignores the fact that they are simply devoting their energies to other, more profitable work.

In his article on the American use of convenience foods, "Science Has Spoiled My Supper," Philip Wylie commits the error of drawing an irrelevant conclusion from the evidence given:

> Without thinking, we are making an important confession about ourselves as a nation. We are abandoning quality—even, to some extent, the quality of people. The "best" is becoming too good for us. We are suckling ourselves on machine-made mediocrity. It is bad for our souls, our minds, and our digestions. It is the way our wiser and calmer forebears fed, not people, but hogs; as much as possible and as fast as possible, with no standard of quality.
>
> The Germans say *"Mann ist was er isst*—Man is what he eats." If this be true, the people of the U.S.A. are well on their way to becoming a faceless mob of mediocrities, or robots. And if we apply to other attributes the criteria we apply these days to appetite, that is what would happen! We would not want bright children any more; we'd merely want them to look bright—and get through school fast. We wouldn't be interested in beautiful women—just a good paint job. And we'd be opposed to the most precious quality of man: his individuality, his differentness from the mob.[4]

Although Wylie may make a good case that the frozen and packaged foods described in the essay are inferior, he establishes no necessary or even probable link between Americans' eating processed food and their loss of individuality and good taste—qualities which, by the way, he does not prove they had before they started eating convenience foods.

Drawing an irrelevant conclusion about convenience foods does

[4]Philip Wylie, "Science Has Spoiled My Supper," *Atlantic Monthly*, April 1954, reprinted by permission of Harold Ober Associates Incorporated. Copyright © 1954 by the Atlantic Monthly Company, Boston, Massachusetts.

*Consequences of
invalid induction*

no great harm, but misusing the inductive method can have more serious consequences. Probably you know of instances in which unthinking people have made rash and sometimes harmful judgments on the basis of wholly inadequate evidence. Beliefs many people share about welfare furnish one example. An individual may know or hear of one or two families on welfare who have color television sets. When driving through the poorer areas of a city, this person may also see expensive cars parked along the curb and several apparently able-bodied men standing around talking and laughing with each other. On the basis of these observations, none of which have been investigated—it isn't known, for instance, if the family won the television in a supermarket promotion contest, who actually owns the cars, or whether the observed men are on the night shift or are construction workers not currently employed—this person may conclude, however, that all people on welfare are freeloaders who are defrauding the state. Moreover, this person may not hesitate to use this so-called evidence to justify strong opposition to all welfare programs.

Equally faulty inductive reasoning led many nineteenth-century defenders of slavery in this country to assert confidently that a slave was really happier and better off living as a slave than as a free person competing in the mainstream of society. Because most slaves did not dare express their discontent, such defenders were hardly getting either an accurate or random sample of the slave population as a whole. Furthermore, the relatively few slaves an average Southerner knew well scarcely constituted an adequate sample from which to generalize. Yet many of the people who took a proslavery stand genuinely thought that they were making valid arguments based on solid evidence.

These kinds of conclusions illustrate one of the major pitfalls of inductive reasoning: selecting and interpreting evidence in such a way that it will confirm a bias already held. Individuals who do this may honestly believe that they have solid grounds for their opinions; what they do not realize is that they are reasoning from a priori premises, premises formed before the evidence was examined. Consequently, if they are called upon to defend those opinions, they select evidence that reinforces their premises and reject or ignore that which does not. This process cannot be called valid induction.

*Be sure evidence is
not selected to
support a bias*

There is, of course, nothing inherently wrong with forming a

*Forming a
hypothesis*

hypothesis before examining the evidence. Much scientific research begins in this just way because if investigators do not have
some idea of what they are looking for, they don't know where to
start gathering data. Nevertheless, the person using the inductive
method should hold a hypothesis only tentatively and be willing
to alter or modify it when conflicting evidence is found. The person who is committed to a theory before beginning research must
be particularly scrupulous both in selecting and evaluating evidence in order not to succumb to the temptation to find what is
desired.

Using Inductive Arguments

Judging the arguments of others By now, this analysis of the
ways in which inductive arguments can go wrong may have you
ready to challenge any that you encounter and even a little dubious about the wisdom of trying to use the method yourself. A
challenging attitude is healthy if you don't carry it to extremes. If
writers or speakers give you a reasonable number of examples that
seem to be accurate and randomly selected and their conclusions
are statements of probability rather than sweeping generalizations, give them the benefit of the doubt. After all, we can

*Give writers the
benefit of the doubt*

scarcely expect rhetoricians to present *all* the relevant data on an
issue; if they were to attempt to do so, the audience would become so bored it would never hear the argument to the finish.
Furthermore, we must accept generalizations and hypotheses
from qualified, reliable people if we are to learn anything. Your
best approach to the inductive arguments of others is, then, to be
receptive but not gullible, open minded but not naive. Be alert to
possible bias, omission, or distortion but don't assume that everyone seeks to deceive.

*Have confidence in
your ability to use
evidence*

Constructing your own arguments You should not assume,
either, that the task of constructing a respectable inductive argument is too complex and difficult for you to master. It is not. You
have access to perfectly good evidence on a variety of topics, and
you now have some guidelines for shaping it into an effective
argument.

For example, you could write a paper demonstrating that the

people in your home town or city are or are not serious about conserving energy by using what you already know about the city and supplementing it with data gathered in a survey that wouldn't take more than a few hours. For instance, if you know that your city has one or more enclosed shopping malls that are heated in winter and cooled in summer—one of them may even operate a skating rink all year round—you have one strong piece of evidence that energy is being wasted. You can also observe how many stores leave their show windows lighted all night, and how many lighted billboards or other lighted displays you have seen late at night. You could go into several public buildings chosen at random and check to see how warm or cold they are being kept. You could sit on a bench and count the number of passengers in the first fifty cars that pass. If most cars have only a driver, again you can conclude that a lot of energy is being wasted. You could get more data by asking several friends if the heat or air conditioning is kept on over the weekends in their schools or office buildings.

All this kind of evidence is specific and relevant to the topic, and you can draw a legitimate conclusion on the basis of it. The same kind of investigative techniques could furnish data for papers on study conditions in the library, living facilities for married students, or even broader topics, such as public transportation in your city or low-cost child-care facilities for student mothers.

Making the "inductive leap" As long as we are working from a sample rather than examining every single unit of the whole that we are generalizing, the inductive method cannot yield perfect results. For instance, we cannot prove beyond any doubt that attending college in the North or East is always more expensive than attending college in the South unless we have data on every single school. The possibility of error is always present when we are projecting from a sample—even the voter profile analysis is wrong sometimes. Nevertheless, we can, by careful sampling, establish high probability: a survey of representative institutions in the North, South, and East would show that going to college in New York or Minnesota is very likely to cost more than going to a school in Alabama or Louisiana. Moving from an examination of some of the available evidence to a generalization about the whole population from which that evidence is drawn is known as

Moving from evidence to conclusion

the "inductive leap." If our sample is sufficient, random, accurate, and relevant, we can be confident that the leap is warranted. If the sample does not meet these criteria, we are not reasoning, but jumping to conclusions.

Deduction

Deduction goes from the general to the specific

The study of classical deductive logic is a complex process that, if done properly and thoroughly, takes several weeks and involves learning many rules and definitions. But it is not really necessary that you learn all the intricacies of the deductive method in order to understand how it works or how to use it in arguments. In practice, you have been both encountering and using deductive logic, or syllogistic reasoning for a long time, so in this section you will be simply examining and evaluating a procedure you are already familiar with.

The three principal forms of deduction are the *categorical syllogism*, the *hypothetical syllogism*, and the *alternative syllogism*. Each does what its name suggests. The categorical syllogism sets up classes or categories and, by showing that an individual case does or does not fit into a class, affirms or denies that the individual case has the same characteristics as the class. The hypothetical syllogism sets up a hypothesis, an "if—then" statement, and by showing that the "if" part of the statement is or is not true, it leads to a conclusion. An alternative syllogism sets up two opposing alternatives in one sentence, then goes on to show that only one can be true.

Here are examples of each of the three kinds of syllogisms:

Categorical

middle term
Major premise   All persons born in the United States are eligible

major term
to be United States citizens.

minor term   middle term
Minor premise   Hans Krueger was born in the United States.

	minor term
Conclusion	Therefore Hans Kruger is eligible to be a
	major term
	United States citizen.

Hypothetical

Major premise	If a person has been convicted of a felony, that person may not be a lawyer.
Minor premise	Jane Ferguson has been convicted of a felony.
Conclusion	Therefore Jane Ferguson cannot be a lawyer.

Alternative

Major premise	A whale is either a mammal or an amphibian.
Minor premise	A whale is not an amphibian
Conclusion	Therefore a whale is a mammal.

Concrete examples and diagrams will help to clarify how these syllogisms work. Let's begin with some definitions of key terms:

Major term The term that describes the largest class in the syllogism; it is always the last term (predicate) of the conclusion.

Middle term The term that describes the class that appears in both the major and minor premise; it does *not* appear in the conclusion.

Minor term The term that describes the individual thing, person or group about which a generalization is being made; it is always the *subject* of the conclusion.

Major premise The first statement of a categorical syllogism. It makes a statement about the relationship between two classes.

Minor premise The second statement of a categorical syllogism. It makes a statement about an individual object, person, or group and one of the classes mentioned in the major premise.

Conclusion The third and last statement of a categorical

syllogism. It makes a statement about an individual object, person, or group and the *other* class mentioned in the major premise.

The following examples and diagrams illustrate how these terms are used in actual syllogisms.

The Categorical Syllogism

Affirmative syllogisms A typical affirmative categorical syllogism (that is, one in which both the major and minor premises are affirmative) would look like this:

	middle term	major term
Major premise	All United States astronauts have college degrees.	

	minor term	middle term
Minor premise	Robert Crippen is a United States astronaut.	

	minor term	major term
Conclusion	Therefore, Robert Crippen has a college degree.	

What we have done here is set up three classes: A—People with a college degree; B—United States astronauts; and C—Robert Crippen. All of class B is included in class A; therefore, the individuals in B share the characteristic of those in A. Class C is included in class B, thus it too must share the characteristic of A, that is, a college degree. Diagrammed, the syllogism looks like this:

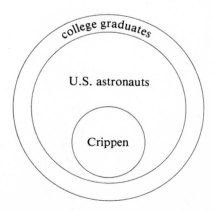

All affirmative syllogisms that are valid, that is, show positive proof, *must* look like the above figure when they are diagrammed. The *minor term*, that is, the subject of the conclusion, must be enclosed within the circle representing the *middle term*, the term that appears in both premises but not in the conclusion. The circle for the middle term must be completely within the circle representing the *major term*, that is, the term that is the predicate of the conclusion. If an affirmative syllogism is valid, you will be able to draw a straight line that runs through the centers of all the circles representing the various terms.

Negative syllogisms Negative categorical syllogisms make negative assertions about classes. A typical one would look like this:

	major term	middle term
Major premise	No Eskimos have blond hair.	

	minor term	middle term
Minor premise	Jones has blond hair.	

	minor term	major term
Conclusion	Therefore, Jones is not an Eskimo.	

Diagrammed, the syllogism looks like this:

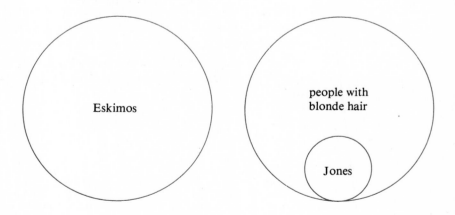

Notice that here there are two circles and that they must not touch, since by definition Eskimos are completely excluded from the class of people with blond hair. The circle representing Jones, or the minor term, comes wholly within the circle representing people with blond hair, or the middle term. Therefore, Jones cannot have the characteristics of a class from which he is necessarily excluded.

Affirmative/negative syllogisms Another kind of categorical syllogism has an affirmative major premise, but a negative minor one. A typical syllogism of this type might look like this:

	major term middle term
Major premise	All Texans are wealthy.
	minor term middle term
Minor premise	George is not wealthy.
	minor term major term
Conclusion	Therefore, George is not a Texan.

Diagrammed, it would look like this:

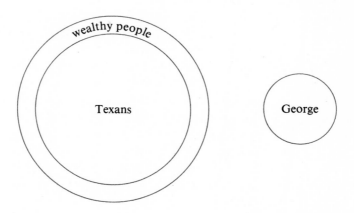

Again, the diagram proves the syllogism is valid because the circle representing the minor term, George, must come completely outside of the circle representing wealthy people. Since Texans cannot, by the definition in the major premise, be outside of that circle, George cannot be a Texan.

Testing validity—the concept of distribution Although there is more than one way that a categorical syllogism can be invalid— that is, lead to a faulty conclusion—the chief reason, and the only one to be discussed at any length here, is that it contains an undistributed middle term. Students seem to have more trouble grasping the concept of *distribution* than they do any other terms about syllogisms, so I will try to explain it as carefully as possible.

The meaning of distribution

As it is used in logic, the term *distributed* means including or excluding every single member of a group or class. When a quality or characteristic—intelligence, for instance—is distributed throughout a class, then each member or unit in that class is, by definition, intelligent. Thus the phrase "all intelligent people" or "every intelligent person" indicates a distributed term. The phrases "some intelligent people" or "most intelligent people" indicate an undistributed term. When you have a phrase that indicates *all*, then, you have a distributed term. When you have a phrase that indicates *part*—some, most, few, the majority, several—you have an undistributed term.

Distribution can also be negative; that is, it can *exclude* every person in a class. For example, the phrase "no Germans" indicates a distributed term. So does "no atheists," or "no reasonable person." "Not a single Irishman," "No one who is a patriot," or "None of the students" are also distributed terms, variations of the phrases "No Irishmen" "no patriots," or "no students."

Problems in recognizing distributed terms

Your chief problem in recognizing whether a term that describes a class is distributed or undistributed comes when writers or speakers use labels without any qualifying words to go with them. For instance, if a writer uses the term *professors* or *bricklayers*, you don't know if the word means *all* professors and *all* bricklayers or most or some or a few. The context of the statement the writer is making should give you some clue about what is intended, but you will need to decide whether the term applies to all or part before you can judge how good the syllogism is. And you need to be alert for the writer who *implies* that all members of a class are included in an accusation, when the statement actually applies only to a small part of the class.

You will also be able to handle problems of identifying distributed and undistributed terms if you memorize the following rules:

1. The middle term (that is, the term that appears in both major and minor premises, but not in the conclusion) must be distributed at least once in a valid syllogism.
2. No term that has not been distributed in the premises may be distributed in the conclusion.
3. The *predicate terms* of all *affirmative premises* are *undistributed*.
4. The *predicate terms* of all *negative premises* are automatically *distributed*. (Remember that a predicate term is one that completes the verb *to be* or another linking verb.)

Examples

distributed   undistributed
All Austrians are lovers of whipped cream.
undistributed   distributed
Most women are not ardent women's libbers.
distributed   distributed
No dogs are five-legged creatures.
undistributed   undistributed
Some brilliant people are poor.
undistributed   undistributed
Few illiterates are qualified to vote.
distributed   distributed
No one under thirty is a person who can be trusted.

Try your hand at labeling the following:

No satellites are planets.

Most atheists are radicals.

All borogroves are slithy toves.

Most people are not concerned about international affairs.

All A is Z.

The reason for all this fuss about distributed and undistributed middle terms is that, as Richard Weaver says in his book *Rhetoric and Composition*, "The fallacy of the undistributed middle is probably responsible for more faulty reasoning than is any other of the formal fallacies." (Another name for this kind of faulty reasoning is "the fallacy of the shared characteristic"; it will be mentioned again in a few pages.) So you need first to be able to recognize the middle term in a syllogism and second to be able to tell whether or not it is distributed. When you determine whether it is distributed, you can tell exactly what the class you are making generalizations about includes. If it includes *all* of a certain group, then your generalization is sound; if it includes only *part* of that group, then your generalization is faulty.

Notice that the term "Communists" in the following syllogism is the middle term. It is, however, the predicate term of both the major and minor premises; therefore, by definition, it is undistributed. The syllogism must be faulty and the diagram shows that it is.

Major premise	All members of the Politburo are Communists.
Minor premise	Sergei is a Communist.
Conclusion	Therefore, Sergei is a member of the Politburo

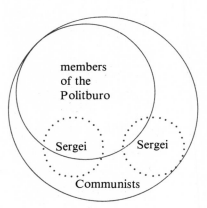

Sergei, the minor term, can go anywhere in the large circle that designates Communists; it does not *have* to go within the Politburo circle and, consequently, Sergei does not *have* to be a member. It is true that he may be, but it is not proved that he is. Because the middle term in both premises is undistributed, the syllogism is invalid. Moreover, the diagram proves it. Whenever the circle for the minor term can be put in more than one place in a diagram or whenever it overlaps a larger circle rather than coming completely within or without it, the syllogism is invalid. Here is another example:

Major premise   Most United States senators are wealthy.
Minor premise   Collins is a United States senator.
Conclusion   Therefore, Collins is wealthy.

The middle term, United States senator, is not distributed in either premise. You know then, that the syllogism is invalid. You can prove it with a diagram:

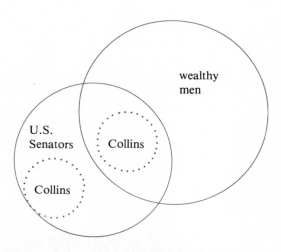

The following invalid syllogism works a little differently:

Major premise   All southerners are gentlemen.
Minor premise   McKinney is not a southerner.
Conclusion   Therefore, McKinney is not a gentleman.

The problem here is that a term that is distributed in the conclusion is not distributed in the premises, but even if you do not see precisely what is wrong, diagramming the syllogism will reveal that it is invalid:

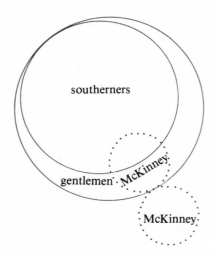

After you draw the first two circles and look for the correct place to put the circle representing McKinney, you realize that it could go either outside southerners or gentlemen. It might go outside gentlemen, but it does not have to; thus, you know the reasoning is invalid because there is more than one place to put the circle. Here is another example:

Major premise   Not all politicians are dishonest.
Minor premise   Clark is a politician.
Conclusion   Clark is not dishonest.

The middle term, politician, is not distributed in either premise, so the syllogism is invalid. You know this as soon as you make the following diagram:

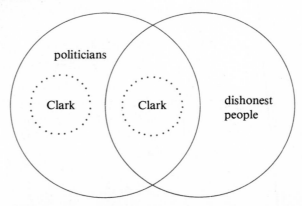

Diagramming is your quickest way to detect the fallacy of the undistributed middle term, which can also be labeled "the fallacy of the shared characteristic." It is closely related to the "guilty-by-association" fallacy. Notice how this works:

Radicals study the works of Herbert Marcuse.
Professor Schwartz studies the works of Herbert Marcuse.
Therefore, Professor Schwartz is a radical.

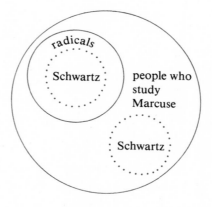

Most liberals are fuzzy thinkers.
Gerald is a liberal.
Therefore, Gerald is a fuzzy thinker.

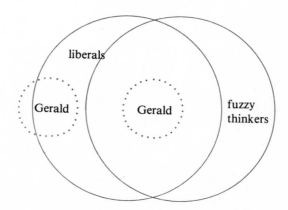

Ignorant people are racists.

Jackson is a racist.

Therefore, Jackson is an ignorant person.

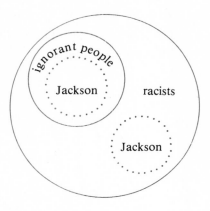

*Truth and validity
are not the same*

The difference between truth and validity So far we have been considering only the *form* of syllogisms. We have been asking whether the various statements are related in such a way that a diagram proves the minor term can go in only one place. If they are, the syllogism is valid; if they are not and the minor term can be put in more than one place, the syllogism is invalid. Obviously, this is a mechanical process, a matter of observing the rules. It shows us what we can and cannot actually *prove* beyond any doubt. If, for example, parents know that all individuals studying for the Catholic priesthood are males, they can prove to a daughter who says she wants to be a priest that her goal is logically unattainable. The circle representing candidates for the priesthood is completely enclosed by the circle representing males. The daughter cannot enter the circle of males so there is no way she can enter the circle of priesthood candidates. In this same way, parents could demonstrate to a son who aspired to be an astronaut that he must get a college education.

This kind of proving is useful and often enlightening. But a syllogism can be *valid*, that is, in the correct form, and be quite useless and even deceptive because its premises are not true. You may have suspected this earlier when you saw the example of the syllogism beginning, "All Texans are wealthy." They are not, of course, but the *form* of the syllogism is correct. So is the form of the following syllogisms even though the major premise of both is absurd.

All cows have purple wings.

Bessie is a cow.

Therefore, Bessie has purple wings.

No red-headed woman is trustworthy.

Millie is a red-headed woman.

Therefore, Millie is not trustworthy.

Two tests for acceptable syllogisms

An acceptable syllogism, then, must pass two tests: first, its form must be valid; second, its premises must be true. When a deductive argument satisfies these two requirements, then you, as a rational person, are bound to accept the conclusion. To quote Lionel Ruby again, "It is not the mark of the rational mind to say, 'Your argument is valid, and your premises are true, but I refuse to grant the truth of your conclusion.' "

Checking truth of premises

Testing for validity is fairly simple, but unfortunately, we cannot diagram for truth. To test for that we must examine the premises and decide whether, in the light of our knowledge and common sense, they seem to be reasonable statements. Assessing the truth of the major premise is especially important because usually it is the one that contains the chief generalization or definition on which the conclusion is based. For example, if a person argues that Byron White must be a brilliant man because he was a Rhodes scholar, the major premise is that all Rhodes scholars are brilliant men. The strength of the conclusion depends on the truth of the major premise. Someone who asserts that Tom Harris is a bigot because he comes from Mississippi is using as the major premise the generalization that all people from Mississippi are bigots. In the same way, the person who argues that Julie Harris must be a poor wife because she favors women's liberation is backing the argument with the major premise that no advocate of women's liberation can make a good wife.

The minor premise that puts an individual person or unit into a specific class can usually be quickly checked—after all, you probably know whether Byron White was a Rhodes scholar or if Tom Harris is from Mississippi—but the major premise is not so easy to verify, particularly because it is often an a priori premise. Moreover, when we use or encounter syllogistic reasoning in everyday discourse, frequently the major premise is not directly stated because the categorical syllogism appears in the form of an *enthymeme.*

Enthymemes

Enthymemes are condensed syllogisms

Enthymemes (pronounced ĕn-thĭ-mēmes) are condensed syllogisims from which one premise, usually the major one, has been omitted. In actual conversation the syllogism used earlier to demonstrate that Mr. Jones is not an Eskimo might sound like this: "Jones an Eskimo? Nonsense! He's a blond." The speaker thinks that the major premise, "No blondes are Eskimos," is so obvious that it is not worth mentioning. Some other syllogisms condensed into enthymemes might look like this:

We can count on McGinnis to support the tax reform bill because she is a liberal.

Unstated premise All liberals will support the tax reform bill.

The Smiths must be rich. They sent their daughter to Radcliffe this year.

Unstated premise All families who send their daughters to Radcliffe are rich.

Playboy is sent through the United States mails, so obviously it's not hard-core pornography.

Unstated premise No hard-core pornography is sent through the United States mails.

All of us revert constantly to this abbreviated form of the deductive method, both to save time and because it would be impractical and tedious always to spell out the assumptions and generalizations that underlie our reasoning. And there is nothing basically wrong in arguing in enthymemes; in fact, we must have them. We should, however, make a habit of identifying the miss-

Learn to look for the missing premise
ing premise, both in our own arguments and those that are directed to us, because anyone who works from poorly thought-out premises will necessarily come to dubious conclusions.

For example, the premise "All families who send their daughters to Radcliffe are rich" is false because some students get scholarships, some parents begin saving money for their children's education as soon as the children are born, and some college students at expensive schools receive grants that pay most of their expenses. Similarly, if someone asserts that a person is a convert to Zen Buddhism simply because there are many books on the subject on that person's shelves, he or she is arguing from a false premise. Simply owning books on any philosophy—socialism, anarchy, existentialism, or Marxism—does not identify a convert to that belief. It shows only interest, and perhaps a hostile interest.

In practice, what we usually do when we reason from enthymemes is to establish probability. For example, if the subject of politics were to come up when you were talking to a medical doctor, you might reason that he or she would be a conservative on most issues. The unstated premise backing your conclusion would be that most doctors are political conservatives. You could not be absolutely sure that the doctor you are talking to is a conservative because your middle term, medical doctors, is not distributed. Good sense would tell you that anyway; you can scarcely generalize about the opinons of *all* of any class. Nevertheless, you would be justified in your conclusion if your reading, personal experience, and observation provided solid backing for your major premise.

We argue in the same way, and with about the same degree of probability, when we try to persuade a potential high school dropout that the person who does not finish high school is sacrificing the chances of finding an interesting and high-paying job. We are making the same kind of argument when we take the position that people who eat, drink, and smoke too much damage their health. Not everyone who drops out of high school will do poorly in later life, and not everyone who overindulges is going to end up in poor health. But that's the way to bet, because the probability is very high. And that is what most enthymemes are—deductive arguments of a high probability, provided that the unstated premises are sound, if not absolutely airtight.

Enthymemes best for showing probability

Using Categorical Syllogisms

Checking your own arguments

Understanding categorical syllogisms and enthymemes can help your writing in two ways. First, it will allow you to trace the pattern of your own thinking and test both its truth and validity; thus you can correct weaknesses before you actually put them in writing. Suppose, for example, that you are petitioning the dean of your school to be exempted from the freshman mathematics requirement on the grounds that algebra will be of no use to you in your chosen profession of nursing. Your argument would look like this:

Major premise   Students should have to take only those courses which are directly useful in their careers.

Minor premise   Algebra is not directly useful to this student (me).

Conclusion   Therefore I should not have to take algebra.

Once you wrote out your argument, you would probably realize that you could not convince the dean of the major premise. The dean might reply that if the major premise were granted, requirements in history, government, English literature, and several other courses would be dropped and the college would become little more than a vocational training school.

You can also make good use of syllogistic reasoning in constructing arguments. Notice, for example, how the author Virginia Woolf uses it in her long essay *A Room of One's Own*, in which she undertakes to answer the frequently made claim that women must be intellectually inferior to men because there have been so few women writers, artists, and scientists.

> . . . It is unthinkable that any woman in Shakespeare's day should have had Shakespeare's genius. For genius like Shakespeare's is not born among labouring, uneducated, servile people. It was not born in England among the Saxons and the Britons. It is not born today among the working classes. How, then, could it have been born among women whose work began . . . almost before they were out of the

nursery, who were forced to it by their parents and held to it by all the power of law and custom?[5]

Here is her syllogism:

Major premise No genius is born among laboring, uneducated, servile people.

Minor premise Women have historically been laboring, uneducated, servile people.

Conclusion No geniuses have been born among women.

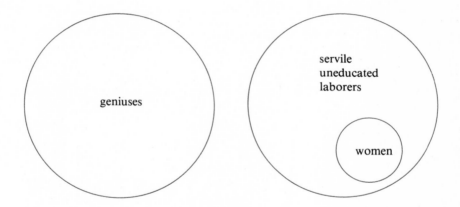

Of course, Woolf is making an argument of high probability, not absolute certainty. She would probably not put "All" before "Women" in the minor premise because there were some women, even in the sixteenth century, who were not uneducated and servile laborers—for example, Queen Elizabeth. But almost all women fit into that category, at least until the nineteenth century, and most stayed in it well into the twentieth century. So she does make a good circumstantial argument that the lack of women geniuses was due to circumstances beyond their control, not natural inferiority.

You can adapt this technique for your own arguments once you

[5] Virginia Woolf, *A Room of One's Own* (New York: Harcourt, Brace & World, 1929), p. 50.

Adapting syllogisms for your own arguments

get in the habit of thinking in syllogisms. The trick is to start by thinking of your conclusion first—that's usually not hard to identify, since we all are full of opinions. When you have identified your conclusion, go back and try to find the basis for it and in most cases you will find that you can make a generalization that includes the specific case you are arguing. Then you can work out your syllogism. Here are some examples:

Major premise	All cruel and unusual punishment is unconstitutional.
Minor premise	Capital punishment is cruel and unusual punishment.
Conclusion	Therefore capital punishment is unconstitutional.

The major part of your paper would have to be spent proving, by reasoning or by example—say instances taken from Capote's *In Cold Blood* or Camus' *The Rebel*—that capital punishment is cruel and unusual.

Major premise	Tests that discriminate against minority groups should not be used to determine who is admitted to professional schools.
Minor premise	The Law School Admission Test (LSAT) and the Medical School Admission Test (MCAT) discriminate against minority groups.
Conclusion	Therefore the LSAT and the MCAT should not be used to determine who is admitted to professional schools.

To write an argument on this syllogism, you would have to expand on and support both your major and minor premises. The major premise is a matter of opinion, and you could use arguments of definition and cause and effect to support it. The minor premise is based on data, and you would have to argue from evidence and authority to demonstrate it.

Major premise	Any business whose products are essential to the survival of our country should be subsidized by the federal government
Minor premise	Farming is a business whose products are essential to the survival of our country.
Conclusion	Therefore farming is a business that should be subsidized by the federal government.

In this paper you would have to spend most of your time and effort convincing your audience that the government should subsidize certain businesses. Probably the best way to do that would be by cause-and-effect arguments, showing what could happen if some essential businesses were to fail. The rest of the paper should be fairly easy to do.

Working an argument out in this way is more than an exercise in organization; it is also an exercise in applied reason. If after you finish the study of the categorical syllogism, you forget the precise meaning of *undistributed middle, validity,* and *enthymeme,* but you remember always to look for the basic premises on which you base your conclusions, you will have taken a major step toward improving both your writing and your thinking.

The Hypothetical Syllogism

The hypothetical syllogism also consists of a major premise, a minor premise, and a conclusion, but, as the name suggests, the major premise is a hypothesis, a conditional statement that asserts that if a certain condition or event occurs, it follows that another condition or event will also occur. The minor premise asserts that the first condition or event did or did not occur; the conclusion states that the second condition did or did not follow. The first condition in the major premise is called the *antecedent,* and the second condition is called the *consequent.* For example:

Antecedent Consequent
If a book wins the Pulitzer Prize, it must be a good book.

Antecedent Consequent
If the Labor party wins the election, wages will go up.

                    Antecedent   Consequent
If racial prejudice were a natural emotion, no one could overcome it.

Two kinds of valid minor premises

Testing validity: form There are two and only two kinds of minor premises that lead to valid conclusion for a hypothetical syllogism. In the first, the minor premise affirms the antecedent; that is, it says "yes" to part A of the major premise. In the second, the minor premise denies the consequent; that is, it says "no" to part B of the major premise. Another way of saying this is that if you can show that the statement made in part A is true, then the statement in part B must also be true. Or if you can show that the statement made in part B is *not* true, then the statement in part A cannot be true either. In practice the method works like this:

> If a book wins the Pulitzer Prize, it must be a good book.
> *Guard of Honor* won a Pulitzer Prize.
> Therefore *Guard of Honor* must be a good book.

Here the minor premise affirms the antecedent, so the conclusion is valid.

> If the Labor party wins an election, wages go up.
> Wages did not go up.
> Therefore the Labor party must not have won the election.

Here the minor premise denies the consequent, so the conclusion is valid.

> If racial prejudice were a natural emotion, no one could overcome it.
> People do overcome racial prejudice.
> Therefore racial prejudice is not a natural emotion.

Here the minor premise denies the consequent, so the conclusion is valid.

To repeat, a hypothetical syllogism is valid *only* if the minor premise affirms the first statement in the major premise or if it denies the second statement in the major premise.

Denying the antecedent makes the conclusion invalid

If either process is reversed, the syllogism becomes invalid. If the minor premise denies the antecedent, that is, says "no" to part A, the conclusion is incorrect; it is also incorrect if the minor premise affirms the consequent, that is, says "yes" to part B. A common-sense analysis will show why setting up a hypothetical syllogism in which the minor premise does either of these things will invalidate the conclusion, for instance:

> If a book wins the Pulitzer Prize, it is a good book.
> This book did not win the Pulitzer Prize.
> Therefore, it is not a good book.

The minor premise denies the antecedent, and the conclusion therefore is invalid. The reason is that the formula "if A, then B" is not necessarily reversible into "if not A, then not B." In many cases, B can exist independently of A, that is, A's *not* happening will not prevent B from existing. In this case, obviously a book can be good and not win a prize. In this next syllogism you have the same kind of invalid form:

> If Carl cuts all his classes, he will flunk out of school.
> Carl does not cut all his classes.
> Therefore, he will not flunk out of school.

A will produce B, but many students who attended class regularly have still flunked out of school. Excessive cutting is not the only reason for failure.

Affirming the consequent makes the conclusion invalid

Affirming the consequent produces the same kind of fallacy; that is, B's being true does not prove that it was caused by A, because the valid formula "if no B, then not A" cannot be reversed into "if B, then A." For example, the following syllogism is invalid because the minor premise affirms the consequent:

> If a car runs out of gas, it will stop.
> The car has stopped.
> Therefore, it has run out of gas.

The syllogism is invalid not only because it breaks a rule but because it violates the rational precept that though a certain cause may produce a predictable effect, the presence of that effect does not necessarily indicate that cause. There are many reasons why a car may stop:

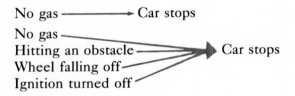

Similarly, if we were to affirm part B of the second and third hypothetical premises on page 336 we would get invalid syllogisms.

False premises ruin the argument

Reasoning about the truth of premises Formal validity by itself, however, does not make a hypothetical syllogism persuasive; we must also be convinced of the truth of the premises. If a person bases the reasoning on a flimsy or deceptive hypothetical proposition, we will reject it no matter how logically the point is argued. Simplistic assertions such as "if he is over thirty, he is a reactionary" and "if a person is loyal to her country, she does not criticize it" cannot form the basis for legitimate arguments because they are false. If, however, you accept the major premise as reasonable and the minor premise as true, a properly developed hypothetical syllogism can be an extremely effective rhetorical device.

Using hypothetical syllogisms Hypothetical syllogisms are particularly useful in arguing about intangible concepts. Arguments for the existence of God often take this form:

If there is order in the world, there must be a God who established it.
There is order in the world.
Therefore, there must be a God.

C. S. Lewis uses a hypothetical syllogism to "prove" that there is a natural law of right and wrong;

If people quarrel, they must have a common standard of right and wrong.

People do quarrel.

Therefore, they must have a common standard of right and wrong.

Using hypothetical syllogisms You can put the hypothetical syllogism to good use in your own papers, particularly when you are setting up cause-and-effect arguments. You might choose to assert, "If the grading system promotes dishonesty and destructive competition, then it should be abolished" or "If efficient public transit systems would help to solve our air pollution problems, then we should use public funds to build such a system." In either paper your two chief tasks would be, first, to support the reasoning behind your major premise and, second, to give evidence to show that your minor premise is true. The technique is a comparatively simple way to develop a convincing argument.

The Alternative Syllogism

The third kind of syllogism sets up an either/or major premise, phrasing it in such a way that it is impossible for both of the options to be true. The minor premise then asserts that one of the options is or is not true. The conclusion asserts what the consequence of the minor premise must be. For example:

The governor is either dishonest or naive.

The governor is not naive.

Therefore the governor must be dishonest.

She must either obey her father or leave home.

She will not obey her father.

Therefore she must leave home.

The city must either cut salaries or reduce services.

It cannot cut salaries because of contracts.

Therefore it must reduce services.

*Pitfalls of using
hypothetical
syllogisms*

The alternative syllogism works particularly well when you are trying to get someone to face an issue or accept a decision by pointing out the options. It has, however, two pitfalls. One, the options that the major premise sets up may not be mutually exclusive—perhaps both of the options could exist at once. Two, there may be more than two options—in fact, several choices may be open. So before you accept the conclusion of an alternative syllogism, you must be sure that the major premise is not inaccurate or oversimplified.

For instance, the frequently quoted statement that professors at certain universities must either publish or perish (that is, lose their jobs) is an oversimplified assertion. First, the options may not be mutually exclusive. A professor could publish *and* perish if what she or he published was inaccurate or plagiarized, and the same individual might also publish and perish if the university enrollment were to drop so sharply that even tenured faculty had to be dismissed.

In other cases, the two alternatives given in the major premise might be only two of several. For example, the statement "Either this country must find new sources of oil in the next ten years or reduce its energy consumption fifty percent" probably does not list all the options. Other possibilities are that companies might develop methods of getting more oil from oil sources, find a way to reclaim waste oil, develop sources of energy besides oil, convert some machines to electricity or solar energy, and so on. A spokesperson would have to *prove* that there are no other options before the major premise would be acceptable.

By all means try using alternative syllogisms in your arguments if the options you set up seem to be genuine ones. But too often people who want to force a problem into a pattern that allows two and only two alternatives are oversimplifying badly. It is at such times that you get slogans like "America, love it or leave it" and "Make love, not war." The black/white fallacies that will be discussed in the next chapter are nearly always invalid alternative syllogisms.

The Rogerian or Nonthreatening Argument

For centuries writers and speakers have been using and studying the traditional kinds of argument we have just been considering:

Weaknesses of traditional arguments

definition, cause and effect, circumstance, induction, deduction, and so on. And such arguments often succeed because people frequently do respond to reasoned, carefully supported, and skillfully constructed arguments. Yet we all are aware that sometimes logic doesn't work, that sometimes apparently rational people simply refuse to listen to reason. Ironically, such breakdowns in rational communication seem to occur most often when the arguments concern issues about which we care a great deal—issues involving questions of morality, fairness, or personal or professional standards. Because such issues involve a person's basic values, arguments about them can challenge that person's priori premises (see p. 189). When that happens, a reader or listener is likely to stop reading or listening, and the person who is arguing fails because she has lost her audience.

But the noted psychotherapist Carl Rogers thinks we do not have to admit defeat in such situations. He believes that people can communicate about sensitive issues in a rational manner and move beyond controversy to understand and perhaps accept what another person is saying if they will learn how to engage in *nonthreatening argument*. In order to do that, they need to grasp these principles of communication:

Rogers's principles of communication

1. Threat hinders communication. When a person feels threatened by what another person is saying (or writing), he or she is apt to stop listening (or reading) in order to protect the ego and reduce anxiety.
2. Making strong statements of opinion stimulates an audience to respond with strong opinions. Once people have expressed these opinions, they are more likely to be interested in defending them than in discussing them.
3. Biased language increases threat; neutral language reduces it.
4. One reduces threat and increases the chance of communicating with someone by demonstrating that one understands that person's point of view.
5. One improves communication by establishing an atmosphere of trust.[6]

---

[6] Condensed from Carl R. Rogers, "Communication: Its Blocking and Its Facilitation," reprinted in Carl R. Rogers, *On Becoming a Person* (Boston: Houghton Mifflin Company, 1961) pp.329–337. Used by permission.

In his discussion of communication blocks, Rogers shows how these principles work:

> Although the tendency to make evaluations is common in almost all interchange of language, it is very much heightened in those situations where feelings and emotions are deeply involved. So the stronger our feelings, the more likely it is that there will be no mutual element in the communication. There will be just two ideas, two feelings, two judgments, missing each other in psychological space. . . . This tendency to react to any emotionally meaningful statement by forming an evaluation of it from our own point of view, is, I repeat, the major barrier to interpersonal communication.[7]

Probably you can easily find in your own experience an example of the kind of situation Rogers refers to. For example, if someone says to you "I thought *Ordinary People* was a wonderful movie," your first impulse is probably not to ask why the other person liked it, but to give your own opinion: either "So did I" or "I didn't like it at all." Almost inevitably, once two people have committed themselves to opposing opinions on an issue, even one so trivial as the merits of a movie, they are not likely to keep an open mind on the question. Probably both parties will hasten to justify their opinions instead of listening to what the other person wants to say.

Using the nonthreatening argument

If we unthinkingly throw up this kind of barrier to communication on relatively unimportant matters, how much more likely we are to trigger strong reactions from our audience when we are writing or speaking about controversial ethical, political, or social issues. Suppose, for example, that you are a scientist doing research on lung diseases and you must write a letter to persuade members of the Humane Society not to work for the passage in the state legislature of a bill that would prohibit the use of dogs in laboratory experiments. You have a very tough rhetorical problem on your hands, one that logic alone will not solve. If you simply list the medical advances that have been made possible by laboratory experiments on dogs and suggest, rationally, that ani-

[7] Rogers, "Communication," p. 331.

mals' lives are less important than people's lives, you are not likely to make much impression on your audience because you are ignoring the real source of their opposition, their feelings. If you angrily attack your audience as sentimental and impractical meddlers whose proposals will interfere with important scientific research, you will make matters even worse because you will be threatening your audience. They will refuse even to consider what you are saying and stiffen their opposition. The communication breakdown will be total, and you will have done more to promote the unwanted bill than to stop it.

What can be done about such an impasse? Very little, if you insist that your position is the only rational one and that intelligent people ought to accept it. If, however, you are genuinely interested in solving the communication problem, Rogers suggests that there is much you can do. First, and most important, you can start by looking at the issue from the other person's point of view, that is, by trying *to empathize* with the audience you want to communicate with. As Rogers points out,

Try to emphathize with your audience

> Real communication occurs, and this evaluative tendency is avoided, when we listen with understanding. What does that mean? It means *to see the expressed idea and attitude from the other person's point of view, to sense how it feels to him, to achieve his frame of reference in regard to the thing he is talking about.*[8]

To try to understand the viewpoint of the Humane Society's members, you would probably need to talk to one or two and ask them what their goals are. You would ask them to explain specifically what it is they object to about using dogs in laboratory experiments. You would also ask what they hope to achieve with the legislation and what incidents led them to propose it. During the whole conversation you would have to force yourself to stay calm and really listen instead of getting defensive or pointing out flaws and misconceptions in their statements. Maintaining such calm would probably be the hardest part of the conversation because few people *really* want to listen to opposing views; our instinct is to attack them.

[8] Rogers, "Communication," pp. 331–332.

Once you fully understand the other person's point of view and can genuinely appreciate how he or she feels, even if you don't agree, you are ready to start trying to construct a nonthreatening argument. Remember, though, that the purpose of such an argument should not necessarily be to win. Rather, your first goal should be to increase understanding and improve communication between you and the other party, thus making it more likely that you may agree on some points. If you can establish some common ground and begin to create an atmosphere of trust, it's possible that you may be able to resolve some of your differences.

*Keep an open mind
about issues*

Since the Rogerian approach to argument is heavily exploratory and requires that you keep an open mind about the issues, you shouldn't start writing with a detailed plan in mind. Rather, you should first write down the other side's main concerns; then you can jot down some of the key points you want to make and perhaps also list some of the problems you anticipate. Finally, think about what points you can probably agree on. When you have accumulated this information, you can start writing a first draft and see what develops.

Your notes for the letter to the members of the Humane Society might look like this:

Their Concerns	*Your Points*
cruelty to animals	large animals necessary for testing experimental drugs
lack of restrictions on experiments	dogs used are unwanted strays who often starve
insufficient supervision of experiments	sufficient human volunteers not available
dogs sometimes ill treated	horror stories are exaggerated
many experiments are unnecessary	animals are well taken care of in most labs
laboratories sometimes buy stolen pets—encourage black-market operation in laboratory animals	animals are humanely disposed of after experiments

Problems	*Common Ground*
Convincing society members that animals are not abused	Concern for animals' welfare
	Concern for advancements in medical science
Convincing them that animals are absolutely necessary to medical research	Agree that animals are neglected and mistreated in some labs
Convincing them that scientists are not callous and cruel	Agree that profession needs to establish strict regulations about how animals can be used
	Agree that state should supervise labs more carefully

When you have accumulated this information, you can start writing a first draft of your letter or paper. Certainly there is no prescribed form for nonthreatening argument—the best approach is to let it develop from the material. You should, however, make sure it contains these elements:

Elements of the nonthreatening argument

1. A brief and objectively phrased statement that defines the issue.
2. A complete and neutrally worded analysis of the other side's position. This should demonstrate that you understand their position and their reasons for holding it.
3. A complete and neutrally worded analysis of the position you hold. You should carefully avoid any suggestion that you are more moral or sensitive than your audience.
4. An analysis of what your positions have in common and what goals and values you share.
5. A proposal for resolving the issue in a way that recognizes the interests of both parties.

If you can write an argument that does all these things, you will significantly reduce the threat to your readers and greatly increase the chances that they will read and consider your argument.

Obviously this nontraditional approach to argument requires extraordinary patience and effort, and to undertake it you would have to care deeply about coming to an understanding with a person or group. The approach also requires courage, for as Rogers points out,

> If you really understand another person in this way, if you are willing to enter his private world and see the way life appears to him, without any attempt to make evaluative judgments, you run the risk of being changed yourself. You might see it his way, you might find yourself influenced in your attitudes or your personality.[9]

No one would claim that this approach is easy to work out or even that one can use it consistently in emotionally tense situations. When both you and your audience have serious disagreement and, in some cases, basically different a priori premises, it is difficult to sustain the control and open-mindedness that Rogerian argument requires. Most of us are not good enough—in both senses of the word—to construct a careful but nonthreatening argument very often. And it will not work at all if one party uses the strategy as a trick to win agreement from the other party, then twists that agreement into a point for his or her side.

Advantages of the Rogerian approach

But the Rogerian approach to rhetoric can be effective if you are really more concerned about increasing understanding and communication than you are about scoring a triumph. You may be able to "win an argument" by showing an audience that the person on the other side is foolish and biased and ill informed, but you do *not* convince the person you are criticizing. Threatening and hostile comments only put people on the defensive; you do not persuade people by making them angry. The mature person who realizes this should be ready to try Carl Rogers's approach.

Exercises on Inductive Reasoning

1. The following paragraphs illustrate some patterns of inductive reasoning. From the evidence given or suggested in each one,

[9] Rogers, "Communication," p. 333.

what judgment would you make about the conclusion that is drawn?

a. Both this summer and last, I taught a section of freshman English with an enrollment of twenty students. In each of those sections I had a student who was an active member of the Socialist party. This leads me to believe that 5 percent of the students in summer school are Socialists.

b. At a recent meeting the leaders of our local parent-teacher association expressed concern because the afternoon meetings held on the first Monday of every month do not attract enough parents, particularly fathers. Someone suggested holding the meetings at night, but the president rejected that idea because those present decided two to one, that night meetings would be inconvenient.

c. The Cuban refugees who came to this country after Castro's rise to power have done quite well. A survey by the United States Bureau of Immigration shows that 48 percent of the refugees have entered the professions they were in in Cuba, 35 percent have gone into other businesses, 10 percent are in college or technical training and only 7 percent are receiving aid from a government source or relatives.

d. Our student newspaper recently conducted an experiment that demonstrates rather conclusively that the landlords in the university area are not abiding by the no-discrimination clause required in all leases. The reporters called one hundred apartment houses chosen at random from the yellow pages of the telephone directory asking if they had vacancies and if they rented to students. The supervisors of sixty-seven of those called said they did. Yet when a black couple applied to rent those apartments, in fifty-four instances they were told that there were no vacancies and none was expected.

e. A survey of members of the United States Chamber of Commerce, people who represent the outstanding achievers in our country's free enterprise system, supports this committee's belief that new corporate taxes would seriously impede industrial expansion and new investment in the next fiscal year.

f. A recent grand jury investigation of conditions in the county jail indicates a drastic need for reforms. They found three and four prisoners confined in two-person cells, inadequate lighting and ventilation, no recreational facilities for prisoners, two suicides and nineteen instances of assaults by inmates on other inmates in the past month, and sanitary conditions that one juror described as "simply unbelievable in an institution that is under government supervision."

g. Obviously influence counts more than brains when they're deciding who gets into the service academies. Admiral Crosby's nephew was accepted at Annapolis this year, and his grades weren't as good as those of a friend of mine who was turned down.

2. What kind of evidence would you need to support the following generalizations? Which ones would you phrase in more moderate terms?

a. The college students of the eighties are not interested in protest and social reform.

b. English 101 is a flunk-out course on this campus.

c. The student who graduates from a German high school is much better educated than the average high school graduate in the United States.

d. People who have taken a defensive driving course are much safer drivers than those who have not.

e. Professional football has replaced baseball as the national American pastime.

f. We are living in the most corrupt era this country has ever seen.

g. Television advertising is a major cause of the economic discontent of low-income groups in America.

h. The automobile has caused radical changes in the American way of life in the last forty years.

i. The decline in verbal scores on the Scholastic Aptitude Test may be at least partially due to the fact that we now have a whole generation of students who have been reared on television.

j. Raising and showing Arabian horses is a rich person's hobby.

3. Below are three generalizations, followed by evidence that might be used to support them. For each generalization decide which pieces of evidence constitute good support and which are of dubious value. Give your reasons.

a. Football is a character-building sport.

1. The successful football player must practice self-discipline.

2. Football is the most popular of all high school sports.

3. A good football player learns that teamwork is the key to winning.

4. Learning plays develops the memory, and drills improve the player's physical coordination.

5. A high percentage of football players have been chosen as Rhodes scholars.

b. In the fifty years following the Civil War in this country, a series of scandals occurred that caused many people to feel that the American dream had succumbed to greed and corruption.

1. In 1905 six United States senators were under indictment for fraud.

2. Mark Twain wrote "The Man That Corrupted Hadleyburg."

3. Under the Grant administration cabinet officers sold positions in the Bureau of Indian Affairs.

4. Upton Sinclair's book *The Jungle* revealed that in the meat-packing industry the owners exploited the workers and sold meat from animals that were diseased and condemned as unfit for human consumption.

5. Andrew Carnegie used his fortune to establish free public libraries across the country.

c. During the next decade the make-up of the college population in this country is going to change significantly.

1. Because of the increasing number of community colleges that make it possible for students to go to school at night, more and more adults will be entering college.

2. The open admission policies that are being adopted by many publicly financed colleges will make a college education available to those who were not previously qualified.

3. More and more adults are going to return to school as automation makes many present jobs obsolete.

4. More women want college degrees in order to become independent.

5. Fewer young men will be going to college now that the draft is no longer in effect.

4. Analyze and evaluate this student paper as an inductive argument:

The Fast Food Employee Blues

Over the past fifteen years America has gone fast food crazy. With an explosion of spontaneous growth, mammoth chains like Kentucky Fried Chicken, Jack-in-the-Box, Burger King, and of course, McDonald's, have changed the eating habits of the nation. Today, any town of appreciable size, probably including yours, has its "strip" of fast food eateries, each one in keen competition with its neighbors. The competition, naturally enough, breeds a desire among chain owners for cheap, hardworking labor. That's important—especially for you teenagers. Because believe it or not, the giant fast food industry could not exist without you. That's right—McDonald's doesn't do it all for you, you do it for them. By your need for flexible working hours, by your willingness to work hard for minimum wage, and by your inexperience concerning management tactics, you allow your local hamburger joints to operate at a profit. So if you're thinking about going to work for one of these establishments, you'd be wise to read the following.

Like ten million other teenagers every year, when I was fifteen I went to work for a fast food chain. (The manager who interviewed me kindly promoted me to legal working age with a slash of his pencil.) Like everyone else, I took the job because it was easy to get and no experience was necessary. It fit in well with my school hours, and who cared if I was only making $1.60 an hour? That was $1.60 more than I'd ever made before. I figured I had it made.

But I didn't, and it took me six years to realize why not. It's simple really, so obvious it's hard to convince yourself it's really happening. In the fast food business, company policy dictates the continued exploitation of its own employees until they get smart and quit. Like strip miners ruining a landscape, the industry methodically uses its workers until they are used up.

Don't get me wrong, I'm not going to tell you any horror stories of sweatshop-type forced labor; that simply isn't so. Although the pay is ridiculous, the jobs themselves aren't *that* bad, as far as they go. In fact, they aren't very demanding at all at the nonmanagement level. And all those reasons I gave for taking the job do apply. If they didn't nobody would work there at all. No, the fast food industry exploits young people in ways much more subtle, but almost as damaging. They are successful because, frankly, most teenagers haven't experience enough to realize they are being taken advantage of. They don't have unions to bargain for them, they don't have previous job experience to draw upon, and in most cases, they don't value their own work highly enough. They are anxious to please. High-level management knows this only too well, and predictably enough, manipulates it.

They do this by fostering a cheery, bustling, all-business atmosphere designed to make the uninitiated youngster feel he is a vital part of a larger whole. Unskilled teenagers are hired, given a uniform and an hourly wage. Most are so thankful for the job they don't care what they make. Inevitably, the new employee is given a set of rules to abide by. If the rules are followed, a gracious dime raise is meted out every six months or so. If they are broken, pay is docked or the employee is fired. By this weeding-out process, all remaining employees become cogs in a machine. Each day they perform their particular function in an assembly line of meal construction. Some draw soft drinks, some build sandwiches, some stuff french fry bags. Usually everyone does the same job every day. The advantages of teamwork are highly stressed—motivational posters abound and are changed every month. It's really a very smoothly run machine, and the atmosphere is infectious.

As a fast food employee, you're happy to be there, to be a part of it. You've got job security for the first time in your life. You may not make as much money as others your age, but you're comfortable where you are.

Now some fit into the machine better than others, that's to be expected. The ones who do are usually offered a promotion to crew leader or assistant manager. Here is where the screw is really turned tight. Store level managers are the most important people in the fast food business because they are the ones who actually set the production rate. In spite of this, they are also the most exploited.

Most assistant store managers are 17–20 years old. People this age are dazzled by the opportunity to tell others what to do. I know this because it happened to me and those around me. I was filled with warmth by the thought that the company trusted me enough to run the store. I received a key to the front door, held complete responsibility for operations during my shift, and to top it off I was equipped with a brand new weekly salary—no more punching the time clock for me. This was all pretty heady stuff; I would have done it for nothing. Oh sure, I knew I'd have to work a lot more (six days a week), and that I'd be on call when I wasn't working, and that I'd have to forego much social life. I might have even figured out that my new salary didn't amount to much more than my old hourly wage. But I didn't care, because while my peers were mowing lawns or sacking groceries, I was a *manager*. I figured the advantages outweighed the disadvantages.

I was wrong. To be brief, my working life the next few years was a constant stream of frustrations and letdowns. I couldn't understand why, after working so hard, I never made much more money and never received another promotion. I thought for awhile my problems were due to personality conflicts with my supervisors. Later, much later I caught on. *Nobody* got promoted, nobody got raises. Management vacancies were created solely by firings or resignations. In six years I saw only one store manager get kicked upstairs to the district office, and that was the supervisor's nephew. At that point, at age 21, after delaying my college education for three years because I thought I was doing so well, I walked out and never went back.

My experience is not atypical, nor is it of a type confined to one particular company. Every large fast food chain in the country operates this way, simply because it is the most profitable legal method available. Teenagers are lulled by labor-savvy businessmen into accepting jobs with the lowest possible wage and the least chance for significant advancement. Should employees tire of these conditions and quit, fine. High turnover rates are no big problem; job training is quick, and easy. To make it perfectly clear, it is just not worth these companies' effort to care much about the people who work for them. They know that the profit margin in fast food is relatively low, about twenty per cent. Any kind of incentive programs, or insurance benefits, or profit sharing arrangements would cut into that twenty per cent, so they don't even consider it.

But *you* should consider it. You can avoid the frustrations encountered by millions of young people caught in the fast food trap every year. As one who's been there, I can offer you some valuable advice about working for a fast food chain. Don't. In the long run, and the short run, you'll be better off mowing lawns or sacking groceries.

Paul Geilich

Suggested Writing Assignment

Theme

Purpose To give you practice in gathering and using evidence to construct an inductive argument.

Procedure Gather evidence for a paper on one of the following topics. Include in your theme, but on a separate sheet, a description of your sample, indicating its size and how you choose it. For example, for topic a, you should list the facilities on campus you are including: theaters, gymnasiums, tennis courts, bowling alleys, concert facilities, and so on. For topic d, you should indicate the number of television ads you watched, for how long, and what proportion of the ads was for pills or some other home remedy.

You may state your conclusion first and then give your evidence, or give the evidence first and then draw your conclusion.

Topics
a. Recreational facilities on this campus do (do not) meet the needs of the student body.
b. The newspaper advertisements for movies are (are not) a good indicator of the tastes of the movie-going public.
c. A significant proportion of the students I know feel that they would (would not) get more benefit from their education if they were graded solely on a pass/fail system.
d. Television advertisements do (do not) encourage viewers to take a wholesome attitude toward their health.

Exercises on Deductive Reasoning

1. There are at least three major syllogisms in the following passage: they may not be in absolutely perfect logical form; that is, the middle term may not be distributed, but the form is there. Begin by looking for the conclusions Orwell is trying to prove and then work back through the argument.

   As a matter of fact, very little of the concept of the tramp-monster will survive inquiry. Take the generally accepted idea that tramps are dangerous creatures. Quite apart from experience, one can say *a priori* that very few tramps are dangerous, because if they were they would be treated accordingly. A ward will often admit a hundred tramps in one night, and these are handled by a staff of at most three porters. A hundred ruffians could not be controlled by three unarmed men. Indeed, when one sees how tramps let themselves be bullied by the work-house officials, it is obvious that they are the most docile, broken-spirited creatures imaginable. Or take the idea that all tramps are drunkards—an idea ridiculous on the face of it. No doubt many tramps would drink if they got the chance, but in the nature of things they cannot get the chance. At this moment a pale watery stuff called beer is seven-pence a pint in England. To be drunk on it would cost at least half a crown, and a man who can command half a crown at all often is not

a tramp. The idea that tramps are impudent social parasites
. . . is not absolutely unfounded, but it is true in only a few
percent of the cases. Deliberate, cynical parasitism is not in
the English character. The English are a conscience-ridden
race with a strong sense of the sinfulness of poverty. One
cannot imagine the average Englishman deliberately turning
parasite. And this national character does not necessarily
change because a man is thrown out of work. Indeed, if one
remembers that a tramp is only an Englishman out of work,
forced by law to live as a vagabond, then the tramp-monster
vanishes.[10]

2. Test the following categorical and hypothetical syllogisms for
   both validity and truth. Use diagrams when applicable.

   a. All crimes punishable by death are felonies.

      Manslaughter is a felony.

      Therefore manslaughter is a crime punishable by death.

   b. No person who has been divorced can win this election.

      Stevenson has been divorced.

      Therefore Stevenson cannot win this election.

   c. If two people quarrel, they are not in love.

      John and Mary sometimes quarrel.

      Therefore John and Mary are not in love.

   d. No slithy toves are borogroves

      All momeraths are slithy toves.

      Therefore no momeraths are borogroves.

   e. If people do not vote, they have no right to criticize
      politicians.

      Jerry does not vote.

      Therefore Jerry has no right to criticize politicians.

   f. No gentleman would cheat at cards.

      Jeff cheats at cards.

      Therefore Jeff is no gentleman.

   g. All people who are members of Alcoholics Anonymous are
      nondrinking alcoholics.

---

[10] George Orwell, *Down and Out in Paris and London*, copyright 1933 by George Orwell;
copyright 1961 by Sonia P. H-Rivers. Reprinted by permission of Harcourt Brace Jovanovich, Inc., the estate of the late George Orwell, and Martin Secker & Warburg.

Stanley is not a member of Alcoholics Anonymous.

Therefore Stanley is not a nondrinking alcoholic.

h. If someone is a construction worker, he or she will have a weather-beaten face.

Joe has a weather-beaten face.

Therefore Joe is a construction worker.

i. No lawyer is a person who has been convicted of a crime.

Jane is a lawyer.

Therefore Jane has never been convicted of a crime.

j. Most geniuses are fundamentally lazy people.

George is a genius.

Therefore George is a lazy person.

3. Expand the following enthymemes into full syllogisms:

a. It can't be very good because it is made of synthetics.

b. I know she's making lots of money because she is a veterinarian.

c. Since Joe doesn't pay school taxes, he won't care if we have good schools.

d. I know he's a Texan because he's wearing cowboy boots.

e. Of course she supports the ERA. She's an intelligent woman.

f. Jones must have a Ph.D. After all, she's a full professor.

g. With his criminal record he'll never get a decent job.

h. Well, you know that Tom didn't embezzle that money. He's a warden in his church.

i. You can count on Jim's behaving well. He's a graduate of the Naval Academy.

j. Clarence really isn't an alcoholic; he doesn't drink anything but beer.

k. Smith was virtually sure of reelection simply because he was the incumbent.

4. Analyze the following student paper to discover the syllogism that underlies the argument. What are the major premise, the

minor premise, and the conclusion? Do you find it an effective argument?

The Unfair Tax Burden on the Middle Class

For as long as I can remember, April 15 has been a bad word around my house. Weeks before what my father termed the "unholiest day," my family would receive lectures on the evils of the U.S. tax system; he would use phrases like: "rape of the middle class," "unfair taxation," and his favorite, "God-damned bureaucrats." I shall never forget how irate he becomes on Tax Collection Day, U.S.A. as he puts his check in the mail to Uncle $am. I never thought things could be that unfair until I received my first 1040A form and became for the rest of my life—a taxpayer.

For a while, paying taxes didn't bother me. That was until I realized (I never listened to my father's lectures) I was a victim of unfair taxation; I was paying an unproportionate share of taxes relative to other economic groups. Somewhat dismayed, I set out to find exactly how unfair America's tax scheme truly was. The results of my studies are nothing less than outrageous. For instance, according to figures released by the Internal Revenue Service about income taxes paid in 1975, the middle class, people whose taxable income is between 20 and 50 thousand dollars per year, and who make up 15 percent of the total population, paid 57 percent of the total taxes collected. Compare this to the lower class. People with income under 20 thousand dollars per year, and who make up 85 percent of the population, which paid only 43 percent of the taxes. Is this fair? Consider this: These figures represent an effective tax rate (that is, the percentage of an individual's income which is paid in taxes) of 25.9 percent for the middle class, while they show only a 9.4 percent effective tax rate for the lower-income individual; or, in other words, a ratio of almost three to one in the amount of taxes paid by the middle class versus the lower class. Obviously, this isn't fair; it's a clear case of unequal taxation.

Of course, the discrepancy in these rates has not gone

unnoticed by critics of the tax system. For example, Diogenes, an Internal Revenue Service agent states that, "there is something wrong with a tax system that doesn't tax all incomes alike;" and, he even goes on to provide us with "The Middle-Income Taxpayer's Cheating Guide" which offers helpful hints on how to cheat on tax returns. Inevitably, solutions are provided with the criticisms; and occasionally, they are valid. These solutions range from a proposal to sharply increase the tax rate to the lower class to generating a scheme which will increase the importance of making money instead of avoiding taxes. However, I'm not sure this is what's needed.

I have formulated a plan that subscribes to an idea which I call the "Equal-Load Theory," which is founded on the basic belief instilled in all schoolchildren: Share and share alike. This theory is neither profound nor complex. It merely prescribes that all taxpayers pay a percentage of their usable income and that this percentage is the same to all taxpayers. I define usable income as that money which exists after a small amount of needed deductions (such as medical expenses, child support, etc.). Whenever this proposal is mentioned, someone always cries that it is grossly simplistic and could never solve the tax problem. I remind the critics of two things: First, I'm talking about tax on an individual's income, not the complicated taxes of a major oil company. Second, scientists have always agreed that the most simple plan which explains something correctly is the best—even when they are dealing with subjects tremendously more complex than a tax system. Why should this idea not be applied to taxing schemes also? I see no reasons.

Needless to say, myself, my dad, and most everyone else that belongs to the middle class are in an uproar over the present system of non-uniform taxing. I feel my solution to the problem (no doubt it has been suggested before) is simple and fair. Borrowing one of my father's sayings, "the rape of the middle class" has gone on long enough; now is the time for change.

Jeff McDaniel

Suggested Writing Assignments

Theme 1

Purpose To show how an ordinary argument can be built on the basis of a categorical syllogism.

Procedure Construct an argument supporting one of the following propositions. Using the proposition as the conclusion of your syllogism, work backwards to set up the whole syllogism. Your argument should be a supported expansion of the premises of your syllogism.

Example You want to argue against a proposal that the city council is considering that would require all people owning female dogs to either have them spayed or pay a licensing fee of twenty-five dollars.

Major premise	The council should not pass any law that would prevent people in low-income groups from owning pets.
Minor premise	The proposed law would prevent people in low-income groups from owning pets.
Conclusion	The council should not pass the proposed law.

Your paper would support first the major premise, probably with cause-and-effect and definition arguments, then illustrate the minor premise with examples, and treat the conclusion in a few sentences. As an introduction, you might show that you realize that the people who proposed this regulation are doing it out of concern for animals.

Remember that your first step in thinking out your argument is to decide on your conclusion; then work back to setting up your major and minor premises. If you have trouble setting up your syllogism, ask for help before you begin your paper.

Choose one of these topics, taking only *one* side of the issue.

Topics

a. Single people should (should not) be allowed to adopt a child.

   b. An X or R rating should be assigned to any movie that features violence or torture.

   c. Contraceptive devices should (should not) be available to anyone who wants them, regardless of age, marital status, or ability to pay.

Theme 2

Purpose To show how the hypothetical syllogism may be used to work out an argument.

Procedure Choose one of the paragraphs below and read it carefully. Decide how you think the person involved should solve the problem and why you believe that solution is the best. Then put your reasoning into a hypothetical syllogism that summarizes your points. Develop that hypothetical syllogism into a theme.

Example In case A, the major premise of your syllogism might look like this;

> If a person is an elected law official, he or she has an obligation to enforce the law impartially, regardless of who may be affected.

Or this:

> If a person has to choose between loyalty to the family and duty to the profession, he or she should put personal obligations before business obligations.

Or this:

> If a person thinks that a particular course of action is going to corrupt young people, his or her obligation is to stop that action at all costs.

Of course, you may not agree with any of these interpretations. Work out your own for one of the cases, and then develop your theme by expanding and supporting the premises of your syllogism. *Be sure you set up the minor premise so that your reasoning is valid.*

Topics

a. Mr. Chase, the local district attorney, is earning himself a statewide reputation by vigorously tracking down and obtaining convictions of pushers of hard drugs. He is, understandably, proud of his work and feels that he is contributing to cleaning up his town and protecting the young people in it. Just before a planned raid Mr. Chase gets an anonymous phone call that warns him that his son is one of the key figures in the ring of pushers that will be picked up. The phone call may be a trick to get him to call off the raid; on the other hand, when he thinks about some of the strange behavior of his son in past weeks, he realizes that the caller may be telling the truth. The raid is due to start in ten minutes and he could give his men no good reason for calling it off, but if he goes ahead with it, his son may be arrested and sent to prison for ten years. What should Mr. Chase do?

b. Young Jim Dodson is a cadet at the U.S. Air Force Academy, an institution that demands of its students a very strict code of honor. Not only must the cadets pledge not to lie, cheat, or steal, but they must also pledge to reveal any code violation by another cadet. Dodson knew this when he entered the academy and approved of the regulation because he feels that a dishonest man is not fit to be an officer or to lead other men. The night before a final examination he finds that his roommate has made a complete set of crib notes to take into the exam with him and has done it so cleverly that there is little chance that he will be caught. Dodson knows that it is his duty to turn in his roommate; he also knows that if he does the boy will be expelled from the academy and probably will not get an education since his family is very poor. But if the boy is caught and Dodson is asked if he knew about the cheating, he will lose whether he lies or tells the truth. What should he do?

Theme 3

Purpose To help you understand the concept of the Rogerian approach to argument by putting it into practice.

Procedure Write an argument in which you put yourself into *one* of the situations described below and try to persuade your audience to accept your point of view. Consider carefully how and why your audience is going to be threatened by the proposal you are making, and think how you can best alleviate their fears and persuade them to see your point of view. Before you start, reread the text. Organize your paper according to the five phases of argument summarized on pages 341 and 345.

Topics

a. You are a man of thirty-five who makes about $20,000 a year as a salesman, but after ten years of work you have come to detest your job and want to go back to college in order to become an engineer. As a veteran, you will receive about $330 a month while you are in school, but that will not be enough to live on. You want to convince your wife that in the long run you will both be happier if you make this change, but she is skeptical. She has a job that pays $650 a month. You have no children.

b. You are a young psychologist who has just bought a home in one of the old and established neighborhoods in your city. You cannot afford to rent a separate office in a medical complex, and you want to establish your counseling practice in your home. You will be able to do this only if other residents in your block of the street will sign a statement agreeing to let you open a professional office in that block. Write a letter to these neighbors that might persuade them to sign such a statement.

c. You are a college sophomore who cannot decide on a career and you want to drop out of school for a year to rethink your goals and values. You must convince your parents who are very much opposed to the idea.

Fallacies 11
and
Propaganda

How Not to Argue and What Not to Believe

Fallacies are sometimes called *counterfeit arguments*. The figurative description is apt because, like bogus money, fallacious arguments resemble the real thing (logic) but have flaws that cancel their value as sound rhetoric. Fallacies are usually classified as *formal* if those flaws are in form or structure and as *material* if the flaws are in content or matter.

Formal Fallacies

Fallacies of deductive and inductive logic

We have already covered the chief fallacies of the various kinds of syllogisms used in deductive logic. For the categorical syllogism, it is the fallacy of the shared characteristic or the undistributed middle term. For the hypothetical syllogism, it is the fallacy of denying the antecedent or affirming the consequent. For the alternative syllogism, it is the fallacy of insufficient options. The errors of generalizing from an insufficient sample or from a sample that is biased or not randomly selected might be called the *formal fallacies of inductive reasoning*.

Circular arguments

Another kind of formal fallacy is the *circular argument*. This kind of reasoning appears to move from a premise to a conclusion, but in reality it does no more than move in a circle. Such a pseudoargument might go like this: "The proposed gun control legislation is a left-wing plot because only Communists would scheme to take guns away from citizens." "Jones cannot be trusted because she is an unreliable person" is just as circular. The main assertion is not supported but simply repeated.

Students sometimes slip into this kind of fallacy when doing rhetorical analysis. They may, for instance, conclude a theme with a statement like this: "The writer is not persuasive because he does not convince the reader to accept his idea." Unfortunately, their teachers sometimes do no better. Several years ago the authors of an article in an educational psychology journal claimed to have proved that feminine and masculine traits exist among very young children. They cited as evidence for their theory an experiment conducted by putting an equal number of male and female three-year-olds in a room with an assortment of toys. Their observations convinced them that boys had a definite preference for "masculine" toys, and girls showed a marked preference for "feminine" toys. Then they defined "masculine" toys as those preferred by boys and "feminine" toys as those preferred by girls! A government official who replies to a journalist's inquiry about why certain documents have been marked "classified" by saying that they contain confidential information is using the same kind of evasive reasoning.

Informal Fallacies

Faulty Analogy

Two major informal fallacies, *faulty analogy* and *false cause,* have already been touched on in the chapter on modes of argument, but they are important enough to warrant a brief review. Prudent writers seldom use analogy as a main rhetorical device because, although a good analogy can clarify and reinforce an argument, it cannot actually furnish proof. And most analogies break down if they are pushed too far. For instance, proponents of our multibillion dollar space program have sometimes drawn an analogy between that program and the opening of our American frontier to justify the expenditure and human resources that we have invested in space exploration. The comparison is a faulty one, however, because there are far more differences than similarities between the two enterprises. Each may introduce people to an unknown territory, but people cannot journey to space on their own, and they cannot settle and cultivate the area after they get there. The comparison of trips to the moon to Columbus's voyages has the same weaknesses. Analogies of this kind have more emotional than rational force. Because Americans are likely to respond favorably to words such as *exploration, pioneer,* and *frontier,* too often they do not carefully examine the validity of the arguments in which they are used.

Weak analogies hurt arguments

As a precaution against being misled by such easy comparisons, when you use or encounter an analogy you should ask yourself, "Are there enough important similarities between the two things being compared to really support the conclusions that are being drawn?" If a comparison is far-fetched, as it would be if drawn between the president of the United States and the captain of the football team, or if it is trivial, as it would be if it were drawn between learning to fly a plane and learning to ride a bicycle, you should reject it.

False Cause

The informal fallacy of *false cause* (Latin term: *post hoc, ergo propter hoc*) is another form of simplistic reasoning. Human laziness or the desire to see dependable patterns in a complex world tempts us to solve problems by setting up neat cause-and-effect relationships. It is much easier to say "Permissive child rearing causes juvenile delinquency," "The Vietnam War caused our economic problems," or "Pornography causes sex crimes" than it is to try to trace and understand the complicated chain of circumstances that underlies most problems or events.

In the 1950s, shortly after the United States government had conducted a series of hydrogen bomb tests in the Pacific, the country was hit by an unusually severe winter. Despite the meteorologists' protestations that the weather was the predictable result of a change in the Gulf Stream, some people insisted that the bomb tests had caused it. *The New Yorker* magazine satirized this kind of thinking in a cartoon showing two Neanderthal men peering out of a cave at a torrential rain. The caption was, "We never used to have this kind of weather before they started using bows and arrows."

Fallacies common in political rhetoric

Understandably perhaps, people who are running for office rely heavily on the "after this, therefore because of this" strategy. First, most campaigners who are trying to discredit the current officeholders suggest that they are directly responsible for all the bad things that happened while they were in office. If taxes or unemployment or the crime rate or the cost of living went up during an administration, the challenger always blames the incumbent just because he or she was there. The incumbent, of course, oversimplifies in the same way by taking credit for all the good things that happened during the administration. And the "ins" and the "outs" both project their false cause fallacies into the future by predicting with great certainty that certain effects will follow the election: good effects if "we" are elected, bad effects if "they" are elected.

Now not all such reasoning is faulty. We base our votes on the premise that electing particular candidates will at least help cause or prevent certain effects. And if such predictions are backed with reason and evidence, we are justified in believing them. But one should always be careful about claiming that any one person or act caused something complex to happen.

This same technique is used extensively by advertisers, who rely on it heavily to convince their customers that delightful effects will follow their purchase of a certain product. "Drive our car and the girls will swarm all over you," "Bleach your hair and rekindle your husband's lagging affection," "Take our correspondence course and earn $20,000 a year," "Use Endocreme and look young again." What deceptively simple cause-and-effect arguments!

Begging the Question

Another informal fallacy that crops up as often as weeds in a garden is *begging the question*. The term describes the process of assuming in the premises of an argument what you ought to be establishing by proof; another name for it might be *loading the assertion*. It resembles circular reasoning in that the writer does not construct a legitimate argument but merely asserts that something is because it is. For example, the statement "Henry Miller's filthy books should not be allowed in our library," which neither proves that the books are filthy nor shows why they should be taken out of the library, is a loaded assertion masquerading as an argument. So are the following sentences: "Useless courses such as Greek and Hebrew are a waste of time"; "This fine public servant deserves our support"; and "This corrupt official should be thrown out of office." A reader would probably agree that useless courses are a waste of time, fine public servants deserve support, and corrupt officials should be gotten rid of; such statements are almost redundant. But in each case the writer has not proved the allegation.

The fallacy of begging the question creeps into writing in subtler ways as well. A common form is the question-begging epithet, that is, a favorable or unfavorable label attached to the subject of the assertion, for example, "John's *disgraceful* conduct ought to be censured" or "This *treasonable* act must not go unpunished." Such statements substitute connotation for argument.

Other expressions that appear frequently in question-begging arguments are "It is common knowledge," "Everybody knows," "Everyone would agree," "It is obvious," and "The fact is." When these are followed by no more than statements of opinion, the chances are that the writer is trying to evade the burden of proof. Statements like "Everyone knows that socialized medicine has been a failure in England" and "It is common knowledge that the Syndicate controls the numbers racket" prove nothing unless they are followed by supporting evidence.

Argument to the Person

*Argument to the
person instead of to
the issue*

Argument to the person (Latin term: *argumentum ad hominem*) focuses on an individual's character or personal life rather than on the issues involved. If a person is running for office, the debate should center on qualifications, experience, and the kind of program advocated, not on religious beliefs, military record, or marital status. The campaigner who overemphasizes a war record and church affiliation and keeps appearing on television with his or her family, but who says little about taxes or legislation, may reasonably be accused of evading the real issues. That person is trying to appeal to the audience's emotions rather than to its reason. Unfortunately, such tactics often work. Until recent years, a divorced person stood little chance of being elected to public office, and John F. Kennedy was the first successful Catholic presidential candidate. But the thinking person tries to look beyond personalities and personal biases when making a judgment about an individual's qualifications or achievements. To condemn an author's works because she or he is reputed to be a heavy drinker or to say that a person ought not to be elected to Congress because he or she does not belong to a church shows a poor grasp of the real issues involved.

People who want to make thoughful and rational judgments will pay little attention to mudslinging, gossip, or unsupported accusations against office seekers or other public figures. They will try to focus on matters that affect a person's work and official behavior. For this reason you should be wary of anyone who tries to sell you a program or platform not by stressing issues and proposals but by relying on patriotic clichés, such as "he fought for our country" and "she is a devoted wife and mother."

There are times, however, when habits or beliefs can become

Personal matters can be relevant

legitimate concerns. If a person who is running for office actually is an alcoholic, that person may not be able to handle the responsibilities of the office. Or if you want very much for the next legislature to legalize gambling in your state, a candidate's religious affiliation may indeed be pertinent. But everyone should try to distinguish between personal attacks and information that bears on the issue. The following kind of political advertisement illustrates the problem:

Vote for Honesty and Decency

John Q. Candidate stands four-square on his record of thirty scandalfree years as county treasurer. You *know* he's honest. On the other hand, his opponent is a man who declared bankruptcy in 1968, has been married three times, and last year was brought into court twice on charges of reckless driving.

Is it an *argument to the person* fallacy or a justified baring of relevant information?

Argument to the People

Argument to the people (Latin term: *argumentum ad populum*) is similar to the previous one. It takes the form of impassioned emotional appeals "to the people," that is, to the deep biases people have for institutions such as God, motherhood, country, family, and may have against fascism, communism, atheism, or other such abstract concepts. This fallacy too seeks to arouse emotions rather than confront issues. In Albert Camus' *The Stranger*, the state prosecutor pleads to the jury to send the protagonist, Meursault, to the guillotine not so much because he killed a man in a moment of irrationality, but because he did not cry at his mother's funeral and was unmoved when the prosecutor showed him a crucifix. And the jury convicted. As we shall see, propaganda relies heavily on the argument to the people.

"To the people" appeals to deep biases

You're Another

This fallacy (Latin term: *tu quoque*) takes the form of evading the issue or deflecting a hostile charge or question by making a similar charge against the opponent. For example, a person who had been charged with cheating on an expense account might counter the accusation with, "Who are you to criticize me for padding my expense account when I know you cheat on your income tax?" Lionel Ruby quotes a typical *you're another* argument on the issue of the draft. A younger man might say to an older one, "You're in favor of the draft because you're too old to go." The older one might reply, "Maybe so, but you're against it because you're afraid you'll have to go."[1] The so-called argument is entirely beside the point; neither has mentioned the merits or defects of the draft law.

Exchanges on a low personal level are not difficult to spot for the counterfeits they are, but these kinds of arguments sometimes become rather sophisticated—in fact, one finds them in surprising company. Take, for example, this paragraph from a Jean-Paul Sartre essay on existentialism:

> As is generally known, the basic charge against us [Existentialists] is that we put the emphasis on the dark side of human life. Someone recently told me of a lady who, when she let slip a vulgar word in a moment of irritation, excused herself by saying, "I guess I'm becoming an existentialist." Consequently, existentialism is regarded as something ugly; that is why we are said to be naturalists; and if we are, it is rather surprising that in this day and age we cause so much more alarm and scandal than does naturalism, properly so called. The kind of person who can take in his stride such a novel as Zola's *The Earth* is disgusted as soon as he starts reading an existentialist novel; the kind of person who is resigned to the wisdom of the ages—which is pretty sad—finds us even sadder. Yet, what can be more disillusioning than saying "true charity begins at home" or "a scoundrel will always return evil for good"?[2]

Sartre has not at all refuted the charge that existentialism is a gloomy philosophy that focuses "on the dark side of human life." He has only deflected the criticism by saying, in effect, "You call

---

[1] Lionel Ruby, *The Art of Making Sense* (Philadelphia: J. B. Lippincott Company, 1954), p. 89.
[2] Jean-Paul Sartre, "The Humanism of Existentialism," *The Philosophy of Existentialism* (New York: Philosophical Library, Inc., 1965), p. 32.

us gloomy! You're just as gloomy with your cynical slogans and admiration for naturalistic novels."

Black/White Fallacy

*Either/or options
often oversimplify*

This fallacy may also be called the *fallacy of insufficient options* or the *either/or fallacy*. Writers or speakers who use it are trying to force their audience into choosing between two conflicting alternatives by suggesting that there are no other options. In fact, there may be several options or even the option of making no choice. This kind of oversimplification is attractive to people who have what the psychologists call "two-valued orientations"; that is, they see the world in terms of black and white, right and wrong, good and bad. As you can imagine, they don't have many philosophical problems. A typical example of their outlook on life is illustrated by the bumper sticker "America—Love It or Leave It." This kind of attitude is as prevalent on the left as it is on the right. "Either you believe in socialism or you're a dirty fascist pig" is as bad as "If you're not an advocate of free enterprise, you're a communist sympathizer."

Rational thinkers neither rely on this tactic nor allow themselves to be intimidated by it. For example, if they are concerned about industrial air pollution in this country, they do not argue that we have to choose between factories and clean air. They know there are other options: filtering devices and other controls that will give us clean air if we are willing to pay for it, relocating factories to reduce the concentration of pollutants, and so on. They do not subscribe to the simplistic view that the solution to our technological problems is a return to nature. Moreover, they see the flaws in aruments such as the following:

> Johnny goes by the official title of "student." Yet Johnny is the face every professor would prefer to see anywhere but in his classroom where it blocks with its dreary smile, or its stoical yawn, the educational process on which we are proud to spend annually billions of dollars. By his sheer inert numbers he is making the common pursuit of professors and students—real students—impossible.[3]

---

[3] Hugh Kenner, "Don't Send Johnny to College," *Saturday Evening Post*, November 14, 1964, pp. 12–16.

Kenner goes on to define the "real student" as one who insists on knowing:

> . . . What it does not know it will encounter with pleasure. And it *must* learn, as a cat must eat. . . . its tireless curiosity is unmistakable. In time, if all goes well, it will accept training, and the life-long responsibilities of keeping itself trained.
>
> But Johnny has no such appetite, no such momentum. When Johnny applies his brand-new ball-point to his first blue book, each sentence comes out smudged with his unmistakable pawprint.

Throughout the essay Kenner recognizes only two kinds of students: Johnnies and real students. The real student is always described in favorable terms—"tireless curiosity," "a mind that insists on knowing," "encounters knowledge with pleasure"—while Johnny is defined by his "dreary smile," "stoical yawn," and the smudge of "his unmistakable pawprint." The argument is totally black and white; Kenner does not acknowledge the possibility that there may be students who do not fit into one of his categories. As a result his argument, although cleverly written, falls to the ground.

Misuse of rhetorical questions

The loaded rhetorical question that allows for only one acceptable answer is a form of the black/white argument:

> Are we going to take steps to maintain law and order in our community, or are we going to allow the thugs and dope addicts to take over this town and ruin our homes and families?
>
> Shall we vote against this bill for increased welfare payments, or shall we abandon our fight to stop creeping socialism in our society?

The Complex Question

Double questions confuse the issue

The *complex question* is fallacious because it sets up a question in such a way that a direct answer can only support the questioner's assumption. The classic example is "Have you stopped beating your wife?" To answer either "yes" or "no" is incriminating. The deceptive part about this fallacy is that the questioner is apparently asking only one question, but in reality is asking two: "Did you ever beat your wife?" and "Do you now beat your wife?" Other variations of this fallacy might take these forms:

> Does everyone in your town still get drunk and raise hell on Saturday night?
>
> How long have you been consorting with known criminals and other Syndicate types?
>
> What made you think you could get away with plagiarizing that paper?
>
> When did you start cheating on your income tax?

Questions like these are designed to trick an audience and therefore do not deserve a direct answer. You can cope with them only by insisting that the questioner break the question down into two distinct parts to be answered separately and independently.

Red Herring

Bringing in irrelevant issues

This term, which refers to smoked herring, a particularly strong-smelling fish, is a figurative phrase that describes the tactic of bringing in an irrelevant point to divert the audience's attention from the main issue. It refers to the old belief that dragging a red herring across a trail would divert the attention of hunting dogs from the scent they were expected to follow and send them off in another direction. There are many kinds of diversionary tricks used in arguments, but we usually reserve the term *red herring* for the digression a speaker or writer uses to sidetrack an argument.

For example, if a labor leader were arguing that unions ought to be exempt from antitrust laws but spent much of the speech describing the hardships union people endured in the early part of this century, he or she would be employing a red herring fallacy. Labor's fight for the right to bargain collectively is important historically but has nothing to do with the present issue. The fallacy also crops up when a speaker interrupts a debate on a specific issue to bring in matters that are not under discussion. For instance, a college faculty member who tried to sidetrack a discussion about faculty salaries into an attack on the school's publish-or-perish rules would be using a red herring fallacy. The latter problem may be worth discussing, but it is not the issue under consideration.

The Genetic Fallacy

Misleading references to origins

People who argue from the *genetic fallacy* assert that we can predict a person's nature and character if we know that person's origins. They would hold that the same is true for institutions, works of art, or ideas. We often find this fallacy expressed as an enthymeme:

He wouldn't do that because he's from a good family.

Jane must be a racist since she spent her early life in South Africa.

The Reivers must be a Gothic novel since Faulkner wrote it.

Acupuncture cannot be an acceptable technique for modern doctors since it was developed in ancient China.

Jack is bound to be exceptionally bright because his father is a professor.

That radio won't last very long if it came from Japan.

Some of these conclusions *may* be true, but proving them requires evidence, not simply speculation about origins.

Special Pleading

Biased use of evidence

This term describes a totally one-sided argument that is presented as the whole truth. The points that the arguer makes for or against the issue may be quite true, or at least supported with reasonable evidence, but the position is so biased that it cannot be considered valid. Mark Twain used this kind of argument against the church and Christianity in his novel *The Mysterious Stranger*. He focused on the crimes that have been committed in the name of the church, on the misery and injustice that God allows to exist in the world, and on the suffering of good Christians and the triumph of those who flout God's laws. Bertrand Russell took the same approach in his book *Why I Am Not a Christian*. Neither man conceded any good to Christianity. Even those people who are inclined to share the writers' prejudices should realize that their arguments, although supported with examples, are completely unfair. Any argument that concentrates solely on the merits or defects of an institution or system and ignores whatever points may be made on the other side is open to the same charge.

The Appeal to Ignorance

Persons who use the *appeal to ignorance* (Latin term: *argumentum ad ignorantiam*) typically assert that a claim or theory must be right because no one can prove that it is wrong. Thus they try to evade their own responsibility for supporting or proving a point by simply shifting that obligation to their opponents. Frequently, people who argue in this way will make highly dubious cause-and-effect statements and defy their challenger to show that the relationship is impossible. If the challenger cannot, the arguer interprets the response as agreement.

Putting burden of disproof on opponent

For example, someone might claim that wearing a copper bracelet will bring about improvement in people who suffer from arthritis. Although medical specialists have repeatedly pointed out that there is no scientific basis for the claim, the promoters of copper bracelets can say that neither has anyone proved that they *don't* help. Therefore they claim, they have a right to say they do help.

This catalogue of common fallacies by no means includes all the ways in which an argument can go wrong. Studying it, however, should alert you to the more obvious weaknesses in the arguments of others and help you avoid such pitfalls in your own rhetoric. If, while you are constructing an argument, you can spot those places at which an opponent might justly say, "Oh, but you're not being logical" or "Ah ha! Your conclusion does not follow from the evidence you have given," you can strengthen your own writing. But we also have to remember that almost no rhetoric is totally free of fallacy—even Plato or John Stuart Mill could produce arguments that might be justifiably criticized.

Most rhetoric has some fallacies

Don't demand perfect arguments

We cannot demand perfection and unswerving consistency from any speaker or writer; such a demand is in itself a kind of fallacy. What we must do, then, is make a balanced and charitable judgment of other people's arguments. An occasional question-begging epithet or genetic fallacy does not constitute sufficient grounds for rejecting an entire editorial, essay, or speech. If, however, an argument contains blatant false cause fallacies or personal attacks and the author twists the evidence, you have every right to say that it is not a sound or just argument. Finally, you should remember that your opponents are not the only ones who indulge in fallacies. You must be honest enough to search out the fallacies in arguments you agree with, as well as in those to which you are hostile.

Why Not Use Fallacies?

Ethical considerations Students often ask, "Well, what's the matter with using fallacies in an argument if they help you to win?" There are two answers to that question, one ethical, one practical. The first involves definition. Using dishonest means—and that is what fallacies amount to if a person is using them consciously—to attain an end brands you as a dishonest person. A fallacy is a swindle, a counterfeit argument, an evasion of your responsibility to support your beliefs with logical and legitimate methods. Viewed from an ethical standpoint, this question is on the same level as "What is the matter with cheating if it gets you a good grade?" or "Why shouldn't I lie if it's to my advantage?" Deception by any other name remains deception.

Using fallacies deliberately is unethical and hazardous

Practical considerations Viewed from a practical standpoint, fallacies in your argument may contribute to defeating your purpose. If you use fallacies deliberately and cynically, you are assuming that your audience is not very bright and cannot detect twisted reasoning. Even people with untrained minds are not totally gullible; they can recognize loaded statements and spurious appeals to their emotions, and they will realize you are insulting them. People with trained minds will immediately dismiss a fallacious argument as not worth bothering with. If you cannot construct a rational defense for your ideas, they will label you as a sloppy thinker. If they think you are capable of putting together a reasonable and careful argument but prefer to make an irrational one in the hope of winning, you will lose their respect and support.

Propaganda

All rhetoric seeks to persuade, but *propaganda*, as we shall use the term here, seeks to persuade principally by appeals to the emotional, irrational side of our nature. As Lionel Ruby put it:

A propagandist, in the strict sense, is not interested in the truth for its own sake, or in spreading it. His purpose is different. He wants a certain kind of action from us. He doesn't want people to think for themselves. He seeks to mold their minds so that they will think as he wants them to think, and act as he wants them to act. He prefers that they should *not* think for themselves. If the knowledge of certain facts will cast doubts in the minds of his hearers, he will conceal those facts.[4]

Propagandists rely on fallacies

Given these goals, we might expect propagandists to rely heavily on fallacies to achieve their ends. And so they do. Whether they are promoting a product, an ideology, a frame of mind, or a person, they will employ counterfeit arguments designed to short-circuit the reasoning process and go straight to the emotions. Sometimes this technique is employed to achieve useful, even admirable, goals; nevertheless, propagandists quite often reveal a real contempt for their audience. They operate from the assumption that the audience is irrational, shallow-minded, more swayed by myths than by facts, and incapable of abstract or logical thinking. Propagandists who have contempt for their audience agree, in effect, with Adolf Hitler that "the people in their overwhelming majority are so feminine by nature and attitude that sober reasoning determines their thoughts and actions far less than emotion and feeling."[5] These propagandists are confident that they, with their superior intellect and knowledge of human weaknesses, can manipulate and condition the masses into buying what they have to sell.

Commercial Propaganda

Advertisers also use fallacies

In recent years the advertising industry has learned so many ways to use fallacies and to manipulate the language that commercial persuasion has become almost a special branch of communication. As a former adman, Carl P. Wrighter, puts it in his book, *I Can Sell You Anything:*

[4] Ruby, *The Art of Making Sense*, p. 76.
[5] Adolf Hitler, *Mein Kampf*, trans Ralph Mannheim (Boston: Houghton Mifflin Company, 1933), p. 183.

You see advertising is really a science, and it is mostly a science of human motivation and behavior. When we get ready to pitch a new soap to you, we know more about what you do in your bathroom than your own wife or husband. Not only that, we know why you do it, how you do it, and what makes you do it. We know what kind of appeals you will respond to, what kind of emotions you will fall prey to, even the very words which will strike a chord on your heart strings. In short, persuasion in advertising is done not so much by dispensing information publicly as by attacking your weak spots emotionally, and having our products soothe your savage ego.[6]

Ad agencies learn to play on your emotions and ego by spending large chunks of their budgets on motivational research, the systematic study of people's needs, fears, anxieties, hopes, and desires. They hire sociologists to advise them about patterns of behavior and the attitudes of various economic groups. They hire psychologists to tell them what stimuli will trigger favorable responses toward a product and what symbols they can use to set up good associations with their products in the minds of the consumers. And using these insights, they assault each of us, one student of our culture claims, with a minimum of five hundred messages a day.[7]

Arguments to the people, red herrings, and question-begging fallacies abound in advertising; so, of course, does the false cause fallacy that suggests that using a product will cause certain wonderful results. And what almost all advertisements have in common is their heavy load of emotional appeal. Carl Wrighter analyzes it like this:

Ads rely on emotional appeal

Emotionalism is always present in advertising. It is used in two ways: First, as a hook, leading up to the factual message or claim; and second, as a sale all by itself, when no fact, claim or demonstration is available. Generally it relies on buzz

[6] Carl P. Wrighter, *I Can Sell You Anything.* Copyright © 1972 by Ballantine Books, a Division of Random House, Inc. Reprinted by permission of the publisher.
[7] Alvin Toffler, *Future Shock* (New York: Bantam Books, Inc., 1970), p. 167.

words, which trigger emotional responses, and usually occurs in unnecessary products. There are nine basic approaches.[8]

Nine kinds of advertising appeals

Wrighter goes on to summarize the nine categories of emotional gimmicks that advertisers rely on:

1. The family environment. Showing a warm family scene that suggests that the product will give you this kind of life.
2. Motherhood. Appealing to the customer's need for understanding and love; she'll make everything all right.
3. Feeling good. Suggesting that using the product will make the customer happy.
4. Sympathy. Implying that the people who make this product know and sympathize with the client's problems.
5. Identity. Using references and language which make the buyer feel comfortable and at home.
6. Music. Getting the buyer to respond to rhythm and melody and thus feel good about the product.
7. Borrowed interest. Getting the buyer to transfer good feelings about something to the manufacturer's product. The four most common interests used here are babies, animals, sex, and status.
8. Scare tactics. Making customers think something bad is going to happen to them if they don't use the product.
9. People to people. Trying to get the customer to take someone else's recommendation. There are two variations of this: first, bringing in the common everyday person who must be telling the truth; second, getting the endorsement and implied wisdom of someone famous.

Wrighter also warns about the deceptive use of authority figures (ads showing the person in the white coat) and about the *weasel words* of advertising: *fortified, special, different, new, best, helps prevent,* and *lasts up to,* and a multitude of equally slippery terms.

Armed with these tools, the advertisers mount their campaign to persuade the great buying public to part with its dollars. In re-

---

[8] Wrighter, *I Can Sell You Anything,* p. 117.

turn for these dollars, buyers get the manufacturer's product, which to them may represent some of the good things in life: pleasure, love, security, popularity, prestige, new images of themselves. What appeal do you think the following hypothetical ads might have for what types of audiences?

The Jupiter is *the* auto! Built by true craftsmen for those few who demand the finest. And those few who can afford the finest. Its sleek styling, its understated elegance, its unmistakable *éclat* says—but ever so subtly—that you've arrived!

You Can't Afford to Wait! You feel young doing those fun things you love—swimming, skiing, riding. But the sun, the wind, the water are the enemies of that fresh complexion. Don't wait for them to dry out those precious oils your skin must have. Be young! Keep that dewy look your man loves so much! Start today to use Ponce de Leon Essence of Youth. Smoothed over your skin twice a day, it will help to erase those tiny wrinkles that steal away your youth! Only $15 for a half-ounce jar.

Mother McCrea's bread is as good as that wonderful bread your mother used to make. You could make it too, if you had time. But because we know you don't have those hours and hours it takes to make really delicious bread, we want to help you. Just take a Mother McCrea's ready-to-brown loaf, brush a little butter on the top, pop it in the oven and you'll have that delicious, golden-crusted bread you remember. Your family will love it! And you! Because you've taken time to bake for them. (*According to Vance Packard, author of* The Hidden Persuaders, *advertisers use this kind of copy to overcome the guilt women feel about using prepared foods. Notice the emphasis on "you" and "your."*)

VIXEN! It's not for the timid. Only a *real* woman would dare to wear it, dare to hint at that exciting, provocative you that simmers just beneath the surface. But if you're not afraid, VIXEN is your perfume. And you'll find a *real* man.

Do you want to serve a wine to those special guests but are afraid to? Afraid you'll reveal your ignorance when you bring out the bottle? Want to cover up the label for fear it might not be the right kind? Don't be. You'll never be gauche if you choose our *vin extraordinaire*. White or red, it's superb. Serve it proudly—it says all the right things about your taste. And may even get you that promotion.

Not all or even most advertisements are deceptive or contrived wholly to appeal to the emotions. In fact, many advertisers stress information about their product and try to appeal to their audience's reason. Even though words are often connotative and the accompanying pictures may fall into one of the categories that Wrighter mentions, the tone is partially rational. Such ads cannot be called propaganda in the bad sense because at least part of their purpose is informative.

Some commercials play on fears

Commercial appeals like the ones illustrated earlier, however, and the kinds of television ads that play on viewers' fears by showing people who are old or sick or unpopular or alone must be classified as attempts to sell a product by manipulating the audience's insecurities and anxieties. Such ads sell hope and illusions, and perhaps there is nothing wrong with that. The rational woman should know, however, that when she pays fifteen dollars for a half-ounce jar of face cream to make her look ten years younger, she is buying an illusion—nothing more.

Political Propaganda

Political propaganda tries to ignore reason

Political progadandists also sell illusions, but of a potentially more dangerous kind. One of the chief illusions they promote is that there are simple solutions to complex problems. They want people to believe that if they will just put their faith in one party or one candidate or one creed, all their troubles will disappear. By employing almost every kind of fallacy and emotional appeal, they try to short-circuit the voters' intellects and go straight to their biases, sentiments, prejudices, and basic physical drives. They depend on people being so mentally lazy that they are ready to substitute slogans and clichés for thinking.

Although modern propagandists have more sophisticated techniques and technology at their command than did their colleagues of the preelectronic era, their basic methods have changed very

Varieties of techniques

little since 1939, the year the Institute for Propaganda Analysis published the definitive analysis of propaganda techniques. Notice how apt the following categories and descriptions still are:

Name Calling—giving an idea a bad label—is used to make us reject and condemn the idea without examining the evidence.

Glittering Generality—associating something with a "virtue word"—is used to make us accept and approve the thing without examining the evidence.

Transfer carries the authority, sanction, and prestige of something respected and revered over to something else in order to make the latter acceptable; or it carries authority, sanction, and disapproval to cause us to reject and disapprove something the propagandist would have us reject and disapprove.

Testimonial consists in having some respected or hated person say that a given idea or program or product or person is good or bad.

Plain Folks is the method by which a speaker attempts to convince his audience that he and his ideas are good because they are "of the people," the "plain folks."

Card Stacking involves the selection and use of facts or falsehoods, illustrations or distractions, and logical or illogical statements in order to give the best or the worst possible case for an idea, program, person, or product.

Band Wagon has as its theme, "Everybody—at least all of *us*—is doing it"; with it, the propagandist attempts to convince us that all members of a group to which we belong are accepting his program and that we *must therefore* follow our crowd and "jump on the band wagon."[9]

Notice how many of the fallacies go hand-in-hand with propaganda devices; argument to the person, argument to the people, and begging the question with "name calling," "glittering gener-

[9] Alfred McClung Lee and Elizabeth Briant Lee, *The Fine Art of Propaganda* (New York: Harcourt, Brace and the Institute for Propaganda Analysis, 1939, and Octagon Books, 1972; San Francisco, Institute for General Semantics, 1979), pp. 23–24, by permission of the authors who are the copyright owners. Copyright renewed 1967.

alities," and "plain folks"; special pleading, red herring, black/white, you're another, and false cause with "card stacking" and "band wagon."

Fortunately, in this country no single power group has ever totally monopolized the media so that it can pour out a constant stream of fallacies and propaganda that gives us a one-sided simplistic view of politics and effectively prevents criticism or opposition. We also, for the most part, seem to have a tradition of fair play and restraint that keeps all but the most extreme groups and individuals from indulging in the completely irrational, hate-filled propaganda that totalitarian states make use of. But we should not be complacent about our comparative freedom; to retain it, we need to be always alert to the propaganda surrounding us, to have an internal warning system that goes off when adviser, politician, or all-purpose swindler starts using one of the familiar devices. We should analyze the actual meaning of the words and make our decisions based on what we think is right or best and not what others are doing.

Merging of political and commercial propaganda

Unfortunately, in the last decade resisting and analyzing propaganda has become more difficult—but also more important—because the commercial and political propagandists have joined forces. The merger is particularly obvious in that most pervasive branch of all the media, television. Joe McGinniss describes the alliance in his book, *The Selling of the President, 1968:*

> Politics, in a sense, has always been a con game. . . .
>
> Advertising, in many ways, is a con game too. Human beings do not need a new automobile every third year; a color television set brings little enrichment of the human experience; a higher or lower hemline no expansion of consciousness, no increase in the capacity to love.
>
> It is not surprising, then, that politicians and advertising men should have discovered one another. And, once they recognized that the citizen did not so much vote for a candidate as make a psychological purchase of him, it is not surprising that they began to work together.[10]

McGinniss's book is a detailed, documented account of how the professional writers and advertising people who were hired to help with the 1968 presidential campaign "marketed" Richard Nixon to the public through television. Our concern here is not with the merits of the candidate himself—presumably the "salespeople" would have handled Abraham Lincoln or Franklin Roosevelt the same way if they had run those campaigns. Our concern is, rather, with the professional propagandists and their methods. McGinniss quotes one of them as writing,

> "Voters are basically lazy, basically uninterested in making an *effort* to understand what we're talking about. . . . Reason requires a high degree of discipline, of concentration; impression is easier. Reason pushes the viewer back; it assaults him, it demands that he agree or disagree; impression can envelop him, invite him in, without making an intellectual demand. . . . When we argue with him we demand that he make the effort of replying. We seek to engage his intellect, and for most people this is the most difficult work of all. The emotions are more easily roused, closer to the surface, more malleable. . . .
>
> "[Nixon] has to come across as a person larger than life, the stuff of legend. People are stirred by the legend, including the living legend, not by the man himself. It's the aura that surrounds the charismatic figure more than it is the figure itself, that draws the followers. Our task is to build that aura. . . .
>
> "So let's not be afraid of television gimmicks . . . get the voters to like the guy and the battle's two-thirds won." [pp. 32, 33]

The promoters built their campaign on this philosophy. They assumed that voters didn't want to think about the issues, that they wanted to feel, to be impressed, to be swept along in a warm swell of emotions.

The advertising people created a new slogan: "This time vote like your whole world depended on it"—ambiguous, vague, but catchy. Their marketing masterpiece, however, was a series of sixty-second television commercials based on still pictures. McGinniss describes them this way:

Treleaven could use Nixon's voice to accompany the stills but his face would not be on the screen. Instead there would be pictures, and hopefully, the pictures would prevent people from paying too much attention to the words.

The words would be the same ones Nixon always used—the words of the acceptance speech. But they would all seem fresh and lively because a series of still pictures would flash on the screen while Nixon spoke. If it were done right, it would permit Treleaven to create a Nixon image that was entirely independent of the words. Nixon would say his same old tiresome things but no one would have to listen. The words would become Muzak. Something pleasant and lulling in the background. The flashing pictures would be carefully selected to create the impression that somehow Nixon represented competence, respect for tradition, serenity, faith that the American people were better than people anywhere else, and that all these problems others shouted about meant nothing in a land blessed with the tallest buildings, strongest armies, biggest factories, cutest children, and rosiest sunsets in the world. Even better: through association with the pictures, Richard Nixon could *become* these very things. [p. 83]

Eighteen of those sixty-second commercials were produced, each carefully edited to remove anything controversial. They became one of the major propaganda devices used in the last weeks of the campaign. McGinniss reports the comment of one of the people who helped make them:

"You know, . . . what we're really seeing is a genesis. We're moving into a period where a man is going to be merchandised on television more and more. It upsets you and me, maybe, but we're not typical Americans. The public sits home and watches *Gunsmoke* and when they're fed this pap about Nixon they think they're getting something worthwhile." [p. 117]

Did the professional propagandists con the American public? No one knows the answer to that question. Richard Nixon did win in 1968, to be sure, but by a very narrow margin. He did not even receive a majority of all the votes cast, so the propagandists' success was certainly not overwhelming. Moreover, he might well have received all his votes entirely on his own merits, or because of a number of events quite beyond his or anyone else's control. It would be foolish to overestimate the power of the Big Sell. But it would be foolish also to be unaware of the new techniques of propaganda that technology has made possible. Your only weapon against them is reason and critical thinking—and being more perceptive and better informed than some manipulators give you credit for being.

Exercises

1. Identify and analyze the following fallacies. Although you should be able to identify each by name (sometimes more than one designation could apply), the most important thing is that you be able to tell why the reasoning is faulty.

   a. You see, the priests were right. After we threw those virgins into the volcano, it quit erupting.

   b. This campaign to legalize filthy and corrupting movies is the irrresponsible work of a few perverted individuals.

   c. We ought to elect Bill Duncan to the senate because he was a Medal of Honor winner in World War II.

   d. Are all the people in your home town still red necks and bigots?

   e. It is common knowledge that socialized medicine has not been successful in England.

   f. Are we going to vote a pay increase for our teachers, or are we going to let our schools deteriorate into substandard custodial institutions?

   g. The people of Rome lost their vitality and desire for freedom when their emperors decided that the way to keep them happy was to provide them with bread and circuses. What can we expect of our own country now that the government gives people free food and there is a constant round of entertainment provided by television?

   h. Of course, Madame, since you loved your husband so dearly you will want to buy this $2,800 casket, our very finest.

i. The policy that Jones is proposing is unsound because it won't work.

j. Jack must be a very tough young man. He just got out of the Marines.

k. Two kinds of young women go to college: those who want an education and those who want a husband. If a girl drops out without graduating, it is a sure sign that she wasn't really interested in an education.

l. Vote for Burns. She'll make a good governor—honestly.

m. My opponent for the state legislature, Mrs. Jenkins, may be a capable woman, but in my opinion, and I think yours, capable women should be using their talents to provide a good home for their husbands and children. If they have extra time after doing that, they should devote their energies to volunteer work in the community.

n. The question before us today is how we can raise the money to provide this state with a new medical school. I am for a medical school; the citizens of this state need it if we are to have adequate care. But I shall refuse to vote for the appropriation as long as the doctors of this state continue to charge such excessive fees for their services.

o. Women should not be allowed to go to stag parties because they are for men only.

2. Analyze the fallacies in the following paragraphs:

a. Now, in the 1980s, every intelligent person would agree that marijuana ought to be legalized. Only a few puritanical types who think that anything that is fun must be bad for people still want to keep our ridiculous laws on the books. They claim that getting stoned on marijuana now and then is harmful, but they think nothing of tossing off a couple of martinis before dinner every night. As for the argument that smoking marijuana leads to experimenting with hard drugs, I know for a fact that that is not true. I know several people who have smoked pot but as far as I know none of them is on heroin. And studies have demonstrated that there is no necessary connection between the two.

b. There is no doubt that the present deplorable state of morals among our young people is due to the increasing popularity of sex education in the schools. Showing films on sex to youngsters and then expecting them not to experiment with it is like putting them in a room full of food and expecting them not to eat. And statistics prove that one out of every three high school students who has been enrolled in a sex education course had gone on to have intercourse at some time within the next two years. We should realize that one of the avowed aims of the Communists is to weaken the moral fiber of our young people. We must choose: either we return to the old Christian way of chastity and continence before marriage, or we let our society degenerate into a shameless hedonism of the kind that destroyed ancient Rome.

3. For several days read your daily newspaper carefully, particularly the editorials, syndicated columns, letters to the editor, and news stories in which public officials are quoted. Clip and bring to class any fallacies that you may find. Be prepared to say specifically what you think those fallacies are and to make a judgment about whether they seriously damage the effect of the article.

4. Carefully examine the advertisements in two magazines, preferably two with very different audiences. Clip or photocopy advertisements that you think are based on fallacious reasoning or that represent commercial propaganda.

Suggested Writing Assignments

Theme 1

Purpose To give you practice in identifying the kinds of fallacies that may appear in popular writing.

Procedure Begin by summarizing in one short paragraph, and in *your own words*, the main idea of the selection below. Go beyond the assertion that Vilar thinks men are treated badly to show what specific claims she makes.

Then identify and illustrate with brief examples three or four kinds of fallacious arguments Vilar uses to persuade the reader.

Organize your discussion by types of fallacies instead of a paragraph-by-paragraph analysis. That is, show how Vilar uses false cause, question begging, or bad induction in several places.

Conclude with a short statement about the general effectiveness of the passage. Would it persuade the average, reasonably well informed reader? Why or why not?

In your organizing thesis sentence, outline, summary, or list identify the main fallacies you are going to discuss.

Warning: *Do not either argue or agree* with Vilar's view. You should concentrate strictly on her methods of arguing.

From "What is Man?"[11]

A man is a human being who works. By working, he supports himself, his wife, and his wife's children. A woman, on the other hand, is a human being who does not work—or at least only occasionally. Most of her life she supports neither herself nor her children, let alone her husband.

Any qualities in a man that a woman finds useful, she calls *masculine;* all others, of no use to her or to anyone else for that matter, she chooses to call *effeminate.* A man's appearance has to be *masculine* if he wants to have success with women, and that means it will have to be geared to his one and only *raison d'être*—work. His appearance must conform to each and every task put to him, and he must always be able to fulfill it.

Except at night when the majority of men wear striped pajamas with at most two pairs of pockets, men wear a kind of uniform made of durable, stain-resistant material in brown, blue, or gray. These uniforms, or "suits," have up to ten pockets, in which men carry instruments and tools indispensable for their work. Since a woman does not work, her night or day clothes rarely have pockets.

For social events men are permitted to wear black, a color that shows marks and stains, since on those occasions men are less likely to dirty themselves. Moreover, the bright colors worn by women show to advantage against it. The occasional red or green evening jacket worn by men is acceptable,

---

[11] Esther Vilar, *The Manipulated Man* (New York: Farrar, Straus & Giroux, Inc., 1972), p. 51. Reprinted with the permission of Farrar, Straus & Giroux, Inc. from *The Manipulated Man* by Esther Vilar, Copyright © 1972 by Farrar, Straus & Giroux, Inc.

since, by contrast, all the real men present seem so much more masculine.

The rest of a man's appearance is also adapted to his situation. His hair style requires only fifteen minutes at the barber every two or three weeks. Curls, waves, and tints are not encouraged as they might hinder his work. Men often work in the open air or spend a considerable amount of time in it, hence complicated styles would be a nuisance. Furthermore, it is improbable that such styles would make a hit with women since, unlike men, they never judge the opposite sex from an aesthetic point of view. So most men, after one or two attempts at individuality, realize that women are indifferent to their efforts and revert to a standard style, short or long. The same is true of beards. Only over sensitive men—usually ones with intellectual pretensions—who want to appear mentally tough by letting their facial hair grow indiscriminately wear a full beard for any length of time. It will be tolerated by women, however, for a beard is an important indication of a man's character and therefore of the way in which he might be most easily exploited. (His field of work will usually be that of the neurotic intellectual.) . . .

Apart from a wedding ring—worn to show that he is already being used by a particular woman for a particular purpose—a proper man wears no ornaments. His clumsy, functional watch, worn on the wrist, is hardly decorative. Heavy in design, waterproof, shock-resistant, showing the correct date, it cannot possibly be called an ornament. Usually it was given to him by the woman for whom he works.

Theme 2

Write a paragraph similar to those in exercise 2 in which you construct a fallacious argument on some topic of current interest on your campus. Consult the editorials and letters to the editor in your local student newspaper for ideas and, perhaps, for some sample fallacies. Leave a wide margin at the left side of the paper, and in it label each of the fallacies that you have used.

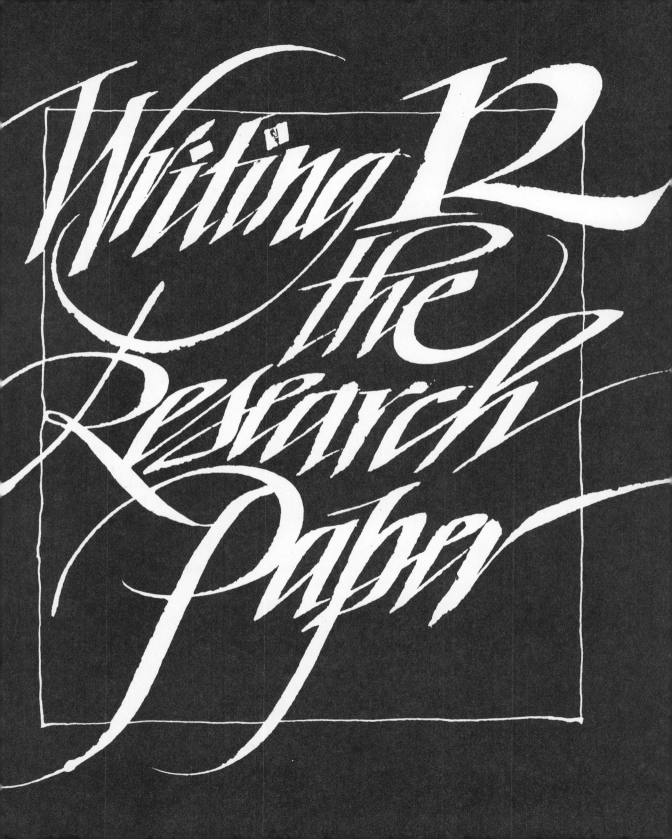

Writing the Research Paper

12

As a college student you will sooner or later probably have to write reports or term papers that require you to do library research and take extensive notes before you begin to write. The process for writing the paper itself will most likely not differ substantially from that which you have been using for other kinds of writing, but the preliminary work of gathering and organizing material and the subsequent task of putting it into properly documented form can present difficulties that you haven't previously encountered. The purpose of this chapter is to help you develop strategies for doing library research and to give you guidelines for shaping your findings into an informative, readable, and well-documented paper. Mastering those strategies at this early stage in your development as a writer will give you tools that will serve you well not only as you continue your college education but later when you enter a business or professional career.

Making a Plan: The Early Stages

Because writing a research paper involves a number of steps and proceeds through several stages, you need to start by working out a master plan that will allow you to see the whole picture before you start and give you a sense of what specific tasks need to be done, in what order, and how long the whole process will probably take. The skeleton of such a working plan might look like this.

1. Clarify your assignment: length, general focus, due date.
2. Make a schedule.
3. Choose a general topic.
4. Find background information on your topic.
5. Narrow your topic.
6. Formulate your thesis and title.
7. Begin focused search for information.

For this chapter I have drawn extensively from the series of excellent study guides and informative pamphlets compiled by the staff of reference librarians at the Undergraduate Library of The University of Texas at Austin. All of them, and particularly Barbara Schwartz, have invested an impressive amount of their time and energy in helping students at Texas become better researchers and better writers. I appreciate the help of this highly competent and professional staff and their generosity in sharing their material.

8. Take notes.
9. Choose a plan of organization.
10. Write first draft.
11. Check documentation.
12. Revise and put into final form.

Clarifying Your Assignment

As in any writing project, you will make your job much easier if you start out by answering these questions fully and precisely.

1. What kind of writing am I doing?
2. Why am I writing?
3. Who is going to read it and why?
4. What specifications must it meet?
5. What is my deadline?

Kind of writing Research papers are, by definition, informative papers. They are the means by which investigators share what they have learned with other people, and as such, they form the foundation of organized education. Although people may do research in order to support opinions or theories, the report on the research should be factual and unbiased, not persuasive. Thus you should keep in mind that your obligation in a research paper is to find facts, present them objectively, and document your sources so that other people can trace them if they wish to.

Purpose of writing You write research papers in college for at least two reasons. First, and primarily, you write to learn; probably you already know from experience that you learn material better and retain it longer when you write about it. Second, you write to demonstrate to your instructors that you can do research in the library and present the results in a readable and carefully documented paper. For this second purpose, you must master the intricacies of the card catalogue system and other reference sources in the library and learn the proper forms for writing footnotes and bibliographies.

Audience analysis If you are writing the research paper for a college course, your only audience may be your instructor. Don't assume, however, that he or she cares only about the form of your paper and whether you have the proper number of sources. Not true at all. Instructors also look forward to learning something from their students' research papers, so you definitely have something to gain by picking an interesting topic and trying to tell your instructor something he or she wants or needs to know.

Even while you are in college, or soon after, you may have to write a research paper for your employer. As a senior, you might work part time for a real estate broker who wants a report on the types and prices of houses in one area of a city, or you might write a report for a health maintenance organization that needs to find out how many women have their children by the Lamaze method of childbirth. When you begin writing research papers in such situations, you will need to analyze your audiences carefully and decide exactly what they want before you begin to write.

Specifications Find out from your instructor approximately how long the research paper should be and translate that into typewritten pages (about 250 words per double-spaced page if you use pica type, 300 if you use elite type). Length makes a difference because it affects your choice of topic. Also find out what format your instructor wants you to use and what style of documentation he or she favors. And be sure to check little details such as where your name should go, what should be on the title sheet, width of margins, and so on. Some instructors are particular about these matters, and it would be foolish to make a bad first impression by not paying attention. If you're writing a report for an employer, be especially careful about details because your attention to them reflects your persona.

Deadline Finally, find out precisely when the paper is due and post the date in some prominent place where it will nag you. You might be wise to phrase the deadline in different ways in order to remind yourself that you need to get started. For example,

April 6

five weeks from date assigned

35 days from date assigned

three weeks before last day of class

Making a Schedule

Your instructor may set up a timetable for you specifying the dates on which you are to hand in your preliminary topic, your limited topic, your thesis statement, the titles of five books, your rough outline, and so on. If so, following that schedule will keep you on track. If, however, you are on your own, you would do well to map out a schedule for yourself to avoid the last-minute panic that is sure to happen if you wait until the last week to do everything. It might look like this:

Week 1: Pick out general topic and look at background material.

Week 2: Settle on a specific topic, write a preliminary title and a thesis statement. Begin research.

Week 3: Check under Subject Headings in card catalogue. Identify books that will be useful.

Week 4: Consult specialized indexes. Take notes. Consult periodical indexes. Take notes. Identify useful articles. Take notes.

Week 5: Write first draft of paper. Draft bibliography. Revise draft, check documentation. Write final draft of paper.

Writing out such a schedule will help you realize how much work is involved in producing the final paper and remind you to give yourself enough time.

Choosing a Topic

Criteria for a good topic

It is particularly important that you give yourself enough time to choose your topic carefully so that you will not get bored while you are working on the paper and so that you can find enough material to write a substantial, well-documented report. You will probably have the best chance of getting an interesting topic that you can work with if you go about it in two stages. First, think of a fairly broad topic that interests you. It should meet these criteria:

1. It should be some topic about which you are really curious; for instance, cattle breeding or professional football or the stock market. If you can think of a topic about which you might need information later in your life, so much the better. Picking a topic because it looks easy usually turns out to be a mistake because you will quickly become bored.
2. Choose a topic on which you will be able to discover facts and concrete evidence and on which you will be able to say something significant in the specified number of pages. The broad topic of socialism or disarmament, for example, probably wouldn't work well for even a long research paper.
3. Choose a topic that can be adequately researched in a library that is available to you. Don't assume that all libraries have a wealth of material available on every possible subject; they don't. If you attend a small college, the library may have limited resources, so you shouldn't assume that you can research in highly specialized areas like Japanese burial customs or the role of women in medieval Germany. Be particularly careful not to pick a topic that is so new that only a few books have been published on it, books which your library may not yet have acquired. Thus you might not be able to find enough material to write a well-documented paper on embryo transplants or microsurgery.

You can take two precautions against choosing a topic on which not enough material is available. First, you can make a preliminary survey in the subject portion of the library card catalogue to see how many books on a specific topic may be available. Second, you can ask the librarians in the reference section of your library. They should have a fairly good idea of what resources are probably available to you. For example, the staff of research librarians in the Undergraduate Library at The University of Texas at Austin compiled the list of 50 topics given at the end of this chapter, carefully selecting ones on which the university library could provide ample material for research. If you are attending a university of comparable size, probably these topics will work for you too. If you are attending a smaller school, however, and don't have time to get materials from interlibrary loan, you should check sources for even these topics before you make a final choice.

Finding Background Information

If you stop at this point in your project to do some preliminary background reading on your general topic, you are much more likely to be able to quickly narrow that topic to a manageable size and focus your reading so that you don't waste your time. You will also get some idea of the scope of the topic and specific leads to follow up in the card catalogue.

Start your search for background material by finding out if your library has *specialized encyclopedias*, reference volumes devoted to particular areas of knowledge. Most libraries do have reasonably substantial collections of such volumes. Listed below are a few with which you might start.

Humanities

Cassell's Encyclopedia of World Literature. 3 volumes.

Encyclopedia of Philosophy. 8 volumes.

Encyclopedia of Religion and Ethics. 13 volumes.

Encyclopedia of World Art. 15 volumes.

Encyclopedia of World History. 1 volume.

International Encyclopedia of Film. 1 volume.

New Grove Dictionary of Music and Musicians. 20 volumes.

Encyclopedia of Pop, Rock, and Soul. 1 volume.

Social Sciences

International Encyclopedia of Social Sciences. 17 volumes.

International Encyclopedia of Psychiatry, Psychology, Psychoanalysis, and Neurology. 12 volumes.

Encyclopedia of Bioethics. 4 volumes.

Encyclopedia of Social Work. 2 volumes.

Handbook of Criminology. 1 volume.

Encyclopedia of the Unexplained: Magic, Occultism, and Parapsychology. 1 volume.

Science and Technology

McGraw-Hill Encyclopedia of Science and Technology. 15 volumes.
Van Nostrand's Scientific Encyclopedia. 1 volume.
Encyclopedia of Bioethics. 4 volumes.

If you can't decide where your chosen topic would fit, ask the librarian. He or she may also be able to give you additional specialized references.

You may also find these general encyclopedias useful.

Collier's Encyclopedia. 24 volumes.
Encyclopedia Americana. 30 volumes.
Encyclopaedia Britannica. 19 volumes.

You can update many of these sources by consulting the following yearbooks, usually issued every year to include the most recent material in a field.

Britannica Book of the Year, 1919 to the present.
McGraw-Hill Yearbook of Science and Technology, 1962 to the present.
Yearbook of Science and the Future, 1971–76, 1979 to the present.

Narrowing Your Topic

When you have done enough general reading on your broad topic to give you a good idea of what kind of material is available, you are ready for the crucial step: choosing a limited and specific topic. Remember, the more specific the better. It is almost always a good idea to write more about less, or as one professor has put it, to pick the smallest possible topic out of which you can squeeze the requisite number of words. If you follow that advice, you are more likely to find a topic that will interest both you and your reader because you'll both be learning new information in a specialized area.

Ways to narrow your topic

Some of the limiting strategies you can use to narrow down your topic are these:

time period	specific classification
occupation	individual example
cultural period	gender
religion	specific region or locale
particular economic group	specific nationality or race
specialized discipline	specific age group

Suppose you wanted to narrow the general topic of divorce down to a specific and manageable topic. You might choose to study the causes of divorce among young American (nationality) women (gender) who married in their teens (age group) in the 1970s (time period) and did not finish high school (educational classification). Other topics can be limited in similar ways. You can also get ideas for limiting your topic by considering the questions that follow each of the suggested paper topics, at the end of this chapter (pp. 418–427), questions that were designed to help you look at a general topic from a specific point of view. And remember that even after you start to do your research and take notes, you may find that you want to narrow or revise your topic again if you make an unexpected discovery.

Formulating Your Thesis

Once you have settled on a topic, it's time to draft a thesis statement for your paper and decide on a tentative title. Though you may want to revise or change both thesis and title when you write your final draft, writing a thesis and title now will help you to anchor your paper and control your writing. It will also give you that starting impetus you need to stir up your creative energies and get going on your research.

You can get ideas for the thesis by asking yourself, "What have I heard about it that might be an interesting line to pursue?" "What kind of issues does it raise and what problems are connected with it?" Try to think with an *exploratory* attitude, not with the assumption that you already know what you think. You'll waste all that energy you're going to put into research if you start with a closed mind. Instead, construct a hypothesis for your thesis, follow it, and see where it will take you. For example, your tentative thesis for the paper on the causes of divorce among teenage American girls might be, "The excessively high divorce rate of teenage American girls who marry before they finish high school probably has economic, social, and emotional causes." Your title might be "Why American Teenagers Divorce."

Beginning Your Focused Search for Information: The Intensive Stages

Books

You will have at least two sources for finding the titles of books about your topic: the bibliographies that accompany articles on your topic in the specialized encyclopedias that you consulted and the Subject section of the library card catalogue. You may already be familiar with this portion of the library, but if you are not and wonder where to start, consult the two-volume reference book *Library of Congress Subject Headings List*; it will list the subject headings and subheadings in the card catalogue and give you cross-references that can save you a great deal of time. Usually these volumes are kept on a shelf or table very close to the card catalogue. Remember that you may also find useful book titles when you are reading magazine articles on your topic, and in some libraries you can do a computer search for material. More on that later in this chapter.

When you begin your search in the Subject catalogue, for most topics you should have no trouble finding the titles of at least a dozen books that sound as if they might yield useful information; in fact, your problem may be that you will find far more books than you can possibly use or even skim. In that case, choose those titles that sound most specifically related to your narrow topic and check publication dates to help you choose the most recent books. Make a list of titles, including the date, author's name, and name of the publisher. Try to include at least twice as many books as your instructor has suggested you consult for your paper because inevitably you will find that some of those you want are checked out or lost.

With list in hand, head for the Author/Title section of the card

catalogue and start your search. Probably it's most efficient to
look for each book by the name of the author. So arrange your list
in roughly alphabetical order for a more efficient search and begin
looking at the catalogue card for each book. That card will give
you specific and useful information that will help you decide if
you want to consult it.

```
  ⎧ TX        Lappé, Frances Moore.
  ⎪ 392           Diet for a small planet / Frances
  ⎨ L27       Moore Lappé ; illustrated by Kathleen
  ⎪ 1975      Zimmerman and Ralph Iwamoto. Rev. ed.
  ⎩ UGL       New York : Ballantine Books, 1975.
                 411 p. : ill. ; 18 cm.




             ⎧ Bibliography: p. 396-397.
             ⎨ Includes index.
             ⎩

                1. Vegetarianism.  2. Proteins.
             I. Title
```

If you decide that you want to consult a book, write the *complete*
call number beside the title of the book on your list and go on.
Later, you can group call numbers together so that if you are
working in an open stack library and are looking for the books
yourself, you can do a systematic search.

Cataloging systems You may have to work in a library that is
currently classifying its books in two ways; by the Dewey Decimal System and by the Library of Congress system. Many large
libraries are now doing this, cataloguing new books that come in
by Library of Congress symbols but keeping old books catalogued
under Dewey Decimal numbers, the kind you may be familiar
with from your previous school. The two kinds of symbols appear
on the next page.

Dewey Decimal call numbers start with *numbers*	Library of Congress call numbers start with *letters*
813 A75	BD 452 S45

Thus it is particularly important that you write down the full call number before you start looking for books, and that you find out where books bearing each kind of symbol are shelved. Books with the Dewey Decimal symbols will be shelved in order according to the *number* on the top line of the call number; books with Library of Congress symbols will be shelved alphabetically according to the *letters* on the top line of the call number, then within that category by the number on the second line.

Probably your library will have good directions explaining the system or systems it uses; if it does not, don't hesitate to ask librarians as often as you need to in order to find what you want.

Magazine and Journal Articles

Anyone who does much research soon realizes that one cannot find everything in books. Sometimes the most up-to-date material on a topic can be found only in articles, and often even important older information has appeared only in a periodical. Your library will probably have the most current magazines and journals on the shelves but the older articles may be in bound volumes on the shelves or on microfilm or microfiche. (Don't be intimidated by the latter forms—you can learn how to use them as quickly as you would a simple camera.)

Finding magazine articles requires that you know how to use the periodical indexes—leafing through the tables of contents of even highly specialized magazines consumes too much time.

Choosing an Appropriate Index

Most people are familiar with the *Readers' Guide to Periodical Literature*, a general index covering current news, hobbies, people, movie reviews, travel, consumer information, and other subjects of popular interest. Other indexes are more specialized and deal with history, psychology, art, or education, for example.

Often you may wish to use several indexes to find articles on a particular topic from different perspectives. For example, in dealing with the issue of abortion you may want to find materials on:

psychological aspects ⟶ *Psychological Abstracts, Social Sciences Index*

moral implications ⟶ *Humanities Index*

legal problems ⟶ *Public Affairs Information Service*

feminist viewpoint ⟶ *Women Studies Abstracts*

Look up your subject in the index Most indexes follow the same general format. Articles are listed alphabetically by subject. If you don't find your subject listed, try looking under related terms. For instance, if you want articles on Dakota Indians, you might find them listed under "Indians of North America," "Dakota Indians," or "American Indian Movement."

Each entry includes the title of an article, the author's name, title of the periodical, volume, page, and date. For example:

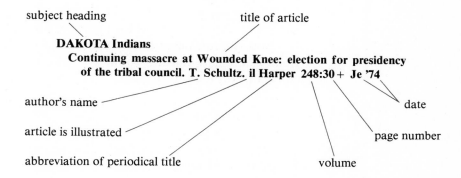

Look in the front of the index volume In order to save space, much of the information in the entries is abbreviated. Look in the front of the volume at the "Abbreviations of Periodicals Indexed" to find the full title of the periodical you want. Finding the full title is very important for actually locating the periodical because journals are listed by title in the serials list and in the name/title catalog. They are also shelved alphabetically by title in your undergraduate library.

ABBREVIATIONS OF PERIODICALS INDEXED

The full title of the periodical in the example above is Harper's Magazine ⟶

Harp Baz — Harper's Bazaar
Harper — Harper's Magazine
Harvard Bus R — Harvard Business Review
Hi Fi — High Fidelity and Musical America

Other abbreviations used in the entries are also explained at the front of the volume.

General indexes

Magazine Index. 1976 to the present.
Start here for recent articles on topics of general interest in popular magazines. Unlike *Readers' Guide* and the more specialized indexes you will use, all the articles indexed from 1976 to the present are in one place, rather than year-by-year. Titles are not abbreviated. This index is in a machine format, so follow the instructions for using it that are located on the front of the machine. Although you will be able to use articles found here as a starting point, you will usually need to use a specialized index to find more professional or scholarly articles.

Readers' Guide to Periodical Literature. 1949 to the present.
Use this index for articles on almost any subject. The periodicals covered in this index are general interest magazines. Although you will be able to use articles found here as a starting point, you will usually need to use a specialized index to find more professional or scholarly articles.

Specialized indexes Listed below are a few of the indexes devoted to particular subjects or disciplines. Many others are available; ask a reference librarian for suggestions.

Humanities

Humanities Index. 1974 to the present.
Use this index for information on archaeology, classics, folklore, history, language and literature, performing arts, philosophy, and religion. (Before 1974 this was called *Social Sciences and Humanities Index.*)

Art Index. 1959 to the present.
Articles indexed here cover photography and films, architecture, city planning, fine arts, graphic arts, and design.

Film Literature Index. 1973 to the present.
This index to international publications covers film reviews and articles about specific films, film genres, directors, cinematographers, screenwriters, and other aspects of the film industry. Look under the title of the film to find a review.

Music Index. 1970 to the present.
Look in this index for articles on popular music, dance, jazz, classical music, radio and television, as well as the business aspects of the music industry. A variety of publications is covered, from *Rolling Stone* to *Opera News* and *Journal of Music Theory.*

Social Sciences

Social Sciences Index. 1974 to the present.
This is a good starting place for articles on anthropology, area studies, psychology, public administration, sociology, and related fields. (Before 1974, this was called *Social Sciences and Humanities Index.*)

Public Affairs Information Service. Bulletin. (P.A.I.S.) 1960 to the present.
This list of articles, pamphlets, and books deals with economic and social conditions, public administration, politics, and international relations. For example, you can use it to find information on the legal aspects of issues like abortion, divorce, child abuse, pollution, and genetic research.

Business Periodicals Index. 1973 to the present.
This index is useful for finding information about business

and industries, computer technology, advertising, and business aspects of other subjects.

Education Index. 1959 to the present.
For material relating to children or to education, this index can be quite helpful. Some examples of subjects covered are busing, child abuse, teenage pregnancy, adoption, and intelligence.

Psychological Abstracts. 1975 to the present.
Left-handedness, body language, ESP, and alcoholism are among the many subjects this index covers from a psychological point of view. Most of the articles listed here are scholarly. In addition to the information indexes usually include, *Psychological Abstracts* provides a summary (abstract) of each article, so you can tell if the article will be relevant to your topic. Ask a librarian to explain how to use this index.

Sociological Abstracts. 1975 to the present.
If you are doing research on any aspect of sociology, including studies on poverty, violence, and feminism, try here. Most of the summaries of articles found here are highly specialized, so you need to have some background knowledge before you will find this a useful source. Ask a librarian to explain how to use it.

Women Studies Abstracts. 1972 to the present.
If your subject deals with women, you may find this source useful. The books, pamphlets, and periodicals listed here are grouped into broad categories, such as family, employment, and sexuality. However, many topics appear in more than one category, so you must still look for your topic in the index at the back of each issue.

Science

General Science Index. 1978 to the present.
This new index covers most of the basic journals in astronomy, biology, chemistry, earth science, environment and conservation, food and nutrition, medicine and health, physics, and psychology. For earlier articles on these topics, select the appropriate index from those listed below.

Applied Science and Technology Index. 1971 to the present.
This publication lists articles on aspects of physics, chemistry, geology, and other industrial and mechanical arts, including the textile industry, computers, the food industry, and energy resources and research.

Biological & Agricultural Index. 1973 to the present.
This indexes scholarly articles in biology, biochemistry, botany, ecology, forestry, nutrition, genetics, zoology, and related sciences. Most of these articles are rather technical and may be found only in specialized libraries.

Computer Searches

An increasing number of libraries have good computer facilities for searching for information, and these facilities are frequently available to students. Many libraries run regular short training sessions that anyone can attend. If your library offers such a service, by all means take advantage of it. It's not difficult to learn the fundamentals, and mastering computer research skills can save you substantial chunks of time, now and later. Keep in mind two potential limitations, however. First, what does a computer search cost and who has to pay for it?; second, would your school library have most of the sources you might turn up with a computer search? If not, the search would not be worth your time.

Serendipity

Finally, when you are looking for material, remember *serendipity* (p. 43). In research, a person often seems to stumble on to the best leads almost by accident rather than through a methodical step-by-step search. For that reason, stay alert for unexpected findings and follow your hunches. Run your eyes over the books shelved next to the one you are looking for and glance at the table of contents in a magazine that contains the article you want. Pay attention to footnotes; sometimes they will lead you to something more interesting than the text itself. Talk to other people about your research project; they may be able to put you on to some source you hadn't realized existed. In other words, cultivate serendipity by extending your intellectual antennas all around you as you work. Frequently you'll find something you didn't know you were looking for.

Taking Notes

Perhaps your instructor requires that you take notes on index cards and turn them in as one part of the research paper assignment. Even if he or she does not, however, you need to start making notes early in your search rather than depend on photocopying long sections from books or magazines. For one thing, when you copy material you only postpone the skimming and condensing you are going to have to do with any information that you gather. Also, if you copy materials, you will find yourself with a stack of unwieldly sheets that are hard to classify and probably don't contain all the information you need, such as publisher, edition, publication date. So the best approach is to make notes on index cards as you work, using a consistent system that will enable you to classify and organize the notes later. In fact, you may want to use two sets of cards, one for information and one for bibliographical information. For example:

Orbiting solar cells

Put collecting stations on space colonies — already know how. 94 colonies in 10 years

Heppenheimer, pp. 74-76

```
TL          Heppenheimer, T. A.
795.7
H 46        Colonies in Space
1980

            New York: Warner Books, 1980

                  Bibliography
```

The double card system will make it easier to compile your bibliography later and is probably more convenient to work with because it separates content from documentation. Thus you can put key words in the left-hand top corner of all cards pertinent to a certain point and put a shorthand notation at the bottom of the card to remind you of its source.

```
            Cost of producing energy

        from coal about 2-3 cents
        per kilowatt hour




    Heppenheimer, p. 236
```

Always remember, however, that when you write out a quotation you may want to use, put down the page numbers immediately after it. If you don't, you will find yourself going back to the library at the last minute trying to find a page reference—and if the book happens to be gone, you're in trouble.

No one else can really tell you what system of taking notes will work best for you; you will probably modify whatever system you begin with as you work. In general, however, your system of note taking should do these things:

1. Give brief summaries of important points in the book or article.
2. Give the specific source of every point with enough information to enable you to document where you found it.
3. Set up categories for the material that is found.
4. Set up some system of putting material in order, such as numbered cards.
5. Put enough information on a card to enable you to remember the important points without going back to consult the source.

Organizing and Writing the Paper

Choosing a plan of organization

As you accumulate material to write your research paper, you may find that a logical way to organize the paper seems to be emerging in your mind. For instance, in the paper on the causes of teenage divorce, it would seem logical to divide the causes into economic, social, and emotional and write about them in that order. Or if you are writing a paper on the effects of legalized gambling, you might want to organize it according to different kinds of gambling: state lotteries, off-track betting, and casino gambling. If you were writing a paper on microcomputers, you might want to organize it chronologically, tracing the development of modern small computers from the huge ones of just a few years ago. If, however, some practical plan of organization has not occurred to you by the time you have accumulated your material, look back over the section on controlling patterns in Chapter 2, page 52. At least one of the patterns listed there—definition, comparison, cause and effect, classification, and so on—should work for your topic.

Since a research paper must usually be longer than the other papers written in a composition course, you probably need to make a rough outline to get your material under control. One good way to organize such an outline would be to use the categories into which you have divided your cards as the main divisions for the outline; then write a generalization or thesis for each division and arrange the material in that category as specific points to be made under the thesis. The section-by-section summary method described in Chapter 2 is also an excellent way to organize a research paper. To write such a summary, separate your cards into categories, read over all those in each category, and make a brief but precise summary of the information. After you have the summaries, you can decide in what order you want to present them.

Use subheads

Finally, when you write your paper make your plan of organization obvious to your reader by using subheadings for each division. Not only do they help your readers see and follow your controlling pattern, but they also break up the text and give your readers signals about what to expect as they read. The subheadings that break up this chapter—Clarifying Your Assignment, Taking Notes, Organizing Your Paper, and so on—illustrate how this device works. You particularly need such subdivisions if your paper runs to more than eight or ten pages.

Preparing to write the first draft

Before you begin to write the first draft, go back and review the summary you made of your writing task, your audience, and your purpose. Remind yourself once more that you are writing in order to share what you have found out with an audience who wants or needs to know about your findings. So you want to present facts as clearly as possible and in an objective tone. You also want to meet the specifications drawn up for the paper as well as have it meet all the criteria for good writing that are outlined in Chapter 1. But remember that a research paper doesn't have to be dull, and you shouldn't lapse into a pretentious and pompous "academic style" because you are presenting facts. Keep your language concrete and simple, use strong verbs, and help your reader *see* what you are explaining whenever possible.

And remember that you are writing a first draft. Don't start worrying about correct spelling and usage at this point, and don't stop to tinker too much with your sentence structure. Just get down your information in an orderly way and decide which facts you are going to use to illustrate your main points. You will probably want to work according to the main subdivisions you have set up but you don't even have to put in your subheadings at this stage; they can be added later. Try to view your plan and thesis as still flexible, open to change if some fresh insight strikes you as you are writing, and try to start writing far enough ahead of time so that you can follow up on any unexpected leads that you might stumble onto. That could be the best part of the whole project.

Learning to Document Sources

The authors of research papers, whether they are writing for a class or on a job, carefully document their sources as fully as possible for two important reasons. First, they want their readers to know what sources they have investigated, where they found them, and how recent their information is. Second, they want to give the readers enough information so that the readers, if they wish, can locate and use the material themselves. After all, people write about their research to share information, and good documentation makes that easier to do. So the question you should keep in mind when you write your footnotes or endnotes and when you prepare your bibliography is this: "Am I giving my readers the kind of information they need in order to track down the source of this reference?" If you do, then you are doing a good job of documenting your paper.

Two Forms of Documentation

When you quote directly from any source, even a personal interview, you need to enclose the quotation in quotation marks in your text and give the source in a footnote or endnote. For quotations of two or more lines, you may use the block indentation method rather than inserting quotation marks (see examples on pp. 148-150), but you still need to put a number at the end of the quote and give its source. You should use the same form for acknowledging oral statements as you would for acknowledging written statements.

Endnotes and footnotes Footnotes are explanatory notes that appear at the bottom of the page on which the source is cited;

thus readers can check the note immediately to find the origin of the writer's information. In some ways this form is more convenient for readers because they don't have to track down references at the end of the chapter or book. But footnotes can be distracting, particularly if several appear on one page, and they make typing a paper slower and much more difficult.

Endnotes, which appear at the end of a paper, are easier to handle; for that reason more and more editors of books and journals are encouraging their writers to use endnotes. If the person reading your paper has no objections, you will probably find it much easier to use endnotes. The forms are the same as they would be for footnotes. Remember that both footnotes and endnotes should be consistently numbered through the paper.

Conventions of Documentation

If you are writing a research paper for a course, check with your instructor to find out what kind of documentation form he or she prefers and which style manual you should consult if you have a question about the correct form of citing your sources. The two most common styles are that of *internal documentation*, with an accompanying bibliography, favored by the social sciences, and *full documentation*, favored by writers in English and many other disciplines. The standard reference manuals for the two forms are these: for internal documentation, the *Publication Manual*, American Psychological Association; for full documentation, *MLA Handbook for Writers of Research Papers, Theses, and Dissertations*. You will find these in the reference room of your library or you can buy them at the bookstore.

Following are examples of the most common kind of footnotes or endnotes written according to the MLA style sheet:

A book by one author:

Arthur Koestler, *The Act of Creation* (London: Pan Books, Ltd., 1975), p. 147.

A book by two authors:

Dorothy G. Singer and Tracey A. Revenson, *How A Child Thinks* (New York and London: New American Library, 1978), p. 41.

A book edited by the author:

Thomas Kuhn, ed., *The Essential Tension: Selected Studies in Scientific Tradition and Change* (Chicago: The University of Chicago Press, 1977), pp. 212–15.

An essay in a book of collected essays:

Stephen Judy, "On Clock Watching and Composing," in *Rhetoric and Composition*, ed., Richard L. Graves (New Rochelle, N.J.: Hayden Book Company, Inc., 1976), pp. 70–78.

A translated book:

L. S. Vygotsky, *Thought and Language*, trans., Eugenia Hoffman and Gertrude Vakar (Cambridge, Mass: The M.I.T. Press, 1962), pp. 39–42.

An edition:

Thomas Kuhn, *The Structure of Scientific Revolutions*, 2nd. ed. (Chicago: The University of Chicago Press, 1971), p. 68.

A piece in a reference book:

"Microcomputers," *Encyclopedia Americana*, 1980 ed. (No page number or volume is necessary since entries in encyclopedias are alphabetically arranged.)

An article in a newspaper:

Joan Didion, "Why I Write," *New York Times Book Review*, December 15, 1975, p. 10.

A magazine article:

Cyndy Severson, "Pack Up Your Troubles," *Texas Monthly*, April, 1981, p. 140.

An article in a journal, usually scholarly or professional:

Richard Braddock, "The Frequency and Placement of Topic Sentences in Expository Prose," *Research in the Teaching of English* Vol. 8, No. 3 (Winter, 1974), p. 291.
(Notice that for this kind of citation you should give the volume and issue number because the collected journals are bound according to those designations.)

An unsigned article in a magazine or newspaper:

"Working the Rigs," *Texas Monthly*, March, 1980, p. 162.

A movie:

Franco Zefferelli, dir., *Romeo and Juliet* with Lennard Whiting and Olivia Hussey, BHE Verona Productions, 1968.

A television interview:

Lauren Bacall, interviewed by Barbara Walters on "Woman of the Year," NBC network, June 9, 1981.

A personal interview:

Personal interview with Alexander Haig, June 15, 1981.

Note that after you have given full documentation for a reference the first time, you can abbreviate your next reference to it. For instance,
[2]Young et al., p. 68.
[3]Vygotsky, p. 46.

Documentation for Bibliographies

A bibliography is an essential part of your research paper if you are using internal documentation; without it your readers would not be able to understand your references. But it is also an important addition to your research paper even when you have already given full documentation in your notes. For one thing, you may have done significant background reading in sources that do not appear in your notes because you do not directly refer to them in your paper; these sources should be listed in your bibliography.

The bibliography also gathers all the sources you have consulted for your paper in one convenient list so that your reader can quickly see the scope of your research. In addition, a full and carefully arranged bibliography makes it easy for readers to find the book or article they want without having to search through footnotes.

Because bibliographical entries should be in strict alphabetical order, they should be written with the author's last name first. If no author's name is given, arrange the entry by the first word of the title, excluding *a*, *an*, or *the*. If you are citing magazine or journal articles, give the inclusive page numbers of the article, but you do not need to give the relevant page numbers for books. Otherwise, bibliographical entries should be written in the same form as the documentation for footnotes, with one exception: bibliographical form does not require parentheses around the location, publisher's name and publication date of books. Here are some sample bibliographical entries:

Koestler, Arthur, *The Act of Creation*, London: Pan Books, 1975.

Judy, Stephen, "On Clock Watching and Composing," in *Rhetoric and Composition*, ed. Richard L. Graves. New Rochelle, N.J.: Hayden Book Co., Inc., 1976.

Severson, Cyndy, "Pack Up Your Troubles," *Texas Monthly*, April, 1981, pp. 140–146.

Finally, when in doubt about the proper form for notes or bibliographical entries, check the appropriate style manual. If you can afford the few dollars such manuals cost, probably you should buy one. It's a comfort to know you have a complete and authoritative guide to documentation sitting on your bookshelf when you need it.

Putting Your Paper in Final Form

Reviewing your paper

When you have written your first draft and accumulated the data you will need to document your sources fully and accurately, read over your paper carefully and ask yourself these questions.

1. Is my thesis clear? Have I stated it early in the paper to let my reader know what to expect?

2. Does the paper have a definite plan of organization that is clearly marked for the reader by subheadings or directional signals? Have I linked the parts of the paper together?
3. Are the sections of the paper in logical order? Would I make the paper easier to follow if I rearranged some parts?
4. Do I have enough data to support each part of the paper? If the assignment requires that I use a specific number and kind of sources, have I done so?

After considering your draft with these questions in mind, you should be able to decide whether you are generally satisfied with the content and organization of your paper. If you sense that you don't have enough supporting evidence for some part or that you have left out an important point, find time to go back to the library and consult some extra sources. You might check the latest issues of *Readers' Guide to Periodical Literature* to see if you can find some up-to-date information on your topic or ask the librarian if there is some specialized reference book you haven't yet consulted. You may be able to add several paragraphs and integrate them smoothly into your paper at this point.

When you think you are reasonably well satisifed with the content of your paper, read it again, this time thinking about style, usage, and spelling. Ask yourself these questions:

Questions for revising

1. Is the paper wordy? Are there phrases or whole sentences that really don't say much and should be cut out?
2. Is my language concrete and clear? In some places have I tried to sound impressive and used fuzzy or pretentious language that I really don't understand? Is the paper visual? Can my reader *see* what I am writing about? Have I used strong verbs when possible?
3. Is my tone objective? Should I change some words to get rid of emotional bias or an unprofessional tone?
4. Do my subjects and verbs agree? Can the reader always tell what my pronouns refer to? Have I put commas where I need them to mark off interrupting phrases or make meaning clear?
5. Have I checked the spelling of any words I'm not sure about? Should I get someone else to read the paper for misspellings?

Finally, when you are satisfied that you have done as well as you have the time and determination to do, type your paper, carefully following the instructor's guidelines for margins, spacing, cover sheet, and so on. And, as a last step, proofread it and neatly mark any necessary corrections before you hand it in.

Suggested Topics and Model Paper

The final section of this chapter includes a list of 50 topics for research papers, a number of which may interest you or may suggest other topics. Following the list is a model research paper.

Suggested Topics for Research Papers

The questions under each topic are intended to serve as probes to help you explore the topic and give you suggestions about various ways in which you might approach your research.

1. *Gambling*
   Why do people gamble? What are the attitudes toward gambling in our society? Do other societies have similar attitudes toward gambling? Is gambling a legal, a moral, or an economic issue? What are some of the consequences of legalized gambling?

2. *Astrology*
   What is the relationship between astronomy and astrology? Does astrology have a scientific basis? Can belief in astrology cause any harm? How widespread is belief in astrology?

3. *Genetic research*
   What is genetic engineering? What legal, ethical, or safety problems are raised by genetic research? Why is "test tube birth" controversial? What are the pros and cons of research with recombinant DNA?

These topics were compiled and annotated by the staff of reference librarians at the Undergraduate Library at the University of Texas at Austin. Copyrighted by the Undergraduate Library, The General Libraries, The University of Texas at Austin, 1980–81.

4. *Animal communication*

   How do animals communicate with each other? Do certain species have the capacity to talk to man? What research has been done on teaching language to such animals as apes and dolphins? What are the implications of this research?

5. *Artificial intelligence*

   What is artificial intelligence? Can machines be built which will solve problems, play games, and even demonstrate the ability to learn? What research has been done in this area? What are the dangers of developing artificial intelligence? What is cybernetics? What is the relationship between cybernetics and artificial intelligence?

6. *Equal Rights Amendment*

   When was the Equal Rights Amendment proposed? What progress has been made? What groups are opposed to the Equal Rights Amendment? For what reasons? What impact would the amendment have on women's rights and legal status if it were adopted?

7. *Television*

   How does television violence affect the public? How do TV watchers differ from nonwatchers? What can children learn from television? Who determines what appears on television: advertisers, producers, network officials, the public? How has television programming changed over the years? What impact will cable TV (community antenna television) have on television viewers of the future?

8. *Income tax*

   What are some of the criticisms voiced about the U.S. income tax system? Do the tax laws favor certain groups, such as corporations, the wealthy, or the unmarried individual? If the laws are unfair, why are they so difficult to change? How does our system compare with that of other countries? How is inflation affecting the income tax structure?

9. *Film*

   How have movies been used to influence public attitudes such as patriotism during wartime? Why did certain types of films dominate the screen in certain eras, such as the gangster movies of the thirties? What kinds of social commentary have movies portrayed? What censorship has been imposed?

10. *Population explosion*

    What solutions have been proposed for overpopulation? What are some of the most promising methods of birth control and the problems associated with them? Should sterilization be used as a method of birth control? Are all countries concerned about limiting their populations? How are population trends in other countries going to affect the U.S.?

11. *ESP*

    What is extrasensory perception? What are some of the forms it takes? What kinds of experiments are used to test its validity? Why is there so much skepticism about ESP?

12. *Aging*

    What is it like to be old in the U.S.? How is the age distribution of the population changing? What problems of income, housing, or medical care do old people face? Is mandatory retirement fair? How does the treatment of old people differ in other countries? What factors in our culture contribute to our attitude toward old age? What is "gray power"?

13. *Death and funeral rites*

    What are some of the historical changes in attitudes toward death and the customs associated with it? How are U.S. attitudes toward death changing? What can be done to help terminal patients prepare for death? What are some ways to cope with grief? What functions do funeral rites and ceremonies serve? How do a society's rites reflect its concept of death? What can be learned about life after death and the moment of death from people who survive an apparent death experience?

14. *Cults and religious movements*

    What accounts for the rise in participation in various evangelical religions and cults? How does the increasing interest reflect American society and its values? What is the "human potential" movement? Is it a new religion in America? What is deprogramming? What are the pros and cons of its use on cult members?

15. *Popular music*

    Choose a form of popular music, for example, jazz, country and western, rock, or blues. How did this type of music originate and develop? How has it changed from its original form? What influence has it had on other forms of music? How does it reflect other aspects of contemporary society?

16. *Life on other planets*

    What evidence exists to suggest the possibility of life on other planets? Is the search for extraterrestrial life an important goal in our space program? What methods are used to detect life? What forms is life elsewhere likely to take? Have recent planetary explorations changed our views? What can we learn from contact with other life forms?

17. *Parent and child*

    What role does each parent have in the child's development? How have ideas about raising children changed in the last twenty years? How has our changing society affected the family? Is the family becoming obsolete? What new roles is the father playing in child rearing? Why? What special problems does the single parent face in raising a family?

18. *Utopia*

    What is utopia and how did the term originate? Do ideas of utopia change as society changes? What are some of the famous utopian experiments? Were they successful? Did they have any impact on society? What are some of the famous literary utopias?

19. *Pesticides, herbicides, and industrial poisons*

    What are some of the effects of pesticides on the environment? On people and wildlife? What are some of the chemicals being attacked by environmentalists? How important are pesticides and herbicides in protecting our food supply? What are the limitations or advantages of "natural pesticides"? How have government, industry, or farmers reacted to the controversy? What are the risks or dangers of chemical waste disposal, such as at Love Canal?

20. *Solar energy*

    Is solar energy a feasible alternative to fossil fuels? How does it work? What are its limitations? What is the government doing to stimulate research into solar energy? What are the merits of passive design? How has architectural design been affected by solar energy use?

21. *Computers*

    How has the computer changed since its invention? What impact has the computer had on business, education, communication, or other aspects of society? What benefits does the computer bring? What problems? How has the invention of the microprocessor revolutionized the computer industry?

22. *Contemporary sexual ethics*

    How are sex customs changing in the U.S.? How has sex research contributed to our understanding of human sexuality? What are the pros and cons of sex education in the schools? Are men feeling threatened by changing sex roles?

23. *Wiretapping and the right to privacy*

    What legislation has been passed to protect the right to privacy? Is it legal for private citizens to tap, bug, or record private conversations? When did government wiretapping originate? Is it legal? Is it justified?

24. *Endangered species*

    What species are endangered? What is being done to save rare animals or plants? What is the history of an animal that is either already extinct or in danger of extinction? Are zoos part of the answer or part of the problem? What is the role of the sportsman? Conservationist? Government?

25. *Photography*

    Is photography an art or a technology? Trace the development of a style or movement in the history of photography. Who were some of the earliest photographers and how do their methods compare with today's? What is photojournalism? How can it influence the public's perception of current events? How do photographers choose and compose a subject for a photograph? How has photography portrayed various eras in American history, such as the Western expansion or the Depression?

26. *Vampires*

    What is the origin of the vampire legend? Who was the original Count Dracula? What does the vampire represent? How have vampires been portrayed in nineteenth and twentieth century literature and in films? Is there any factual data to support the existence of vampires?

27. *Gun control*

What are the arguments for and against gun control? Does the availability of guns lead to their use in crime? How is the phrase "the right to keep and bear arms" interpreted by the National Rifle Association or by gun control advocates? Why is gun control such a controversial issue in the U.S. when it is practiced successfully in many other countries?

28. *The press and politics*

What effect does television and radio coverage have on elections? Have campaign strategies changed as a result? Does television, radio, and newspaper coverage make politicians more open to ridicule and scandal? What effect does television, radio, and newspaper coverage have on political events? Is legislation to control the political use of the press desirable? Can the press "make" or "break" a political figure?

29. *Sports and society*

What are some of the psychological and sociological aspects of being a participant or spectator of sports? How and why have some sports ceased to be "fun" and become big business? Is violence in sports becoming excessive? What are the advantages and disadvantages of amateur versus professional status in various sports? How important are sports and its heroes to the public? Do world political conflicts endanger international sports competitions such as the Olympics and similar events?

30. *Inflation*

What is inflation? What causes it? Is it a recent phenomenon or an historic one? What are its effects? What has the U.S. done to reduce inflation? How do the opinions of particular politicans or economists differ? What effect does the status of the dollar abroad have on the economy here?

31. *Adoption*

Why do people decide to adopt a child? What difficulties are they likely to encounter before and after adopting? What special considerations are involved in the adoption of multiracial, handicapped, or other "special" children? What problems are created for the adopted parents and the birth parents when adopted children search for their "roots"? What obstacles do the children face in their search?

32. *Pyramids and ancient megaliths*
Who built the pyramids of Egypt or Stonehenge in England or the great stone faces on Easter Island? How do these ancient monuments reflect the cultures of their makers? What is one theory of how the pyramids were built? What are some of the legends and curses of the pyramids? Do these structures indicate high levels of civilization? What happened to the builders? What is the relationship between astronomy and these ancient monuments?

33. *Divorce*
How are patterns of marriage and divorce changing in the U.S.? What changes have there been in attitudes toward divorce? What kinds of psychological, legal, financial, or social problems does divorce cause and what help is available to deal with these problems? How does divorce affect children? How should child custody be handled? How can problems in marriage be resolved without divorce?

34. *Origin of the universe*
What are some of the scientific explanations for the origin of the universe? What theory does most of the available evidence seem to support? Is there agreement on the way planets are created? What new evidence has been turned up by the space program?

35. *Consumer protection*
What rights do consumers have? Historically, how has the government regulated such things as food, appliances, alcohol, cars, and cigarettes? What effects has Ralph Nader had on American consumer protection? If a product or service has been unsatisfactory, what can a consumer do about it? Are laws necessary to protect consumers?

36. *Laughter*
What makes people laugh? What are some of the theories of humor? What is the difference between humor and comedy? What role does laughing play in the release of tension? Are some things universally funny? What comparisons can be drawn between contemporary jokes, comedy films, or TV shows and those in the past?

37. *Body language*
    What is nonverbal communication? Can you really read a person like a book? How does nonverbal communication differ in other cultures, for example, Latin America? What effect can this have on inter-cultural communication? Of what practical use is the study of nonverbal communication? What has research on kinetics contributed to understanding the importance of body movement in communication?

38. *Cancer*
    What do doctors think causes cancer? Is there likely ever to be a single cure or treatment? What are some of the most promising areas of cancer research? Can cancer be predicted? Can it be prevented?

39. *The airplane and society*
    How safe is flying? What are the major causes of aviation accidents? What are some of the safety measures being taken to prevent accidents? What impact has the development of aviation had on business, warfare, or public transportation? What are the pros and cons of deregulation for the airline industry?

40. *Suicide*
    Is suicide on the increase? In what groups of people is it most common? Have recent social attitudes toward suicide changed? How do attitudes toward suicide differ among cultures?

41. *Animals that capture the imagination*
    Choose an animal and discuss its habitat, behavior, or position in the world today. For example: What is the controversy surrounding whale hunting? Should there be a moratorium on the killing of seals? What has research discovered about the intelligence of dolphins or chimpanzees?

42. *White collar crime*
    What is white collar crime? How does it differ from other crime? Do white collar criminals receive special treatment? What are some of the most famous cases of white collar crime? Is white collar crime on the increase in this country? Do computers provide more opportunities for white collar crime?

43. *Child abuse*
    How widespread is the problem of child abuse? What are its

causes? Is it a moral, legal, or psychological problem? What is being done to prevent child abuse and help the abuser? What are the various forms child abuse can take, such as physical, emotional, or sexual abuse? How does one kind of abuse, such as incest, affect the child in later life?

44. *The twenty-first century*

What are some of the predictions about life at the end of this century and in the twenty-first century? How should we prepare for the future now? Does our future depend on space exploration, increased technology, or new constraints on our use of resources? Which nations will be most affected by the future? Who will fare best? Why? What changes will the future bring in terms of social attitudes, such as the changing nature of sex roles or the function of the family?

45. *Smoking*

How serious a health hazard is smoking to smokers and non-smokers? Has smoking always been considered unhealthy? How influential is the tobacco industry? What impact has the U.S. Surgeon General's report *Smoking and Health* had on smoking habits? What are some of the methods recommended for people trying to give up cigarettes, and how effective are these methods?

46. *Prison reform*

Why do U.S. prisons need reform? What are some specific reforms suggested? What part have the prisoners themselves played in the demand for reform? What are the "liberal" and "conservative" views on this issue? How do penal systems differ in other countries? What progress has been made to improve conditions?

47. *Vitamins*

How do vitamins affect people's health? How accurate is the Minimum Daily Requirement? Does mega-vitamin therapy work? What are the diseases it is being tried on? What are the arguments against it? How do natural and synthetic vitamins differ?

48. *Art forgeries*

What have been some notorious art fakes and hoaxes? How can forgeries be detected? What are some of the methods used in art forgery? Is there a way to protect valuable art from forgery?

49. *UFO's*

    What are some current theories about the existence of UFO's? Do UFO sightings follow a pattern? Is there any evidence of government cover-up of UFO sightings? What serious research has been done on UFO's?

50. *Climatic change and weather modification*

    Is man inadvertently changing the earth's climate? How can pollution, industrialization, or urbanization influence the weather? What do scientists predict the impact of a worldwide climatic change would be? In what cases would weather modification be beneficial? What are the limits of weather modification technologies?

SOLAR POWER: A USABLE ENERGY SOURCE?

The twentieth century has been a time of growth for America, where more is produced each year than was produced the year before. Production requires energy, and Albert Bartlett tells us in the *American Journal of Physics* that all the oil, our predominant source of energy, could be depleted as soon as the year 2000.[1] Therefore, if growth is to continue, a lasting source of energy must be found. The major candidates for this role are fusion, coal, natural gas, and, some ecologists believe, tidal and wind power. But the energy source which is cheapest and least damaging to the environment is receiving the least attention. That source is solar power, transmitted from orbit via microwave.

Currently, on earth we have two methods of solar collection, termed passive and active. The passive method of collecting solar energy, which is used in today's solar homes and businesses, works by using mirrors to concentrate the sunlight onto pipes containing water. The intense light heats the pipe and boils the water, forcing it to move through the pipes so that it can be stored for later use in a household as hot water. The heated water can also be passed through pipes in the walls, heating the building during the night and in the winter, thereby cutting fuel costs for the owner. Passive solar systems are designed to take the place of electricity, gas, and oil for heating purposes, but unfortunately, they don't actually produce the electricity needed for everyday living. Though a system could conceivably be built to produce electricity, such a system would take miles of pipe, thousands of square yards of mirrors, and many thousands of gallons of water. It would heat the water in the same way as the passive system described above, but on a much grander scale. The water in the pipes would be heated to very high temperatures by the sunlight and would become a high energy steam. The steam would be used to turn a conventional turbine generator which would produce the electricity, Unfortunately, even if the mirrors were perfectly clean and focusing the light exactly on the pipes, and the pipes were perfectly straight and the turbine were in perfect working order, only a small percent of the energy in the sunlight hitting the mirrors would be converted into electricity. Also, the amount of room needed to power each city with this system would be prohibitive, so no one takes the system seriously.

The alternative to passive solar systems are active systems, where instead of pipes and turbines, solar cells are used to convert sunlight directly into electricity, skipping all of the inefficient intermediate steps. Laboratory tests have obtained efficiencies above 70 percent with solar cells, but field conditions are much filthier than those in laboratories and the efficiency of the cells plummets when they get dirty. Experts estimate that an active solar system located on earth would produce electricity at a cost of 7 to 20 cents per kilowatt-hour as compared to an average between 1.8 and 3.0 cents for the energy sources available today.[2]

The biggest problem inherent in both passive and active systems is that the sun does not sit still in the sky, nor does it shine all the time. Therefore, expensive equipment would be needed to allow either system to track the sun as it moves across the sky. But that still doesn't solve the problem that the sun goes down long before peak rates of consumption of electricity are over. The sunniest portions of the United States receive sunlight less than 17 percent of the time,[3] and even during that time they are exposed to sunlight which has been filtered by the atmosphere so that the solar cells are not working anywhere near their capacity. The only way to reach these capacities is to take the cells above the atmosphere and out of the earth's day-night cycle.

Most of the satellites in orbit today have a few square yards of solar cells glued to their outer skin to provide the electricity needed for each satellite on its own. In contrast, a solar power satellite would consist almost solely of solar cells, and would spread out over as much as twenty square miles. It would have very little supporting structure because the satellite would be in "free fall," or zero gravity, where there are few stresses to disturb a satellite. There are many possible orbits into which a Solar Power Satellite (SPS) could be placed, but by far the best would be a geosynchronuous orbit. This is an orbit in which the satellite takes exactly one day to circle the earth in the same direction the earth spins, so the earth always shows the same face to the satellite, and the satellite appears to hover in one spot above the earth. In this orbit, the satellite would spend 99 percent of its time in sunlight, the other 1 percent being when it was eclipsed by the earth's shadow, once a day for several days in the spring and fall.[4, 5]

But once we have collected all that useful energy in orbit with the solar cells, how do we get it down to earth? The cheapest answer, using today's technology, is via microwaves. Today "microwave" is a word usually associated with ovens, but solar power satellites utilize the microwave beams in a very different manner from microwave ovens. If we wished, we could use a very tight and powerful beam to transmit power from the satellite; it would wreak havoc on the environment near the collection facilities. Obviously, we are not going to do that. Instead, we will spread the beam out to insure the safety of anyone or anything which happened across the beam. It is quite possible to design the system so that the density of microwave energy on top of the receiving antennae (rectennae) would be no more than ten times the U.S. standard of exposure to microwave radiation. Such an exposure would have no disastrous side effects, such as mutation or broiling an animal in its own juices, but, instead, the microwaves would only produce a slight warmth.[6] Below the rectennae, the land is so safe (and receives plenty of sunlight, since the rectennae is merely a wire grid) that cattle could be raised on pastures grown there.[7]

A good analogy to the danger of burning down the countryside with microwaves using an SPS, would be a comparison of the chance of injury when using a 100 watt light bulb and a navy searchlight. If you put your hand next to a 100 watt light bulb, it is possible to burn yourself, but you almost have to try to do so. If you stood in front of a searchlight, however, you would fry just as if you were in a big oven (microwave or wood burning). The SPS's would be comparatively as dangerous as a light bulb.[8]

While it has been easy to prove that SPS's are safe, the point means little if they are not cost effective. Surprisingly, capital costs for SPS's can be kept comparable to those of other energy systems at the same amounts of power output. If we used only materials from the earth to build SPS's, the costs would be literally astronomical. But through the Apollo missions we have learned that the moon is very rich in most of the minerals needed to build space colonies and SPS's. Thus, with the moon's lower gravity, an SPS project becomes very economically attractive.[9]

The technical details of moving material from the surface of the moon into orbit around the earth are beyond the scope of this essay, but the following is a short description of how the process would work. First, several tons of lunar rock, to be refined in orbit, would be scooped up and put in an open-ended bucket. The bucket would then be put on a "mass driver," a monorail-like track, and sped up to about 6000 mph. Then the bucket would be jerked to a stop, and the rock would fly out the open end to literally soil over the horizon. The rock would orbit the moon several times before passing through a point above the far side of the moon where a mass catcher would be waiting. The mass catchers (there would be two, one on station while the other is en route to the space colony) would be giant garbage sacks, a football field wide and a quarter of a mile long, made out of the exceptionally strong material, kevlar.

When a catcher has collected several thousand tons of lunar material, it will begin a trip of several weeks to get from its station above the far side of the moon to the orbit the space colony will be following about the earth. There, the lunar ore will be refined and used to build SPS's. The space colony will be a wheel a mile in diameter, with six spokes, each a half mile tall. The outer ring will be about 400 feet thick. Crops will be grown in the colony and it will house as many as 10,000 colonists. Each colony could build either two SPS's a year or one colony per year. Therefore, if we start with two colonies and each year put half the colonies to building SPS's and the other half to building more colonies, by the end of ten years we would have 94 colonies and 194 SPS's.[10]

These ideas are not science fiction. We can do it. If we started working tomorrow, we could have the first SPS by 1990 and the first colony by the year 2000. We know more about how to build space colonies today than we knew about how to put men on the moon when President Kennedy set that as our goal. Even the price is easily within our grasp. Separate studies have produced capital outlay estimates at under $110 billion, spread out over 20 years, with a peak yearly cost of $8 billion, a mere 3.5 to 4 percent of the U.S. national budget.[11] Peter Glaser, the man who first suggested the SPS system, feels that, in the interest of world politics, no one country should monopolize the energy source, thereby cutting capital costs on the American taxpayers.[12] Getting started on the SPS system would be an Apollo-sized project which would pay for itself by the year 2005 and would reap benefits of $200 billion per year by the year 2112. The price of electricity for consumers would start at eight-tenths of a cent per kilowatt-hour and drop to below four-tenths of a cent, less than half of the price of the cheapest power available today.[13]

We can build SPS's, but are they the best answer?

Some ecologists feel that the winds and tides could power the world. Quick calculations, though, show that the wind in the U.S. can provide only 5 percent of the energy consumed in any one year. As for tides, if we build a dam around the entire continental U.S. (and what would that do to the ecology?), the resulting electricity would just about power the city of Boston. So much for the winds and tides.[14]

A lot of hope is being placed on nuclear fusion, the process which powers the sun. The big problem with relying on fusion for the next century's need is that fusion plants don't work yet. What fusion engineers are trying to do is create, here on earth, the pressure and temperature conditions found in the middle of stars, and then control the reaction enough to be able to extract useful energy from it. No one knows how to do this yet, and there is no guarantee that anyone will have the correct answer when fusion power is needed. Congress, though, is apparently looking for a breakthrough, because last October they signed into law a bill guaranteeing $20 billion over the next 20 years for fusion research.[15]

Many people are looking to fossil fuels such as coal and natural gas as a solution to our energy shortage because they see vast quantities of each in relatively easily accessible places. They perform projections using today's rate of consumption of energy against the energy content in these two fossil fuels and conclude that together they will last thousands or even millions of years. These people totally ignore growth rates, thinking that a mere 7 percent increase in consumption each year is too small to be important. A 7 percent growth rate yields a doubling period of ten years.[16]

Many experts erroneously feel that there is enough coal in the U.S. to power the world for millions of years:

"The trillions of tons of coal lying under the United States will have to carry a large part of the nation's increased energy consumption," says (the) Director of the Energy Division of the Oak Ridge National Laboratories. He estimated America's coal reserves are so huge, they could last "a minimum of 300 years and probably a maximum of 1000 years."[17]

But compare the above statement of the life expectancy of U.S. coal reserves with the results of simple calculations given in Table I.

TABLE I

Rate of Growth (%)	High Estimate (yr)	Low Estimate (yr)
Zero	2878	680
1%	339	205
2%	203	134
3%	149	102
4%	119	83
5%	99	71
6%	86	62
7%	76	55
8%	68	50
9%	62	46
10%	57	42
11%	52	39
12%	49	37
13%	46	35

No matter what anyone may say to the contrary, there is enough coal to get into the twenty-first century, but not past it at present rates of growth.[18]

But even if we had enough coal for millions of years, would we really want to use it? Each 1000 megawatt coal plant dumps into the atmosphere approximately nine million tons of carbon dioxide, 157,000 tons of sulfur dioxide, and 474,000 tons of assorted ashes. These would combine to make beautiful sunsets but at the same time would cause acid rains and widespread cancer. Also, a buildup of carbon dioxide could cause a greenhouse effect on the earth, thereby raising the temperature, of the earth, melting the ice caps, and possibly turning the earth into a hot, dark hell similar to the planet Venus.[19]

About the only advantage of using coal as an energy source is that the price of producing power is 1.8 to 3.0 cents per kilowatt-hour.[20] That price makes it the cheapest earthbound energy source available today.

The final source of energy which many feel could power the earth is natural gas. The estimated reserves of gas in conventional fields measures approximately six billion cubic meters, not overly abundant. But recently, domes of pressurized water have been found under the sea which may contain as much as 1300 trillion cubic meters of natural gas mixed with the water. The energy content in that much natural gas is almost equal to the total U.S. coal reserve, and would give us only one more doubling period if we used all of our coal and then switched to natural gas. And natural gas is another energy source which adds carbon dioxide to the atmosphere.[21]

Unlike other potential energy sources, the SPS system is the only energy source which is clean, able to keep up with the growth of energy consumption, and obtainable with today's technology. The only limit to how many SPS's we can build is the total of all the building material available in the solar system. Exhaustion of that much material will not be a problem for thousands of years.

Drake Christensen

NOTES

1. Albert Bartlett, "Forgotten Fundamentals of the Energy Crisis," *American Journal of Physics,* 46 (1978), p. 879.
2. T. A. Heppenheimer, *Colonies in Space* (1978; rpt. New York: Warner Books, 1980), p. 259.
3. T. A. Heppenheimer, p. 46.
4. T. A. Heppenheimer, p. 47.
5. Jerry Pournelle, *A Step Farther Out* (New York: Ace, 1980), p. 366.
6. T. A. Heppenheimer, pp. 48–49.
7. Jerry Pournelle, pp. 256–257.
8. Jerry Pournelle, p. 39.
9. T. A. Heppenheimer, p. 102.
10. T. A. Heppenheimer, pp, 102–121, 157–161.
11. T. A. Heppenheimer, pp. 72–75.
12. Douglas Collogan, "Interview: Peter Glaser," *Omni,* Apr. 1981, pp. 114–116.
13. T. A. Heppenheimer, p. 73.
14. Jerry Pournelle, p. 317.
15. "The McCormack Fusion Bill: Victory and Challenge," Editorial, *Fusion,* Jan. 1981, pp. 4–5.
16. Albert Bartlett, p. 880.
17. Albert Bartlett, p. 879.
18. Albert Bartlett, p. 880.
19. Jerry Pournelle, p. 358.
20. T. A. Heppenheimer, p. 259.
21. Jerry Pournelle, p. 364.

BIBLIOGRAPHY

Bartlett, Albert. "Forgotten Fundamentals of the Energy Crisis," *American Journal of Physics,* September, 1978, pp. 876–888
Collogan, Douglas. "Interview: Peter Glaser," *Omni,* April, 1981, pp. 114–116
Heppenheimer, T. A. *Colonies in Space,* Warner Books, New York, 1980
"The McCormack Fusion Bill: Victory and Challenge," *Fusion,* January, 1981, pp. 4–5
Pournelle, Jerry. *A Step Farther Out,* Ace, New York, 1980

Writing About Literature

13

At some time in your college career you will almost certainly face the assignment of writing one or more papers about literature. If most of the writing you have done up until that time has focused on argumentation and factual material, you may feel unprepared to meet this new challenge. Analyzing a poem or comparing two characters in a play seems, at first glance, to call for different skills and tactics than arguing for additional services at the student health center or analyzing an editorial that calls for student participation in faculty promotions. Actually, the two kinds of writing are more similar than you might realize. Both call for you to make an assertion and support it; both require that you use language precisely and clearly and that you understand how other people are using it; and both demand that you reinforce your statements with examples and concrete evidence. In practice, then, the approach and techniques that you have been using for writing exposition and argumentation will, with certain limitations, serve you well in writing about literature.

Understanding effects

Your study of rhetoric can help you with literary assignments in other ways. Probably nothing is more crucial to an appreciation of literature than a sensitivity to language; therefore, your study of diction—connotation, figurative language, concreteness, tone—will help you understand how poets, playwrights, or novelists achieve their effects. You can also use rhetorical analysis to find the themes or main ideas of works, and the habit of analyzing the evidence writers bring in to support their assertions will aid you in tracing the devices authors use to develop these themes.

Finding the theme

Discovering purpose

Authors of fiction, like essayists or orators, have a purpose; at times, especially if they are writing suspense or adventure stories, it may be no more than to entertain. More often, however, the writers that you are likely to study in college have a moral purpose. They want to persuade you that some ways of behaving are good, some ways are bad; they want you to admire certain characters, dislike others. They may want to persuade you of the need for change. Sometimes they simply want you to understand people and their problems. Unlike writers of nonfiction, however, they do not usually announce their purposes. You must infer them from internal evidence in the work. In Mark Twain's *Huckleberry Finn*, for example, the theme of Huck's gradual disillusionment with conventional morality is developed by incident after incident in which so-called good people act selfishly and cruelly. The ability to recognize and evaluate this kind of evidence is invaluable in writing about literature.

Finding your Purpose, Audience, Persona, and Argument

Purpose and Audience

Preparing to write a paper about literature involves going through the same preliminary steps that you would take before beginning any other writing assignment: deciding on your purpose, deciding who is your audience and what its expectations of you are, choosing a persona or voice, and deciding on the main points of your argument. Your immediate purpose is to demonstrate to your instructor that you understand the literature you are working on and can articulate your ideas about it. A corollary purpose should be to learn more about the literature by writing about it. Obviously you know that your audience is your instructor (and perhaps the class), but analyzing that audience's expectations may require some reflection.

Preliminary steps

You can begin by assuming that unless an instructor specifically says so, he or she does *not* want your paper to be merely a summary of the literary work you are writing on. You can also assume that most teachers do *not* expect your paper to be solely a subjective emotional response to the work. Although your emotional response to literature is important, an instructor cannot very well evaluate your understanding of a literary work on the basis of your feelings about it. Probably what your instructor does expect from you is this: first, that you understand the theme of the work; second, that you have some insight into the way the author achieves the effects; and third, that you can make a supported judgment about its quality. These expectations, of course, closely parallel the formula we have been using in rhetorical analysis: what is the author's main idea, what means are used to communicate that idea, and is the author successful?

Persona and Argument

Establishing a persona

Choosing your argument

Deciding on your persona should not be difficult; you are in the straightforward role of student, and your tone will probably be objective and informal. The kinds of argument or expository techniques that you decide to use in your paper will depend, at least partially, on the assignment, but you may be surprised at how readily you can adapt the rhetorical modes to developing the topics most frequently assigned for literary papers. For example, if you are asked to analyze the character of Oedipus in *Oedipus Rex* and to relate his character to his fate in the play, the logical way to develop your topic would be by using arguments of definition and cause and effect. If you are asked to evaluate a short story, you can use deductive reasoning: a good short story has traits, A, B, and C; this short story has these traits; therefore, this is a good short story. If you are asked to discuss the effect of imagery in a poem—for example, T. S. Eliot's "The Hollow Men"—you can argue inductively. By listing the main images from the first stanza—"stuffed men," "hollow men," "leaning together," "filled with straw," "dried voices," "wind in dry grass," "rats' feet," "broken glass," and "dry cellar"—you can demonstrate that Eliot is trying to create a depressed and sterile atmosphere, and then go on to support your thesis with examples from other stanzas. In a theme on character motivation, you may want to show how the author builds an argument from circumstance. In William Faulkner's *Light in August*, for instance, the author develops a complex and almost air-tight circumstantial argument to explain why Joe Christmas murders a woman.

Preparing to Write Literary Papers

Rough out a plan

For some reason, literary topics tempt many students just to start writing with little real idea of what they are going to say. The result is often a collection of random comments that does not even qualify as a good book report. Such a paper has almost no value for either you or your teacher. To avoid this kind of disaster, begin by narrowing your topic to a manageable size. If, for instance,

Narrow the topic the assignment is to write on the significant character traits of Jay Gatsby in F. Scott Fitzgerald's novel *The Great Gatsby,* you would not describe his actions through the entire book in order to show his character. You need to focus on a few key traits, but in order to choose those traits, you should write down everything you can remember about him.

Ambitious—wanted to be rich, hard working as boy

Dishonest—tells lies about war experiences, shady business deals

Materialistic—likes big cars, big house, parties, fancy clothes

Naive—believes Daisy perfect, no social sense

Romantic—impossible dreams, wants to sacrifice self for Daisy

Out of this list you choose materialism and romanticism as the most interesting, particularly because the combination is paradoxical. Now you can go on to plan what is essentially a theme of definition. You can define Gatsby by his possessions—fancy car, gaudy clothes, pretentious mansion—by his actions toward Daisy, and by his dreams, giving examples to illustrate all your points. Your thesis sentence could be: "Jay Gatsby's character is a paradoxical combination of the materialistic and the romantic."

A rough outline would look like this:

I.   Gatsby's Possessions
   A.   Clothes
      1.   White suit, silver tie
      2.   Dozens of flashy shirts
   B.   Pretentious mansion
      1.   Twenty-room house
      2.   Library with fake books
      3.   Swimming pool
   C.   Large, ostentatious car
II. Gatsby's Actions Toward Daisy
   A.   Arranges secret meetings
   B.   Wants to rescue her from her husband
   C.   Takes blame for her killing Myrtle

III.   Gatsby's Dreams
    A.   Boyhood dream of wealth
    B.   Plans to marry Daisy; thinks of her as still a virgin

Another assignment might be to discuss conflict in *Othello*. If you try to discuss all the conflicts in *Othello* in one short paper, you're going to have trouble organizing your ideas and finding room to bring in the supporting details you need. Therefore, in order to focus your paper you need to review the conflicts in the play and decide which one you want to deal with: Iago and Othello, Othello and Desdemona, Desdemona and Iago, or the conflict within Othello himself. Since the last is really the crux of the play, you choose that. Your thesis sentence might read: "Despite the abundance of killing, plotting, and fighting in *Othello*, the major conflict in the play is within Othello himself: the conflict between honor and love."

Limiting your topic presents less of a problem when the assignment is to write about a short poem, because you have a comparatively small amount of material to work with. Nevertheless, you need to decide on the main points you are going to make, in what order you are going to discuss them, and which examples you are going to use to support your ideas. Suppose, for example, you were asked to analyze the following poem:

A Fire Truck[1]

Right down the shocked street with a siren-blast
That sends all else skittering to the curb,
Redness, brass, ladders and hats hurl past,
   Blurring to sheer verb.

Shift at the corner into uproarious gear
And make it around the turn in a squall of traction,
The headlong bell maintaining sure and clear,
   Thought is degraded action.

Beautiful, heavy, unweary, loud, obvious thing!
I stand here purged of nuance, my mind a blank.
All I was brooding upon has taken wing,
   And I have you to thank.

As you howl beyond hearing I carry you into my mind,
Ladders and brass and all, there to admire
Your phoenix-red simplicity, enshrined
   In that not extinguished fire.

Probably the main points you would want to bring out about this poem would be its dominant impression, the tension in it, and the poet's theme. Your working notes might look like this:

Dominant impression *action;* motion—noise—power

Support	shocked, siren-blast, skittering, hurl past—uproarious gear, squall of traction, headlong bell, howl, brass, red, beautiful, heavy, loud, obvious
Tension	Contrast of fire engine and poet's mind; motion vs. reflection and inaction
Support	action verbs vs. "stand here," "purged of nuance," "mind a blank," "brooding"
Poet's theme	Action is easier than thinking; temptation to avoid reflection and thought and just *do*. Italicized phrase "Thought is degraded action" obviously important but can't be sure statement represents poet's beliefs since he says only that it is the message he gets from the engine's bell.

More consideration of the poem would probably give you additional ideas, but with these points you have a good basis to begin writing. Your thesis sentence might read, "In 'A Fire Truck' Richard Wilbur contrasts the sensations of watching a fire truck in motion with the persona's melancholy frame of mind to show the temptation the persona feels to abandon the intellectual life for a life of action." A specific outline would follow the pattern of your working notes.

Finding Evidence

When you are writing a paper on a literary topic, you are, after all, still writing an expository theme; that is, you are making assertions about that literature, and you must support and develop them in the same way that you would handle assertions in argumentative writing. You can look for supporting evidence in several places: the author's use of connotation and imagery, his or her attitude toward the characters, the value statements of characters who seem to speak for the author, and the attitudes expressed toward institutions, beliefs, manners, or morals.

Connotation and Imagery

In *Sister Carrie* Theodore Dreiser repeatedly uses the terms *drift, swept along, carried on the tide,* and *a moth of the lamp* in describing his heroine, a woman who has little control over her life. You could assert, on the basis of this connotative evidence, that the author sees this character as a victim of circumstances. You might make the same assertion about a character who is described by words like *pawn* and *puppet,* terms such as *defeated, helpless,* or *beaten,* or associated with jail or trap imagery.

Attitude Toward Characters

Characters whom the author obviously either admires or dislikes furnish you with strong supporting evidence for statements about the theme of a book or story. In *The Scarlet Letter,* for example, Hawthorne portrays Chillingsworth as contemptible and Dimmesdale as weak and hypocritical (the names themselves are connotative). You could assert, therefore, that he disapproves of cowardice, rigid codes of morality, the motive of revenge, and a religion that concerns itself more with punishment than with love. His obvious approval of Hester indicates that he believes in the values she represents: courage, fortitude, loyalty. Thus, Hawthorne's attitude toward his characters provides evidence for the assertion that a major theme in the book is the destructive effect of judgmental, narrow morality. In *Babbitt* Sinclair Lewis criticizes small-town mores by portraying an outstanding citizen as a ridiculous and pompous person.

Spokesperson Characters

You should be cautious about assuming that an important character in a book or story is the spokesperson for the author, but if the ideas expressed by that character seem consistently to be a reflection of the philosophy you think the book is expressing, you can probably use that character's speeches as supporting evidence in a paper. It is obvious, for example, that Hank Morgan's comments on slavery in *A Connecticut Yankee in King Arthur's Court* are an accurate statement of Mark Twain's own views; therefore, we can reason that other attitudes he expresses are also Twain's. John Steinbeck comments on the actions of his characters in *In Dubious Battle* through the philosophical doctor; the events in the book reinforce the impression that the doctor/observer speaks for the author.

Finding Evidence in Poetry

Evidence in poetry may be more subtle and therefore more difficult to extract because usually it consists of image clusters and the general tone that the poem conveys. Nevertheless, it is there in the form of connotation, metaphor, and the author's attitude toward the material. Look, for example, at the two final stanzas from Matthew Arnold's "Dover Beach":

The Sea of Faith
Was once, too, at the full, and round earth's shore
Lay like the folds of a bright girdle furled.
But now I only hear
Its melancholy, long, withdrawing roar,
Retreating, to the breath
Of the night wind, down the vast edges drear
And naked shingles of the world

Ah, love, let us be true
To one another! for the world, which seems
To lie before us like a land of dreams,
So various, so beautiful, so new,
Hath really neither joy, nor love, nor light,
Nor certitude, nor peace, nor help for pain;
And we are here as on a darkling plain
Swept with confused alarms of struggle and flight,
Where ignorant armies clash by night.

The lines reveal Arnold's sense of despair and desolation and also hint at his loss of faith in God and his failure to find anything to replace it. The metaphor of faith as a sea that once surrounded him like a "bright girdle" conveys the spiritual support he felt in the past; the slow tempo and the negative words "melancholy," "retreating," "night wind," "drear and naked shingles" in the following lines reveal his present mood. In the next stanza a key word is "seems": the world may "seem" various and beautiful and new, but the next two lines deny that this is so. The negative phrases "darkling plain," "confused alarms of struggle and flight," and "ignorant armies clash by night" complete and reinforce the total impression of despair.

Diction and tone

Thus, the diction in a poem is evidence, evidence as substantial as examples or data that you might use to support another kind of argument. The associations that we attach to words have a kind of reality, and we cannot ignore that reality when interpreting poetry or any other kind of literature. A poet's figurative language is similar evidence. Shakespeare's metaphors comparing age to autumn, sunset, and a dying fire leave little doubt that the persona has a melancholy view toward aging. When Gerard Manley Hopkins writes in his sonnet "God's Grandeur," "The world is charged with the grandeur of God./It will flame out, like shining from shook foil," we must recognize that he is a religious man who wants the reader to be awed by God's power. The rest of the imagery in the poem supports the interpretation.

Figurative language

It is simply not true, then, to say, as readers sometimes do, that a poem can mean anything you want it to mean. It is true that a poem may have more than one fixed meaning or that it can mean different things to different people. A valid interpretation, however, cannot contradict the evidence. Given the imagery we quoted earlier from the first stanza of Eliot's "The Hollow Men," one can scarcely assert that it is a cheerful poem. All the evidence is against such an interpretation. Nor could one find evidence in "A Fire Truck" to claim that it is somber or dismal, although there may be a faint undertone of discontent.

What it comes down to is this: in searching for the meaning of a poem—or any other literary work—you go through the same intellectual process that you would use in any other field. You look at the material before you, form a hypothesis, and then look for evidence to confirm it. If the evidence supports your hypothesis, it is valid; if it does not, you should reexamine your data until you find a hypothesis that fits the facts. The main difference between interpreting literature and writing an account of other kinds of material is that in literature there may be more than one hypothesis that fits the evidence.

Making Judgments About Literature

Finally, in writing a theme about literature, you will probably have to give a supported answer to the question: "Is this a good piece of literature; why or why not?" The question is one that many of us would prefer not to face. We would rather say simply we like the book, play, or poem and not have to justify our opinion. Nevertheless, if we study literature seriously, we must make judgments about it and try to analyze the grounds for those judgments. Only in this way can we develop our tastes and learn to make intelligent distinctions about what is worth reading and what is not.

Fortunately, we can use many of the same techniques that we have been using in judging other kinds of rhetoric. We can fashion a yardstick of values and determine in what ways the work measures up and in what ways it does not. Such a yardstick would have much in common with the ones we have been already using, and it would also contain some other features. Criteria for judging literature should include at least these points:

1. *Timelessness* Is the work of lasting interest? Are the comments the author makes about people, about the pressure, rewards, and problems of life still relevant? Is the theme of the work as pertinent now as it was at the time it was written? *Oedipus Rex*, for example, was written over two thousand years ago, but we are still awed and moved by its portrayal of the inner conflicts of a proud ambitious man who brings on his own doom.

2. *Universality* Does the work, regardless of when and where it was written, have meaning for people throughout the Western world? (I specify "Western" because most of us are not sufficiently familiar with the Asian cultures to judge the impact a piece of literature might have on them.) *Huckleberry Finn*, for example, although it has been called the first truly American novel, deals with a universal theme, the loss of innocence.

3. *Truthfulness* Is the work credible? Does the author make us believe what is being said? Such a standard cannot, of course, be applied literally. We do not believe in the literal truth of *Gulliver's Travels* or *Candide*, but we understand that the authors are using fantasy and exaggeration to communicate basic truths about humanity. Moreover, a good novel, story, or drama should give us the feeling that what happened to the characters was inevitable; that, given their temperaments and the situation in which they were placed, the outcome could not have been otherwise. Everything we know about Willie Loman in *Death of a Salesman*, for instance, makes his suicide inevitable. A different ending would have been disappointing and untrue.

4. *Effective language* This is a matter for which it is difficult to set precise standards. The study of such authors as James Joyce, William Faulkner, Mark Twain, and Henry James reveals that writers can use language effectively in a variety of ways. In general, however, we can expect the language in any literary work to be forceful, fresh and unhackneyed, and suitable to the purposes of the work. Thus, the gentle style of Washington Irving would be as unsuitable for *Gulliver's Travels* as the complex, ornate style of Henry James would be for *Huckleberry Finn*.

5. *Morality* This may seem like a strange requirement, somewhat as if I were saying, "Good stories should have a moral to them." The term *morality*, however, is intended in the much broader sense of "sense of value." Applied to literature, this

standard means that a work of art should say something of value. It should draw attention to human problems, say that some things are worth doing or believing in, condemn or applaud certain ways of living or certain viewpoints; in sum, it should make a statement that is more significant than the "Chocolate cake is the world's best dessert" kind of comment we talked about in an earlier chapter. We cannot, however, require that the statement the author makes be one that we agree with. We cannot, as we can with arguments, challenge a creative artist's a priori assumptions. The work is an author's own creation, and he or she is entitled to personal values. Although we may not, like Voltaire, believe that human beings are basically foolish or selfish and we may not agree with Dreiser that people are simply victims of circumstance, we must grant any author the right to personal opinion. If our criticism is truly objective, we should judge only the way an author expresses and illustrates that viewpoint. This critical tenet is, needless to say, difficult to observe.

If a work of literature meets most of the standards set forth here, we can judge it as "good" and support that judgment with concrete evidence. Making judgments about the relatively few works that measure up to all these requirements or the great body that meet almost none of them is comparatively easy. A play like Eugene O'Neill's *Long Day's Journey into Night* and a poem like Robert Frost's "After Apple Picking," immediately impress us as fine works. And it doesn't take much critical perception for most of us to realize that the run-of-the-mill "entertainments" ground out for the mystery, science-fiction, and adventure-story market are poorly done. The real problem comes in deciding about the many pieces of literature that fall somewhere in between, books, for example, like Ken Kesey's *One Flew over the Cuckoo's Nest* or William Golding's *Lord of the Flies*. We feel that in many ways such books are good but also suspect that they have defects, that they are less than great. Such uncertainty, however, should not prevent you from attempting a judgment. There is, after all, no reason why you cannot make a qualified statement: "This book measures up on points 1, 3, and 4 but lacks the qualities given in points 2 and 5." Give reasons for your judgment, and no one can ask more of you.

Two final points on both reading and writing about literature

Do not confuse taste and judgment

are important. First, do not confuse these two statements: "I like this book" and "This is a good book." If you say, "I like this book," you are expressing your taste, making a statement of preference. You may want to defend your preference, but you do not have to prove that the book is a good piece of writing. If, however, you assert, "This is a good book," you have an obligation to support that statement by showing how it meets the standards that are generally set forth for good literature. Nor should you be ashamed of liking books that cannot be classified as "good literature." Almost all of us enjoy some kinds of so-called escape literature: romances, mysteries, or science fiction. If you enjoy them, read them and make no apologies.

Do not be intimidated by labels

Second, do not be intimidated by a famous name or by any literary work that has long been labeled a "classic." Though it is true that works by authors whose reputations have endured for decades or centuries are more likely than not to have value, you should judge the work on its own merits. Shakespeare did write some mediocre plays, and both Faulkner and Hemingway have more than one second-rate novel to their credit. The following poem is a good example of a bad work by a renowned poet:

> *All the breath and the bloom of the year in the bag of one bee;*
> *All the wonder and wealth of the mine in the heart of one gem;*
> *In the core of one pearl all the shade and the shine of the sea;*
> *Breath and bloom, shade and shine—wonder, wealth,*
> *and—how far above them—*
> *Truth, that is brighter than gem,*
> *Trust, that's purer than pearl—*
> *Brightest truth, purest trust in the universe—all were for me*
> *In the kiss of one girl.*

The alliteration in the poem is overdone, the imagery hackneyed and fuzzy, the meter singsong, and the whole effect painfully sentimental. Yet the poet was one of the finest of his century: Robert Browning. (In his defense, it should be pointed out that the poem was written when he was seventy-seven, in the year of his death.)

*Trust your own
judgment*

Finally, then, you should trust your own critical faculties. There is no reason why you cannot make sound judgments about literature if you read carefully and apply common-sense standards to what you read; nor is there any reason why writing persuasively about literature should be any more difficult than writing about any other topic. You have the tools that you need.

Writing Critical Analyses

The following two papers on a well-known poem, "To His Coy Mistress" by Andrew Marvell, illustrate the advantages of using the rhetorical approach to write about literature. The papers were done in response to that familiar assignment, "Write a short critical analysis of a poem." The writer of the first paper started by asking these questions: What is the poet's purpose? That is, what thesis or main idea does he want to express in the poem? What means does he use to achieve that purpose? Is he successful? Why or why not? The writer of the second paper, understandably confused about what constituted a "critical analysis," began with no particular purpose or approach in mind and simply wrote about the poem.

Here is the poem:

To His Coy Mistress

Had we but world enough, and time,
This coyness, lady, were no crime.
We would sit down and think which way
To walk and pass our long love's day.
Thou by the Indian Ganges' side
Should'st rubies find; I by the tide
Of Humber would complain. I would
Love you ten years before the flood:
And you should, if you please, refuse
Till the conversion of the Jews.
My vegetable love should grow

Vaster than empires, and more slow.
An hundred years should go to praise
Thine eyes, and on thy forehead gaze.
Two hundred to adore each breast;
And thirty thousand to the rest.
An age at least to every part,
And the last age should show your heart.
For, lady, you deserve this state;
Nor would I love at lower rate.
    But at my back I always hear
Time's winged chariot hurrying near;
And yonder all before us lie
Deserts of vast eternity.
Thy beauty shall no more be found;
Nor in thy marble vault shall sound
My echoing song; then worms shall try
That long preserved virginity;
And your quaint honor turn to dust;
And into ashes all my lust,
The grave's a fine and private place,
But none, I think, do there embrace.
    Now therefore, while the youthful hue
Sits on thy skin like morning dew,
And while thy willing soul transpires
At every pore with instant fires,
Now let us sport us while we may;
And now, like am'rous birds of prey
Rather at once our time devour,
Than languish in his slow-chapt pow'r.
Let us roll all our strength, and all
Our sweetness, up into one ball;
And tear our pleasure with rough strife,
Through the iron gates of life.
Thus, though we cannot make our sun
Stand still, yet we will make him run.

Andrew Marvell, c. 1681

Paper I

In this poem Andrew Marvell seems to be addressing himself to young ladies who think that it is romantic and amusing to tease their lovers by insisting that they pay court to them for months and flatter them with extravagant compliments in order to win their sexual favors. He wants these young women to realize that their coyness is follish and unrealistic: while they are playing their games, time is running out. Rather than waste their youth and beauty in "playing hard to get," they should enjoy life now. In order to convience his audience, Marvell constructs a careful, concretely supported argument, which vividly illustrates his point.

Marvell's persona in the poem is a devoted but impatient lover; his persuasive purpose is frankly seduction. To achieve it, he sets up an argument from circumstance and reinforces it by appeals to his mistress's vanity and fears. The argument itself is built on an "If—but—therefore" structure: If we had unlimited time, I would be happy to court you for an eternity; but we, being only mortal, are going to age and die; therefore, let us take our pleasure while we can.

Much of the force of the argument comes from the contrast of tone and imagery in the three sections. In the first part, the persona flatters his mistress by using a lofty tone and extravagant phrases to show that his love really is high-minded: "I would/love you ten years before the flood:" "An hundred years should go to praise/Thine eyes," "Two hundred to adore each breast;/And thirty thousand to the rest." His phrases suggest that his adoration is so great it would last for an eternity.

In the second stanza, however, the persona begins his argument from circumstance: because of time, he is *forced* to forget about eternity and think about the present. He brings in images of death to make his point: "thy marble vault," "worms," "dust," "ashes," and "the grave." What lies ahead is not unending pleasure, but "deserts of vast eternity." He tries to frighten the girl by suggesting that her beauty will be gone and that that virginity which she has preserved so carefully will be destroyed by worms, not a man. He plays on her fear of being alone by suggesting that in the grave, none embrace.

In the last stanza, the persona uses images of lust and violence to contrast with the repulsive circumstances he has pictured in the previous section. He is saying, "While we are young and passionate, let us seize the day!" The phrases "instant fires," "am'rous birds of prey," and "tear our pleasure with rough strife" conflict dramatically with the lofty, leisurely tone of the first stanza. And he makes what he is suggesting here sound much more attractive than languishing by the Ganges gathering rubies.

Although we cannot know whether the persona's appeal was literally successful—or whether this particular situation really existed—the poem itself is certainly a success. The poet has taken a theme which is so common that he ran the danger of writing a hackneyed poem, and through vivid diction and contrast of tone and imagery made his message seem fresh. His skillful use of traditional rhetorical techniques clothed in poetic language is one of the chief strengths of the poem.

Paper II

Andrew Marvell's famous poem "To His Coy Mistress" tells the story of a young man who is trying to persuade his girl to go to bed with him. He starts out by saying that he would be glad to spend as much time as she liked in praising and admiring her if they had thousands of years to waste. Apparently the girl is more interested in getting compliments than she is in having the man make love to her.

In the second part of the poem the man explains why he thinks they cannot afford to waste time with his talking and admiring her. When he says that he hears Time's chariot at his back, he means that time is going by faster than they think. If they aren't careful, they'll both be old or dead and they never will have the chance to enjoy sex. He talks about the girl being in a marble vault and the worms eating on her. This is an ugly picture but he uses it to scare the girl into giving in to him.

In the last part of the poem he tries to persuade the girl that while they are still young, they ought to enjoy sex now. He says they ought to have "sport" and "pleasure" while they can and concentrate all their strength on having a good time. If they do this, the time will go by quickly.

The meaning of this poem seems to be that young men are going to get very impatient with girls who lead them along but don't want to give in to them sexually. Under those circumstances, a man is going to try to talk a girl into sex by saying there isn't much time or by insinuating that they are missing a lot of pleasure. Girls should know that they can't expect men to wait indefinitely; either they should marry them or quit going with them.

The poem is a good one because Marvell is writing about something that has been going on for a long time; men always try to talk girls into sex and girls try to put them off. Marvell does a good job of showing the man's point of view. The first stanza of the poem makes girls who tease men and play hard to get look silly and immature. The reader doesn't have much sympathy for the "coy mistress." Then the talk about death in the second part makes Marvell's argument seem reasonable. The reader tends to sympathize with the lover and think at the end that he is right. For this reason I would call the poem a successful one.

The difference in the quality of the two papers is partially the result of the first writer's using a rhetorical approach to a writing assignment. That writer had a sense of purpose to writing and a plan for supporting the analysis. Not only was evidence from the poem used throughout the paper, but the writer continually kept in mind the effect that the poet was trying to achieve with the audience and discussed the way those effects were achieved. The result is a well-organized and solid critical analysis.

The writer of the second paper, although seeming to have some appreciation of the poem, has done a poor job of analyzing or evaluating. Moreover, almost no internal evidence is used to support points and thus this writer has missed the opportunity to discuss one of the poem's major strengths, its imagery. The result is a rather dull paper that does credit neither to the poem nor to the reader's appreciation of it.

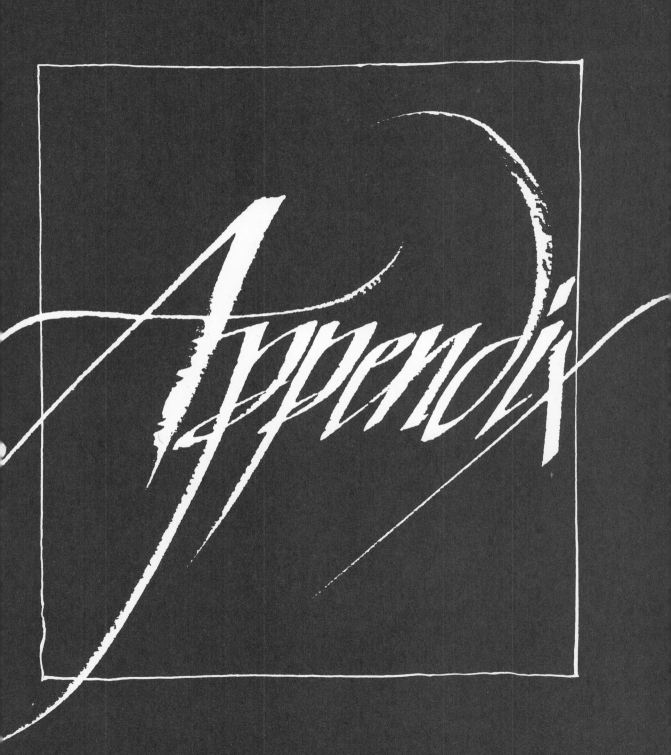

Sample Passages for Rhetorical Analysis

1 / The Great Barbecue

Congress had rich gifts to bestow—in lands, tariffs, subsidies, favors of all sorts; and when influential citizens made their wishes known to the reigning statesmen, the sympathetic politicians were quick to turn the government into the fairy godmother the voters wanted it to be. A huge barbecue was spread to which all presumably were invited. Not quite all, to be sure; inconspicuous persons, those who were at home on the farm or at work in the mills and offices, were overlooked; a good many indeed out of the total number of the American people. But all the important persons, leading bankers and promoters and business men, received invitations. There wasn't room for everybody and these were presumed to represent the whole. It was a splendid feast. If the waiters saw to it that the choicest portions were served to favored guests, they were not unmindful of their numerous homespun constituency and they loudly proclaimed the fine democratic principle that what belongs to the people should be enjoyed by the people—not with petty bureaucratic restrictions, not as a social body, but as individuals, each free citizen using what came to hand for his own private ends, with no questions asked.

It was sound Gilded Age doctrine. To a frontier people what was more democratic than a barbecue, and to a paternalistic age what was

From *Main Currents in American Thought*, Vol. III, pp. 23–24, by Vernon L. Parrington, copyright 1930 by Harcourt Brace Jovanovich, Inc.; renewed 1958 by Vernon L. Parrington, Jr., Louise P. Tucker, Elizabeth P. Thomas. Reprinted by permission of the publishers.

more fitting than that the state should provide the beeves for roasting. Let all come and help themselves. As a result the feast was Gargantuan in its rough plenty. The abundance was what was to be expected of a generous people. More food, to be sure, was spoiled than was eaten, and the revelry was a bit unseemly; but it was a fine spree in the name of the people, and the invitations had been written years before by Henry Clay. But unfortunately what was intended to be jovially democratic was marred by displays of plebeian temper. Suspicious commoners with better eyes than manners discovered the favoritism of the waiters and drew attention to the difference between their own meager helpings and the heaped-up plates of more favored guests. It appeared indeed that there was gross discrimination in the service; that the farmers' pickings from the Homestead Act were scanty in comparison with the speculators' pickings from the railway land-grants. The *Credit Mobilier* scandal and the Whisky Ring scandal and divers other scandals came near to breaking up the feast, and the genial host—who was no other than the hero of Appomattox—came in for some sharp criticism. But after the more careless ones who were caught with their fingers where they didn't belong, had been thrust from the table, the eating and drinking went on again till only the great carcasses were left. Then at last came the reckoning. When the bill was sent in to the American people the farmers discovered that they had been put off with the giblets while the capitalists were consuming the turkey. They learned that they were no match at a barbecue for more voracious guests, and as they went home unsatisfied, a sullen anger burned in their hearts that was to express itself later in fierce agrarian revolts.

2 / You Are What You Ride

To the deep disgust of every outlaw biker, Japanese motorcycles have taken over the American market. Their advertising is everywhere, always insinuating that if you own a Kawasaki, a Suzuki, or a Honda, you will be popular and meet interesting people who, no doubt, are vegetarians and joggers. The slogan "You meet the nicest people on a Honda" may have sold lots of bikes to respectable suburbanites, but it also explains why most outlaw bikers would never ride a Honda. Horses made the Comanches the masters of the plains, and Harleys give their riders

Dick Reavis, "You Are What You Ride," reprinted with permission from the May 1979 issue of *Texas Monthly.* Copyright 1979 by *Texas Monthly.*

superiority over all living creatures. Right-thinking Americans, especially Bandidos, know this is true.

Lone Star drinkers, Adidas wearers, and Fleetwood Mac fans sport their loyalties and good taste on T-shirts, but no cult compares with Harley-Davidson's. Without any authorization from the motorcycle maker, devotees and profiteers have spawned a thriving commerce in rings and earrings, caps and gloves, ashtrays and beer steins, patches and hashish pipes, even panties and bras, all emblazoned with the winged Harley trademark. As a tattoo, the Harley emblem is more in demand than the Navy anchor or the Marine Corps bulldog—or even "Mother."

The machine behind the Harley mystique is a 650-pound roaring motorcycle with a two-cylinder engine. Like that other air-cooled classic, the 1200cc Volkswagen engine, the Harley motor can be endlessly rebuilt. Thousands of forty-year-old Harleys are still on the road, but there is no such thing as a vintage Honda (the first one wasn't built until 1948), and there never will be. Honda has produced so many models that none of its dealers can afford to keep all parts in stock. Harley produces only three motors. Some parts for it can be found at auto supply houses, and nearly all are on the shelves of dealerships. Bikers hoard and trade old Harley parts; junkyards take in old Hondas, which are built to sell, not to last. Harley handlebar tubing is bigger, so the bars won't break. Airplane bolts with reinforced heads are used on Harleys, but not on Hondas; many who have worked on the rice-burners have had stove-bolt heads break off in a wrench. There are plastic body parts on Hondas, but not on Harleys. The gearshift, clutch, and brake levers on Hondas are likely to bend or crunch off in a spill, but Harleyites ride away from accidents. A Harley is a machine your grandchildren can inherit when you've ridden it to your grave. About the only thing a Honda is good for is riding to work, because Hondas don't break down—for three years, after which they rapidly turn to trash. But real bikers don't work, or ride disposable motorcycles, either.

Honda now makes a machine with a 1047cc displacement that some misguided people claim rivals Harley's performance. Of course, if you want a four- or six-cylinder engine that sounds like a sewing machine, has a *radiator*, a fuel gauge, and little lights to tell you what gear you're running in, then, yes, you do want a Honda. Nobody who rides a Honda smokes *real* cigarettes, but if you want a Honda and you do smoke, you'd better get a purse to carry your low-tar brand in, for a very simple reason: Harley T-shirts, made only in black, all come with cigarette pockets. But Honda T-shirts come in white and rainbow colors, and you'll have a hard time finding one with a pocket. And that explains the difference between Honda and Harley—Honda has no class.

3 / *Little Red Owes Her Troubles to Attaining Interface with Lupine Perpetrator*

In an effort to make the classics accessible to contemporary readers, I am translating them into the modern American language. Here is the translation of "Little Red Riding Hood":

Once upon a point in time, a small person named Little Red Riding Hood initiated plans for the preparation, delivery and transportation of foodstuffs to her grandmother, a senior citizen residing at a place of residence in a forest of indeterminate dimension.

In the process of implementing this program, her incursion into the forest was in mid-transportation process when it attained interface with an alleged perpetrator. This individual, a wolf, made inquiry as to the whereabouts of Little Red Riding Hood's goal as well as inferring that he was desirous of ascertaining the contents of Little Red Riding Hood's foodstuffs basket, and all that.

"I see you indicating," the wolf said, "but what I don't see is whatever it is your're indicating at, you dig?"

Little Red Riding Hood indicated more fully, making one think perfectly clear—to wit, that it was to her grandmother's residence and with a consignment of foodstuffs that her mission consisted of taking her to and with.

At this point in time the wolf moderated his rhetoric and proceeded to grandmother's residence. The elderly person was then subjected to the disadvantages of total consumption and transferred to residence in the perpetrator's stomach.

The wolf had adopted the abdominal-distress recovery posture when Little Red Riding Hood achieved his presence.

"Grandmother," she said, "your ocular implements are of an extraordinary order of magnitude."

"The purpose of this enlarged viewing capability," said the wolf, "is to enable your image to register a more precise impression upon my sight systems."

"In reference to your ears," said Little Red Riding Hood, "it is noted with the deepest respect that far from being underprivileged, their elongation and enlargement appear to qualify you for unparalleled distinction."

Russell Baker, "Little Red Riding Hood Revisited." *The New York Times*, January 13, 1980. © 1980 by The New York Times Company. Reprinted by permission.

"I hear you loud and clear, kid," said the wolf, "but what about these new choppers?"

This observation was followed by the adoption of an aggressive posture on the part of the wolf and the assertion that it was also possible for him, due to the high efficiency ratio of his jaw, to consume little persons, plus, as he stated, his firm determination to do so at once without delay and with all due process and propriety, notwithstanding the fact that the ingestion of one entire grandmother had already provided twice his daily recommended cholesterol intake.

There ensued flight by Little Red Riding Hood accompanied by pursuit in respect to the wolf and a subsequent intervention on the part of a third party, heretofore unnoted in the record.

Due to the firmness of the intervention, the wolf's stomach underwent ax-assisted aperture with the result that Red Riding Hood's grandmother was enabled to be removed with only minor discomfort.

4 / The Chemistry of Brain Clocks

First the movie then the dinner, and then, when the aircraft cabin is finally dark and you have managed to fall asleep at last, the incredible brilliant-orange North Atlantic sunrise murders your dreams. Up go the shades, the orange juice and stale Danish appear, and shortly, it's time to stagger out of Heathrow Airport into London's rush-hour traffic—drooping, depressed, and desynchronized. This is jet lag, a disturbance in our biological rhythms that nothing in man's evolutionary history has equipped him to cope with. We can set the hands of our watches forward five hours, but the clock in our brains remains set on home time for days. Now, clues to the working of this clock have suggested to neuroscientists that drugs useful in treating psychological depression may help us set our biological clock ahead, as well.

Like a clock on a home thermostat, brain clockwork turns down body temperature at night and turns it up at dawn. Adrenal-cortical and other hormones, sodium and potassium salts, and many other substances are similarly regulated through a daily cycle. The clock appears to run a little slow, normally—about an hour later every day. This tendency for the clock to run a little slow is corrected daily at sunrise, when the brain resets it for the correct time.

To the traveler flying westward from New York to California, the sun appears to rise at a later hour, and the brain merely receives the reset-signal a little late, affording another hour or two of sleep. Since we naturally function on a 25-hour free-running cycle, it is not surprising that most people adjust to westward travel and a longer day easily.

Flying eastward—to Europe, for example—is more stressful. The sun appears to rise earlier: six, seven, or more hours before the brain is ready to begin a new day. At that point, the sunrise may not be very effective in setting the hands of the brain's clock ahead. The traveler is awake and eating, the sleep and feeding cycles being fairly flexible, but body temperature, hormones, and other vital functions—still on home time—lag behind. It is the desynchronization of those physiological functions that causes loss of appetite, lethargy, disturbances of sexual function, and the other peculiar feelings of jet lag.

Early risers, who probably have natural cycles of 25 hours or less, may have an easier time adjusting to eastward flight than do late risers, but both may experience difficulty. Five days to three weeks may pass before all the cycles synchronize.

How can the traveler avoid a bad case of jet lag in flying east? A strong signal to the brain's clock is important. Raising the blinds and looking out the airplane windows at the sun can help. Coffee or tea, which contain caffeine and other stimulants, may help make the inner clock run faster. Eating a regular breakfast on an overnight flight further reinforces the signals to the biological clock that a new day has started; a big midnight dinner probably won't help. Alcohol slows the free-running clock, so the traveler who must drink should do so on the way to California, not London.

Some psychiatrists who have noted similarities between the symptoms of depression and those of jet lag suggest that a desynchronization of basic biological rhythms may be partly responsible for depressive disorders.

Evidence for the correlation is not direct, but it is intriguing. Depressed patients show disturbances in the timing of their sleep; they wake up with depression at its most severe in the early morning and show abnormalities in the daily rhythm of their excretion of many hormones. If the connection between depression and rhythm desynchronization is valid, then might not drugs used to treat depression be useful in treating jet lag?

Lithium carbonate, widely used for manic-depressive illness, appears to slow biological clocks and might assist westbound travelers. Imipramine, another type of antidepressant, may speed the biological clock, advancing morning awakening to better coincide with other physiological functions. Experiments with rats have shown that imipramine speeds adjustment to a sudden reversal of the day-night cycle. And, in a remarkable clinical study, psychiatrist Thomas Wehr and coworkers at the National Institute of Mental Health brought temporary relief to a depressed manic-depressive woman by advancing her sleep period so that she rose six hours earlier than usual—thus simulating the jet-lag shift.

Whether the use of imipramine to help the holiday traveler with jet lag is really practical or worthwhile, given the often mild and transient nature of the illness, awaits further study and consideration. But jet lag is not a frivolous concern for the pilot of the aircraft facing the complexities of a Heathrow landing, or for intensive-care-unit nurses on rotating work shifts caring for cardiac emergencies. New knowledge about resetting brain clocks may not only help the occasional traveler, but also may aid in the medical care of travel crews and shift workers, as well as provide a clue to understanding the darkness of depression.

5 / Shoes

They are one of the most ordinary types of working shoe: the blucher design, and soft in the prow, lacking the seam across the root of the big toe: covering the ankles: looped straps at the heels: blunt, broad, and rounded at the toe: broad-heeled: made up of most simple roundnesses and squarings and flats, of dark brown raw thick leathers nailed, and sewn coarsely to one another in courses and patterns of doubled and tripled seams, and such throughout that like many other small objects they have great massiveness and repose and are, as the houses and overalls are, and the feet and legs of the women, who go barefooted so much, fine pieces of architecture.

They are softened, in the uppers, with use, and the soles are rubbed thin enough, I estimate, that the ticklish grain of the ground can be felt through at the center of the forward sole. The heels are deeply biased. Clay is worked into the substance of the uppers and a loose dust of clay lies over them. They have visibly though to the eye subtly taken the mold of the foot, and structures of the foot are printed through them in dark sweat at the ankles, and at the roots of the toes. They are worn without socks, and by experience of similar shoes I know that each man's shoe, in long enough course of wear, takes as his clothing does the form of his own flesh and bones, and would feel as uneasy to any other as if A, glancing into the mirror, were met by B's eyes, and to their owner, a natural part though enforcement of the foot, which may be used or shed at will. There is great pleasure in a sockless and sweated foot in the fitted leathers of a shoe.

The shoes are worn .for work. At home, resting, men always go barefooted. This is no symptom of discomfort, though: it is, insofar as it is conscious, merely an exchange of mutually enhancing pleasures, and is at least as natural as the habituated use and laying by of hats or of "reading-glasses."

So far as I could see, shoes are never mended. They are worn out like animals to a certain ancient stage and chance of money at which a man buys a new pair; then, just as old Sunday shoes do, they become the inheritance of a wife.

Ricketts' shoes are boldly slashed open to accommodate as they scarcely can the years of pain in his feet. The worst of this pain is in stirrup corns, a solid stripe of stony and excruciating pearls across the ball of each foot; for two years, years ago, he rode mules all of the day. Recognizing my own tendency half-consciously to alter my walk or even to limp under certain conditions of mental insecurity, and believing Ricketts to be one of the most piteously insecure men I have ever known, I suspect, too, that nervous modifications in his walking have had much to do with destroying his feet.

6 / The Company Man

He worked himself to death, finally and precisely, at 3:00 A.M. Sunday morning.

The obituary didn't say that, of course, It said that he died of a coronary thrombosis—I think that was it—but everyone among his friends and acquaintances knew it instantly. He was a perfect Type A, a workaholic, a classic, they said to each other and shook their heads—and thought for five or ten minutes about the way they lived.

This man who worked himself to death finally and precisely at 3:00 A.M. Sunday morning—on his day off—was fifty-one years old and a vice-president. He was, however, one of six vice-presidents, and one of three who might conceivably—if the president died or retired soon enough—have moved to the top spot. Phil knew that.

He worked six days a week, five of them until eight or nine at night, during a time when his own company had begun the four-day week for everyone but the executives. He worked like the Important People. He had no outside "extracurricular interests," unless, of course, you think about a monthly golf game that way. To Phil, it was work. He always ate egg salad sandwiches at his desk. He was, of course, overweight, by 20 or 25 pounds. He thought it was okay, though, because he didn't smoke.

On Saturdays, Phil wore a sports jacket to the office instead of a suit, because it was the weekend.

He had a lot of people working for him, maybe sixty, and most of them liked him most of the time. Three of them will be seriously considered for his job. The obituary didn't mention that.

But it did list his "survivors" quite accurately. He is survived by his wife, Helen, forty-eight years old, a good woman of no particular marketable skills, who worked in an office before marrying and mothering. She had, according to her daughter, given up trying to compete with his work years ago, when the children were small. A company friend said, "I know how much you will miss him." And she answered, "I already have."

"Missing him all these years," she must have given up part of herself which had cared too much for the man. She would be "well taken care of."

His "dearly beloved" eldest of the "dearly beloved" children is a hard-working executive in a manufacturing firm down South. In the day and a half before the funeral, he went around the neighborhood researching his father, asking the neighbors what he was like. They were embarrassed.

His second child is a girl, who is twenty-four and newly married. She lives near her mother and they are close, but whenever she was alone with her father, in a car driving somewhere, they had nothing to say to each other.

The youngest is twenty, a boy, a high-school graduate who has spent the last couple of years, like a lot of his friends, doing enough odd jobs to stay in grass and food. He was the one who tried to grab at his father, and tried to mean enough to him to keep the man at home. He was his father's favorite. Over the last two years, Phil stayed up nights worrying about the boy.

The boy once said, "My father and I only board here."

At the funeral, the sixty-year-old company president told the forty-eight-year-old widow that the fifty-one-year-old deceased had meant much to the company and would be missed and would be hard to replace. The widow didn't look him in the eye. She was afraid he would read her bitterness and, after all, she would need him to straighten out the finances—the stock options and all that.

Phil was overweight and nervous and worked too hard. If he wasn't at the office, he was worried about it. Phil was a Type A, a heart-attack natural. You could have picked him out in a minute from a lineup.

So when he finally worked himself to death, at precisely 3:00 A.M. Sunday morning, no one was really surprised.

By 5:00 P.M. the afternoon of the funeral, the company president had begun, discreetly of course, with care and taste, to make inquiries about his replacement. One of three men. He asked around: "Who's been working the hardest?"

7 / The Right Stuff

A young man might go into military flight training believing that he was entering some sort of technical school in which he was simply going to acquire a certain set of skills. Instead, he found himself all at once enclosed in a fraternity. And in this fraternity, even though it was military, men were not rated by their outward rank as ensigns, lieutenants, commanders, or whatever. No, herein the world was divided into those who had it and those who did not. This quality, this *it*, was never named, however, nor was it talked about in any way.

As to just what this ineffable quality was . . . well, it obviously involved bravery. But it was not bravery in the simple sense of being willing to risk your life. The idea seemed to be that any fool could do that, if that was all that was required, just as any fool could throw away his life in the process. No, the idea here (in the all-enclosing fraternity) seemed to be that a man should have the ability to go up in a hurtling piece of machinery and put his hide on the line and then have the moxie, the reflexes, the experience, the coolness, to pull it back in the last yawning moment—and then to go up again *the next day*, and the next day, and every next day, even if the series should prove infinite—and, ultimately, in its best expression, do so in a cause that means something to thousands, to a people, a nation, to humanity, to God. Nor was there *a test* to show whether or not a pilot had this righteous quality. There was, instead, a seemingly infinite series of tests. A career in flying was like climbing one of those ancient Babylonian pyramids made up of a dizzy progression of steps and ledges, a zigurat, a pyramid extraordinarily high and steep; and the idea was to prove at every foot of the way up that pyramid that you were one of the elected and anointed ones who had *the right stuff* and could move higher and higher and even—ultimately, God willing, one day—that you might be able to join that special few at the very top, that elite who had the capacity to bring tears to men's eyes, the very Brotherhood of the Right Stuff itself.

8 / Marrying Absurd

To be married in Las Vegas, Clark County, Nevada, a bride must swear that she is eighteen or has parental permission and a bridegroom that he is twenty-one or has parental permission. Someone must put up five dollars for the license. (On Sundays and holidays, fifteen dollars. The Clark County Courthouse issues marriage licenses at any time of the day or night except between noon and one in the afternoon, between eight and nine in the evening, and between four and five in the morning.) Nothing else is required. The State of Nevada, alone among these United States, demands neither a premarital blood test nor a waiting period before or after the issuance of a marriage license. Driving in across the Mojave from Los Angeles, one sees the signs way out on the desert, looming up from that moonscape of rattlesnakes and mesquite, even before the Las Vegas lights appear like a mirage on the horizon: "GETTING MARRIED? Free License Information First Strip Exit." Perhaps the Las Vegas wedding industry achieved its peak operational efficiency between 9:00 P.M. and midnight of August 26, 1965, an otherwise unremarkable Thursday which happened to be, by Presidential order, the last day on which anyone could improve his draft status merely by getting married. One hundred and seventy-one couples were pronounced man and wife in the name of Clark County and the State of Nevada that night, sixty-seven of them by a single justice of the peace, Mr. James A. Brennan. Mr. Brennan did one wedding at the Dunes and the other sixty-six in his office, and charged each couple eight dollars. One bride lent her veil to six others. "I got it down from five to three minutes," Mr. Brennan said later of his feat. "I could've married them *en masse*, but they're people not cattle. People expect more when they get married."

What people who get married in Las Vegas actually do expect—what, in the largest sense, their "expectations" are—strikes one as a curious and self-contradictory business. Las Vegas is the most extreme and allegorical of American settlements, bizarre and beautiful in its venality and in its devotion to immediate gratification, a place the tone of which is set by mobsters and call girls and ladies' room attendants with amyl nitrite poppers in their uniform pockets. Almost everyone notes that there is no "time" in Las Vegas, no night and no day and no past and no future (no Las Vegas casino, however, has taken the obliteration of the ordinary time sense quite so far as Harold's Club in Reno, which for a while issued, at odd intervals in the day and night, mimeographed "bulletins" carrying news from the world outside); neither is there any logical sense of where one is. One is standing on a highway in the middle of a vast hostile desert looking at an eighty-foot sign which blinks "STARDUST" or "CAESAR'S PALACE." Yes, but what does that explain? This geographical implausibility reinforces the sense that what happens there has no connection with "real" life; Nevada cities like Reno and Carson are ranch towns, places behind which there is some historical imperative. But Las Vegas seems to exist only in the eye of the beholder. All of which makes it an extraordinarily stimulating and interesting place, but an odd one in which to want to wear a candlelight satin Priscilla of Boston wedding dress with Chantilly lace insets, tapered sleeves and a detachable modified train.

And yet the Las Vegas wedding business seems to appeal to precisely that impulse. "Sincere and Dignified Since 1954," one wedding chapel advertises. There are nineteen such wedding chapels in Las Vegas, intensely competitive, each offering better, faster, and, by implication, more sincere services than the next: Our Photos Best Anywhere, Your Wedding on a Phonograph Record, Candlelight with Your Ceremony, Honeymoon Accommodations, Free Transportation from Your Motel to Courthouse to Chapel and Return to Motel, Religious or Civil Ceremonies, Dressing Rooms, Flowers, Rings, Announcements, Witnesses

Available, and Ample Parking. All of these services, like most others in Las Vegas (sauna baths, payroll-check cashing, chinchilla coats for sale or rent) are offered twenty-four hours a day, seven days a week, presumably on the premise that marriage, like craps, is a game to be played when the table seems hot.

But what strikes one most about the Strip chapels, with their wishing wells and stained-glass paper windows and their artificial bouvardia, is that so much of their business is by no means a matter of simple convenience, of late-night liaisons between show girls and baby Crosbys. Of course there is some of that. (One night about eleven o'clock in Las Vegas I watched a bride in an orange minidress and masses of flame-colored hair stumble from a Strip chapel on the arm of her bridegroom, who looked the part of an expendable nephew in movies like *Miami Syndicate*. "I gotta get the kids," the bride whimpered. "I gotta pick up the sitter, I gotta get to the midnight show." "What you gotta get," the bridegroom said, opening the door of a Cadillac Coupe de Ville and watching her crumple on the seat, "is sober.") But Las Vegas seems to offer something other than "convenience"; it is merchandising "niceness," the facsimile of proper ritual, to children who do not know how else to find it, how to make the arrangements, how to do it "right." All day and evening long on the Strip, one sees actual wedding parties, waiting under the harsh lights at the crosswalk, standing uneasily in the parking lot of the Frontier while the photographer hired by The Little Church of the West ("Wedding Place of the Stars") certifies the occasion, takes the picture: the bride in a veil and white satin pumps, the bridegroom usually in a white dinner jacket, and even an attendant or two, a sister or a best friend in a hot-pink *peau de soie*, a flirtation veil, a carnation nosegay. "When I Fall in Love It Will Be Forever," the organist plays, and then a few bars of Lohengrin. The mother cries; the stepfather awkward in his role, invites the chapel hostess to join them for a drink at the Sands. The hostess declines with a professional smile; she has already transferred her interest to the group waiting outside. One bride out, another in, and again the sign goes up on the chapel door: "One moment please—Wedding."

I sat next to one such wedding party in a Strip restaurant the last time I was in Las Vegas. The marriage had just taken place; the bride still wore her dress, the mother her corsage. A bored waiter poured out a few swallows of pink champagne ("on the house") for everyone but the bride, who was too young to be served. "You'll need something with more kick than that," the bride's father said with heavy jocularity to his new son-in-law; the ritual jokes about the wedding night had a certain

Panglossian character, since the bride was clearly several months pregnant. Another round of pink champagne, this time not on the house, and the bride began to cry. "It was just as nice," she sobbed, "as I hoped and dreamed it would be."

9 / Women Fight Back

The psychologic edge men hold in a situation characterized by sexual aggression is far more critical to the final outcome than their larger size and heavier weight. They know they know how to fight, for they have been trained and encouraged to use their bodies aggressively and competitively since early childhood. Young girls, on the other hand, are taught to disdain physical combat, healthy sports competition, and winning, because such activities dangerously threaten the conventional societal view of what is appropriate, ladylike, feminine behavior. . . .

Unthinkingly cruel, because it is deceptive, is the confidential advice given from men to women, or even from women to women in some feminist literature, that a sharp kick to the groin or a thumb in the eye will work miracles. Such advice is often accompanied by a diagram in which the vulnerable points of the human anatomy are clearly marked— as if the mere knowledge of these pressure spots can translate itself into devastating action. It is true that this knowledge has been deliberately obscured or withheld from us in the past, but mere knowledge is not enough. What women need is systematic training in self-defense that begins in childhood, so that the inhibition resulting from the prohibition may be overcome.

It would be decidedly less than honest if at this juncture I did not admit that my researches for this book included a three-month training program in jujitsu and karate, three nights a week, two and a half hours a night, that ended summarily one evening when I crashed to the mat and broke my collarbone. I lost one month of writing and the perfect symmetry of my clavical structure, but I gained a new identification with the New York Mets' injury list, a recognition that age thirty-eight is not the most propitious time in life *to begin* to learn how to kick and hit and break a stranglehold and a new and totally surprising awareness of my body's potential to inflict real damage. I learned I had natural weapons that I didn't know I possessed, like elbows and knees. I learned how to kick backward as well as forward. I learned how to fight dirty, and I learned that I loved it.

Most surprising to me, I think, was the recognition that these basic aggressive movements, the sudden twists, jabs and punches that were so foreign to my experience and ladylike existence, were the stuff that all little boys grow up learning, that boy kids are applauded for mastering while girl kids are put in fresh white pinafores and patent-leather Mary Janes and told not to muss them up. And did that early difference in rearing ever raise its draconic head! At the start of our lessons our Japanese instructor freely invited all the women in the class, one by one, to punch him in the chest. It was not a foolhardy invitation, for we discovered that the inhibition against hitting was so strong in each of us that on the first try none of us could make physical contact. Indeed, the inhibition against striking out proved to be a greater hindrance to our becoming fighting women than our pathetic underdeveloped muscles. (Improvement in both departments was amazingly swift.)

Not surprisingly, the men in our class did not share our inhibitions in the slightest. Aggressive physical grappling was part of their heritage, not ours. And yet, and yet . . . we women discovered in wonderment that as we learned to place our kicks and jabs with precision we were actually able to inspire fear in the men. We *could* hurt them, we learned to our astonishment, and hurt them hard at the core of their sexual being—if we broke that Biblical injunction.

Is it possible that there is some sort of metaphysical justice in the anatomical fact that the male sex organ, which has been misused from time immemorial as a weapon of terror against women, should have at its root an awkward place of painful vulnerability? Acutely conscious of their susceptibility to damage, men have protected their testicles throughout history with armor, supports and forbidding codes of "clean," above-the-belt fighting. A gentleman's agreement is understandable—among gentlemen. When women are threatened, as I learned in my self-defense class, "Kick him in the balls, it's your best maneuver." How strange it was to hear for the first time in my life that women could fight back, *should* fight back and make full use of a natural advantage; that it is in our *interest* to know how to do it. How strange it was to understand with the full force of unexpected revelation that male allusions to psychological defeat, particularly at the hands of a woman, were couched in phrases like emasculation, castration and ball-breaking because of that very special physical vulnerability.

Fighting back. On a multiplicity of levels, that is the activity we must engage in, together, if we—women—are to redress the imbalance and rid ourselves and men of the ideology of rape.

Hints for Polishing Your Writing

Writers who have learned to write clear, well-organized, and correct but rather drab prose frequently want to know what they can do to make their writing more vigorous and interesting. Probably the best habit they can form is to develop an acute sense of audience, to be able to anticipate how their writing affects the reader. They can also learn these specific revision strategies:

1. Check your writing for abstract sentence subjects, particularly for nouns that have been derived from verbs or adjectives, for instance, *particularity, qualification, adherence, obtainment,* and so on. If you have more than a few words of this kind in a paragraph, tinker with it to see if you can get rid of them. If possible, rewrite your sentences to make people the subjects. For example:

Original More attractiveness is sometimes given an act when it is made illegal.

Revision When an act becomes illegal some people find it more attractive.

Original The instability of the agricultural market exists despite all government reforms.

Revision Despite government reforms, farmers still face an unstable market.

2. Check your sentences to see if you have begun them with unnecessarily wordy phrases such as "They are desirous of . . . " or "It is the case that. . . ." When possible, substitute one-word shorter or more direct constructions. For example:

Original They are desirous of . . .

Revision They want . . .

Original The inspector took cognizance of . . .

Revision The inspector recognized . . .

Original The regulations imply their incapability of doing it themselves.

Revision The regulations imply that they cannot do it themselves.

Original There is as yet no general consensus as to what stage of fetal development constitutes human life.

Revision People do not yet agree on the stage at which a fetus becomes a human.

3.   Review all your verbs, looking for passive verb constructions (those in which the subject is acted upon instead of acting) and weak verbs, verbs like *seems, exists,* and all forms of *is.* Think about ways to change passive verbs to active verbs and to substitute strong verbs for weak ones. For example:

Original Inflation exists as a threat to our economy.

Revision Inflation threatens our economy.

Original The city government is full of graft.

Revision Graft permeates the city government.

Original Differences of opinion on the issue are found between business and labor.

Revision Business and labor differ on the issue.

4.   Watch for those stretcher phrases, *it is* and *there are,* that writers often use to get started on a sentence. Too many of them will devitalize your writing because they take the place of stronger, more interesting verbs. For example:

Original There were several reasons for the United States' entrance into the war.

Revision The United States entered the war for several reasons.

Original There was a long counter on one side of the room.

Revision A long counter stretched along the side of the room.

Original There is support being given this candidate by radical groups.
Revision Radical groups support this candidate.

5.   Don't overload your sentences with prepositional phrases; they slow them down and can create a monotonous effect. For example:

In the event of a drop in enrollment . . . could be phrased:
If enrollment drops . . .
The element *of time* is *of interest to everybody* . . . could be changed to:
Time interests everybody.

6.   Whenever possible, *show* your audience rather than tell them. That is, depend on images rather than adjectives to carry your meaning, particularly vague adjectives such as *pathetic, gigantic,* and *grotesque.* Notice, for example, how George Orwell gets his effect in this sentence without using adjectives:

When the corpse went past the flies left the restaurant table in a cloud and rushed after it, but they came back a few minutes later.

When you do use adjectives, as often you must, choose words that are sharp and precise. Avoid all-purpose, fuzzy intensifiers like *marvelous* and *fantastic.*

7.   Try to avoid *doubling*, that is, writing pairs of words that mean almost the same thing. For example, "fitting and appropriate," "wretched and miserable," "happy and content," and so on. When you do write such pairs, stop to think if you really need both words.

8.   As you revise, get rid of phrases or figures of speech that are so overused that they have deteriorated into clichés, for example, "cream of the crop," "flat as a pancake," "rat race."

9.   Learn to get rid of sexist language. Don't consistently use *he* as an all-purpose pronoun or write *man* or *men* when you are referring to people in general. For example, this is a sexist paragraph:

If a man is a research scientist whose work will aid many people, he should be chosen [for a kidney transplant] over a man who is simply not able to do as much for society. This does not mean that one man is any better than another in the moral sense or that a man should be able to buy his life with wealth and power.

It could be rewritten like this:

> If a person is a research scientist whose work will aid other
> people, that person should be chosen [for a kidney transplant] over
> one who is not able to do as much for society. This does not mean
> that one person is better than another in a moral sense or that a
> wealthy person should be able to buy his or her life when a poor
> one cannot.

Also work consciously in your writing to avoid sex stereotyping by categories; for example, don't give the impression that all doctors are male
and all secretaries are women.

10. Go back over your writing to see if you can condense it and
eliminate all excess words. Ask yourself, "If I were paying fifty cents a
word to get this typed, would I insist that all these words are necessary?" Then cut out any words and phrases that you really don't need.

Tips for Reading Expository Prose

Many of the difficulties that students encounter in college courses are directly connected to reading. They find themselves responsible for understanding, analyzing, and writing about a new kind of material—essays and books that focus on ideas rather than on information. Mastering such material requires more than routine reading; it requires careful, active reading, reading that is purposeful.

The first step is to ask yourself what you expect to get out of your reading. The answer should include at least four points:

1. To discover and be able to state in one or two sentences the author's main idea. What is the thesis or principal point of the book or essay?
2. To understand why the author has taken this position. You should be able to state the chief reasons that the author gives to support the thesis.
3. To decide whether the author's approach is primarily rational, emotional, or some combination of the two. If it is rational, is the reasoning sound? If it is emotional, what specific emotions are appealed to?
4. To evaluate how well the author presents and supports the thesis. Is the writing effective? Why or why not?

Next, before you begin on the text itself, take time to examine whatever nontextual material accompanies the article. You should look for the following information:

1. The name of the author. Is he or she living? If not, what are the dates of birth and death? What is the author's nationality? What

qualifications does this person have to write on this particular topic? What else has he or she written? Information of this kind may be in a footnote, in the preface, in a special biographical section of the book, or at the beginning or end of an article.

2. Date and place of publication. You should know this in order to put the work in its historical context.
3. Title. Does it seem to have special significance? Does it give you a clue to the content of the book or essay?
4. Titles of subdivisions, sections, or chapters. Can you tell from this what points the author is going to make?

Begin reading the text itself with the assumption that you will have to read it at least twice, probably three times if the material is difficult. Although the first reading should be more than just a skimming, you can do it fairly quickly. Read the introduction carefully to get an idea of the author's purpose; then read through the rest of the essay or chapter without stopping to underline or make notes. As you read, note key words that recur frequently because they will give you a clue to the author's chief concern. Pay special attention to italicized words or phrases, noting if possible why they have been stressed. Carefully read the concluding paragraph or section because it is here that the author will probably pull together the main points.

If you find that your mind is wandering as you read and that you are covering large sections without really absorbing the content, make yourself stop and go back to the point where your attention began to wander. Sometimes you may have to take a break, get up and move around for a few minutes, before you go back to refocus on the task at hand. And if on this first reading you encounter words you don't know, stop and look them up. This is particularly important when you are reading expository material, for although you may be able to skip over unfamiliar words in fiction and still grasp the meaning, when you read nonfiction the very word you failed to look up may be essential to understanding the essay.

After reading the whole essay over once, you should have a reasonably good grasp of the author's main idea, but you are probably not prepared either to write on the essay or to discuss it intelligently. In order to do that you need to reread the material slowly and actively with a pencil or highlighter in your hand. I prefer a pencil because I can use it to make notes as I go along; I also use a six-inch plastic ruler as a pacer and an aid to underlining.

Begin your second reading with the conscious intention of stopping at frequent intervals in order to absorb the material and make notes on what you have read. You should time your pauses according to the difficulty of the material. If it is clearly written and deals with relatively simple ideas, you may be able to read several paragraphs or even a whole section at once; if, however, the ideas are complex or totally unfamiliar and the writing rather abstract, you will probably need to stop after each paragraph.

As you are reading, ask yourself these questions. What is the main assertion in this section? What are the key words? Which sentences in the material are primary and which sentences are secondary in the sense that they restate, expand, illustrate, or support the main idea? In all expository writing, much of the material is illustrative or explanatory, and it is essential that you learn to distinguish between the main statements and elaborations on them. Fortunately, authors often give you useful clues that help you to spot important sentences or passages. Watch for signal words and phrases such as *It is essential, An important point, The primary reason, significantly;* watch for definitions and for words that announce conclusions: *consequently, therefore, as a result, thus,* and *we must conclude;* also look for words signaling order: *first, second,* and *finally.*

When you have finished a unit of the reading, stop and force yourself to summarize what you have just read. If you cannot do it or are confused about the author's meaning go back and reread; then try again. As tedious as this method may seem, this *immediate recall,* as it is labeled by educators, is probably the most important step in your reading. Experiments have shown that most forgetting takes place immediately after one learns something; thus, in the long run you will save yourself time and retain far more of what you read if you reinforce your learning by stopping to summarize as you go along. Moreover, as writers develop a thesis, they build on and refer back to concepts they have set forth earlier. If you have not grasped those concepts, you will have to go back and reread in order to understand the whole. So make it a rule to understand every paragraph and section as you read.

When you are sure you understand a unit of the material, *and only then,* stop to underline or mark and take notes. If you stop to underline before you have fully grasped the key points in a section, you may find that you have emphasized the wrong things, and the work will have to be done again. Waiting to underline until you are sure what is important will ensure your marking your book in a way that will be instantly useful to you when you want to review for a paper or exam. Underline thoughtfully but sparingly, marking only crucial passages. If you find that you are underlining half the sentences on a page, you are probably not reading as carefully as you should. Occasionally, of course, an entire paragraph or passage contains essential material. In that case, draw a line down the margin and star the section.

Writing notes and capsule summaries in the margins of your book is another major aid to comprehension and review. Sometimes a note may be just a reminder about the contents of a section: for example, if you are reading an essay on existentialism, you might jot down "despair," "anguish," and "forlornness" in the margins beside the sections dealing with those concepts. Such notes would help you remember the author's main points. More extensive notes that sum up content are an even greater help for both immediate retention and future review. For instance, you might expand your note on existentialism by writing "anguish; uncertainty and distress about decisions and their consequences." Or you might sum up key ideas in an essay by S. I. Hayakawa with notes like these: "hasty judgments block thinking"; "need to be aware of basis of our inferences." *Studying* a book or essay almost necessarily involves making these kinds of marginal notes. Ask your teacher to show you the teaching copy of the text you are using, and you will find a book that is underlined and annotated. From long experience your teacher has learned that the quickest and surest way to comprehend an essay thoroughly is to read it slowly, actively, and with a pencil in hand.

When you have finished this step-by-step reading of an essay, you should then go back and view the material as a whole. Think about what you have read and reflect on it. What have you learned? Was it worth reading? Why do you think so? Do you agree or disagree with the author? Why? Finally, ask yourself the questions that you started out with. By now you should be able to answer them clearly and make a thoughtful, supported criticism of what you have read.

The initial reaction of a student who has never done this kind of reading is nearly always, "But it's so slow!" I'll never get through all I have to read if I go at it this way." Well, it is slow; there is no denying that. It is also, however, remarkably efficient. When you have prepared a reading assignment in this way, you have learned it thoroughly. You are ready for class discussion, a quiz or exam, or writing a paper. If you need to review the material for a major examination, you can do so quickly by rereading underlined portions and marginal notes. In the long run the process takes less time and produces far better results than the kind of passive reading and rereading that many students depend on.

Sample Passages of Annotated Reading

purpose: to state rule of way society should deal with individual

1. The object of this essay is to assert one very simple principle, as entitled to govern absolutely the dealings of society with the individual in the way of compulsion and control, whether the means used be physical force in the form of legal penalties, or the moral coercion of public opinion. That principle is, that the sole end for which mankind are war-

assertion: only reason soc. can interfere with liberty is self-protection

expansion

can't interfere for his own good

ranted, individually or collectively, <u>in interfering with the liberty of action of any of their number, is self-protection</u>. That the only purpose for which power can be rightfully exercised over any member of a civilized community, against his will, is to prevent harm to others. <u>His own good, either physical or moral, is not a sufficient warrant</u>. He cannot rightfully be compelled to do or forbear because it will be better for him to do so, because it will make him happier, because, in the opinions of others, to do so would be wise, or even right. These are good reasons for remonstrating with him, or reasoning with him, or persuading him, or entreating him, but not compelling him, or visiting him with any evil in case he do otherwise. To justify that, the conduct from which it is desired to deter him, must be calculated to produce evil to some one else. <u>The only part of the conduct of any one, for which he is amenable to society, is that which concerns others.</u> In the part which merely concerns himself, his independence is, of right, absolute. Over himself, over his own body and mind, the individual is sovereign.

only conduct soc. should control is what hurts others

rule applies only to mature people not children

It is, perhaps, hardly necessary to say that <u>this doctrine is meant to apply only to human beings in the maturity</u> of their faculties. We are <u>not speaking of children</u>, or of young persons below the age which the law may fix as that of manhood or womanhood. Those who are still in a state to require being taken care of by others, must <u>be protected against their own actions</u> as well as against external injury. For the same reason, <u>we may leave out of consideration those backward states of society</u> in which the race itself may be considered as in its nonage. The early difficulties in the way of spontaneous progress are so great, that there is seldom any choice of means for overcoming them; and a ruler full of the spirit of improvement is warranted in the use of any expedients that will attain an end, perhaps otherwise unattainable. <u>Despotism is a legitimate mode of government in dealing with barbarians</u>, provided the end be their improvement, and the means justified by actually effecting that end. Liberty, as a principle, has no application to any state of things anterior to the time when mankind have become capable of being improved by free and equal discussion. Until then, there is nothing for them but implicit obedience to an Akbar or a Charlemagne, if they are so fortunate as to find one. <u>But as soon as mankind have attained the capacity of being guided to their own improvement by conviction or persuasion</u> (a period long since reached in all nations with whom we need here concern ourselves), <u>compulsion</u>, either in the direct form or in that of pains and penalties for noncompliance, <u>is no longer admissible as a means to their own good</u>, and <u>justifiable only for the security of others</u>.[1]

not savages or the uncivilized

despotism OK for barbarians

when people are rational and civilized

compulsion not legit except to protect others

[1] John Stuart Mill, *On Liberty* (Indianapolis: The Bobbs-Merrill Co., Inc., 1956), pp. 17–18.

2. The Yeoman and the Myth

The United States was born in the country and has moved to the city.
From the beginning its political values and ideas were of necessity
shaped by country life. The early American politician, the country editor, who wished to address himself to the common man, had to draw
upon a rhetoric that would touch the tillers of the soil; and even the
spokesman of city people knew that his audience had been in very large
part reared upon the farm. But what the articulate people who talked
and wrote about farmers and farming—the preachers, poets, philosophers, writers, and statesmen—liked about American farming was not,
in every respect, what the typical working farmer liked. For the articulate people were drawn irresistibly to the noncommercial, nonpecuniary,
self-sufficient aspect of American farm life. To them it was an ideal.
Writers like Thomas Jefferson and Hector St. Jean de Crèvecoeur admired the yeoman farmer not for his capacity to exploit opportunities
and make money but for his honest industry, his independence, his
frank spirit of equality, his ability to produce and enjoy a simple abundance. The farmer himself, in most cases, was in fact inspired to make
money, and such self-sufficiency as he actually had was usually forced
upon him by a lack of transportation or markets, or by the necessity to
save cash to expand his operations. For while early American society was
an agrarian society, it was fast becoming more commercial, and commercial goals made their way among its agricultural classes almost as rapidly as elsewhere. The more commercial this society became, however,
the more reason it found to cling in imagination to the noncommercial
agrarian values. The more farming as a self-sufficient way of life was
abandoned for farming as a business, the more merit men found in what
was being left behind. And the more rapidly the farmers' sons moved
into the towns, the more nostalgic the whole culture became about its
rural past. The American mind was raised upon a sentimental attach-
ment to rural living and upon a series of notions about rural people and
rural life that I have chosen to designate as the agrarian myth. The
agrarian myth represents a kind of homage that Americans have paid to
the fancied innocence of their origins.

Like any complex of ideas, the agrarian myth cannot be defined in a
phrase, but its component themes form a clear pattern. Its hero was the
yeoman farmer, its central conception the notion that he is the ideal
man and the ideal citizen. Unstinted praise of the special virtues of the
farmer and the special values of rural life was coupled with the assertion
that agriculture, as a calling uniquely productive and uniquely important
to society, had a special right to the concern and protection of govern-

Margin notes:

U.S. political values shaped by country life

writers and politicians liked self-sufficient aspect of farm life

but farmers more interested in money

American mind raised on agrarian myth

ingredients of agrarian myth

1. farmer ideal man

2. agriculture special right to govt. protection

3. farm life wholesome and pure

4. yeoman best citizen

agrarian myth came from upper class

strong in U.S. late 18th cent.

ment. The yeoman, who owned a small farm and worked it with the aid of his family, was the incarnation of the simple, honest, independent, healthy, happy human being. Because he lived in close communion with beneficent nature, his life was believed to have a wholesomeness and integrity impossible for the depraved populations of cities. His well-being was not merely physical, it was moral; it was not merely personal, it was the central source of civic virtue; it was not merely secular but religious, for God had made the land and called man to cultivate it. Since the yeoman was believed to be both happy and honest, and since he had a secure propertied stake in society in the form of his own land, he was held to be the best and most reliable sort of citizen. To this conviction Thomas Jefferson appealed when he wrote: "The small land holders are the most precious part of a state."

In origin the agrarian myth was not a popular but a literary idea, a preoccupation of the upper classes, of those who enjoyed a classical education, read pastoral poetry, experimented with breeding stock, and owned plantations or country estates. It was clearly formulated and almost universally accepted in America during the last half of the eighteenth century. As it took shape both in Europe and America, its promulgators drew heavily upon the authority and the rhetoric of classical writers—Hesiod, Xenophon, Cato, Cicero, Virgil, Horace, and others—whose works were the staples of a good education. A learned agricultural gentry, coming into conflict with the industrial classes, welcomed the moral strength that a rich classical ancestry brought to the praise of husbandry. In France the Physiocrats preached that agriculture is the only true source of wealth. In England the rural entrepreneurs, already interested in breeding and agricultural improvements, found the praise of husbandry congenial.[2]

[2] From *The Age of Reform*, pp. 23–25, by Richard Hofstadter. Copyright © 1955 by Richard Hofstadter. Reprinted by permission of Alfred A. Knopf, Inc.

Journals

Many writers, both amateur and professional, find that keeping a journal helps them get started writing and also helps them keep writing once they have worked up momentum. Writing in a journal between other, more structured, writing assignments, keeps the juices flowing and the inspiration from drying up.

Although most writers who have gotten into the journal-keeping habit try to write something in their journal every day, a journal is not a diary. Rather, it is a record of the impressions, reflections, reactions, or even speculations that a person experiences from day to day. It is *reflective* writing in which one sets down thoughts and responses. The topic can be almost anything—movies, concerts, scenes noticed while walking or driving, advertisements, stories, television programs, conversations, books, classes, meals. Whatever you respond to makes a good journal topic, and since the writing is primarily for you and no one is going to grade it, you can put down those responses any way you want to.

People who get into the habit of writing in a journal may gain several things from the activity. First, they may discover that writing is a creative act—writing freely about ideas and responses generates more ideas and responses. Also a person who relaxes and starts putting down words and sentences without worrying about whether everything is "correct" may find that writing is easier than she or he thought possible. And once one gets into the habit of writing for oneself, it usually becomes easier to write for other people.

Daily writing also helps most people become more perceptive about their world and more receptive to new experiences. And, particularly important for people who are trying to improve their writing, keeping a journal makes one aware of what an abundance of material for writing there is in everyday experience. You can use that experience to illustrate, support, and expand on your ideas. Not only will having written down your impressions help you to remember them, but you will have a ready-made source to consult when you need an idea.

In some writing classes, instructors have students keep journals and turn them in to be read, and if there is time, to be responded to. Such a writing exchange can help students and teachers to get to know each other better. It can also give students a chance to write on free topics, to be whimsical or frivolous or poetic, and not worry about a grade. Sometimes that kind of writing is fun and productive for both students and professors.

But the most important thing about keeping a journal is that when you do so you are practicing your writing—and that is what you have to do if you want to write well.

A Glossary of Usage

accept—except

Accept means "receive" or "agree to."
Except as a preposition means "excluding"; as a verb it means "omit" or "make an exception."

Examples:
They *accept* the conditions of the treaty.
Everyone came *except* John.
The registrar *excepts* handicapped students from the schedule.

access—excess

Access means "admission to" or "approach."
Excess means "too much" or "more than is necessary."

Examples:
He has *access* to the building.
The accident happened on the *access* road.
She smokes to *excess*.
There will be an *excess* profits tax.

affect—effect

Affect is a verb meaning "change" or "influence."
Effect may be a verb meaning "bring about," but in most writing is used as a noun meaning "result."

Examples:
Changes in the weather *affect* his mood.
The black lights produced a startling *effect*.

aggravate

In formal usage *aggravate* means "to make worse" or "intensify." Informally it is used as a synonym for "annoy" or "exasperate."

Formal:
His insolence *aggravated* an already difficult situation.

Informal:
George's habits *aggravate* me.

all right—alright

All right is the preferable spelling for this phrase indicating agreement. Many dictionaries now give alright as acceptable, but your audience might not agree. It is best to remember that *all right* takes the same form as "all wrong."

Example:
Mary is *all right* now.

allusion—illusion

The similarity in sound between these two words sometimes confuses students. *Allusion* means "reference"; *illusion* means "misconception" or "misleading image."

Examples:
The author's *allusion* to Prometheus was confusing.
He is under the *illusion* that she loves him.

already—all ready

Already means "prior to a certain time"; *all ready* means "prepared."

Examples:

John was *already* in bed.
The train had *already* left.
The car is *all ready* to go.

A lot—alot

A lot is a colloquialism that is acceptable in informal writing, but it must be written as two words. *Much, many,* or another modifier expressing quantity is preferable in more formal writing.

Formal:
He has *many* friends.

Informal:
She went to *a lot* of trouble to arrange the party.

among—between

See **between.**

amount—number

Amount generally refers to a bulk quantity or to a mass; *number* refers to several units. *Number* as a subject takes a singular verb.

Examples:
The *number* is rising steadily.
He has a large *number* of friends.
He has a large *amount* of money.

as—like

See **like—as.**

as—that

The use of *as* as a substitute for *that* in introducing a clause is too colloquial for most writing.

Colloquial:
I don't know *as* I will go.

Acceptable:
I don't know *that* I will go.

bad—badly

Bad is an adjective that modifies nouns or acts as a complement to linking verbs. *Badly* is an adverb used to modify verbs or adjectives. People who are trying too hard to speak elegantly frequently make the mistake of completing a linking verb such as *feels* or *looks* with badly.

Correct:
Jim feels *bad* about the accident.
George looks *bad* since his illness.
The team played *badly* tonight.

Incorrect:
Joan looks *badly* without make-up.
I feel *badly* about not going.

between—among

Purists use *between* when referring to two persons or objects, *among* when referring to more than two. The distinction is a comparatively minor one.

Examples:
The quarrel was *between* Joe and me.
The money was distributed *among* the members of the team.

can—may

Traditional grammarians specify that *can* should be used only to indicate capability, and *may* to indicate permission: The distinction is rapidly disappearing, and in all but the most formal writing, the terms may be used interchangeably.

Examples:
John *can* lift a 150 pound weight.
You *may* take the book home with you.

center around—center on

Center around is an illogical expression.
Center on is preferable.

Illogical:
The talk *centered around* the war.

Preferable:
The talk *centered on* the war.

cite—site—sight

Students frequently confuse these three words. *Cite* is a verb meaning "refer to," *site* is a noun meaning "location" or "place," and *sight* as a noun means "view" or "spectacle."

Examples:
He will *cite* two other occasions on which the play had been used.
Fred showed them the *site* of the new building.
The children had never seen such a wonderful *sight*.

collective noun

A collective noun refers to a group of individuals or things considered as a single entity, for example, *team, platoon, congregation, jury*. It may take a singular or plural verb according to the context of the sentence.

Examples:

The *team* is going to win.

The *jury* were divided in their opinion.

complement—compliment

Complement as a verb means "complete" or "fit with"; as a noun it means a "word or phrase that completes."

Compliment as a verb means "speak favorably of"; as a noun it means "favorable remark."

Examples:

That dress *complements* her dark hair.

Linking verbs must be followed by a *complement*.

He *complimented* them on their foresight.

Jack is always ready with a *compliment*.

could of

An incorrect form of "could have."

Correct:

We *could have* taken the bus.

Incorrect:

We *could of* taken the bus.

data, media, criteria, phenomena

These are plural forms of the singular nouns *datum*, *medium*, *criterion*, and *phenomenon* and take plural verb forms. Except in formal usage, however, a singular verb is acceptable with *data*.

Acceptable:

The *data are* inaccurate.

The *data is* reliable.

Correct:

The mass *media are* influential in our culture.

His *criteria are* clearly stated.

These *phenomena indicate* the presence of oxygen.

different from—different than

The preferred usage is "different *from*," but most dictionaries give either form as acceptable.

double negative

Regardless of its acceptance in other languages, the construction is considered substandard in English. *Hardly* and *scarcely* are negative words and should not be used with other negatives.

Unacceptable:
He *didn't* do *nothing* wrong.
Jane *can't hardly* pass English

Correct:
He *did nothing* wrong.
Jane *can hardly* pass English.

due to

Although widely used, this phrase is usually avoided by careful writers. *Because of* is preferable.

Acceptable:
Due to icy roads, she could not come.

Preferable:

She was unable to come *because* of icy roads.

effect

See **affect—effect.**

etc.

Etc. is a contraction of the Latin Phrase *et cetera*, meaning "and other things." Although it is acceptable in informal speech, too often it is a lazy substitute for writing out a full list. Because many teachers find the expression unacceptable, students would do well to avoid it.

except

See **accept—except.**

fact

Use *fact* only to refer to that which can be tested and verified. *The fact that* is an overworked and often inaccurate phrase that should be avoided whenever possible. When you do use it, be sure that it refers to something that is indisputably true, not a matter of opinion.

Incorrect:
The *fact* that busing to integrate schools is a failure was mentioned again and again.

Acceptable:
The *fact* that Germany was defeated at Stalingrad changed the course of the war.

Preferable:
Germany's defeat at Stalingrad changed the course of the war.

fewer—less

Fewer should be used when one is referring to individual units, *less* when one is referring to a smaller amount of a substance or quality. The distinction is a comparatively minor one.

Examples:
They had *fewer* applicants this year.
He had *less* money than he realized.
A Ford costs *less* than a Buick.

first—firstly; second—secondly

The *-ly* form for numerals is awkward and unnecessary. The straight form is preferable.

Awkward:
Firstly, I should say thank you to my colleagues.

Preferable:
First, I should thank my colleagues.

formally—formerly

Formally means "in a proper manner"; *formerly* means "at a previous time."

Examples:
We have not been *formally* introduced.
He *formerly* played football for Alabama.

infer—imply

Although one major dictionary suggests that these words may be used interchangeably, the practice is not generally accepted. *Infer* means "conclude from the evidence," and *imply* means "suggest" or "hint." In college writing you should observe the distinction.

Examples:

He *inferred* from conversation that Jones was a Democrat.
The article *implied* that the students were responsible.

irregardless

An incorrect form of *regardless*; not acceptable in standard English.

its—it's

Confusion of these two forms causes one of the most common student writing errors. *Its* (in spite of its not having an apostrophe) is a possessive pronoun; *it's* is a contraction of *it is*.

Examples:

The company increased *its* profits.
It's time that something was done.

lay—lie

Lay is a transitive verb that must take an object; it means "place" or "put." Its principal parts are *lay, laid, laid.*
Lie is an intransitive verb that means "recline"; its principal parts are *lie, lay, lain.*

Correct:

The dog *lay* peacefully on the floor.
She *laid* the pattern on the material.

Incorrect:

I *lay* the book on the table yesterday.
He *laid* on the ground for an hours.

like—as

The confusion of these words causes great distress to purists. In formal English *like* should be used only as a preposition, not as a conjunction to introduce a clause. *As, as if,* or *as though* should be used before clauses. The distinction is disappearing, but your teacher may want you to observe it.

Informal:

It looks *like* there will be trouble.

Formal:

It looks *as if* there will be trouble.

Correct:

He looks *like* an athlete.

Mary talks *like* her mother.

loose—lose

Confusion between these terms causes one of students' most common spelling errors. *Loose*, although it can be used as a verb to mean "release" or "make loose," is most often an adjective meaning "unconfined." *Lose* is a verb only.

Examples:

The bindings were too *loose*.

John may *lose* his scholarship.

media

Media is a plural noun and takes a plural verb; see **data**.

myself

Myself should not be used as a substitute for *I* or *me*. Its proper uses are (1) as a reflexive pronoun and (2) as an intensive pronoun.

Correct:

I build it *myself*.

I cut *myself* badly.

Incorrect:

Mary and *myself* are going to do it.

He gave instructions to Jim and *myself*.

one

An impersonal pronoun used more often in formal than informal writing. In strictly formal writing it must be used consistently and not mixed with *his* or *hers*.

Formal:

One has the feeling that *one* is helpless.

Informal:

One has the feeling that *he* is helpless.

only

An adverb or adjective meaning "solely" or "exclusively." It should always come next to the word it modifies.

Correct:

He has *only* two more years of college.

John comes *only* in the mornings.

Incorrect:

He *only* has two more years of college.

John *only* comes in the mornings.

prepositions

There is nothing inherently incorrect about putting a preposition at the end of a sentence if the context seems to call for it. "These were the only figures he had to work *with*" is a perfectly good sentence. So is "There is the man you need to speak *to*."

principal—principle

These two quite different words are often confused. *Principal* may be a noun or an adjective. As a noun it means "chief administrative officer of a school," "leading character," or "sum of money." As an adjective it means "first" or "main."

Examples:

Jones is the *principal* of the high school.

Fonteyn was the *principal* in Swan Lake.

He invested the *principal*.

Clark is the *principal* suspect in the case.

Principle is a noun only; it means "a rule" or "theory."

Examples:

We must act according to our *principles*.

The *principle* of economy should come first.

reason is because—reason is that

The reason is because is an awkward and redundant construction. *The reason is that* is preferable.

Awkward:

The *reason* John didn't come *was because* his car wouldn't start.

Preferable:

The *reason* John didn't come *was that* his car wouldn't start.

shall—will

Trying to make a distinction between these forms is no longer realistic or useful. They may be used interchangeably in both formal and informal writing.

should of

An incorrect form of *should have*.

Correct:
We *should have* gone yesterday.

Incorrect:
We *should of* gone yesterday.

supposed to—used to

See **used to**.

sure—certainly

Sure should be used to express certainty or assurance.

Example:
I am *sure* that his report is accurate.

Sure should not be used in formal or informal writing to replace *certainly*.

Colloquial:
Alabama *sure* has a great team.

Informal:
Alabama *certainly* has a great team.

their—there—they're

Students sometimes fail to distinguish between these homonyms. *Their* is a possessive pronoun.

Tom and Jane will drive *their* own car.

There is a demonstrative pronoun.

There is the woman we saw yesterday.
Tell me when we get *there*.

They're is a contraction of *they are*.

They're scheduled to arrive at noon.

to—too—two

This is another set of homonyms that is often confused.
To is a preposition.

We are going *to* Chicago tomorrow.

Too means "also" or "in addition."

Jane will be there *too*.

Two is a numeral.

There are *two* mistakes on that page.

unique

Unique, like perfect, describes a condition that is absolute. Modifiers should not be used with it.

Correct:
Her problem is *unique*.

Incorrect:
Her problem is *rather unique*.
This dress is *more unique*.

used to—supposed to

Because the final *d* of these verbs disappears when they are pronounced, students sometimes forget to write the complete form.

Correct:
He is *used* to starting on time.
We *used* to get there early.
This is *supposed to* be an open meeting.

Incorrect:
We *use* to get there early.
John is *suppose* to serve as president.

where—that

The colloquial construction *I saw where* or *I read where* should not be used in writing, formal or informal.

Colloquial:
I heard *where* the chairperson died.

Acceptable:
I heard *that* the chairperson died.
I read *that* the building had burned.

who—whom

Who is the nominative pronoun and should be used when the noun it is replacing would be acting as the subject of a sentence or clause.

Example:
This is the man *who* came with Joe.

Whom is the objective form and should be used when the noun it replaces would be an object.

Example:
There is the man *whom* we saw Friday.

In practice, *who* is generally acceptable in informal writing except when it occurs directly after a preposition.

Acceptable:
There is the man *who* I need to see.
Jones is the man to *whom* I will write.

will—shall

See **shall—will**.

-wise

Avoid attaching *-wise* to a word as a suffix.

Jargon:
Moneywise she is having troubles.
Gradewise Joan is doing well.

Correct:
She is having money troubles.
Joan gets good grades.

would of—would have

Would of is an incorrect form of *would have*.

Correct:
We *would have* come if we had known.

Incorrect:
We *would of* come if we had known.

Would have should not be used to replace *had*.

Correct:
If I *had* known, I would have told you.

Incorrect:
If I *would have* known, I would have told you.

An Index to Grammatical Terms

Active verb The verb form used when the subject of the sentence is the doer of the action.

George *caught* the calf.
Molly *left* the gate money on the counter.

Adjective clause An adjective clause is a dependent clause, usually introduced by a pronoun, that modifies a noun or pronoun.

There is the person *whom I came to see.*
London is the *city that has most to offer.*
My son, *who is now a veterinarian,* studied at Cornell.

Adverb clause An adverb clause is a dependent clause that modifies a verb or a verbal phrase. Adverb clauses can be moved around more freely than adjective clauses.

Although he has not yet been nominated, Black will be the new judge.
Let me know *when you are finished.*
Jones failed the course *because he never came to class.*

Agreement We speak of *agreement* between subject and verb and between pronoun and their antecedent. For rules governing subject-verb agreement see Handbook, pp. 524–526; for rules governing pronoun-antecedent agreements, see Handbook, pp. 531–532.

Antecedent The antecedent of a pronoun is the noun that the pronoun refers to or substitutes for. The antecedent can be in the same sentence as the pronoun or in a previous sentence, but a sentence should be written so that there can be no confusion about which noun is the antecedent for pronouns that follow.

Appositive A word, phrase, or clause inserted after a noun to give more information about it.

Auxiliary verb A "helping" verb that combines with other verbs, usually to show tense. The most common auxiliary verbs are the various forms of *is*, *to be*, and *have*. For example:

George *is* coming tomorrow.
I *am* studying for my algebra test.
We *have been* sailing out at the lake.

Comma splice The use of a comma rather than a conjunction or semicolon to join two closely related independent clauses. See text, pp. 130–131.

Complement A word or phrase that completes a verb. (Notice the term is spelled with an *e* rather than an *i*.) It can be a noun that gives more information about the subject (George is the *captain*) or an adjective that completes a linking verb and gives information about the subject (The storefront is *false*).

Complex sentence A sentence made up of one independent clause and one or more dependent clauses. See text, pp. 104–106.

Compound sentence A sentence made up of two or more independent clauses joined by conjunctions or a semicolon. See text, pp. 106–108.

Conjunction A word that acts as a joiner within a sentence. There are two principal kinds of conjunctions: (1) coordinating conjunctions used to connect independent clauses (*yet, moreover, and, therefore, then, besides,* etc.) and (2) subordinating conjunctions used to introduce dependent clauses (*although, because, after, unless, if, when,* etc.).

Demonstrative pronoun A pronoun that points out a noun. The four demonstrative pronouns are *this, that, these,* and *those.* Also called *demonstrative adjectives.*

Dependent clause A group of words that contains a subject and a verb but that could not stand alone as a sentence, and thus is joined by a subordinating conjunction to an independent clause to form a complete sentence. See text on sentence fragments, pp. 123–129.

Gerund One of the verbals (see p. 125 in text). Gerunds are formed by adding *-ing* to the verb stem, and they function as nouns. For example:

Swimming is my favorite sport.
We must realize that good *thinking* is basic to good *writing*.
Be sure to ask him about *renting* the house.

Independent clause A group of words with a subject and a verb that could stand as a sentence by itself but is acting as a part of a sentence.

Infinitive Another verbal form (see p. 125 in text). Infinitives are formed by adding *to* to the base part of the verb. The infinitive can act in several ways in a sentence. For example:

Subject To ski is not really difficult.
Adverb He struggled *to achieve* fame. (*Modifies "struggled"*)
Adjective I must find a way *to bring* them together.

Intransitive verb A verb that expresses action but does not take a direct object. Intransitive verbs cannot be used in the passive voice.

Linking verb A verb indicating one of the senses or a condition of being. If you can substitute the verb *is* for a verb and have the meaning remain virtually the same, the verb qualifies as a linking verb. For example, "I feel fine" translates to "I am fine"; "The sky seems overcast" translates to "The sky is overcast." Linking verbs should be completed with an adjective or a noun, *not* an adverb. For instance, "I feel bad," *not* "I feel badly." The most common linking verbs are the forms of *to be, feel, look, seem, become,* and *appear*.

Modifier A word, phrase, or clause that gives you information about another word or group of words.

Nonrestrictive clause A modifying clause within a sentence that could be taken out without seriously affecting the meaning of the sentence. It should be set off by commas (see Handbook, p. 510).

Noun clause A group of words that has a subject and verb but is a dependent clause; it can serve most functions that a noun has: subject, object, appositive, complement, or object of a preposition. For example, *"That money was not important to him* soon became obvious."

Noun phrase A group of words, usually a noun with modifiers, that acts as a noun. For example: *"Great white clouds* covered the moon" or "He flung himself upon the *desperate rogues.*"

Parallelism The term for maintaining the same structure and kind of words, phrases, or clauses within a sentence (see pp. 518–519 in the Handbook).

Participle A word that comes from a verb but acts as an adjective. There are two kinds: those made by adding *-ed* to a verb stem (past participle) and those made by adding *-ing* to a verb stem (present participle).

Passive verb A verb form that indicates the subject is being acted upon rather than acting. For example: "Rocks were thrown at the car" or "Men have been shot for saying less than that."

Phrase A group of two or more words that does not have a subject and verb.

Predicate The verb in a sentence or clause. The term *simple predicate* refers only to the verb or verbs in a sentence or clause; the term *complete predicate* refers to the verb and any modifiers, complement, or object that may go with it.

Predication The relationship that exists between the subject, verb, and complementary elements of a sentence (see Handbook, p. 519).

Restrictive clause A modifying clause giving information that is necessary to the meaning of the sentence; it should not be set off by commas because it could not be omitted without altering the point of the sentence. For example:

Only a person *who can speak French* can do the job.
The book *that contains that information* has been stolen.

Sentence fragment See text, pp. 123–129.

Subjunctive mood A form of verb used when one wants to express a wish, a hypothesis, or a condition contrary to fact. The most common forms are *were, would,* and *should.* Careful writers make a point of using the form after *if.* For example:

If I *were* you, I wouldn't consider leaving.
What *would* you do if you *were* I?
If that *should* happen, tell me immediately.

Subordinate clause See *dependent clause.*

Transitive verb An action verb that takes an object.

Verbal A word formed from a verb stem but functioning as a subject, object, or modifier; see *gerund, infinitive,* and *participle.*

A Brief Handbook of Grammar

Mechanics

Capitalization

The conventions of capitalization are so familiar to most of us that we put capitals in the right places without even thinking about what we are doing. Assuming, then, that most students need little help with capitalization, in this section I will review the principal rules quickly, concentrating on the few instances that may cause problems.

1. Capitalize all proper nouns and the words that are derived from them.

> *George* is a native of *Chicago*.
>
> *France* is a member of the *United Nations*.
>
> The *Mississippi* flows into the *Gulf of Mexico* at *New Orleans*.
>
> His command of *English* is poor.
>
> *New Mexico* and *Arizona* were the last states to join the union.
>
> The *United States* entered *World War II* in 1941.
>
> My *German* class is boring.

2. Capitalize the first word of each sentence.
3. Capitalize words referring to God or other deities: *Christ*, the *Virgin Mary*, *Buddha*, and *Him* and *He* (when referring to God).
4. Capitalize proper names, the days of the week, months, and holidays.

5.   Capitalize titles when they are used with a name.

Admiral Zumwalt, Governor Smith, Chief Justice Hughes, Professor Baird, Dr. Watkins, Senator Strong, President Carter.

6.   Capitalize the names of organizations, but not a common noun that designates a type of organization.

The American Red Cross, the United States Senate, the University of Georgia, the Better Business Bureau, the National Association for the Advancement of Colored People, United States Steel.

But,

A university, a corporation, the federal government, a fraternity, the state hospital.

7.   Capitalize the most important words (usually that means all words except prepositions and articles) in the titles of books, plays, poems, magazines, short stories, chapters, and subdivisions of chapters.

The Return of the Native
Death of a Salesman
"To His Coy Mistress"
Saturday Review

Commas

We use commas for two reasons. First, they help to clarify writing by preventing possible ambiguities or misinterpretations; second, they make writing easier to read by marking natural pauses and separations. Ideally, writers would not worry about the rules that govern proper use of the comma but would simply insert them as they felt they were needed for clarity or proper emphasis. In practice, however, it is useful to know the chief rules and to get in the habit of observing them almost mechanically.

1.   Use commas to set off items in a series. Most authorities specify that one should insert a comma after each element in the series except the last; however, omitting the comma after the word that comes before the conjunction is permissible.

Standard The early explorers were searching for gold, spices, and precious gems.

Acceptable The early explorers were searching for gold, spices and precious gems.

Further examples

The recipe called for cream, cheese, onions, and marjoram.

Jack was willing to go to Memphis, Houston, New Orleans, or Atlanta but not to a northern city.

The campaign was tailored to appeal to middle-aged people, workers, and retired people.

The semester had been exhausting, frustrating, and generally depressing.

2.   Use commas to set off subordinate clauses that come at the beginning of a sentence. This usage is conventional but not mandatory.

If that pipeline is not repaired, the city will soon run out of fuel.

Whenever a university sets excessively high standards, it will gain professors but lose students.

Until we have settled that issue, there can be no peace.

As we drove over the river, we saw that it was flooded.

If the subordinate clause comes after the main clause, a comma is not necessary.

We will be there if the plane gets in on time.

I cannot come until I have finished my work.

3.   Use a comma to indicate a pause in a sentence that might be misinterpreted if it were read without interruption.

John stationed himself by the door Joe had entered, and waited. *(If the comma is omitted, one gets the impression that it was Joe who waited.)*

If grumpy, Henry forgets his manners. *(If the comma is omitted, the sentence may be read as an introductory clause or a sentence fragment.)*

To the insecure, female education may pose a great threat. *(If the comma is omitted, "insecure" may be mistaken for the modifier of female.)*

Badly wounded, Charles slumped to the ground. *(Without the comma, the introductory phrase becomes an adjective.)*

4.   Use a comma to separate two independent clauses that are joined by a conjunction. In some cases a comma is not absolutely necessary to clarify the meaning, but it is just as well to form the habit of using it to avoid possible ambiguity.

> He was an ambitious man, but he was not a scrupulous one.
>
> I hope she is in class today, for her report is the one that interests me.
>
> He will either honor the contract, or we will file suit.
>
> The defense lawyer withdrew the objections, and agreement was quickly reached.

5.   Use a comma to set off interrupting, nonrestrictive phrases in a sentence. A *nonrestrictive phrase* is one that gives information supplementary, rather than essential, to the main idea of the sentence; a *restrictive phrase* is one that cannot be omitted without seriously altering that main idea. The following examples should help to clarify this distinction, not always an easy one to make:

> *Restrictive clause* Anyone *who has been convicted of a felony* may not serve on a jury.
>
> *Nonrestrictive clause* A convicted felon, *no matter how good his record*, may not serve on a jury.
>
> *Restrictive clause* Students *who have been on scholastic probation for two semesters* will not be allowed to reregister.
>
> *Nonrestrictive clause* Students, *who compose one-third of the voting age population in this precinct*, will not be allowed to vote in city elections.
>
> *Restrictive clause* The document *that is the foundation of liberty in this country* is the Constitution.
>
> *Nonrestrictive clause* There are millions of Americans who know almost nothing about the Constitution, *the document that is the foundation of liberty in this country*.

Notice that in each of the sentences with restrictive clauses, the italicized portion could not be eliminated without drastically altering the meaning of the sentence. Therefore, those portions are not interrupters and should not be set off in commas. The nonrestrictive clauses, on the other hand, could be omitted; therefore, they should be set off by commas.

6. Use commas to set off other kinds of interrupting elements in a sentence: appositives, words or phrases of connection or transition, and terms of address.

Appositives (words or phrases that give us additional information about a term)

> Her uncle, *the chairman of the committee*, gave her that information.
> Blacklock, *an ex-policeman*, has been elected sheriff.
> Tokyo, *the largest city in the world*, has unbelievable traffic problems.

Connectives (words and phrases of transition)

> *Needless to say*, you cannot expect a college to show a profit.
> At the second meeting, *however*, they decided the scheme was impractical.
> *For example*, Russia was once our ally but is now an opponent.
> Japan, *on the contrary*, turned from an opponent to a friend.

Terms of address

> *Madame Chairperson*, I would like to submit my report.
> May I say, *your honor*, that this has been a difficult decision.
> *Overpunctuated* Last night, when the meeting was over, Randall, tired and, therefore, irritable, made a serious, although not fatal, error.
> *Acceptable* Last night when the meeting was over, Randall, tired and therefore irritable, made a serious although not fatal error.
> *Overpunctuated* Of course, the solution is not the best one possible, but, under the circumstances, we can live with it.
> *Acceptable* Of course the solution is not the best one possible, but under the circumstances we can live with it.

The Semicolon

Learning to use semicolons properly can solve many of your punctuation and transition problems.

1. Use a semicolon to connect clauses that are independent but very closely related.

Jarvis is not at his best when he lectures; he communicates better in seminar classes.

The issue is not who is right and who is wrong; it is who can make his or her views prevail.

Yesterday we were confronted with the waste of our natural resources; today we are confronted with pollution as well.

Any of these sentences could be separated by a period, but the two ideas expressed in each are so closely related that a semicolon makes for tighter construction.

2.   Use a semicolon to precede a transition word that connects independent clauses.

Hawkins will probably be our next district attorney; moreover, she will make a good one.

My opinion will not make any difference; nevertheless, I feel that I must express my views.

The statute of limitations on that crime expired a year ago; as a result, Miller cannot be tried.

3.   Use a semicolon to separate a series of clauses or phrases that have internal commas.

Those who participated in the meeting were Gerald Young, the man who had been present at the first test of the plane; Peter Whipple, the pilot who had flown it on the first mission; Robert Mills, the financier who had underwritten the project; and Mrs. Herbert Conn, the wife of the man who designed the plane.

4.   Use the semicolon to separate a series of closely related parallel clauses linked together into a long sentence.

All Christians believe that blessed are the poor and humble, and those who are ill-used by the world; that it is easier for a camel to pass through the eye of a needle than for a rich man to enter the kingdom of heaven; that they should judge not, lest they be judged; that they should swear not at all; that they should love their neighbors as themselves; that if one take their cloak, they should give him their coat also; that they should take no thought for the morrow; that if they would be perfect, they should sell all they have and give it to the poor.

This sentence from John Stuart Mill's *On Liberty* is a model of organization because he has taken advantage of the semicolon to tie several separate ideas together as economically as possible. A student might not want to attempt anything so elaborate, but the technique can be used on a less ambitious scale. For instance:

> There are several advantages to the plan: if we lose our director, we can easily find another one; if one of the participants drops out, we will still have enough members to work with; if we should fail, we will not have a great deal of money invested.

The Colon

The uses of the colon are few, but they are important.

1. Use the colon as the end punctuation for an independent clause that introduces an explanation, an example or illustration, or a list that enumerates or gives a catalogue. For example:

> One quality is essential to the person who wants to be a successful scientist: patience.

> Geneticists insist that acquired characteristics cannot be transmitted from one generation to another: for instance, one's conscience is not a hereditary trait.

> These cities participated in the training program: Chicago, Dallas, New Orleans, Omaha, St. Louis, and Los Angeles.

Remember that you should *not* use a colon after a preposition or a linking verb.

> *Incorrect* The conditions of employment are: union membership, five years' experience, and a high school diploma.

> *Incorrect* The movie is about: organized crime, corruption, drug smuggling, and graft.

2. Use a colon to indicate that an amplification or explanation of your first statement will follow.

> Johnson will give his consent on one condition: all royalties from the article must be contributed to charity.

> The expedition faced almost insuperable problems: there were no maps of the territory, the Indian tribes in that region were hostile,

and the eastern banks refused to advance any money to buy supplies.

3.   The colon is one method of introducing a quotation.

The opening words of the Declaration of Independence give the justification for the document: "When in the course of human events, it becomes necessary for one people to dissolve the political bands which have connected them with another, and to assume among the powers of the earth, the separate and equal station to which the laws of Nature and of Nature's God entitle them, a decent respect to the opinions of mankind requires that they should declare the causes which impel them to the separation."

Kennedy's inaugural address closed with this statement: "With a good conscience our only sure reward, with history the final judge of our deeds, let us go forth to lead the land we love, asking His blessing and His help, but knowing that here on earth God's work must truly be our own."

Dashes and Dots

Make sparing use of dashes as punctuation because it is all too easy to slip into the habit of relying on a dash instead of stopping to think what kind of punctuation would best meet your needs. Probably you should limit them to three functions.

1.   Use dashes to set off parenthetical material when you want to emphasize the contrast between that material and the rest of the sentence.

To lose one's temper because of a slighting remark—and certainly there are times when it is difficult not to do so—is a self-defeating indulgence.

In spite of the delays and interruptions—and God knows we had plenty of them—we managed to finish the project on time.

2.   Use a dash to indicate any sudden change in the structure or direction of a sentence.

As a stern Calvinist, Jordan believed in predestination, original sin, the election of saints—and his own infallibility.

Michael had everything she admired in a man: humor, ability, elegant manners, rugged good looks—and a great deal of money.

If you look at the issue from the Communists' point of view—but then we are not capable of doing that.

3.   Use a dash to indicate that what follows is a summary of the previous material in the sentence. For example:

Too much rain, insects, an early frost—all contributed to the crop failure that year.

Good grades, high test scores, strong recommendations—the person who hopes to get into graduate school must have all these.

When you are writing a paper in longhand, use a line about twice as long as a hyphen to indicate a dash. If you are typing, indicate a dash by two hyphens with no space between the word before or after.

Dots, the symbol of an ellipsis or omission, have only one major function in writing, but it is an important one. You should use three separated dots (. . .) to indicate that you have omitted something from a quotation. If what remains forms a complete sentence, add a fourth dot (. . . .) to stand for the period of that sentence. It is essential that you use this symbol to indicate any omissions; otherwise you may mislead your audience by giving the impression that you are quoting in full. Here are two examples of its use:

Unless anyone who approves of punishment for the promulgation of opinions flatters himself that he is a wiser and better man than Marcus Aurelius . . . let him abstain from that joint assumption of infallibility of himself and the multitude, which the great Antoninus made with so unfortunate a result.

John Stuart Mill

I believe that no people ever groaned under the heavy yoke of slavery but when they deserved it. This may be called a severe censure upon by far the greatest part of the nations of the world who are involved in the miseries of servitude. But however they may be thought by some to deserve commiseration, the censure is just. . . . The truth is, all might be free, if they valued freedom and defended it as they should.

Samuel Adams

Quotation Marks

1.   Quotation marks are used around all quoted material that is within the text of any writing.

Eldridge Cleaver says, "There is in James Baldwin's work the most grueling, agonizing, total hatred of blacks . . . that one can find in the writings of any black American writer of note in our time."

If, however, a quotation runs to more than three lines, it may be indented and single spaced in the text and the quotation marks omitted. There are numerous examples of that form in this text. If you are giving a quotation within another run-in quotation, single quotation marks should go around the inside quotation.

James remarked, "My father's favorite slogan was 'There's a sucker born every minute.' "

2.   Occasionally you may want to use quotation marks to set off a word that you are using humorously or ironically. Use this device sparingly because too often it gives the impression you are apologizing for your diction. If you think a word is unsuitable, get rid of it rather than put it in quotation marks.

Acceptable Their "benefactors" absconded with the last of their savings.

The language of the petition was, you might say, "down-to-earth."

Apologetic My roommate is a real "nut."

3.   You may use quotation marks to identify a word or term to which you wish to call special attention.

"Hopefully" is a word often used incorrectly.

In this context the word "discipline" refers to a special field of study.

4.   Use quotation marks around the titles of articles, short stories, short poems, essays, and sometimes chapter headings.

"The Fall of the House of Usher"

"To His Coy Mistress"

"The Double Standard of Aging"

5.   Commas and periods always are placed inside quotation marks. Semicolons and colons are placed outside quotation marks. Question marks and exclamation points may be placed inside or outside the quo-

tation marks, depending on the context. If they belong to the quoted portion, they go inside; if they belong to the sentence as a whole, they go outside.

> He made frequent use of the terms, "hip," "square," and "cool it."
>
> "If I come," he said, "it will be after lunch."
>
> Marx always thought of himself as a "man of reason"; nevertheless, his philosophy is not always a rational one.
>
> She said, "He is absolutely insane!"
>
> Is this an instance of "checks and balances"?

The Apostrophe

1. The apostrophe is followed by an *s* to form the possessive of single nouns.

> the cook's apron
>
> a bride's book
>
> our doctor's daughter
>
> that child's toy

2. An apostrophe is placed after the *s* to form the possessive of plural nouns ending in *s* or of most names ending in *s*.

> the boys' meeting
>
> those students' books
>
> Charles' graduation
>
> the Jones' house

3. The apostrophe followed by an *s* is used to form the possessive of compound or group nouns or irregular plural forms.

> the team's record
>
> his sister-in-law's car
>
> the women's luncheon
>
> children's clothing

Notice that possessive pronouns are complete as they stand and do not take an apostrophe. *His, hers, their, its, our, my, mine, yours,* and so on.

4. An apostrophe is used to signal the omitted letter or letters in a contraction.

They're going to be late.

We're not interested in opera.

We shouldn't be here.

Jim just can't cope with exams.

5. An apostrophe is used to form the plural of individual letters or numbers.

She consistently mispronounces her *s*'s.

Jerry confuses his 6's and his 9's.

Italics

In writing or typing, an underlined word is considered to be italicized; in print, the italicized words appear in a special kind of print. There are four principal uses for italics.

1. Use italics to indicate the names of books, magazines or newspapers, movies or plays, long poems or musical compositions, and in most cases, the names of ships or special airplanes.

Camus' *The Stranger*

Williams' *The Glass Menagerie*

Milton's *Paradise Lost*

New York Times

Air Force One

U.S.S. *Enterprise*

The Barber of Seville

Playboy

2. Use italics for foreign words and phrases that are not widely used in English.

au courant

deus ex machina

machree

hubris

bête noire

3. You may use italics instead of quotation marks to call special attention to a word.

One variety of jargon is called *cant*.

The concept of *due process* is of particular significance here.

4. Use italics to emphasize a word.

His remarks cannot be called simply dissent; they must be called *treason*.

Justice, not legality, is the issue before us.

Be careful not to overuse this technique of italicizing for emphasis. A passage that is loaded with underlined words gives the reader the feeling of being shouted at.

The Hyphen

Except for the stipulation that a hyphen is used to divide a word at the end of a line, there are few absolute rules for the use of the hyphen. There are some useful conventions.

1. Use a hyphen to divide a word that comes at the end of a line or to show the division of a word into syllables. There are correct and incorrect ways to divide words; when in doubt, check a dictionary for the correct form.

2. Use a hyphen in most common compounds.

mother-in-law

ten-year-old

button-down collar

sergeant-at-arms

self-help books

lieutenant-governor

3. Use a hyphen to connect the elements of a compound modifier.

a go-to-hell attitude

a self-styled liberal
a hang-dog look
down-at-the-heel appearance
a run-of-the-mill movie
a play-by-play description

4.   Use a hyphen between the prefix *ex* and a noun and after a prefix that comes before a proper noun.

ex-football player
ex-husband
a pro-Japanese article
anti-Russian feelings
pro-Texan attitude
super-American

Problems with Sentence Structure

Sentence Fragments

See text, pp. 123–128.

Run-on and Fused Sentences

See text, pp. 129–130.

Comma Splices

See text, pp. 130–131.

Dangling Modifiers

See text, pp. 131–133.

Faulty Parallelism

The elements of a sentence that are alike in function should also be alike in form. For example, if you were writing about the responsibilities of a jury, you might do it like this:

The jury's job is to listen to the evidence, to consider it fairly and impartially, and to render a verdict that is just to both parties.

Or if you wanted to combine several ideas in one sentence you might do it like this:

The United States' ten-year involvement in the Vietnam war caused dissension in this country, aggravated inflation, and diverted resources from our domestic programs.

Sentences in which the structure is not parallel may be understandable, but often they are awkward, difficult to read, and not as unified or smooth as they might be. Notice these examples of faulty parallelism from student themes.

Original The author's comparison of frozen meat to leather reminds one of toughness, dryness, unchewable, and not very tasty.

Revision The author's comparison of frozen meat to leather suggests that the meat is tough, dry, unchewable, and not very tasty.

Original After going through many frustrations and problems and then you find happiness, you will enjoy it more.

Revision Going through many frustrations and problems and then finding happiness makes the happiness more enjoyable.

Original The word *humanitarian* suggests the best qualities of humanity: tenderness, merciful, and considerate.

Revision The word *humanitarian* suggests the best qualities of humanity: tenderness, mercy, and consideration.

Original The teachers were making him compete against others instead of to teach him anything.

Revision The teachers were making him compete against others instead of trying to teach him anything.

Original The main assets of a state university are economical, convenience, and the atmosphere is friendly.

Revision The main assets of a state university are economy, convenience, and a friendly atmosphere.

Predication Problems

The verb is the key part of any sentence. If it is an action verb, it tells what the subject is doing or having done to it and, in the case of transitive verbs, what is being done to the object. If the verb is a linking verb, it makes the connection between the subject and the word that completes or describes it. These relationships between the verb and the other elements in the sentence are called *predication*, and when a sentence is put together in such a way that the relationship between subject and verb or verb and complement or object is confusing or illogical, we describe the error as a *faulty predication*.

Predication problems fall into three classes: (1) faulty subject/verb combinations, (2) faulty verb/object combinations, and (3) faulty linking verb/complement combinations.

Faulty subject/verb combinations seem most apt to occur when a writer has chosen an abstract subject and fails to realize that the subject cannot logically perform the action suggested by the verb. Notice, for example, that the subject/verb relationship indicated by the italicized words in these examples is not logical.

> The *wishes* of the majority *approved* the Articles of Confederation but then *changed* their minds after it was adopted.

> Athletic *scholarships* promote personal accomplishment and *seek out* people of high quality.

> The audience's *racial characteristics contained* Anglo and Hispanic people.

Usually the quickest way to solve this problem is to rewrite the sentence with a concrete or personal subject.

Other faulty subject/verb relationships occur because the writer doesn't really think about what kinds of actions a subject can logically do. Such lapses produce sentences like these.

> Larger *cars respect* Volkswagens because they can get in and out of tight parking places.

> One of the most important purchases of a person's life *is made* by a car's *image*.

Notice that a passive verb probably caused the mistake in the second sentence.

Faulty predication between verb and object occurs less often, but failing to think about what the verb you have chosen can logically do can cause awkward combinations like these:

The company *disconnected people* who hadn't paid their bills.

Such policies *intimidate* the *applications* of minority candidates.

The most common kind of faulty predication is that which occurs when writers use a linking verb to connect a subject and noun complement that cannot go together logically. When writers make this kind of mistake, it is often because they fail to realize that they are setting up a kind of equation; that is, because the noun complement of a linking verb indicates, in a sense, that the subject and complement are equivalents—the words that fill those slots must be capable of being equated. For example, you can logically say, "My mother is a doctor," but you cannot logically say, "My mother is a medical profession," because a person cannot equal a profession. Here are some typical examples of this kind of faulty predication:

Pollution, space, and *energy* are becoming near *tragedies*.

The mere *cost of living* is a *task* in itself.

From television young people get the idea that *hate* is acceptable *behavior*.

Notice that mistakes like these are most likely to occur when either the subject or complement is an abstraction.

Finally, you should be careful to avoid the common predication error that comes from using the phrase, "Something is when . . ." For example:

An example of early *conditioning* is *when* small children are taught to hate people of other races.

The worst *situation* is *when* people ignore warning signals.

Plagiarism is *when* you use someone else's words without giving credit.

In this kind of construction, you are saying that a thing or concept equals a time. The way to correct this error is simply to make it a rule never to use the phrase "is when."

Verbs

For help with identifying different kinds of verbs and verb forms, see Index to Grammatical Terms. Other common usage problems follow.

Problems with Verbs

Disagreement between subject and verb in number and person
Although almost every college student knows that the subject and verb of a sentence should agree in number and person, agreement errors seem to be a persistent problem with some writers. The following rules cover those constructions that cause most of the difficulties.

1.   If two or more subjects in a sentence are connected by *and*, the verb should be plural.

> *Incorrect* Overthrowing the present government and replacing it with a people's democracy *is* two of his major objectives.
>
> *Correct* Overthrowing the present government and replacing it with a people's democracy *are* two of his major objectives.
>
> *Incorrect* Sylvia, Grace, and I *was* going to town.
>
> *Correct* Sylvia, Grace, and I *were* going to town.

There is an exception. If the two subjects connected by *and* are considered a unit, a singular verb should be used.

> *Correct* "Law and order" *is* a popular slogan.
>
> *Correct* Gin and tonic *is* considered a sophisticated drink.

2.   If two or more subjects in a sentence are joined by *or, nor,* or *but,* the verb should be singular.

> *Incorrect* Either Stanley or Roger *are* to be nominated.
>
> *Correct* Either Stanley or Roger *is* to be nominated.
>
> *Incorrect* Not prudence, but courage *are* needed here.
>
> *Correct* Not prudence, but courage *is* needed here.

3.   When a modifying phrase comes between the subject and the verb, the verb should agree with the subject of the sentence.

> *Incorrect* A person in one of these occupations *have* to be pleasant and friendly.
>
> *Correct* A person in one of these occupations *has* to be pleasant and friendly.

Incorrect Words such as "stuffy," "bleak," and "dreary" *connotes* unpleasantness.

Correct Words such as "stuffy," "bleak," and "dreary" *connote* unpleasantness.

Incorrect Other high-quality colleges in Texas, such as Rice, Baylor, Texas Christian, and Southern Methodist, *costs* thousands of dollars more in tuition.

Correct Other high-quality colleges in Texas, such as Rice, Baylor, Texas Christian, and Southern Methodist, *cost* thousands of dollars more in tuition.

4. When a sentence begins with *there* or *here* followed by a linking verb, the verb should agree with the subject that follows the verb.

Incorrect There *is* many things about this program that concern us.

Correct There *are* many things about this program that concern us.

Incorrect *Is* there a lot of children in your neighborhood?

Correct *Are* there a lot of children in your neighborhood?

Incorrect Here *is* the rules of the game.

Correct Here *are* the rules of the game.

5. Pronouns that refer to individual units take a singular verb; the most common of these pronouns are *each, everyone, nobody, somebody, everybody, anybody, one, either,* and *neither.*

Incorrect Everyone of them *are* guilty.

Correct Everyone of them *is* guilty.

Incorrect Neither of them *admit* the error.

Correct Neither of them *admits* the error.

6. The pronouns *any* and *none* may take either singular or plural verbs.

None of the boys *was* responsible for the theft.

None of the boys *were* responsible for the theft.

Any of the answers *is* acceptable.

Are any of the answers acceptable?

7.   In a sentence of the subject/verb/complement pattern the verb agrees with the subject rather than the complement.

Incorrect One characteristic of jargon *are* euphemisms.
Correct One characteristic of jargon *is* euphemisms.
Incorrect Too many absences *was* the chief problem.
Correct Too many absences *were* the chief problem.

8.   Collective nouns may take a singular or plural subject, depending on the context in which they are used. If the noun refers to a unit, a singular verb should be used; if the context suggests several individuals considered separately, a plural verb should be used.

The congregation *wants* a new minister.
The congregation *were* divided on the issue.
The team *has* a wonderful record.
The winning team *divide* the gate receipts among the members.

9.   Some nouns that appear to be plural in form are, in practice, singular and should take singular verbs. Some of the more common nouns of this kind are *linguistics, ethics, mathematics, physics, news, economics,* and *electronics.*

The news tonight *is* depressing.
Ethics *is* the study of the good life.

The use of nonstandard forms for the past tense or past participle of irregular verbs. The only practical way to avoid using nonstandard verb forms is to memorize the principal parts of the most common irregular verbs so well that their use becomes automatic; for less common ones such as *abide, strive,* or *tread,* check the dictionary if you are in doubt. If the verb is regular, the dictionary will give only the present form; if it is irregular, all three forms will be given. Be particularly careful to avoid substituting the past form of a verb for the past participle form when the two are different. The following examples are incorrect:

I *have* already *ate.*
Jack *had ran* out of money.

Principal Parts of the Common Irregular Verbs

Present	*Past*	*Past Participle*
awake	awoke, awaked	awoke, awaked
be	was	been
bite	bit	bitten
blow	blew	blown
break	broke	broken
bring	brought	brought
buy	bought	bought
catch	caught	caught
choose	chose	chosen
come	came	come
cost	cost	cost
cut	cut	cut
do	did	done
dive	dove, dived	dived
drag	dragged	dragged
drink	drank	drunk
drive	drove	driven
eat	ate	eaten
fall	fell	fallen
freeze	froze	frozen
give	gave	given
grind	ground	ground
grow	grew	grown
hang (execute)	hanged	hanged
hang (suspend)	hung	hung
hurt	hurt	hurt
keep	kept	kept
know	knew	known
lay	laid	laid
lead	let	let

Present	*Past*	*Past Participle*
leave	left	left
let	let	let
lie	lay	lain
lose	lost	lost
ride	rode	ridden
ring	rang	rung
rise	rose	risen
see	saw	seen
shake	shook	shaken
shrink	shrank	shrunk
sing	sang	sung
speak	spoke	spoken
steal	stole	stolen
swear	swore	sworn
swim	swam	swum
swing	swung	swung
take	took	taken
write	wrote	written

Inconsistency of verb tenses Keep the tenses of verbs in a paper or theme consistent, switching from past to present only if the logic of your writing requires it.

1. Make the tense of a subordinate clause logically consistent with that of the main clause.

Consistent After they heard the main speaker, they were ready to leave.

Inconsistent After they heard the main speaker, they are ready to leave.

Consistent As the crowd gathers, Jim becomes more and more excited.

Inconsistent As the crowd gathers, Jim became more and more excited.

2. Do not switch back and forth from past to present tense when you are writing straight expository prose.

Inconsistent The author's examples *are* not randomly chosen. He [present] *told* of conversations with several officers, but he *does not* [past] mention [present] any conversations with enlisted men. This kind of sampling technique *invalidated* his reasoning. [past]

Consistent In 1973 the gasoline consumers of this country faced a bitter choice. They had to decide whether they were going to pay exorbitant prices for their gasoline or whether they were going to accept rationing.

If, however, the logic of your exposition demands that you speak of certain events in the past, you may mix your tenses without being inconsistent.

We now know that Hitler was more than a tyrant; he was a master psychologist as well.

It is customary to use the present in writing of documents or works of literature, regardless of when they were written.

In the *Republic* Plato asserts that all art is inherently inferior because it is, by definition, an imitation.

The Constitution of the United States sharply restricts the power of the individual states.

In his novel *Herzog* Saul Bellow writes with contempt of people he calls "reality teachers."

Use of the subjunctive mood of verbs When the context of a sentence calls for it, use the subjunctive mood of a verb. By contemporary standards of usage, the subjunctive mood is necessary in only a few instances.

1. Use the subjunctive mood to express a wish or to make a statement that is contrary to fact.

Colloquial If I *was* you, I would refuse to go.

Preferable If I *were* you, I would refuse to go.

Colloquial We wish that it *was* possible to compromise.

Preferable We wish that it *were* possible to compromise.

2. Use the subjunctive mood in *that* clauses which follow verbs indicating requests, orders, or suggestions.

I suggest that he *be given* another chance.

Stiles moved that the committee *adjourn*.

The judge ordered that the prisoner *be executed* on May 1.

Pronouns

The Terminology of Pronouns

Agreement The rule stating that pronouns must agree with their antecedents means that a pronoun must be of the same gender, number, and person as the noun for which it stands.

Case Pronouns have three categories of syntactic relationship, or cases: subjective, objective, and possessive. Subjective pronouns function as subjects and as subjective complements; they are *I, you, he, she, it; we, you, they,* and *who.* Objective pronouns function as objects; they are *me, you, him, her; us, you, them,* and *whom.* Possessive pronouns show possession: they are *my (mine), your (yours), his, her (hers), its; our (ours), your (yours), their (theirs),* and *whose.*

Demonstrative pronouns Demonstrative pronouns indicate or point out; they have the special function of specifying relative position. The singular demonstrative pronouns are *this* and *that;* the plural forms are *these* and *those.*

Indefinite pronouns Indefinite pronouns have no gender or case. They include *any, anyone, anybody, anything, all, another, both, each, either, everybody, everyone, everything, nobody, none, no one, one, other, several, some, somebody, someone, something.*

Interrogative pronouns The interrogative pronouns are *who, whose, what,* and *which* when these are used in questions, but the same words act as relative pronouns when they introduce an adjective clause.

Reciprocal pronouns Two pronoun phrases indicate action between or among individuals or groups and thus are called reciprocal pronouns. They are *each other* and *one another.*

Reflexive pronouns Reflexive pronouns are created by adding *-self* to personal pronoun forms. They are *myself, yourself, himself, herself, itself; ourselves, yourselves, themselves*. Avoid the nonstandard forms *hisself* and *theirselves*.

Reference The rule stating that pronoun reference cannot be faulty means that a pronoun must take the place of an identifiable unit, a word or clause, in the same sentence or in a previous sentence.

Relative pronouns Relative pronouns introduce phrases or clauses. They are *that, what, which, who, whom,* and *whose*. The *-ever* forms of interrogative pronouns also act as relative pronouns.

Problems with Pronouns

Probably the most common pronoun errors result from writers' not observing the convention that a pronoun must agree with its antecedent in person, number, and gender. Although that convention is violated frequently in informal speech, it is well to observe it in all but the most informal writing. The rules governing pronoun usage in those constructions that cause the most difficulty are as follows:

1. Pronouns that refer to plural subjects, whether they are plural in form or two subjects connected with *and*, must be plural.

> *Incorrect* To me, *every* person is an individual and *they* should be treated as one. ("Every" *is singular, but the pronoun* "they" *is plural.*)
>
> *Correct* To me, *every* person is an individual and *she* or *he* should be treated as one.
>
> *Incorrect* The author explains how children are taught to have feelings that are not *his*. ("His" *refers to children; thus it should be replaced by the plural form.*)
>
> *Correct* The author explains how children are taught to have feelings that are not *theirs*.
>
> *Incorrect* Students should attend a college or university that best meets *his* needs and where there are other students like *him*. ("Students" *is plural, but* "his" *and* "him" *are singular.*)
>
> *Correct* Students should attend a college or university that best meets *their* needs and where there are older students like *them*.

2. The indefinite pronouns *anybody, anyone, everyone, everybody, each, nobody, no one, either,* and *neither* are singular in form and should be fol-

lowed by singular pronouns. Constructions in which these pronouns are followed by a prepositional phrase with a plural word are particularly troublesome.

Incorrect Everyone feels that *their* rights have been violated.

Correct Everyone feels that *his* or *her* rights have been violated.

Incorrect Neither of the suspects was told of *their* rights.

Correct Neither of the suspects was told of *his* or *her* rights.

Incorrect Anybody who invested in that stock lost *their* money.

Correct Anybody who invested in that stock lost *her* or *his* money.

3. The indefinite pronouns *both, all,* and sometimes *none* are plural in form and should be followed by plural pronouns.

Incorrect Both the boys won *his* match.

Correct Both the boys won *their* matches.

Correct None of the contestants had *their* entries returned.

Correct Not *all* the soldiers have received *their* orders.

4. The pronouns that follow collective nouns may be either singular or plural in form, depending on the context of the sentence. If the collective noun seems to refer to a unit, use the singular pronoun; if it seems to refer to several individuals, use the plural pronoun.

The *committee* went beyond the instructions that were given *it.*

The *committee* complained that the work took an excessive amount of *their* time. *(Notice that inserting "members" after committee would remove any possible confusion.)*

That *team* always rose to any challenge that was given to *it.*

The *teams'* uniforms were given to *them* yesterday.

5. Use the relative pronoun *who* when the antecedent is a person; use the relative pronoun *which* or *that* if the antecedent is an animal or thing. The use of *that* to refer to people is now generally accepted, but *who* remains preferable.

Incorrect Those are the sailors *which* were decorated.

Acceptable Those are the sailors *that* were decorated.

Preferable Those are the sailors *who* were decorated.

There is an exception. Because there is no possessive form of the pronoun *which*, the possessive form *whose* may sometimes be used to avoid awkward constructions.

Awkward The Bureaus of Agriculture and Labor were among those the appropriations *of which* were cut.

Preferable The Bureaus of Agriculture and Labor were among those *whose* appropriations were cut.

Another common error in pronoun usage results from the writer's failing to distinguish between the subjective and objective forms of pronouns when they are used in phrases or as the object of pronouns or transitive verbs. To choose the correct form you must determine how the pronoun is functioning in the phrase or sentence. If it is functioning as a subject or as a predicate nominative, use the subjective form of the pronoun; if it is functioning as an object or in apposition with an object, use the objective form. Mastering the following guidelines should help to clarify the problem.

1. Use the subjective form for a pronoun that is the subject of a sentence.

Incorrect The Cooks and *us* are going to the ballet next week.
Correct The Cooks and *we* are going to the ballet next week.
Incorrect Jeffrey and *him* were given special recognition.
Correct Jeffrey and *he* were given special recognition.

Note that the problem here is caused by the plural subject. Almost no one would write "Us are going to the ballet." Therefore, to test your construction, phrase the sentence as it would be phrased if the pronoun were the only subject.

2. Use the subjective form for a pronoun that is acting as the subject of a clause.

I feel that *he* will be our next president.
We will be notified when *she* receives the award.

A perennial problem in this kind of construction is the who/whom confusion. The rule is that you should use *who* when the pronoun is acting as a subject, *whom* when it is acting as the object of a preposition or verb. The best way to determine which pronoun you should use is to recast the sentence or question using another kind of relative pronoun. For example,

There is the man (who, whom) we met yesterday.

Ask yourself, "Would I say 'I met he'?" Since the answer is obviously, "No, I would say 'I met him'" you should use the objective form, *whom*. Imagine you wanted to express the thought: This is the man (who, whom) will run for president next year. You should ask yourself, "Would I say 'He will run for president' or 'Him will run for president'?" Since you would choose the former construction, you should use the subjective form, *who*.

Incorrect May is the girl *whom* entered the convent last spring.

Correct May is the girl *who* entered the convent last spring.

Correct Jenkins is the man *who* they claim is the brains behind the organizations. *(Notice that the intervening phrase "they claim" does not affect the case of the pronoun.)*

3. Use the subjective form of the pronoun when it is in apposition with the subject of a sentence.

Incorrect The subcommittee—Joe, Bob, and *me*—submitted a report yesterday.

Correct The subcommittee—Joe, Bob, and *I*—submitted a report yesterday.

4. Use the subjective form of the pronoun if it is the complement of a linking verb.

Incorrect The principal knew instantly that the culprits were Jim and *me*.

Correct The principal knew instantly that the culprits were Jim and I

Incorrect Delegates to the convention are Harold, Clarence, and *me*.

Correct Delegates to the convention are Harold, Clarence, and *I*.

5. Use the objective form of a pronoun that functions as the object or indirect object of a verb.

Incorrect The judge appointed Walton and *I* to the board.

Correct The judge appointed Walton and *me* to the board.

Incorrect Marshall will send a copy to Kenneth and *I.*

Correct Marshall will send a copy to Kenneth and *me.*

6. Use the objective form of a pronoun when it is the object of a preposition.

Incorrect The prize was divided between *he* and Carlos.

Correct The prize was divided between *him* and Carlos.

Incorrect That is the man *who* I wish to speak to.

Correct That is the man to *whom* I wish to speak.

Incorrect Wilson is the person *who* Jones chose as his successor.

Correct Wilson is the person *whom* Jones chose as his successor.

7. Use the objective form of a pronoun when it is in apposition with an object.

Incorrect He selected three people, Johnson, Clark, and *I,* to prepare the report.

Correct He selected three people, Johnson, Clark, and *me,* to prepare the report.

8. Use the objective form of a pronoun when it acts as the subject or object of an infinitive phrase.

Correct Creighton is to notify *him* at once.

Correct Lewis was surprised to see *him* at the opera.

9. Use the possessive form of a pronoun when it precedes and modifies a gerund.

Justin is angry about *his* having lied.

Our going to the exhibit proved to be a mistake.

The third common problem that crops up with pronouns is faulty or vague references. By definition, a pronoun must refer to a word or group of words that has preceded it. Usually the referent (what the pronoun is substituting for) is a noun or noun clause in a previous clause or sentence, but sometimes it may be an idea expressed in a previous sentence. In either case, unless the reader can immediately identify the thing to which the pronoun refers, the sentence is faulty and should be revised. Errors of this kind usually fall into two classes.

1. Faulty pronoun reference caused by using *this, that, it,* or *which* to refer ambiguously to a sentence or long clause. For example:

Ambiguous Existentialists believe that man is totally responsible for what happens to him *which* I cannot accept.

Clear I cannot accept the existentialists' belief that man is totally responsible for what happens to him.

Ambiguous The author's stories about teen-age drug addicts and young criminals are particularly effective because *this* happens every day.

Clear The author's stories about teen-age drug addicts and young criminals are particularly effective because one hears about such cases every day.

Ambiguous Biologists may soon know how to control the sex of a baby, but *it* is not an acceptable practice yet.

Clear Biologists may soon know how to control the sex of a baby, but people are not yet ready to accept such control.

2. Faulty pronoun reference caused by having more than one possible referent precede the pronoun. For example:

Ambiguous The gambler convinced his banker that he was a lucky man.

Clear The gambler convinced the banker that he (the gambler) was a lucky man.

Ambiguous Freud first met Jung when he was a student.

Clear Freud first met Jung when the latter was a student.

Remember that your reader should never have to guess what any pronoun refers to.

Adjectives and Adverbs

Adjectives may modify only nouns and pronouns; adverbs, however, may modify adjectives, verbs, prepositions and conjuctions, and other adverbs. Although there are a few words that function as both adverbs and adjectives—*fast, slow, better, worse, early,* and *late* are the most common—most adverbs are formed by adding *-ly* to the adjective form: *quick, quickly; clear, clearly; exact, exactly.* Adjectives are compared by adding *-er* or *-est* to the base word when the word is short and by putting *more* or *most* in front of the word if it is comparatively long: *shorter, shortest; meaner, meanest;* but, *more* miserable, *most* miserable and *more* precise, *most* precise. Except for a very few words—*fast, well, early, late, soon,* and *slow*—the comparative forms of adverbs require inserting *more* or *most* before the word: *more* clearly, *most* clearly and *more* swiftly, *most* swiftly. A very few rules govern the correct use of adverbs and adjectives.

1. Adjectives should not be used to modify verbs.

Incorrect The Coxes were *real* upset about the accident.
Correct The Coxes were *really* upset about the accident.
Incorrect The legislators passed the law as *quick* as possible.
Correct The legislators passed the law as *quickly* as possible.

2. Adjectives should not be used to modify adverbs or other adjectives.

Incorrect The story was *reasonable* accurate.
Correct The story was *reasonably* accurate.
Incorrect The officer spoke to us *real* sharply.
Correct The officer spoke to us *very* sharply.

3. If a modifier follows the verb but refers to the subject of the sentence, use the adjective form.

The corners must be kept *clean.*
The measurement was thought *accurate* at the time.

4. When the main verb is a linking verb or one that describes sensory actions, an adjective rather than an adverb should complete it. Verbs in this category are *is, feel, look, appear, sound, taste, become, seem,* and *smell.*

Incorrect That color looks *well* on her.
Correct That color looks *good* on her.
Incorrect Keith's voice sounds *weakly* this morning.
Correct Keith's voice sounds *weak* this morning.